SEASONAL SOCIOLOGY

EDITED BY

TONYA K. DAVIDSON
AND ONDINE PARK

UNIVERSITY OF TORONTO PRESS
Toronto Buffalo London

Toronto Buffalo London
utorontopress.com
Printed in Canada

ISBN 978-1-4875-9409-1 (cloth) ISBN 978-1-4875-9410-7 (EPUB)
ISBN 978-1-4875-9408-4 (paper) ISBN 978-1-4875-9411-4 (PDF)

Library and Archives Canada Cataloguing in Publication

Title: Seasonal sociology / edited by Tonya K. Davidson and Ondine Park.
Names: Davidson, Tonya K., 1979– editor. | Park, Ondine, 1974– editor.
Description: Includes bibliographical references and index.
Identifiers: Canadiana (print) 20200289195 | Canadiana (ebook) 20200289268 | ISBN 9781487594091 (hardcover) | ISBN 9781487594084 (softcover) | ISBN 9781487594107 (EPUB) | ISBN 9781487594114 (PDF)
Subjects: LCSH: Seasons – Social aspects – Canada. | LCSH: Canada – Social conditions. | LCSH: Seasons – Canada.
Classification: LCC HN103.5 .S43 2020 | DDC 508.20971 – dc23

We welcome comments and suggestions regarding any aspect of our publications – please feel free to contact us at news@utorontopress.com or visit us at utorontopress.com.

Every effort has been made to contact copyright holders; in the event of an error or omission, please notify the publisher.

University of Toronto Press acknowledges the financial assistance to its publishing program of the Canada Council for the Arts and the Ontario Arts Council, an agency of the Government of Ontario.

Part opener images: iStock.com/alexiesko

Canada Council for the Arts Conseil des Arts du Canada

Funded by the Government of Canada Financé par le gouvernement du Canada | Canada

Contents

SUMMER

Figures

Tables

Preface

TONYA K. DAVIDSON and ONDINE PARK

Seasonal Sociology as an Introduction

Sociology helps us to make sense of ourselves and our social worlds. The goal of this book is to inspire readers with the fundamental richness of sociology. The editors and most of the authors in this book teach introduction to sociology in Canadian universities. We came together because we wanted a book that could introduce readers to the liveliness of sociology through the use of interesting, contemporary Canadian sociology.

This book is an introduction to sociology through the seasons *and* a seasonal sociology. It has the following goals in mind: to introduce readers to the academic discipline of sociology; to introduce readers to contemporary, Canadian, sociological studies; and to present a way of thinking sociologically about the seasons. In the following chapters, you will find robust, contemporary examples of sociology in action (case studies) that help bring the subject matter to life written in authors' distinctive voices. The authors in this collection use, develop, and explain theoretical ideas, methodological approaches, and sociological concepts in their work, giving readers an understanding of how sociology is done and what it can do. The authors' research methods include participant observation, demographic analysis, archival research, content analysis, discourse analysis, and mixed methods. The authors in this collection live and work across Canada and further afield, and they do a wide variety of sociological research. The chapters reflect this diversity of locations, spanning much of the country and including rural and urban case studies.

We are also forwarding a new way of thinking both about the seasons and about sociology. One of the themes to which authors return again and again is the basic sociological insight that, while there is a materiality to the world, things, and people with whom we engage, our interactions with each other and with this materiality – and the meanings and interpretations that we derive through those engagements – are always fundamentally social. What better way to illustrate the social nature of the human world than to consider the seasons? Seasons and seasonality are ordinary concerns – we must adapt to the specific environmental and cultural situation in which we find ourselves at any particular time to do any particular thing and largely don't think about this adaptation when it constitutes our ordinary, daily background context. But as we describe in the introduction, the seasons also mediate and are mediated by complex social interactions, managed by social institutions, and experienced through socially organized life opportunities.

Acknowledgements

We would like to express our sincere thanks to our editors, Anne Brackenbury, Carli Hansen, and Robin Studniberg, at the University of Toronto Press, each of whom provided keen and insightful support to help shepherd us through this complex project. Thanks to Kiley Venables and Julia Cadney who coordinated the image permissions – not an easy task with so many contributors. Thanks also to Jenn Harris for her thorough and thoughtful copy-editing.

Thank you to our many hard-working assistants along the way. Stefanie Martin and Archana Sivakumaran were excellent research assistants in the early stages of this book project. Christian Pasiak provided discerning reading and invaluable editing. Jasmeet Bahia and Delphine Brown did great work on the instructor's manual.

We are grateful to have received financial support from the Department of Sociology and Anthropology at Carleton University, Teaching and Learning Services at Carleton University, Ryerson University's Undergraduate Research Opportunities Program, the Government of Alberta's STEP program, and MacEwan University's Faculty of Arts and Science.

Tonya would also like to thank Kris Gies – who, when working for the University of Toronto Press, showed enthusiasm for this project in its earliest stages and got this ball rolling – and Morgan Rooney at Carleton University for his insights on learning outcomes.

A huge and heartfelt thank you to all of the contributors to this book. We appreciate their wonderful insights, enthusiasm, patience, and willingness to participate in an unconventional kind of project that required a certain leap of faith. Finally, many, many thanks to the sociology students in all of our classes, who kept us motivated and inspired throughout this process.

Introduction

TONYA K. DAVIDSON, TARA MILBRANDT, and ONDINE PARK

On a drizzly Sunday morning in November, one of the authors of this introduction went with her family to join a crowd of locals along the side of a busy secondary highway on the suburban outskirts of London, Ontario, waiting for Santa Claus and his crew of elves, reindeer, and other jovial friends to parade down the road. Like many others of its kind, at this Santa Claus parade, there were floats of community organizations and **institutions** matched in equal number by floats created by large corporations. People in the parade threw candy to the children in the crowd, sang, danced, and stopped traffic in a display of seasonal conviviality. In culturally and religiously diverse twenty-first century Canada, the beginning of winter is still marked annually in many communities, small and large, rural, suburban, and urban, by this ritual. Such celebrations intermingle folkloric and religious traditions with commercial and consumer interests and civic **culture**. This phenomenon, cherished by many, can be interpreted as a public ritual that reinforces a Christian civil religion as dominant and thus marginalizes many other religious traditions. It can also be interpreted as yet one more of the many consumer events that fill peoples' calendars. However, the parade could also work simply as a good excuse, irrespective of its Christian roots or consumerist co-optation, for a diversity of people to join in an enactment of community when there are not many other good reasons to stand around outside together in cold, darkening November. In the face of these many possible competing interpretations, enjoying a Santa Claus parade with family, friends, and neighbours continues to be a common occurrence; it also inspires us to ask the larger sociological question: What do seasonal traditions and activities – and, more broadly, the ways in which we collectively mark, accommodate ourselves to, and make sense of the different seasons – say about and do in contemporary society?

As you're reading this, what season is it? How do you know? Would seasons exist if humans did not name them as such? These might seem like strange questions, but as you will see, sociology is an invitation to ask strange questions, and it challenges us to seek answers that imaginatively go beyond what might be thought of as normal, natural, and common-sense answers. Provoked by such questions, in this book, we offer an introduction to sociology through the seasons. We invite you to think differently about the social world and reflect upon your own life in relation to something that is both exceedingly familiar and taken for granted: the seasons. While seasons and seasonal changes correspond with cycles originating in the natural world, they are also interpreted through, and marked by, social traditions and collectively established ways of doing things. This book is an invitation to consider how, why, and to what degree our experiences, activities, interactions, expectations, and patterns are shaped both seasonally and socially. We ask you to consider how such seemingly different things as private moods, large-scale manifestations of a collective spirit or group conflict, assumptions that we make when we venture outside, and the physical things that are available to us in the material world can all be understood as shaped by seasonal and social conditions.

What is Sociology?

Sociology can be defined most simply as the systematic study of social life. Its primary goal is to understand and explain the social world, from small-scale interactional processes between individuals and groups to large-scale macro **structures** that organize and give a degree of stability to social life. Sociologists examine such things as the formation, renewal, and conflicts of groups and cultures, the structure and effects of formal institutions, the enactment of social forces and relations of power, and even the patterns of our most mundane thoughts, feelings, and social interactions.

Sociologists are interested in studying all things human, taking the perspective that to understand what and why people do what they do, one must always contextualize what people do within a social framework. That is, sociology begins with the assumptions that the social world is not reducible to its individual parts and that new social phenomena emerge out of the innumerable ways that people combine, create, change, dismantle, and remake a world together, in both cooperation and conflict. The scope of sociology as a field of study is extremely broad, and sociologists use many different theoretical perspectives and methodological approaches to investigate aspects of society that concern and fascinate them, as found in this collection. Sociology's diversity reflects the nature and complexity of its subject matter, for the social world is dynamic and multi-layered, and the history of the human condition is a record of change and difference, collaboration and struggle. Amid all of its diversity, there is something that all sociologists share: a concern with the uniquely social facets of human existence – even in aspects of our lives that don't appear to be social (such as nature or even one's innermost desires).

The Emergence of Sociology

Sociology's birth occurred during a time of massive political, economic, and technological change and upheaval in Europe. Its emergence was part of a significant span of European history known as the **Enlightenment** period, which occurred in the late seventeenth century and eighteenth century. An important development during this time was the rise of science and **empiricism** as the primary basis for knowing the world; this accompanied the decline of religious belief as the dominant source of authority and knowledge about the world. The term "sociology" was coined in 1839 by French philosopher Auguste Comte (1798–1857). The thrust of Comte's intervention was that the social world could be the object of systematic study, much as the biological sciences treated the natural world as an object of systematic study. While philosophers, theologians, and innumerable others had been contemplating human existence for centuries prior, the designation of a formal science of society was a development that helped to crystallize a unique object of inquiry: the *social* world. Since this time, sociology has developed into a highly complex, variegated, and influential discipline within the social sciences. Its growth is reflected in the development of various subfields (such as the sociology of health, the sociology of media, the sociology of childhood, and the sociology of law, to name a few introduced in the chapters that follow).

The Power of the Social

Building on this legacy, the French sociologist Émile Durkheim (1858–1917) sought to demonstrate the power of social forces that shape human lives in myriad ways and to further legitimate a formal science of society. Durkheim's (1982) concept of the **social fact** refers to how conventions of "thinking, acting, and feeling" express social institutional practices (e.g., **religion**, media, family, law) (52). Social facts are powerful and exist externally to the individual; they offer resistance to the individual who violates, or appears to violate, them. For example, what would happen if you forgot, or refused to send your mother a card on Mother's Day?

One of Durkheim's (1997) most influential works is a book called *Suicide: A Study in Sociology* (originally published in 1897). Here, with extraordinary nuance, he took something that seemed on the surface to be an eminently individual act explainable primarily through psychological categories, and he demonstrated its complex social underpinnings. With the research assistance of his nephew, sociologist and anthropologist Marcel Mauss, Durkheim analyzed the difference of and change in rates of suicide across various social groups as the manifestation of collective phenomena. They found that differences in the patterns of suicide from community to community related to differences in social life in those communities and how they affected individuals within those communities. This study shed important light onto the efficacy of social institutions like religion, family, politics, and the economy in people's lives, and Durkheim developed significant insights into the relationship between human well-being and relative levels of social integration and regulation. Too much or too little of either contributes to higher rates of suicide. While it was not the central focus of his study, Durkheim also found significant seasonal variations in rates of suicide, including a peak in the spring, which he also accounted for in terms of social phenomena, especially relative density and frequency of human interaction. This study can be seen as an early form of the seasonal sociology demonstrated in this volume: In chapter twelve, Rania Tfaily details these types of seasonal social patterns throughout the year, wherein seemingly individual decisions (e.g., whether or not to divorce) and activities (e.g., having babies or dying) are shaped by larger social and seasonal forces, while Jen Wrye, Michael Graydon, and Patricia Thille describe, in chapter eight, the ways in which the deeply personal feelings people have about their bodies and the New Year's resolutions they individually devise to change their physiques in fact reflect social and cultural values around ideals of body shape as well as historically formed ideas about the capacity and responsibility of individuals for self-improvement.

Social Life and History as Dynamic

Other important early sociological thinkers were the German theorists Karl Marx (1818–1883) and Friedrich Engels (1820–1895). Marx and Engels's work (1967 [1848], 1970 [1845–1846]) emphasizes the importance of situating analysis of any social phenomenon in the particular historical and material conditions in which it is located to properly understand that phenomenon and to be able to recognize the emergence of new forms of human consciousness (Marx 1967 [1867], Marx and Engels 1967 [1848], 1970 [1845–1846]). They understood history and social life as dynamic. For Marx and Engels, social life is characterized by the **stratification** of classes and the struggle between these classes. They argued that the socio-economic structures of any given historical period are ones that reflect the interests and influence of the ruling material **class**, which wishes to maintain its position of power at the expense of the oppressed class. Marx and Engels focused, in particular, on analyzing social life in the context of **capitalism**, in which there is a struggle between the bourgeoisie and the proletariat. The bourgeoisie is the class that owns and controls the **means of production** (those things that enable the production of goods and services) and takes possession of the surplus value that is derived from productive activity. Surplus value is the profit that the bourgeoisie appropriates for themselves after paying for the means of production and the cost of labour. The proletariat is the class of workers whose labour produces value. In order to appropriate as much surplus value as possible, the bourgeoisie exploit the proletariat, denying the proletariat the true value of their labour. Instead, the bourgeoisie tries to pay as little as possible for the workers' labour by constantly driving up their productivity, driving down their wages, or both. It is the bourgeoisie, as a class, that stands to profit from commercial production in general. Thus, as Jenna Hennebry, David Celis Parra, and Rachelle Daley describe in chapter four, seasonal migrant workers produce many of the foods Canadian rely on for sustenance, yet they are subjected to extremely harsh conditions of labour that enable their employers to derive as much profit as possible. Stratification is also evident in unequal access to valued resources in a society. Thus, the different experiences of summer leisure activities – luxuriating in private cottages for some, while making do with underfunded public pools for others – described by Tonya K. Davidson in chapter seventeen are also an expression of contemporary social stratification in Canada.

Marxist theorists such as scholars of the Frankfurt School and those within the field of cultural studies argued that not only are the oppressed classes denied the true value of their labour as workers but they are also seduced into spending their money on products as consumers, further entrapping them into supporting the interests of the dominant class and subordinating them to their rule. Both processes contribute to the increased wealth and power of the ruling class and reveal the interest that the ruling class has in commercializing seasonal rituals and activities. Sociological analyses that are based in this analytic approach are critical in that they seek to uncover and critique the conditions of social life, especially the inequalities that tend to be obscured within the structures of social life. Thus, as Benjamin Woo shows in chapter nineteen, the film industry has manufactured and, in turn, benefited from creating the new summer ritual of going to blockbuster films. Similarly, as Nathaniel Laywine and Alan Sears argue in chapter thirteen, the travel industry and educational businesses benefit from turning the week-long university study break into the hedonistic, beach-destination "spring break" or the well-meaning but poverty-seeking "alternative spring break," both of which contribute to ongoing global inequalities.

For sociologists who take up Marxist theoretical approaches, the conflict between classes of people due to their competing interests and competing access to the limited resources of society inevitably brings about change in society. From this perspective, social life is dynamic and therefore open to transformation and liberation.

The Sociological Imagination

Drawing on this critical sociological tradition, mid-twentieth-century American sociologist C. Wright Mills (1916–1962) developed the concept of the **sociological imagination** (1959). The sociological imagination refers to a particular "quality of mind" (4) through which one begins to grasp the interrelation between socially structured realities and individual lives. Developing a sociological imagination enables us to meaningfully differentiate between two kinds of problems. Personal troubles are difficulties for which the cause and resolution can be found at the individual level and in the "immediate milieu" of the individual (Mills 1959, 8). In contrast, **social issues** are problems that reflect the organization and operation of larger social structures (e.g., law, the economy, the school system, dominant **norms** and **values**) within particular historical circumstances that require collective action for resolution (Mills 1959). A sociological imagination makes it possible to recognize the social structural underpinning of difficulties that many individuals may experience on their own as private matters – and understand that these are, in fact, social issues and public concerns. In this book, sociologists explore many different problems that initially appear to be personal troubles: parents trying to find constructive and affordable summer activities for their children, as described by Patrizia Albanese in chapter twenty; seniors coping with environmentally enforced isolation during a cold and snowy Edmonton winter, as illustrated by Tara Milbrandt in chapter seven; or one high school girl's frustration at consistently playing the games of her many sports teams in the worst time slots with few audience members, as Nicole Neverson recounts in chapter ten. Analyzed sociologically, these scholars discover that rather than being located randomly or idiosyncratically within individual lives, these problems reflect patterned social relations: socio-economic status has a significant impact on how parents are able to organize their children's summers; seniors and others are lonely and alienated from each other during winter in part because of widely shared attitudes and municipal policies that largely render snow clearing and urban mobility as individual concerns rather than addressing these as a collective duty toward inclusion. And terrible game times for girls' and women's sports reflect social (and sexist) interpretations about the value of girls and women in society.

As Mills (1959) writes, the sociological imagination has both "terrible" and "magnificent" implications: terrible because it makes you realize that you are not solely in charge of your own destiny and that there is a limit to individual agency; it is, however, also magnificent because it means that although our social world and history come to us and limit our agency in significant ways, as members of society, each of us also shapes our own society and has an impact on how history might unfold (5–6). By recognizing the limits and possibilities posed by social life, the sociological imagination enables us to see that there may be solutions to even seemingly insurmountable social problems through collective will and action.

Equipped with this orientation, we can begin to understand how our experiences of the social world – including the seasons – are always shaped by our own particular location within a larger, historically conditioned, and socially structured world. Social structures of **gender**, **race**, class, age, (dis)ability, sexuality, and so on shape our experiences and **life chances** in the same world. Sociologist Max Weber (1864–1920) introduced the concept of life chances (1968) to describe people's unequal access to social resources like food, health care, education, leisure opportunities, respect, **social status**, and satisfaction. As Weber explains, life chances are influenced by **social class** position and status group; thus, different life chances are due to socially structured inequality, not differences in individual talents, personalities, or effort. Just as social structures shape life chances, they also shape our experiences of the various seasons in vastly different ways. So, while seasons are social facts, they are not necessarily experienced in the same way, even within a single community, within the same family, or for the same person over the course of their lifetime. Thus, for example, both Matthew P. Unger in chapter nine and Heather Rollwagen in chapter two demonstrate how individuals' experiences with the law are *patterned*, reflecting the colonial, racial, and gender biases built into the legal and policing systems.

The Relationship between the Individual and Society

An important component of thinking sociologically is recognizing that each of us is constituted in and through the social world in which we grow up. At the same time, the social world is not self-perpetuating; it requires our active and continuous collaboration. This includes the ways in which seasons are accomplished and reconstituted at different times and by different groups.

One of the key concepts that sociologists use to explain how individuals become members of a social world is **socialization**. This term refers to the ongoing, lifelong process in which every member of society participates, as both a learner and a teacher. This process involves actively and (often) unconsciously learning the social values, beliefs, patterns of behaviour, language, and culture that bind people together as members of *a* society. In addition to integrating new members, socialization is also a critical process for reproducing (and recreating) the society by passing on its ways to (and also modifying them for) the next generation and to newcomers. Whether one is very young or very old, inclusion in a group or society includes ongoing socialization into its norms and values. Socialization occurs throughout the **life course**, or the different periods or phases of an individual's life.

An aspect of socialization not generally addressed is that this process is also seasonal. In Canada, children and newcomers are socialized into orientations toward the seasons and how to live in them year-round. This seasonal socialization often includes learning how to survive in the different seasons (proper winter clothing, keeping mittens together with a long string of yarn pulled through the sleeves of a winter jacket), how to enjoy the seasons, and the symbolic meaning of the seasons. For one of this introduction's authors (Tonya), childhood socialization in fall in southwestern Ontario involved competing in cattle shows in a circuit of fall agricultural fairs. Through this socialization process, she became part of a particular rural social world, actively learning how to become a beef farmer, interact with other rural folk, and contribute to this small society. She was socialized into dominant gender norms through witnessing the local fair's princess competitions, and she noticed the tag on her Carhartt overalls that infuriatingly read, at that time, "rugged as the men that wear them." This was also a seasonal socialization, as she learned that fall was a season for rural competitions, socializing, hard work, family time, and candy apples. Similarly, in chapter fifteen, Bonar Buffam describes how his childhood socialization involved participating in the annual spring "Tea Party" in his neighbourhood of Oak Bay, Victoria. Here, he notes, he was being socialized into a local, and national, community that celebrated British cultural traditions and values to the exclusion of others. In his contemporary sociological analysis, Buffam demonstrates how today the annual spring Vaisakhi parades created by the Sikh communities in Vancouver offer ongoing socialization into multiple versions of multiculturalism.

Making the World Unfamiliar

One of the hallmarks of thinking sociologically is to question what is taken for granted – those aspects of the familiar social world, and the familiar explanations for the way things are, that seem so obvious as to go without saying; the things that, from birth (or from whenever one enters into a particular social milieu), one has been socialized to accept as natural, self-evident, or simply the way it is (Berger 1963; Berger and Luckmann 1966). German-American sociologist Peter Berger (1929–2017) describes this sociological orientation as looking at what is familiar in a way as to make it unfamiliar and even strange (1963). Alissa Overend, for example, describes the familiar way in which difficult human emotions are increasingly understood as individual medical problems by examining seasonal affective disorder in chapter six and asks how social expectations and social definitions of normalcy might be better sites of investigation and questioning. Another important and related element of thinking sociologically, which Berger also emphasizes, is the ability to see the general conditions and broader social patterns that inform and produce – but also arise out of – a particular, seemingly idiosyncratic, situation. In this vein, chapter eighteen's author, Paul Joosse, while analyzing the summer bombings of pipelines in a small BC town, shows that even such extreme and seemingly isolated acts – typically framed in public discourse as random or unpredictable – can be understood as informed by larger patterns of community relations, state formation, and structures of power.

The shift of orientation involved in thinking sociologically can be illuminating and transformative in both liberating and existentially disruptive ways. As Berger highlights, the orientation to estrangement can engender a type of culture shock from within. It compels you to ask strange, new, uncomfortable, possibly forbidden questions. Ideally, it places you in a new and critical relationship to the familiar world in which you may have always lived, opening up a critical space to ask different kinds of questions and also, perhaps, to do things differently. Additionally, it enables the possibility of recognizing that seemingly unique or individual occurrences can reveal broader social realities and patterns. For example, as you read through this book, we hope you find yourself asking questions like: how do corporations find a way to co-opt the most ancient folk traditions as well as the most recent grassroots seasonal flavours and trends? Why and how have we come to expect produce from all seasons year-round in our grocery stores? Why is summer marketed as the season of freedom and leisure? Why do divorce rates increase in the fall and winter?

Season

Each major season approximately corresponds with distinctive patterns of temperature, weather, and light that are caused by such things as the position of the sun relative to the tilt of the orbiting Earth, as well as geographical and longer-term geological patterns and conditions. Marked on our calendars and ritualized in various ways throughout the year, these divisions are organized around forces and rhythms of nature that exist above and beyond human volition. Seasons and their associated natural forces and conditions can be considered agents in their own right. Indeed, if humans do not physically accommodate and adapt ourselves to the climatic conditions around us, we can suffer from what is most simply called exposure. For most of us, because they concern patterns in nature, seasons feel like obvious physical facts that simply exist as the objective conditions of the natural world, which in turn seems to determine the conditions of human living. As seasons appear to be just the reality of nature, in many parts of Canada, as throughout much of the temperate zones of the Earth, the idea of the four seasons – spring, summer, autumn, and winter – is taken for granted as being natural.

But seasons are social.

Seasons as Social Categories

Physical, natural conditions by themselves do not produce seasons. The Earth, its systems, and its beings undergo gradual or sudden changes all the time. The identification, division, and categorization of these continual changes into specific seasons are social. Identifying particular sets of natural conditions as belonging to the same category (that is, season) is a collective decision that is culturally and socially determined. Seasons are also social because the very idea of taking note of time, dividing it up into smaller units, and ascribing meaning to these categories, are social activities. Beyond the act of imposing a meaning system on our natural world, seasons are social because they are classifications that are derived from, reflect, and help produce patterns, rhythms, and cycles of collective life. As Durkheim observed in *The Elementary Forms of Religious Life*, divisions of time and space emerge out of group life. The many ways that time and space come to be organized, differentiated, represented, and expressed are rooted in the life energies of the collective: "The division into days, weeks, months, years, etc., corresponds to the recurrence of rites, festivals, and public ceremonies at regular intervals. A calendar expresses the rhythm of collective activity while ensuring that regularity. The same applies to space" (Durkheim 1995 [1912], 10). The chapters of this book illustrate this notion that seasons are socially derived, socially meaningful, and social ordering: these are distinctions that are produced through meaning-making interpretations, which both express and coordinate group life. For example, Heidi Bickis, in chapter five, and Susan Machum, in chapter eleven, examine the historical emergence and social production of particular types of time in their discussions of Thanksgiving and agriculture, respectively.

Seasons are dependent on both natural and social conditions; thus, different human communities pay particular attention to the specific natural conditions that are considered important for their collective life. The orientation to the four seasons, for example, is based on agricultural cycles in the temperate zone (particularly the northern temperate zone), and each season roughly corresponds to the different phases of annual agricultural life. Indeed, the English words "season" (and French *saison*) and "spring" (typically thought to be the first season – or, literally, first time, *printemps*, in French – of the annual seasonal cycles) both derive from the Latin word for "sowing" – scattering seeds in or on the earth in order to grow plants. Sowing is a human activity that takes place at a certain time of the year, when the natural conditions are deemed to be suitable. If you've ever tried to grow a plant from seed, you know that the activity of sowing merges human creativity and natural energies. Seeds are sown through human effort, by hand or by human tool, deploying and adding to knowledge from your cultural and social context. In sowing a seed in the physical world, you also sow hope in your mental and social worlds that something will grow, knowing this can only happen should the weather, the land, animals, weeds, and the seed itself co-operate. While it may be a human and social act to sow, the natural rhythms of the seed in growing and becoming a full-grown plant that is cared for and then harvested help produce the patterns of collective life. From these seeds, the possibilities of holiday dinners, bountiful farmer's markets, and inspiration for pumpkin-spice lattes all become possible. So, cultivating the soil and crops also is a cultivation of a particular kind of culture.

Seasonal Effects Demonstrate Social Inequality

Once the social processes of categorizing time and nature into seasons are in place, the climatic facts of a season are rendered meaningful and taken up in ways that are stamped by the social. Reflecting on seasons makes visible the nature of our collective life, including inequalities in life chances. As the sociological approach that we take to the seasons emphasizes, forces of nature do not in themselves dictate who is most likely to experience what kinds of effects – adverse, positive, or a bit of both – that stem from these recurrent and somewhat predictable conditions. How different people experience and inhabit the naturally occurring seasons is shaped by socially organized differences and divisions. For example, in the summer of 2018, over 70 people in Quebec died during a weeks-long heat wave (Laframboise 2018). In 1995, during a two-day heat wave in Chicago, 700 people perished (Klinenberg 2002). Deaths were not uniformly spread across the entire respective Quebec and Chicago populations, nor were they random. Sociologist Eric Klinenberg (2002) found that people who were most likely to die from the Chicago heat wave were those who came from groups that were socially marginalized and disadvantaged. They had lower life chances. Those who had less access to life-saving social goods during the heat wave were those who, in everyday life, systematically had less access to these social goods, such as health care, welcoming community centres, and social supports, because of the way that social life was structured. Paying attention to seasons and seasonal effects can reveal different life chances.

Seasons Express Collective Values

Seasons help to define and illuminate the shape of our shared world in ways that express and reveal collective values. How any particular group of people recognizes seasons depends on what is important to that society, which, in turn, helps define what should be important and ought to be marked through rituals and in other ways. Seasons are collectively agreed-upon orientations to and interpretations of the cosmos, the Earth-bound natural world, and the social world. They are culturally specific ways of making sense of time, temporality, and duration within the context of the natural and social world. Seasons and how they are collectively imagined and enacted inspire certain forms of social interaction and meaning. Seasons are likewise marked by social rituals, which involve collective affirmations of shared values. Such affirmations can potentially be simultaneously celebratory and oppressive, creative and constraining, moments of social solidarity and social exclusion. For example, summer weddings can bring families and communities together as collective celebrations. But as Ondine Park explains in chapter sixteen, when the dominant form of weddings continues to follow and model expectations of heterosexual romantic love expressed through extravagant consumer spending as the cultural norm, the repetition of attending weddings summer after summer reliably reinforces gendered social norms rooted in a rigid two-gender hierarchical worldview that deeply structures gendered inequality into social life.

Seasons and Their Traditions Change in Relation to Social Change

Like other social constructions, seasons are not universal, timeless, or essential. Our definitions of seasons in general and of each season specifically, our collective and individual relationship to them, and to each other within the context of seasonality, adapt to societal changes. This can be seen, for example, in shifting customs that mark or shape our relation to seasonal rituals such as Halloween, one of the key events of autumn, which has changed markedly, even within the (relatively) short lifespan of this introduction's authors. Children dressing up, going door to door, and asking neighbours for candy has customarily been a time for children and adolescents to play with or break cultural norms with some degree of social permission. Yet layered in with this temporary loosening of ordinary social norms is the persistence of individual and collective fear of strangers expressed, for example, in the annually debunked myth that razor blades have been found in trick-or-treaters' apples. New social practices form in response to new social conditions. The spiked apple myth still circulates, speaking to the tenaciousness of the fear of the stranger. New Halloween practices also reflect an increase in these urban fears. One such newly invented Halloween tradition is the "trunk or treat," where kids gather in parking lots and visit decorated car trunks for a trick-or-treating experience that appears safer and certainly is expedited (Costanzo 2016). Seasonal traditions change in relation to wider social changes, changing our relation to the seasons in turn.

Doing Sociology

Social Theory

Theory and theorizing are important and defining components of doing sociology. All sociological inquiry involves a guiding framework, a perspective through which the sociologist interprets some aspect of social reality: in other words, a theory. A social theory is a system of concepts, ideas, principles, and propositions that is used to make sense of – and explain patterns, regularities, and relationships observed in – the social world. The word theory derives from the Greek term *theoria*, which refers to the activities of contemplation and speculation. When you attempt to account for something you have encountered, or try to explain how something has come about in the way that it has, in your life or in the world, you are theorizing. What distinguishes formal sociological theorizing from everyday theorizing is that sociological theorizing aims to be explicit, consistent, and rigorous in how it deploys concepts, categories, and distinctions to interpret and explain different patterns, tendencies, events, and transformations in the world. Everyday theorizing, by contrast, is typically based on "implicit assumptions and unacknowledged presuppositions" (Edles and Appelrouth 2015, 2). In making their assumptions about the world explicit through formal academic writing, sociological theorists necessarily open their ideas and assumptions up to critical engagement, scrutiny, and revision. It is in this sense that social theory can be considered an ongoing and unfinished conversation about the nature and consequences of socially organized reality.

Theoretical perspectives and leanings open up particular lines of questioning that guide thinking and research along particular lines. There are many different theoretical approaches within sociology, and they vary in their degree of compatibility with one another. Each theoretical approach is rooted in a different set of assumptions about the social world and the workings of society. Theoretical differences and debates within sociology reflect the richness and complexity of our subject matter, and no single approach can encompass the many different facets of social existence. As societies change and as more diverse voices enter the conversation, older theories are reinterpreted and new theoretical approaches emerge.

Classical Theory

Social theory is often differentiated in terms of **classical** and **contemporary theory**. Generally, the classical tradition refers to theorizing from the eighteenth to early twentieth centuries; classical theorists' writings helped to establish the discipline of sociology and make the case that the social world has unique properties that can be studied systematically. The major theorists whose works are most often considered as part of the classical canon are Émile Durkheim, Karl Marx, and Max Weber. Other important classical theorists, whose work has often been under-acknowledged in discussions of classical theory, include Harriet Martineau (1802–76), Georg Simmel (1858–1918), Charlotte Perkins Gilman (1860–1935), Jane Addams (1860–1935), Ida B. Wells (1862–1931), George Herbert Mead (1863–1931), and W.E.B. Du Bois (1868–1963).

Classical sociological theorists lived in Europe and North America during times of rapid and dramatic transformation from largely rural, agrarian societies to urban societies developing industrial capitalist economies through increasingly mechanized and centralized factory work. Much has changed in the world between the mid-nineteenth century and the early twenty-first century, yet many of the major social changes and challenges that engaged the classical theorists' attention continue to shape people's lives in contemporary societies, from the ever-growing influences of **urbanization**, **individualism**, capitalism, bureaucratization, and technological development, to inequalities and forms of marginality stratified according to gender, race, class, and an expanding range of differences. Accordingly, many contemporary sociologists, including some of the authors in this collection, build upon the conceptual approaches from classical theory to explore different aspects of the current social world. The classical sociological tradition, as we contend and as many of the contributors to this volume agree, continues to yield important questions, insights, and avenues for exploring different facets of contemporary social life.

Contemporary Theory

Contemporary theory is much broader and significantly more heterogeneous than classical theory. In social theory, contemporary generally refers to works from the early to mid-twentieth century to today. Whereas in the classical tradition, key figures or works are easily identified (although this is increasingly being challenged), contemporary theory is characterized by a vast and ever-expanding number of theorists and works, none of which are widely agreed upon as canonical or fundamental to the discipline. Whereas classical theory is more connected to particular social thinkers, contemporary social theory is more concentrated around particular schools of thought that reflect broad sets of concerns and categories, such as **feminist theories**, **social constructionism**, micro-sociology (symbolic interactionism, dramaturgical sociology phenomenology, ethnomethodology), **critical theory**, neo-**functionalism**, relational sociology, **poststructural theory**, queer theory, postmodern theory, **globalization** theory, critical race theory, and **Indigenous** social theory, to name just a few. While there is much variation between them, contemporary theorists are typically reflexive, which means that they try to be explicit about the criteria they are using to interpret and explain social phenomena, including normative assumptions and sometimes political commitments. Many are concerned with issues around the production of knowledge, identity, and shared social conditions, which operate within a given set of historical conditions and relations of power.

Many contemporary sociologists engage productively with both classical and contemporary theories, often creating unique syntheses for understanding continuities and differences in the social world across places and times. Sociologists regularly draw upon, critically engage with, and sometimes challenge existing and established theories, new and old. This may be quite explicit, or it may be more implicit. These exchanges contribute to the strengthening of perspectives and/or the development of novel approaches toward and insights into the ever-changing world around us.

The authors in this book have drawn upon a range of classical and contemporary theories, and many engage with multiple theoretical approaches in their analyses. This reflects the dynamism of sociology's theoretical tradition and the rich complexity of the social world. Given this diversity and dynamism, sociologists do not always agree with each other. You will find points of both theoretical agreement and contestation across the different chapters as the authors work from their own theoretical commitments.

Methods and Methodology

Theoretical perspectives and leanings guide the kinds of questions a sociologist asks. Social theory emerges from engagement with data and interpretations of the social world. At the same time, data and interpretations are used to develop, compare, and sometimes test social theories. Sociologists employ a variety of different **methods** for studying the social world. Methods are the specific techniques and processes researchers use to collect, generate, or analyze data about their subject matter. A research method may be **qualitative** or **quantitative** in approach. Qualitative studies focus on meaning and on gathering rich detail and are generally smaller in scale. There are a wide range of methods available for qualitative research, but commonly used methods include various forms of interviewing (e.g., chapter eighteen), observation (e.g., chapter fifteen), **archival research** (e.g., chapter nine), textual or discourse analysis (e.g., chapter six), or a combination of methods (e.g., chapters four and seven). In contrast, quantitative studies translate social phenomena into numerical form and are often large in scale. These studies use methods such as surveys (e.g., chapter two), which can include censuses, and the statistical analysis of these (e.g., chapter twelve), content analysis (e.g., chapter fourteen), and sometimes experimentation. Some researchers use multiple or mixed methods, using a combination of methods both quantitative and qualitative (e.g., chapter nineteen). Research might be intended for description, interpretation, or critique, or it may be social change-oriented. It can be conducted by a researcher working alone or collaboratively with other researchers, community members, or organizations.

The method or combination of methods that researchers employ depends on both the subject matter at hand as well as the **methodology** informing the research study. The methodology is a plan to use specific methods to be able to discover or produce certain kinds of knowledge about a particular facet of social life. The methodology of a study is based on answering larger, more abstract questions pertaining to how one understands the nature of their object of inquiry. In asking, "What is it that I wish to know?," the researcher, either implicitly or explicitly, must contend with questions about what they ultimately believe exists. What is the nature of reality? Questions such as these, about existence and the nature of existence, are ontological questions. **Ontology** is the study of being or a theory of existence. Further, the researcher must ask if what exists is something that can be known. Generally, what is it possible to know? But more specifically, what can be known about what exists? Questions about knowledge are epistemological questions. **Epistemology** is the study of knowledge, or a theory of knowing. Methodology, then, seeks to answer the question: How can I come to know about that which I believe exists? In other words, what specific tools and procedures (i.e., methods) should I use to be able to gain knowledge about the thing I believe exists (e.g., phenomenon, idea, entity, relationship). Zoe Todd discusses these questions in chapter one as she describes a visit to the Rideau Canal.

Conclusion

This collection emerges during a time in which there is considerable concern, debate, and social unrest due to **climate change**, the enduring effects of **colonialism**, the politics of resource extraction, and the impacts of unbridled capitalism on the natural world. The viability and sustainability of our shared environment has never been less certain. Intellectuals, activists, some politicians, civil society organizations, citizens, and communities in Canada and around the world are seeking to intervene in, disrupt, and reverse some of these disastrous trends through the shaping of public policies and through forms of civil disobedience and direct action. Meanwhile, powerful global actors – including the leaders of democratic states and corporations – commonly dismiss unwelcome criticism and warnings supported by evidence-based research on such matters, thereby sowing confusion and dissensus. This particular political-economic-environmental context makes the analysis of seasons important in urgent ways, since changes to both the planetary ecology and local environments threaten to further destroy physical life forms and ecosystems, cultures, and traditions.

One thing that is true about all social (and seasonal) crises is that they offer potent opportunities to examine the ordinary structuring conditions and everyday functioning of society. Thus, with respect to the Chicago heat wave mentioned earlier, Klinenberg (2002) observed that the conditions of inequality that were revealed by the extreme weather did not go away once the temperatures returned to seasonal. But the way in which these ordinary conditions of unequal life chances are invisible "makes them all the more dangerous in the daily life of the city" (Klinenberg 2002, 24). Seasonal crises reveal the failures of society but can also produce moments for people to come together. In her analysis of a series of human-made and natural disasters, Rebecca Solnit (2009) found that in almost all cases of people coming together, people later quickly became nostalgic for the time of the disaster – not for the devastation, but for the feeling of being a part of a community. In these cases, crises are similarly revealing of what modern society lacks. As Solnit found, the disasters revealed that the ordinary, everyday life of disconnection and increased privatization – not just of goods and services, but of aspirations and investments – was the ongoing disaster. But in coming to recognize this everyday disaster, it is possible to begin to imagine other, more livable conditions of social life.

In each of the following chapters, we approach the seasons and the ritualized passage of time as means by which to explore issues of sociological interest and to look more specifically at seasons as social agents themselves; that is, the different seasons create conditions to which we must collectively adapt and respond whether in how we organize and make sense of time, institutions, activities, or interpersonal or intergroup relations, or our own bodies and feelings. We treat seasons and seasonality as phenomena and conceptual devices that bridge, in complex and fascinating ways, natural phenomena, the small-scale personal interactions and processes of meaning making, and formal and institutional structures. The authors in this collection present sociologically diverse ways to think about how seasons are a means of organizing ourselves.

The seasonal sociology in this text attends to the simultaneously terrible and magnificent lessons of the sociological imagination. Terribly, we can realize that our fate is mostly done to us – that climate change, the commercial co-optation of seasonal joys, and the gendered, racialized, and otherwise stratified structuring of labour and leisure impact our individual experiences in ways that are often beyond our individual control. Yet, magnificently, each individual and community contributes to make our social world and history. Enduring seasonal rituals of social cohesion show the ongoing possibilities of social life, while challenges to these and new seasonal traditions and adaptations express possibilities for rethinking and reshaping ways of being together.

References

Berger, Peter. 1963. *Invitation to Sociology: A Humanistic Perspective.* New York: Doubleday.

Berger, Peter, and Thomas Luckmann. 1966. *The Social Construction of Reality*. New York: Doubleday.

Costanzo, Roslyn. 2016. "Trunk or Treat: New Tradition Could Change Halloween As We Know It." *Huffington Post,* September 29. https://www.huffingtonpost.ca/2016/09/19/what-is-trunk-or-treat_n_12086634.html.

Durkheim, Émile. 1982. *The Rules of Sociological Method and Selected Texts on Sociology and its Method,* edited by Steven Lukes, translated by W.D. Halls. New York: Free Press.

———. 1995 [1912]. *The Elementary Forms of Religious Life,* translated by Karen Fields. New York: The Free Press.

———. 1997. *Suicide: A Study in Sociology.* New York: Free Press.

Edles, Laura Desfor, and Scott Appelrouth. 2015. "Introduction." In *Sociological Theory in the Classical Era,* 3rd Ed., 1–19. Thousand Oaks: SAGE Publications.

Klinenberg, Eric. 2002. *Heat Wave: A Social Autopsy of a Disaster in Chicago*. Chicago: University of Chicago Press.

Laframboise, Kalina. 2018. "Deadly Heat Wave Blamed for up to 70 Deaths in Quebec." *Global News,* July 9. https://globalnews.ca/news/4321912/quebec-heat-wave-70-deaths-2018/

Marx, Karl. 1967 [1867]. *Capital: A Critique of Political Economy,* edited by Friedrich Engels. New York: International.

Marx, Karl, and Friedrich Engels. 1967 [1848]. *The Communist Manifesto.* New York: Pantheon.

———. 1970 [1845–1846]. *The German Ideology,* Part 1, edited by C.J. Arthur. New York: International.

Mills, C. Wright. 1959. *The Sociological Imagination.* New York: Oxford University Press.

Solnit, Rebecca. 2009. *A Paradise Built in Hell: Extraordinary Communities that Arise in Disaster.* New York: Viking.

Weber, Max. 1968. *Economy and Society: An Outline of Interpretive Sociology.* Edited by Guenther Roth and Claus Wittich. Translated by Ephraim Fischoff et al. New York: Bedminster.

Fall

Fall is a season of returning and gathering. After Labour Day, many return to schedules of school and work after the long days of summer activities have wound down. Cooler weather returns. Migrating animals head back to their other home places. And, many in Canada gather food and folk together for Thanksgiving dinner and Halloween fun. The chapters in this section contemplate various forms of seasonal autumnal returns and gatherings.

How do you know it's autumn? Is it when the first leaves begin to fall, a date on the calendar, or the sudden abundance of pumpkin spice everything? While this might seem like a trivial question, it can inspire us to think about a bigger question: How do we know anything? How do we know what exists? And, how do we know that we know? Although these seem like abstract philosophical concerns, how we each answer these questions form the basic assumptions upon which all other sociological work is built. In chapter one, Zoe Todd tackles these questions by introducing us to the important philosophical concepts of **ontology** (the study of what exists, or theories of being) and **epistemology** (the study of knowing, or theories of knowledge) in relation to the annual expulsion of fish from Ottawa's Rideau Canal in late autumn. Todd offers a discussion of **Indigenous ways of knowing** that contrast the **Western** philosophical history that underpins the logic of **settler colonialism**. Settler colonialism refers to the practices of land **dispossession** and genocide of Indigenous peoples that was central to the processes of creating Canada as a white settler society. Settler colonialism also refers to a set of ideas, logic, or ideologies that have shaped how knowledge is created, understood, and disseminated in Canada.

One of the main sites where we develop and learn shared epistemological and ontological orientations is school. School is one of the key **agents of socialization** through which individuals learn how to be members of **society**. **Socialization** involves learning skills and knowledge for how to live life competently within a given society. School is a site in which children formally learn these skills and knowledge. Students are also socialized into a whole range of intersecting sets of ideas and expectations about who we are or ought to be, how we should act, and even what we should like, value, or desire. Children learn these in informal ways at school through **interactions** with each other, teachers and authorities, course material, and the institution of education itself. In chapter two, Heather Rollwagen explains that when students come back to school in September, after summer holidays, they return to a social context of **crime** that is embedded within the **social bonds** that youth have within schools. Socialization into gender **norms** often means adopting dominant views that boys and men are naturally more aggressive and more prone to criminality. Meanwhile, dominant beliefs about **race** means that racialized students are disproportionately negatively impacted by **zero-tolerance** policies and what sociologists call the **schools-to-prison pipeline**. A fall return to school can mean a return to all of these socially produced **structures** and social norms.

In chapter three, Sonia Bookman discusses the experience of fall as a season increasingly shaped by marketing and corporate branding; fall is the pumpkin spice latte-branded season. Bookman shows that this has not been an accidental, natural, or inevitable development but one intentionally brought about by companies. Although this might seem like a troubling manipulation of public taste motivated by profit, Bookman argues that it is important to consider **agency** and the flexibility of **culture**.

In chapter four, Jenna Hennebry, David Celis Parra, and Rachelle Daley make sense of the conditions of labour for Canada's seasonal agricultural migrant workers – workers who must return to their home countries in the fall. Hennebry and her collaborators engaged in extensive **participant observation** and **interviews** with **seasonal migrant workers** to get to know their experience and delve into how these workers experience these conditions. Hennebry, Celis Parra, and Daley reveal these experiences to be full of difficulties and exploitation as a result of a combination of structural and interactional processes.

In chapter five, Heidi Bickis analyzes Thanksgiving and **holiday body work**, a term she uses to describe the unpaid and largely under-appreciated labour that goes into gathering people together, preparing and cooking meals, and doing all of the other work that goes into enabling others to rest. Women remain disproportionately responsible for this invisible labour; so, while holidays are imagined as a time of rest and renewal, some bodies emerge more refreshed while others are depleted. In many ways, this fall holiday is a return to **gendered** patterns of family and work relations established in the wake of society-wide changes brought about by the **Industrial Revolution** and its reshaping and dividing of time, space, and labour.

Fall invites reflection and re-examination. In this contemplative spirit, the chapters here offer much to mull over, from the nature of being and knowledge itself to crime and criminogenic environments, from how our bountiful fall harvest and restful Thanksgiving are produced and who does this invisible work, to the appeal and significance of the now omnipresent pumpkin spice latte.

1 The Rideau Canal in Fall: Understanding Ontology and Epistemology with Indigenous Ways of Knowing

ZOE TODD

LEARNING OUTCOMES

After reading this chapter, you should be able to:

- define ontology and epistemology
- explain how the concept of the "pluriverse" relates to systems of power
- explain the relationship between ontology, epistemology, and colonialism
- explain Vanessa Watts's principle of Indigenous Place-Thought and how this relates to Anna Tsing's concept of the arts of noticing
- be able to distinguish between different types of epistemologies and ontology

Field Trip: The Rideau Canal and the Ontology of Fish in Late Autumn

Arts of Noticing

I teach at Carleton University, which is nestled between the Rideau River and the Rideau Canal in Ottawa, Canada. In the autumn of 2016, I taught a graduate seminar called "Decolonizing the Anthropocene," which is about non-**Western** philosophical perspectives on the Anthropocene epoch, ecological crises, and **climate change** in the twenty-first century. You don't need to worry about what the Anthropocene is to read this chapter, so don't panic! My students and I were doing our best to understand how different nations and societies of humans are implicated in current ecological crises on the planet. And we were doing our best to approach these questions by reading work by thinkers, activists, and other knowledge keepers working and/or situated outside of North America and Europe. In this course, one of the main texts we read is anthropologist

Anna Tsing's *The Mushroom at the End of the World.* In this work, she, too, is trying to understand how humans are implicated in current environmental changes, and also how humans and non-human beings work together to exist within spaces marked by ecological destruction caused by current economic and political forces. In this particular book, she advances her principle of the **arts of noticing**, which she employs as a tool to help us make sense of the world around us. Why does this matter? Well, Tsing (2015) argues that "there is a rift between what experts tell us about economic growth, on the one hand, and stories about life and livelihood, on the other. This is not helpful. It is time to reimbue our understanding of the economy with arts of noticing" (132). In other words, we need the arts of noticing in order to help us pay closer attention to the world(s) around us and to better understand how we exist within the world.

When I read Tsing's argument for us to practise arts of noticing, I was reminded of the tireless work of my stepfather, Wayne Roberts, a fisheries biologist and naturalist who dedicated his whole life to observing the well-being of fish, amphibians, and other creatures in the ecosystems of our home province, Alberta. I am also reminded of my childhood spent fishing and outdoors in central and north-central Alberta, where my Métis dad taught me about the history of local plants, animals, and the traces of colonial history in local landscapes. My mom, an avid gardener, was a volunteer steward for an Alberta natural area near Baptiste Lake, west of the town of Athabasca, where she was tasked with observing recreational and industrial impacts along a cutline next to the prairie lake. I spent my childhood learning to observe and pay attention to the habitat and living conditions of amphibians and fish in Alberta waterways, as well as plant and other non-human life. Wayne led annual spring "frog and toad walks" at the Wagner Bog natural area outside of the town of Stony Plain, where he would bring local citizens along to learn to listen to and observe the habitat and conditions of frogs and toads. He also fished extensively throughout central Alberta, collecting a lifetime's worth of knowledge of the well-being of prairie fish throughout the Red Deer River and North Saskatchewan River watersheds (and beyond). Sometimes, on summer evenings, I could find my mom and stepdad on the banks of the North Saskatchewan, right in the heart of Edmonton, checking up on the fish conditions. Throughout my childhood, we regularly ate the whitefish, northern pike, and rainbow trout that Wayne fished from Alberta waterways. Wayne imbued in me a deep responsibility to always give due consideration to the fish. This work was strengthened by my time conducting ethnographic research on human-fish relationships in the Inuvialuit community of Paulatuuq, in the western Canadian Arctic, where Inuvialuit fishermen, including Andy and Millie Thrasher, taught me about the long history of monitoring and observing fish health and water quality in their territories. Whether in Arctic watersheds or in the heart of a southern Canadian **city**, my entire life has been imbued with this work of *noticing* fish and their well-being. Surely I could teach my students to notice and pay attention to the lives and movements of fish and their habitats, as kin and interlocutors had taught me to do from my early childhood. To do this, I decided to take my class to the Rideau Canal to observe the fish.

The Field Trip

The timing and seasonality of the graduate seminar matters in this particular field trip. If we were taking the class in winter, spring, or summer, we would be observing very different relationships and conditions for the fish. It was a bit of serendipity that we visited the canal during the week that it was drained. The water levels of the canal are altered to accommodate different seasons in the waterway. For example, the canal is drained in the fall in preparation for the winter skateway, and water levels fluctuate through manual manipulation of the waterway throughout other parts of the year (Ottawa Sun 2014).

I *had* intended on showing my students the ways fish make the canal their home. As we set out toward the canal, I was giddy with the hope of showing my students how the hardy fish make lives and meaning of their own in the canal. However, we arrived to find that the National Capital Commission, which oversees maintenance of the canal, had drained it to prepare it for winter. The draining of the canal left a sizeable number of fish – we counted at least 30 (including sunfish, carp, and other fish we were unable to identify from our elevated position on the path next to the canal) – to die in the mud below. Stunned by the senseless death of these fish, we could do nothing but film and document the fish kill. As I filmed the carnage in the canal, I thought back to what my colleague, Gwich'in historian Crystal Fraser, had pointed out in a talk at Carleton University in March 2016 (Fraser 2016): when **Indigenous** peoples fish in Canada, they are held to very strict quotas and limits under state laws. As Fraser explained, if an Indigenous fisherman exceeds a fishing quota by even *one* fish, they risk very serious legal ramifications. So, to observe at least 30 fish killed in one single location as authorities prepared the canal for the winter (and to prepare the canal for its function as a public skateway) incensed me as an Indigenous woman. There were myriad ontologies at play here: in one world, the fish were mere *collateral.* Their death was merely the cost of doing business in this nineteenth-century military infrastructure of the Rideau Canal. From my perspective as a Métis woman who studies human-fish relations, these fish were and are kin to local Algonquin peoples, tied into relationships to this land and its waters that bind humans and non-humans to specific reciprocal responsibilities. To simply drain the water and life out of the fish was an affront to these reciprocal duties. Further, nobody would go to jail for killing 30 fish to drain a man-made, colonial era military canal for the winter, but if I had fished these fish out of the canal without a licence and left them to die in the mud, I would be liable for prosecution for violating the state's wildlife conservation laws. My mind raced as I considered all the contradictions and paradoxes of the scene before me. Who gets to decide when a fish lives or dies in the heart of Ottawa, and what constitutes lawful killing of this many fish in the canal? In one onto-epistemology, fish death is an excusable and unavoidable cost of the settler colonial state's operations of its infrastructure. In another configuration, the fish were busily preparing for the winter, and were surely unable to consent to this death as they went about their fishy lives on their own terms in the canal's waters.

This visceral or **embodied** form of noticing became a foundational part of my teaching of this course again in the 2017 fall term. This time, returning to the water that October, I was more familiar with the seasonality and rhythm of the canal. I knew to anticipate the drainage, and I alerted my Twitter followers to keep an eye on the canal and to report any more instances of fish being left to die in the mud. In this way, my students and I were becoming sensitized to the seasonality of the canal. We observed the water intently as we moved about the city, paying closer attention to fluctuations in its levels, observing man-made pollution in the waters, and visiting the fish throughout the year. As fall approached, I became extra vigilant, making an extra effort to walk to the canal when I could, doing what I could to notice the fish and their conditions. My students and I made a point of walking the same section of the canal the week before the anticipated drainage of the canal, and again the week of the draining. We also made several visits to the Rideau River to observe its seasonal changes over the term. We were doing our best to notice the water, the fish, and what is going on with them, using the tools we had available to us: our senses, our cameras on our smartphones, and our collective ability to observe the environment as a group.

As we peered over the edge of the canal's stone walls in 2017, we noticed two large carp swimming against the current, refusing to be sucked into the cavernous outfall that bypasses the lock and shoots out some 20 metres away, opening into the waterways heading to the small urban lake contiguous with the Rideau Canal – Dow's Lake. My students and I struggled to contain our emotions as we watched these two carp enact their visceral and insistent refusal (Simpson 2014) to be drained. We were alarmed at the notion of fish as collateral damage in the canal's human operations. Unable to physically help the fish (given the steep fall into the industrially contaminated mud below us), we were forced to only notice their suffering. We moved down to the outfall, and I gave each student tobacco to place in the canal, to enact a small ceremony for the fish. This was our small effort to acknowledge the dominant **ontology** of canals and military infrastructure as well as their impacts on the thinking and sentient fish within the canal. In this way, our arts of noticing are not entirely empirical, or wed solely to the notion of the **scientific method**, as we were not only documenting the fish and the water conditions, but also performing our own small ceremony in honour of the fish. This approach melds and intertwines onto-epistemologies.

The work of coming to know these fish and the plural ontologies that shape their lives (existing as they do at the intersections of many different realities and worlds) forced us to enact plural epistemologies or arts of noticing (Tsing 2015). Each one of us at the canal's edge experienced a different reaction to the sight of the dead fish in October 2016. Some students looked away, some became angry, others snapped into documentation mode and took note of the number, location, and condition of the fish – each response a unique way of engaging with and making meaning (**epistemology**) of the death of the fish. In October 2017, we again manifested multiple epistemological responses. For example, some students asked if they could leap into the contaminated mud eight feet below to help the struggling carp (I had to say no, for safety reasons). To bear witness to the death and struggle of non-human beings because of very human infrastructure is to contend with the worlds that are made through canals and all the other products of Euro-Western ontologies and epistemologies. These forms and arts of noticing are not tidy or clinical. But these forms of noticing have power, as they bring us into worlds we might otherwise refuse to acknowledge or engage with in contemporary dominant Western **society**. In the following section, we will explore some of the theoretical terms introduced in this short "virtual field trip" in the autumn to visit the fish in the Rideau Canal. Specifically, in the following sections we will explore what the terms *ontology* and *epistemology* mean, and then we will explore how Indigenous scholars and thinkers in North America approach these two concepts.

Ontology and Epistemology

As you read this chapter in your course, there is a good chance that it is in the autumn, during a very special time of year: the Earth is spinning in the vast expanse of space, with one pole tilting ever so slightly away from the sun, calling autumn into life in your neck of the woods. As the days shorten, the trees and other plants stop photosynthesizing, and their leaves turn to various shades of vermillion, mustard, and auburn. As the world slowly turns inwards, preparing for the winter to come, droves of students file back into the lecture halls of universities across the continent, readying for another year of mid-terms, textbooks, and midnight scrambles to finish term papers. If you're especially lucky, you might be asked to write a paper on questions of philosophy and the meaning of the world around you – including the nature of being and reality that we encounter as fallible humans spinning around on this slightly wobbly globe. When such a task arises, there are perhaps no two words that strike greater fear in the hearts of a budding sociologist or anthropologist than "ontology" and "epistemology." I remember the first time I heard these terms: it was in second year, when I was floundering through my arts electives during my biology undergraduate degree. "Onto-what?" I asked myself. "Episte-why?" I spat out under my breath. It was a bit of an uphill journey to make sense of these grandiose terms. But trust me: as someone who failed biochemistry twice and barely squeaked through first-year calculus, I swear that ontology and epistemology are much friendlier concepts to wrangle than CAMK pathways or vertical asymptotes. In this chapter, I explain the Western philosophical metaphysical concepts of ontology and epistemology. I then explore Indigenous philosophical perspectives that challenge Western understandings of ontology and epistemology. Ontology, put simply, is about *what is*, or, as the Oxford Dictionary states: "the branch of metaphysics dealing with the nature of being." And epistemology is about *how we come to know what is*. Put in other terms, the Oxford Dictionary defines epistemology as: "the theory of knowledge, especially with regard to its methods, validity, scope, and the distinction between justified belief and opinion."

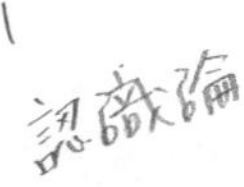

So, that is pretty much it. I could just finish the chapter here and you could have more time to watch *Friends* reruns on Netflix or whatever streaming service you are using when this textbook enters its fifth reprinting. However, as your favourite Indigenous killjoy feminist scholar (a.k.a. a Métis feminist scholar who is not going to sugar-coat the legacies of **colonialism** here in Canada for you), I am here to drop some inconvenient truth: we cannot assume that all thinking and being for every society and **culture** around the world can be split into the universalizing Western philosophical categories of ontology and epistemology. Not everyone divides their world(s) and praxis (i.e., action) into the categories mobilized in Euro-American philosophical **traditions**. People around the world have different ways of explaining the nature of "understandings of being and knowing," and sometimes this means that being and knowing are not even considered separate categories (a topic we will explore in this chapter). While Western philosophy would sometimes have you believe that all thought is universal and therefore all you really need to do to get a sense of human reasoning and struggle is to read some Hegel and Heidegger and smoke clove cigarettes in a dimly lit café in Berlin, there are myriad non-Western ontologies and epistemologies (or, to disrupt the use of these Euro-American philosophical framings, we could say instead "understandings of being and knowing") that jostle for attention in the world.

Think about *being* and *knowing* this way: They are – and they shape – the entirety of everything we are moving through and thinking with. For example, my colleague Dr. Karen Drake opened a talk on Indigenous (specifically, Anishinaabe) law in Ottawa in January 2016 with a quote from author David Foster Wallace (2008):

> There are these two young fish swimming along and they happen to meet an older fish swimming the other way, who nods at them and says, "Morning boys, how's the water?" And the two young fish swim on for a bit, and then eventually one of them looks over at the other and goes, "What the hell is water?"

What the hell is water indeed. For the purposes of this analogy, think of water as *ontology (the proposed reality within which we move)*, and the fish asking what the hell it is as *epistemology (how we come to question, query, and understand the medium or milieu we are moving within and/or living in)*. And, sometimes, when we are moving through a particular society, era, or geography, we may not consciously reflect on the nature of *being* or *knowing, or how we come to understand these phenomena.* Now, nobody could
[…]re swimming in the same water – that is, the water is
[…] we operate (ontology) and you assumed that we are
[…]eworks to come to understand the nature of living and
[…]tions about water are epistemology). There are histori-
[…]phy that argue this very idea – that there are specific
[…]bout the world and, by extension, specific accepted
[…] through empirical methods of research and study).
[…] reality shared by all members of a particular group,

But are we all swimming in the same water?

⇒ There are many ways of being and knowing, and not every culture imagines these as separate things as explained through Western philosophy and Western empirical methods of inquiry, is understood as **universality** (Oxford Dictionary; Mignolo 2013). The scientific method is premised on this principle of universality – that one can apply systematic forms of observation (i.e., gather empirical evidence) to uncover universal truths/phenomenon in the world around us. **Empiricism** is the idea that we can rely on observation and experience to derive knowledge about a phenomenon in the world (Merriam-Webster). To extend the previous analogy – universality and the scientific method argue that there are systemic and uniform ways to study "what the hell" water is, and these empirical scientific methods will uncover universal, irreducible truths about "what the hell" water is, "what the hell" water does, and "what the hell" we should do about these aspects of water. Together, the scientific method and empiricism inform and are informed by very particular worldviews and understandings of the reality we inhabit (for more on the uses of the scientific method in sociology, see Unger, chapter nine).

However, as we develop our understanding of ontology and epistemology as concepts relevant to sociology, it is important for us to ask if a **Eurocentric** perspective of being, knowledge, and existence is indeed the only one. As I note above, there are other thinkers who argue we are not living in one singular or universal understanding of being and knowing. There are scholars who challenge Eurocentric philosophical models by arguing that in fact there are multiple ontologies operating in this world and that people come to understand these plural ontologies according to plural epistemologies (Povinelli 2016; Tsing 2015; Watts 2013). In other words, there are potentially many waters and many "what the hell" moments to contend with.

Why does it matter that there are myriad ontologies and **epistemes** operating in this world? Well, to be blunt: it is a question of power. The dominant (i.e., Euro-Western) forms of ontology (understandings of the nature of *being*) and epistemology (*knowing*) in the world are those that operate to reproduce systems of power (see Povinelli 2016). The specific forms of *being* and *knowing* we choose to embrace, reproduce, and exalt shape how the world is understood, as well as how systems within it and that comprise it are reproduced over time. But it is not always that easy to see ontology and epistemology operating around us, because we are constantly immersed in the worlds they structure and create for us as humans living here on Earth.

Sometimes, when power imbalances privilege one world (ontology) or one way of understanding the world (epistemology) over another, we get the uneven intersections (Crenshaw 1989) of multiple ontologies and epistemologies. That is, in some situations, Western ontologies and epistemologies are afforded more power and significance in global social, cultural, and political systems. As Elizabeth Povinelli (2016) explains, Western metaphysics (including ontology and epistemology) are the dominant ways through which the world is understood in global systems, leading to the violent suppression of other worlds and the beings, relationships, and stories that comprise these worlds.

This imbalance between dominant Western ontology and epistemology and other realities and knowledges can create what scholar Anna Tsing (2005) calls *friction.*

The dominance of Western ontology (*being*) and Western epistemology (*knowing*) is employed to discredit other ways of existing and thinking in the world, but marginalized and oppressed people/societies resist these efforts to displace their ontologies and epistemologies. Through this resistance, there is friction. Where there is friction, there is movement (in this case, of people, resources, and capital), heat, and the possibility for transformation of social, political, and cultural arrangements. This suggests, then, that ontology and epistemology are not static or unchanging, nor that the dominance of a Western order of being and thinking is destined to forever tower over other ontologies and epistemologies. For these reasons, it is also useful to point out here that not everyone likes to use the terms *ontology* and *epistemology*. These Euro-Western concepts are rooted in their Eurocentric origins and do not necessarily make room for other worldviews. It can be helpful to think of ontology in terms of the realities it creates, reproduces, and makes. As Tsing (2015) notes, reality is created through the action of many phenomena and agents; or, as she states, ontology is one form of "world-making." This term, *world-making*, which Tsing (2015, 292) argues can be used "in dialogue with what some scholars are calling 'ontology,'" helps us focus on the notion of ontology as an *action* or a *verb* (something that people actively *do* and *create*) as opposed to a static or politically neutral *noun* or *thing* (something unchanging and inert that people interact with). In other words, ontology, or world-making, shapes everything from how we see the world to the way we measure things around us, to how we explain what is going on politically, socially, physically, economically, spiritually, and culturally. Further, ontology, or world-making, also shapes how we envision how to *change* the worlds we live in. In Tsing's (2015, 293) words: "World-making projects ... show that other worlds are possible."

Let me go one step further. We know now that ontology is *being* and epistemology is *knowing*. We also know that there are multiple ontologies and epistemologies operating here on Earth (and maybe also in outer space, but I will leave that for your generation and your robot kin to figure out!). We know that the intersections of these forms of being and knowing can create what Tsing (2005) calls *friction* and that another way we can talk about ontology and epistemology is as a form of world-making.

Ontology (*being*) and epistemology (*knowing*) tend to be conceived in Western philosophy as two separate entities/phenomena. According to this separation, there is a duality between reality and coming to understand and know reality. Anishinaabe and Haudenosaunee scholar Vanessa Watts (2013) teaches us that this binary in Western philosophy emerges from seventeenth-century French philosopher René Descartes's mind-body dualism. Descartes separates the human mind from nature, arguing "one's perception of the world as being distinct from what is in the world, or what constitutes it" (Watts 2013, 24). This Cartesian dualism between humans and their environment has perpetuated the idea that only humans can think – or only humans are capable of epistemology, generating epistemes, and understanding the nature of being. Watts (2013) calls this divide between knowing and being the "epistemological-ontological divide" (24). This divide stresses the separation between mind and body, human and non-human, and firmly situates the business of metaphysics solely in the realm of humans. As Watts (2013) explains, the epistemological-ontological divide in Western philosophy renders all other beings as inert or static substances being acted *upon*, and frames non-human beings as unable to perceive the world around them in a *sentient* way. In other words: ontology and epistemology are reserved solely for "higher-order" beings in the Western sense (i.e., humans), and everyone else is just along for the ride.

Indigenous Place-Thought

However, there are other ways to think about the nature of being and knowing outside of the binary or the epistemological-ontological divide. Vanessa Watts (2013) contests the binary between being and knowing in her work on Indigenous relationships to land and place in North America, offering a different perspective on who can think, who can know, and how *being* manifests. As Watts (2013) notes, in Anishinaabe and Haudenosaunee cosmology (i.e., the whole entirety of being and knowing that informs Anishinaabe and Haudenosaunee philosophy, law, culture, society, politics, and spirituality), being and knowing inform one another, and the ability to perceive the world and understand it on a philosophical level, and to consciously shape it on an onto-epistemological level, is not restricted solely to human actors or to the realm of human consciousness. As Watts (2013) explains:

> habitats and ecosystems are better understood as societies from an Indigenous point of view; meaning that they have ethical structures, inter-species treaties and agreements, and further their ability to interpret, understand and implement. Non-human beings are active members of society. Not only are they active, they also directly influence how humans organize themselves into that society. (23)

In this quotation, Watts (2013) draws our attention to the fact that in Indigenous worldviews, non-human beings have **agency** and are capable of interpreting the world (existence) in their own ways. This perspective engages more than just humans, and positions questions of being and knowing as activities that involve myriad actors – including humans and non-humans alike! Drawing on these relationships, Watts (2013) presents the principle of **Indigenous Place-Thought**, a concept that fundamentally refuses the divide between thinking and being, human and nature, mind and body (21). She argues instead that being and knowing are interrelated, and they engage not only humans perceiving the world around them but are in fact phenomena co-created by thinking beings (humans and non-humans) entangled in the world, together. She explains the principle of Indigenous Place-Thought:

> Place-Thought is the non-distinctive space where place and thought were never separated because they never could or can be separated. Place-Thought is based upon the premise that land is alive and thinking and that humans and

> non-humans derive agency through the extensions of these thoughts. (Watts 2013, 21)

Let me unpack this a bit. As I explained earlier, ontology and epistemology, in Western philosophical terms, rely on the human ability to perceive the world around us (including, as mentioned, through the paradigms of empirical observation and science). As Watts (2013) further demonstrates, this Eurocentric understanding relies on restricting perception, thinking, analysis, and knowledge synthesis solely to human minds. Indigenous Place-Thought, however, distributes thinking to human *and* non-human beings, including the land itself. Thought is co-constituted by the beings within it, and humans think together *with* land, water, and other non-human beings within these places.

Watts's arguments are helpful to employ when we begin to examine the multiple ontologies and epistemologies that operate in Canada. Unlike a hundred years ago, when you could have comfortably studied the writings of social theorists Marx, Durkheim, and Weber at any old university around the globe without considering the landscapes within which you would have been enmeshed, Canadian sociology students have a responsibility today to consider their relationships to the unceded (and Treaty) Indigenous territories your academic institutions are embedded within.

At this point, let us return to the little virtual field trip to the Rideau Canal that we went on at the beginning of the chapter to see if we can puzzle out what *being* and *knowing* look like when we are contending with the collision of multiple ontologies in a colonial landscape in Ottawa, Canada.

Understanding Plural Ontologies through the Autumn Case Study

One could understand the fish in the canal in several ways. We can understand these fish existing as *pluralities* in their own right, representing and creating different aspects of their being and meaning on their own terms (Todd 2014). Or, as Law and Lien (2013) argue, we can interpret the multiple ontologies of fish – which the fish both inhabit *and* make – as *multiplicities.* The fish in the canal do not exist or "world-make" solely in a Western philosophical paradigm, but rather, exist and manifest their being across, between, and within multiple onto-epistemologies. Let us break this down further: in one onto-epistemology, the fish we observed in the Rideau Canal are objects of scientific study. In Western philosophical terms, these fish are not "persons," but, as Watts (2013) argues, non-thinking beings who live their lives according to the limited conditions accorded to non-human life by Western thinking. As Watts (2013) teaches us, in a Western philosophical onto-epistemology, the fish, water, mud, stones, invertebrates, plants, and other non-human beings in the canal are not capable of thinking. In this onto-epistemology, the only thinking beings present in the autumn visit to the drained or draining canal are the human beings (including myself and the students in the class).

Therefore, the only way to *come to know* about the condition of the fish, the water, the contaminants, and the mud is to observe or measure the conditions using external and "objective" human scientific metrics and tools.

Another ontology offers this: the fish are sentient beings with agency and they are **kin**. They are related to human and non-human beings in this **territory**, and as such, these fish are embedded in complex relationships informed by the legal traditions, languages, and histories of the Algonquin people whose territory this section of the Rideau Canal bisects. As neither the students nor instructor of the course are Algonquin, we engaged in this relationship as outsiders. We do not know the stories, names, histories, or legal traditions that inform the relationships between Algonquin people and these fish. But we can be cognizant of this relationship and do our best to honour its existence. In this context, we can return to Watts's (2013) point that from the perspective of Indigenous Place-Thought, the fish, water, mud, and other components of the canal *are also thinking and knowing beings* who co-constitute knowing and being together. In this sense, agency and knowledge is not limited solely to the human actors at the canal's edge, but actually distributed among the humans and non-humans present in the autumn field trips. In this sense, the fish have a pretty good sense of "what the hell" is going on – as we saw with the two large carp refusing to be drained through the outfall in October 2017.

As we conduct our arts of noticing of the fish and water, we can mobilize plural understandings of the fish as non-human kin to local Indigenous nations *and* as beings who move through and are shaped by Euro-Western onto-epistemologies. In other words: the fish are both "specimens" of study in the Western sense *and* political agents and kin in Indigenous legal orders (Todd 2016). In yet another plurality
(onto-epistemology), the fish are fleshy
and pollution. In this sense, the fish carr
exploitation of local waterways – both l
stories they are communicating throug
human and non-human kin with whon

The point I am making here is that
by a universal or singular onto-episten
non-human) at the canal's edge carriec
that shaped their engagement with the
the world and our social, political, ec
world, it is important for us to unde...
knowing operating throughout every engagement. Another way to look at it is that there are multiple or plural cosmologies operating in framing who the fish are and what they do (i.e., fish are food, fish are collateral to industrial development, fish are kin, and, as David Foster Wallace shows us in the earlier quote in this chapter, fish are philosophers in their own right!).

私たちが魚と水に気づく芸術を行うとき、私たちは、地元の先住民国家にとって非人間的な親類としての魚、そしてヨーロッパ＝西洋の「認識論」を通過し、それによって形成される存在としての魚という複数の理解を動員できる。つまり、魚は西洋的な意味での"標本"であると同時に先住民の法的秩序における政治的主体かつ親族

Philosophers such as Arturo Escobar and Walter Mignolo call this phenomenon the "pluriverse" (Mignolo 2013). Escobar draws on the notion of the pluriverse from the work of the Zapatistas, who define the pluriverse as "a world where many worlds fit" (Escobar 2016, 20). What is also very important for budding sociologists to understand is that these worlds, and how they fit together, are shaped through ongoing colonial, white supremacist, and capitalist phenomena – as pointed out earlier in the discussion of Anna Tsing's principle of friction. This is why some worlds (i.e., Western, capitalist ones) in the pluriverse dominate over others (Escobar 2016). Or, as Watts (2013) teaches us, this is why Western onto-epistemologies are **naturalized** as universal while Indigenous Place-Thought and other non-Western ways of being and knowing are erased. Walter Mignolo (2013) argues:

> If a pluriverse is not a world of independent units (cultural relativism) but a world entangled through and by the colonial matrix of power, then ... a way of thinking and understanding that dwells in the entanglement, in the borders, is needed. (n.p.)

One way to engage, in a fulsome way, the *pluralities* of the pluriverse, or multiple onto-epistemologies, is to embrace what philosopher Achille Mbembe (2015) articulates as **epistemic diversity**: "It is a process that does not necessarily abandon the notion of universal knowledge for humanity, but which embraces it via a horizontal strategy of openness to dialogue among different epistemic traditions" (19).

So, as we stand at the edge of the canal, it is important for us to consider which worlds, knowing, and being are privileged in the stories we tell about the fish, the water, and the heavy metals left by industrial pasts. If we want to know "what the hell is water," or fish, or colonialism, or infrastructure, we need tools to help us navigate the reality and meaning of these principles across plural worlds.

Conclusion

This epistemic diversity behooves us to be open to the possibility that there are plural or multiple ways of being and knowing in the world, and that to conduct ethical and accountable research, we must engage these pluralities. It means that we cannot automatically default to a Euro-Western onto-epistemology to explain the world and that we are tasked with the work of working across the "many worlds" (Escobar 2016) that operate here on Earth. It also opens doors for really exciting and dynamic thinking and collaborative scholarship that honours the diverse knowledge traditions around the globe.

Now that we have examined ontology, epistemology, the pluriverse, Indigenous Place-Thought, and epistemic diversity through our field trip to the Rideau Canal, I want you to consider how these concepts will help shape your engagement with sociology, with human experiences of phenomena like the seasons, and what you will bring to the experiences of knowing and being as you delve into the discipline. And if you ever figure out what the hell water is, let me know!

Questions for Critical Thought

1. As we leave the edge of the canal and head back to the lecture hall, reflect on what it means to engage plural onto-epistemologies, worlds, and cosmologies in your day-to-day work in the university.
2. Explain ontology and epistemology in your own words. Can you identify the ontological and epistemological assumptions that are made by the author of a textbook you're using for any other course you're currently taking?
3. Compare Anna Tsing's notion of arts of noticing to the sociological perspectives forwarded by C. Wright Mills and Peter Berger described in the chapter introduction. How do they contrast and how might they complement each other?
4. What does it mean to think about the relationships between ontology, epistemology, and colonialism when you think about the perspectives of thinkers like Marx, Weber, and Durkheim introduced in this book's introduction?
5. Can you think of your own personal experience with a situation or place that enables you to apply Vanessa Watts's principle of Indigenous Place-Thought to think through the relationships between being, knowing, and world-making, as we just did with the fish in the Rideau Canal?

References

Crenshaw, Kimberlé. 1989. "Demarginalizing the Intersection of Race and Sex: A Black Feminist Critique of Antidiscrimination Doctrine, Feminist Theory and Antiracist Politics." *University of Chicago Legal Forum* 1 (8): 139–68.

Escobar, Arturo. 2016. "Thinking-Feeling with the Earth: Territorial Struggles and the Ontological Dimension of the Epistemologies of the South." *Revista de Antropología Iberoamericana* 11 (1): 11–32. https://www.aibr.org/antropologia/netesp/numeros/1101/110102e.pdf.

Fraser, Crystal Gail. 2016. "Can Fish Drip with Colonialism? White Privilege, Academia, and Forging Ahead Together." Presentation at *The Next 40: Modern Treaties and Citizenship*, Carleton University, Ottawa, ON, March.

Law, John, and Marianne Lien. 2013. "Slippery: Field Notes on Empirical Ontology." *Social Studies of Science* 4 (3): 363–78. https://doi.org/10.1177/0306312712456947.

Mbembe, Achille. 2015. "Decolonizing Knowledge and the Question of the Archive." Lecture at the Wits Institute for Social and Economic Research, May 2. http://wiser.wits.ac.za/system/files/Achille%20Mbembe%20-%20Decolonizing%20Knowledge%20and%20the%20Question%20of%20the%20Archive.pdf.

Merriam-Webster. s.v. "empiricism." Accessed June 19, 2020. https://www.merriam-webster.com/dictionary/empiricism?src=search-dict-box.

Mignolo, Walter. 2013. "On Pluriversality." *Walter Mignolo* (blog), October 20. http://waltermignolo.com/on-pluriversality/.

Ottawa Sun. 2014. "NCC to Drain Rideau Canal." *Ottawa Sun*, March 25. http://ottawasun.com/2014/03/25/ncc-to-drain-rideau-canal/wcm/a5f02ea7-2d5f-41a0-a23c-d1edc42aeedb.

Oxford Dictionary. s.v. "epistemology." Accessed June 19, 2020. https://www.lexico.com/definition/epistemological.

———. s.v. "ontology." Accessed June 19, 2020. https://www.lexico.com/definition/ontology.

———. s.v. "universality." Accessed July 8, 2020. https://www.lexico.com/definition/universality.

Povinelli, Elizabeth. 2016. *Geontologies: A Requiem for Late Liberalism*. Durham: Duke University Press.

Simpson, Audra. 2014. *Mohawk Interruptus: Political Life Across the Borders of Settler States*. Durham: Duke University Press.

Todd, Zoe. 2014. "Fish Pluralities: Human-Animal Relations and Sites of Engagement in Paulatuuq, Arctic Canada." *Etudes/Inuit/Studies* 38 (1–2): 217–38. https://doi.org/10.7202/1028861ar.

———. 2016. *"You Never Go Hungry": Fish Pluralities, Human-Fish Relationships, Indigenous Legal Orders and Colonialism*. Unpublished doctoral thesis, Aberdeen University.

Tsing, Anna Lowenhaupt. 2005. *Friction: An Ethnography of Global Connection*. Princeton: Princeton University Press.

———. 2015. *The Mushroom at the End of the World: On the Possibility of Life in Capitalist Ruins*. Princeton: Princeton University Press.

Wallace, David Foster. 2008. "Plain Old Untrendy Troubles and Emotions." *Guardian*, September 20. https://www.theguardian.com/books/2008/sep/20/fiction.

Watts, Vanessa. 2013. "Indigenous Place-Thought and Agency amongst Humans and Non-Humans: First Woman and Sky Woman Go on a European Tour!" *Decolonization: Indigeneity, Education & Society* 2 (1): 20–34.

2 Back to School Season: Schools and the Social Organization of Crime

HEATHER ROLLWAGEN

LEARNING OUTCOMES

After reading this chapter, you should be able to:

- consider how social contexts can shape the way individuals define, experience, and respond to crime
- describe two different sociological theories of criminal behaviour and how they can be applied to understand crime within the school context
- explain the way in which broader relations of gender, race, and social class are experienced in the school context
- explain why determining the amount of crime is challenging
- use the concepts of the school-to-prison pipeline, zero-tolerance policies, and codes of conduct to reflect upon and analyze your own experiences in the education system

Introduction

When students prepare to return to school in the fall, their thoughts are likely focused on issues such as purchasing school supplies and books, making necessary financial arrangements for tuition, figuring out their class schedules, or signing up for co-curricular activities. Students may be excited to see old friends or anxious to make new ones. The predominant **narrative** of schooling in Canada is that it is a time of intellectual, personal, and social growth. When you prepared to return to school, you likely did not think too much about **crime**.

When people think about the relationship between crime and schools, they may think about high-profile incidents of school violence, such as the school shootings that have occurred in Parkland, Florida, or Newtown, Connecticut. These crimes, while horrific, are relatively rare; however, more minor forms of crime are fairly common. Some research indicates that minor theft (a type of **property crime**) is experienced by as many as 38 per cent of Toronto students, and 39 per cent of students reported experiencing minor assault (a **personal crime**) (Tanner and Wortley 2002). In my own research with sociologist Joanna Jacob, we found that nearly a quarter of all police-involved incidents of violent crime involving young people took place at a school (Rollwagen and Jacob 2018). Given these numbers, it is likely that you or people you know have experienced crime at school.

As a sociologist, I think a lot about the relationship between crime and other social **institutions**, such as schools. How does the school environment shape the way crime is defined? Do schools create opportunities for crimes to occur? Are all students subjected to school regulations in the same way? What are the implications of bringing police officers into schools? These are just some of the questions that I ask in order to think sociologically about crime. In this chapter, I demonstrate how sociologists think about crime by exploring the different concepts, theories, and issues that arise when we think about crime in the school context. After reading this chapter, you might think a little differently about schools you have attended.

Defining Criminal Behaviour

To study crime, we first have to define exactly what constitutes a crime. In Canada, a crime is defined according to criminal **law**, most of which is outlined in the Criminal Code, the Controlled Drugs and Substances Act, and the Youth Criminal Justice Act (YCJA). While these laws provide a legal definition of a crime, sociologists remind us that these definitions are not natural things that reflect an objective idea of "right" and "wrong" (Frohmann and Mertz 1994). Rather, laws tend to reflect the **values** considered to be held by members of a **society**. Those behaviours that are considered **deviant** – that is, behaviours that violate collective understandings of what is "right" and "wrong" in a particular social context (also called "social norms") – are most likely to be the subject of criminal law. It is important to distinguish between deviance and crime because not all deviant behaviour is criminal. For example, forms of extreme body modification (such as extreme tattooing or body piercings) violate social norms of appearance, but they are not prohibited by law.

When behaviour becomes subjected to regulation through criminal law, this process is called **criminalization**. Sociologists interested in the criminalization of behaviour often consider how social norms (and subsequently laws) change according to the social and political context. To illustrate this further, consider how **bullying** and **cyberbullying** have evolved as categories of behaviour that, according to some people, should be regulated through criminal law. In the past, behaviours such as name-calling, schoolyard fights, and exclusion were considered "schoolyard behaviour" and "kids being kids"

(Limber and Small 2003). These experiences were not considered crimes, and were thought to be best handled by school officials (Campbell 2005). Recently, however, things have changed. As a result of some high-profile incidents of suicide that were connected to bullying, there is increased public awareness of the harmful impacts of bullying on youth mental health (Ortega et al. 2012). We are also more aware and concerned for the way bullying is perpetrated against certain social groups, including LGBT youth and young people of colour (Walton 2004). At the same time, technological changes have meant that many bullying behaviours that were once confined to the school have moved to more public and unregulated online spaces (Modecki et al. 2014; Ybarra, Diener-West, and Leaf 2007). The social context of bullying has changed, and there are now calls for law to address bullying, particularly cyberbullying (Broll and Huey 2015).

Of course, demands for changes to criminal law do not mean that those changes will occur. Many sociologists understand the process of "creating" laws as one in which competing groups advocate for laws that reflect their own values. For example, not everyone agrees that cyberbullying merits a law. While some parents have advocated for changes, some police officers believe these laws are reactive and unnecessarily punitive, and that these behaviours could be addressed using laws that already exist (Broll and Huey, 2015). Therefore, even though the social context of bullying has changed, not everyone agrees that laws need to change. Part of thinking sociologically about crime involves examining whose definitions of crime become law, and how that process occurs. Further, sociologists often question how the resources to fight these battles (including the political connections, financial resources, and public support) are more available to some groups of people than others.

Everyone in Canada is compelled to obey the criminal laws that exist; however, students in most Canadian schools are further governed by additional forms of regulation. Schools often have their own sets of "laws" governing student behaviour, referred to as **codes of conduct**. Student codes of conduct define expectations regarding acceptable and unacceptable student behaviour, as well as penalties for violating the code. You might be tempted to assume that these codes of conduct are not as significant as criminal law since schools cannot impose criminal records or incarcerate students. However, school codes of conduct are powerful tools that are considerably more far-reaching than criminal laws, and they may even regulate students' clothing and language. These regulations often reflect problematic assumptions about the "appropriate" way to dress – assumptions that reinforce inequalities of **gender** and sexuality, **social class**, and **race** (Raby 2005). The clothing of young women in particular is heavily policed through dress codes. In 2014, 30 students at a high school in Labrador City were sent home for violating the school dress code: they were wearing sleeveless shirts with their bra straps exposed. They were told that male students and teachers would find their dress distracting (CBC News 2014). Such incidents demonstrate the way student codes of conduct can reflect **heteropatriarchal** ideas of gender, reinforcing ideas of women as sexual objects who are responsible for the sexual impulses of heterosexual men. Codes of conduct can impose penalties such as suspension and expulsion, and these outcomes have likewise been associated with other detrimental effects on academic achievement, mental health, and future employment prospects (Lee et al. 2011). Even though these regulations may not be considered part of criminal law, they operate in a similar way and carry consequences that can be extremely detrimental to a student's future. When you go back to school each fall, you are also re-entering a world where you are subjected to high levels of regulation and control.

Explaining Crime in Schools: Two Sociological Perspectives

An underlying assumption of the school narrative is the notion that school is a good place to be – a place to better yourself through education. Generally, schools are considered to be institutions that positively impact individuals, as they socialize young people to participate "productively" in society as adults – acquiring the necessary language, attitudes, skills and values that will allow them to participate in society in a socially accepted way. This narrative is supported by research. That is, researchers have demonstrated that low academic achievement (dropping out, poor grades, or truancy) is associated with participation in criminal activity (Zingraff et al. 1994; Sampson and Laub 1993; Healy and Bronner 1936). Thinking sociologically about crime and school requires us to think more carefully about *why* there is an association between school (under)achievement and participation in criminal activity. Unlike other disciplinary approaches to the study of crime, which may locate the cause of crime in an individual pathology, **sociological theories of crime** offer explanations that understand crime as the consequence of social interactions or the broader social organization. There are, however, many different sociological theories of crime. In this section, I introduce just two theories as a way to illustrate the very different ways sociologists might explain the relationship between schools and crime.

Social Bond Theory

The first theory that offers insight into the relationship between school and crime is Travis Hirschi's theory of the **social bond** (Hirschi 1969). For Hirschi, the social bond, which generally refers to individuals' relationships to the society in which they live, consists of four dimensions: attachment, commitment, involvement, and belief. Attachment refers to the sensitivity that individuals have to the expectations of others. Commitment refers to the time and energy devoted to conventional activities, such as academic study, part-time work, or extracurricular activities. Involvement is determined by participation in conventional activities. And belief refers to the extent to which an individual's own attitudes and values conform to the attitudes and values of those whom they respect. Hirschi argues that when these bonds weaken, due to a diminishing of any of these four dimensions, individuals are more likely to engage in behaviours that reflect narrow self-interest rather than behaviours that reflect broader social well-being

(Sacco and Kennedy 2012). Although Hirschi did not develop this theory to explain the relationship between school achievement and crime, part of theorizing involves applying more general ideas to make sense of specific social phenomena.

The first step in applying Hirschi's theory is to think about how the four aspects of the social bond can be understood in the school context. Young people who demonstrate high levels of *attachment* will feel connected to teachers and invested in the opinions that teachers have about them (Jenkins 1997). Those who are *committed* to school will accept and believe in the values of education, such as the merit of academic achievement (Sprott, Jenkins, and Doob 2005). The *involvement* component of the social bond can be conceptualized as participation in school-related activities, including curricular activities (homework and studying) and extracurricular activities (such as sports teams, clubs, or musical ensembles). Finally, *belief* in schooling is exemplified in the extent to which an individual accepts school rules and authority as fair (Sprott, Jenkins, and Doob 2005). According to this theoretical logic, students are more likely to engage in criminal behaviour if they are not connected to their teachers, if they do not value good grades, if they do not participate in school activities, and if they do not respect school authority.

Sociologists have used these theoretical ideas to examine the relationship between the strength of the social bond and involvement in criminal activity. For example, Sprott, Jenkins, and Doob (2005) adopted a **quantitative research** approach to explore this relationship by using questionnaires to collect information from students about their attitudes toward school, their participation in school activities, their relationships to teachers, and their involvement in criminal activity. These questionnaires (called **surveys**) were completed by students at two different points in time: the first time when they were between 10 and 13 years old, and again two years later. The information that students provided is converted into numerical data. With this data, sociologists use mathematical procedures (called **statistical analysis**) to look for evidence that social bonds are related to participation in criminal activity. The researchers found that strong school bonds can actually decrease the chances that students who display early aggression or who have delinquent peers will offend later in their teenage years (Sprott, Jenkins, and Doob 2005). In another study, Sprott (2004) found that strong social relationships within a classroom are associated with a lower risk of violent behaviour at a later age and that strong academic environments are associated with a lower risk of committing a property crime, such as theft or vandalism, later in life. Overall, these findings lend support for Hirschi's theory: strong social bonds are associated with lower levels of criminal behaviour. These findings also have important policy implications: Simply showing up to school is insufficient in reducing the likelihood of engaging in crime; rather, individuals must be invested in the value system attached to schools as well as involved in school-related activities in order to protect against the possibility of criminal involvement.

Social bond theory comes out of a **functionalist** understanding of crime, with its roots in the ideas of sociologists such as Émile Durkheim (1938) and Robert Merton (1967). This perspective makes some fundamental assumptions about the nature of human behaviour and organization of social life. For example, it assumes that individuals make rational decisions based on their own self-interest and on the available information about the situation around them. Understanding school crime from this perspective offers us insight into why students with poor connections to their schools and whose values are not closely aligned with those of educational institutions might be more likely to be involved in crime. At the same time, it does not consider the broader social context (and power relations) that shape how crime is experienced. For example, why is it that most youth crime, particularly violent crime, is committed by men?

Feminist Perspectives

Sociologists reject the view that men are inherently more violent than individuals with other gender identities, but social bond theory does not provide us with the tools to answer this question. This is where feminist perspectives can be useful. While feminism is often misunderstood to mean "just about women," feminist perspectives focus on how categories of social identity, such as gender identity, race, and social class (and the **intersections** of these identities), result in inequalities in the way people understand, experience, and respond to crime. A feminist approach links these inequalities to more systemic issues in the social organization of society, as demonstrated in various studies in this book (see chapters five, six, eight, sixteen, and twenty). Feminist perspectives are diverse and wide-ranging in the ways they think about social issues; therefore, this section represents just a small sample of ways in which a feminist perspective can inform our understanding of how crime is experienced in the school context.

Feminist perspectives illuminate the **gendered** nature of crime – that is, men are disproportionately both the perpetrators and victims of violent acts (Connell 2002). In the school context, the gendered nature of violent crime in particular is highlighted by considering some of the most high-profile shootings that have taken place in schools: the 1989 massacre at École Polytechnique in Montreal in which a man murdered 14 women; more recent events in the United States, such as the 2018 murder of 17 high school students at Marjory Stoneman Douglas High School in Parkland, Florida, by a teenage boy, or the 2012 murder of 23 children at Sandy Hook Elementary School by a teenage boy. When you look to media coverage of these events, a fairly consistent narrative emerges: a bullied and socially ostracized young person kills innocent youth, leaving the community shocked (O'Grady, Gaetz, and Buccieri 2010). While the gender of the offender may be casually mentioned, it is rarely mentioned that in these (and many more), the shooters are young men, and most often they are **white** (Newman 2004). Feminists suggest that the invisibility of gender, race, and other categories of social identity in the discussion about school violence reflects the broader organization of power in our society – one in which **cisgender** heterosexual men have social, financial and political control (heteropatriarchy) (Katz 2012). Within a patriarchal society, school shootings are explained in ways that do not problematize men or white masculinity in any way, instead focusing on how the perpetrators experienced mental illness, had access to weapons, or were bullied by their peers.

Taking a feminist perspective to make sense of school violence makes gender (specifically masculinity) the focus of the analysis. A feminist perspective allows us to think about how bullying in schools is part of a broader cultural value system that teaches young boys how to act. Within a heteropatriarchal system, an idealized form of masculinity is one that reflects physical power, economic success, and (hetero)sexual prowess; boys whose physical appearance or actions challenge this version of masculinity are ostracized, harassed, and may be physically or sexually assaulted. Researchers have noted that while the perpetrators were indeed bullied, the bullying reflected heteropatriarchal values of masculinity, such as power, physicality, and sexual experience with women. For example, Rachel Kalish and Michael Kimmel (2010) suggest that the perpetrators of some of the most high-profile school shootings in the United States were teased and bullied because they were perceived as weak (physically), emotional, submissive, non-athletic, artistic, sensitive, or nurturing. According to Katherine Newman (2004), who studies school shootings and interviewed several perpetrators of these crimes, these boys believe that the act of killing other students was a "manly exit" from the bullying they faced. They thought that by killing other students, they would be able to prove their manliness and thus overcome the perception that they were failures of masculinity. Thus, while bullying of these students is often part of the popular narrative explaining mass shootings, the gendered nature of the bullying is not part of the conversation. A feminist perspective allows us to connect boys' experiences of victimization in school to the broader heteropatriarchal structure of society.

Feminist perspectives are also valuable for understanding everyday incidents of school bullying. Using a feminist approach, we can see how these more common experiences constitute important ways in which **norms** of gender and sexuality are encouraged and regulated. In an in-depth qualitative study of a high school in a suburban town in California, C.J. Pascoe (2011) shows that the use of homophobic slurs, aggressive attempts to engage women in sexual activity, and the physical assault of students who identify as gay are central ways in which high school students who are boys learn to "perform" their gender – ways that reflect and reproduce heteropatriarchal norms and values. Teenage boys learn to avoid being bullied by performing gender in "appropriate" ways. Pascoe's analysis thus demonstrates how feminism is a valuable approach for thinking about how these common and **normalized** forms of harassment and bullying in high school stem from broader norms of gender and sexuality.

When we understand school crime through a feminist lens, we can clearly see the need to develop policy that dismantles the broader ideas that uphold these inequalities, rather than creating laws that punish individual offenders. Pascoe (2011) provides several examples of what this might look like, such as working to enact legislation that protects marginalized groups of students, developing curriculum and instructional resources that help educators disrupt **normative** ideas of gender and sexuality, and eliminating school rituals that reinforce heteropatriarchal ideas of masculinity, such as many hazing and seniority rituals. By fostering a school climate that is more inclusive of diverse expressions of gender and sexuality, feminist perspectives believe acts of violence (both minor and significant) will be reduced.

Reporting and Documenting Crime

Sociologists are also interested in examining how society responds to crime. In order to report a crime, individuals must first define for themselves that a particular incident is a criminal act – a definition that is shaped by the context in which an event takes place. For example, a student who is physically assaulted by peers at school might understand this behaviour to be a normal part of the teenage experience, even if the behaviour meets the legal definition of assault. The context in which an event takes place is central for how individuals make sense of those events for themselves.

If individuals believe a crime has taken place, they must also decide if (and to whom) they will report the incident. This is likewise not a straightforward process, as the decision to report may depend on the severity of the incident, the nature of the crime, and even the relationship between the victim and offender (Rollwagen and Jacob 2018). For example, research suggests that when a victim knows their offender, they are less likely to report the crime to the police because they are hesitant to get the offender in trouble or fear retaliation (Kaukinen 2002). In schools, victims and offenders are likely to know one another, which may reduce the number of criminal events that are reported to officials. When you think back to your own school experiences, you might recall witnessing acts of theft, vandalism, or even assault or harassment. How many of these incidents did you report to officials? Why did you (or didn't you) report them? When you consider your own experiences, it is easier to appreciate how much crime goes unreported.

The crime that is not reported to police is referred to as the **dark figure of crime** because we cannot know how much crime is unreported. Since the 1970s, a significant amount of research on crime has used surveys to try and determine the amount that goes unreported. These surveys ask people about crimes they have experienced or committed, regardless of whether they were reported to the police. For example, the Toronto Youth Crime and Victimization Survey (TYCVS) was conducted in 2000 and asked 3,393 high school students about their experiences of crime, regardless of whether these incidents were reported. These surveys can provide insight into the extent to which individuals experience crime and which crimes are reported less frequently. Further, these surveys provide insight into why individuals are unwilling to report crime to the police. For example, results of the TYCVS have been used to establish that young people of colour have particularly negative perceptions of the police, which may explain reluctance to notify them about crime (Wortley and Tanner 2002).

Even if one chooses to notify the police about a crime, it does not automatically result in a charge being laid. Police exercise a tremendous amount of discretion when they are called to an incident. The officers who arrive at a scene must first agree that a crime has taken place before they decide how to proceed. To make this determination, police rely on **crime scripts**, which are culturally specific ideas about what a so-called normal crime would look like (Miethe 1987). Crime scripts often reflect a stereotypical (but not necessarily accurate) idea of crime. As a result, markers of social identity, such as gender, race, age, social class, ability, and sexuality significantly impact the way officials interpret a criminal event (Lally and DeMaris 2012). According to this script, police officials think of young, racialized men as "normal" perpetrators of criminal behaviour and are therefore likely to charge male students of colour (Murray 1990). Offenders who do not fit these crime scripts, such as more affluent white students, may be less likely to be subjected to criminal charges. As a result, police discretion is not applied equally across social groups.

The school context itself can also play a role in how officials understand an event. My own research (Rollwagen and Jacob 2018) has found that when a crime occurs in a school, police are less likely to lay a charge compared with crimes occurring at home. Why might this be the case? Is it possible that the police rely on other officials (such as school administration) to address the issue? Or does the school context operate in a way that frames the event as "kids being kids" as opposed to behaviour that is violent or harmful? Thinking sociologically about crime allows us to explore how the social context plays a significant role in shaping the understanding of criminal behaviour.

If police determine that a crime has taken place, an official crime report is completed. These crime reports form the basis for **official crime statistics**. Claims about "crime rates" or "crime waves" are often based on official statistics. However, it is important to remember that official statistics count only those events that are (a) legally defined as a crime, (b) come to the attention of police, and (c) are believed by a police officer to have taken place. Events that meet these three criteria reflect a very small proportion of the total crime that occurs. Therefore, if you were to ask me how much crime occurs in schools, I would tell you that it depends on who you ask. Official statistics will report one set of numbers, while surveys of victims or offenders will provide another. Further, many crimes will go unreported in both official statistics and survey results. Counting crime is a complicated process; as a result, sociologists are generally quite wary of any grand statements or claims about "crime problems" that are based solely on official statistics.

Controlling Crime: Surveillance in the School

When someone is found to have committed a crime or violated a code of conduct, that person is generally subjected to some form of punishment. The rationale for punishing people varies, and may include retribution (vengeance to rectify a wrongdoing), behaviour modification (to "teach" someone how to behave according to the law), and symbolism (as a way to communicate to other people that the behaviour will not be tolerated). In a school, responding to crime can be done through the disciplinary tools available to school administrators (based on the code of conduct) or may involve the use of the criminal justice system.

Zero-Tolerance Policies

Since the 1990s, schools have increasingly used disciplinary and surveillance practices that rely on the criminal justice system (Casella 2003). The increased involvement of this system in school discipline has grown out of policy that mandates the involvement of criminal justice officials in school matters. Likewise, **zero-tolerance** policies have become very common. Under these policies, punishment is enacted for all rule violations, regardless of the circumstances or mitigating factors. Punishment can include suspension, expulsion, and criminal charges. Zero-tolerance policies were enacted in Ontario under the Safe Schools Act in 2000 in response to growing concerns about violent crime in schools, but they were found to be ineffective and were later rescinded (O'Grady, Gaetz, and Buccieri 2013). Nevertheless, such policies continue to exist in many Canadian and American schools. Sociologists have noted that the rise of zero-tolerance policies in schools has coincided with increased levels of school-based surveillance (Heitzeg 2009), which employs technology like metal detectors and surveillance cameras. Policies such as mandating that students wear identification badges or school uniforms are other ways in which surveillance is undertaken. However, the most noticeable surveillance policy is the presence of police officers, called school resource officers (SROs), in schools. SROs are not educators, but criminal justice officials with the power to make arrests. As you look around your own school, take note of the different ways in which you are subjected to surveillance. How often are you required to produce your student identification? How many security cameras track your movements? Are you required to conform to a dress code? Are police officers or security guards present in your school? These are all forms of surveillance that are part of the everyday life of students.

The School-to-Prison Pipeline

How can we make sense of the increasing levels of surveillance in schools? Some sociologists suggest that the involvement of criminal justice officials in school disciplinary matters is part of the growing **prison-industrial complex** that exists in many contemporary **Western** capitalist democracies. The prison-industrial complex is a concept that is used by sociologists to think about how the work of criminal justice (including police and prisons) is increasingly performed by corporations interested in generating profit by growing the "business" of criminal justice. As a result, "solutions" to social issues are often located within the criminal justice system (Schept, Wall, and Brisman 2014), and the presence of police officers in schools reflects the growth of that system into the realm of education. Other sociologists have considered the way power works in the school context through these technologies of surveillance. The ideas of Michel

Foucault, a philosopher and social theorist, are particularly useful here. Foucault (1977) suggested that the use of surveillance technologies by authorities to make individuals visible and known at all times (referred to as **panopticism**) renders individuals compliant and conforming since they feel they are constantly being scrutinized by the authorities (whether or not they actually are). This form of social control is not unique to a school, but it reflects modern ways of regulating citizens (for other discussions of Foucault see Overend, chapter six, and Unger, chapter nine). Sociologists, therefore, think about how the changes that are occurring in schools reflect shifts in the broader society.

We must furthermore consider if these forms of surveillance and control are effective in reducing crime. While you might think it's obvious that higher levels of surveillance and police presence will reduce crime in schools, research suggests that it is counter-productive (O'Grady, Gaetz, and Buccieri 2013). For example, serious penalties for crime have either no effect (Chen 2008) or are associated with higher rates of criminal activity in school (Mayer and Leone 1999). These policies may actually do more harm than good, as zero-tolerance policies are largely responsible for the development of the school-to-prison pipeline. This term refers to a pattern in which students are tracked (that is, funnelled) from educational institutions "directly and/or indirectly into the juvenile and adult criminal justice systems" (Heitzeg 2009, 1). The presence of SROs in schools (or the requirement that all suspected crimes be reported to police) *directly* funnels young people into the criminal justice system. This process works *indirectly*, too: Students who are suspended and expelled under zero-tolerance policies are academically disadvantaged: they are likely to drop out of school, which can significantly impact their long-term educational and employment outcomes, putting them at a greater risk for involvement in crime (Heitzeg 2009).

The school-to-prison pipeline is also not impacting all students equally. Rather, students who are already marginalized (namely in terms of race and social class) are far more likely to be entered into the criminal justice system as a result of school-related deviance (Salole and Abdulle 2015). There are a few reasons for this. First, these students are more likely to attend schools located in marginalized neighbourhoods, which tend to have higher levels of surveillance and police presence (Salole and Abdulle 2015). Behaviours that would go unnoticed or unreported in more affluent-neighbourhood schools (or private schools) are more likely to result in criminal charges because of this added surveillance. Second, race- and class-based **discrimination** by school authorities and SROs means that racialized students are more often given penalties of suspension or expulsion (Bhattacharjee and Ontario Human Rights Commission 2003; Skiba and Nesting 2001). For example, disruptive behaviour is more likely to be interpreted as a criminal issue (requiring police) for black youth, but may be interpreted as a psychological illness (requiring a medical doctor) for white youth (Heitzeg 2009). Third, when students are involved with the criminal justice system, students who are poor (who are disproportionately racialized minorities) do not have the financial resources to secure adequate legal representation, which makes them less able to challenge or negotiate criminal charges (Kutateladze et al. 2014). Sociological thinking can help us understand how measures such as zero-tolerance policies, as well as surveillance technologies and personnel, which are enacted to keep students safe, actually serve to reinforce race- and class-based inequalities and reduce students' safety.

Conclusion

Thinking sociologically about crime that occurs in schools means understanding how the school context shapes the way deviant actions are (or are not) defined as criminal, how school codes of conduct regulate student behaviour, how strong school attachments can reduce criminal behaviour, how crimes occurring in school reflect broader social inequalities, and how approaches to school discipline reflect and reproduce broader inequalities and relations of power.

Sociologists also tend to orient their analyses toward shaping policies. Based on the research discussed in this chapter, we might consider how schools have the capacity to reduce crime by creating inclusive social environments and reducing the securitization and criminalization of student misbehaviour. Social bond theory reminds us that policies that promote attachment, commitment, involvement, and belief in school values will promote academic achievement and reduce the desire to be involved in deviant activities. Central to accomplishing this task is ensuring that all schools are well equipped: Teachers and support staff must be provided with sufficient resources, and the curriculum provided to students must connect to students' identities, experiences, and values. Using a feminist perspective reminds us that schools do not exist in a vacuum: the inequalities that exist outside the school, such as those that structure opportunities according to race and social class, are also reflected and reproduced within it. Broader social policies that address structural inequality, such as movements to reduce **poverty**, dismantle the prison-industrial complex, and address gender and racial inequality, will shape the way students experience safety in the school context.

Questions for Critical Thought

1. How much crime do you think occurs on your school campus? What types of crime are under-reported? Why do you think that is?
2. Consider the issue of cyberbullying that was introduced in this chapter. Would the creation of cyberbullying laws do anything to prevent this type of behaviour?
3. How strong is your social bond to school? Compare the strength of your social bond to that of your peers. Do you think that makes you more or less likely to commit a crime or even to violate a code of conduct?
4. How has your own social identity (your gender identity, race, social class, sexuality, ability) shaped your experience of crime in the school context? How might a feminist theory help you make sense of those experiences?

5. Consider the different ways in which you were subjected to surveillance while in high school. Did these forms of surveillance make you feel safer or more fearful? How was your experience of surveillance impacted by your social identity?

References

Bhattacharjee, Ken, and Ontario Human Rights Commission. 2003. *The Ontario Safe Schools Act: School Discipline and Discrimination.* Toronto: Ontario Human Rights Commission. http://www.ohrc.on.ca/sites/default/files/attachments/The_Ontario_Safe_Schools_Act%3A_School_discipline_and_discrimination.pdf.

Broll, Ryan, and Laura Huey. 2015. "'Just Being Mean to Somebody Isn't a Police Matter': Police Perspectives on Policing Cyberbullying." *Journal of School Violence* 14 (2): 155–76. https://doi.org/10.1080/15388220.2013.879367.

Campbell, Marilyn A. 2005. "Cyber Bullying: An Old Problem in a New Guise?" *Australian Journal of Guidance and Counselling* 15 (1): 68–76. https://doi.org/10.1375/ajgc.15.1.68.

Casella, Ronnie. 2003. "Zero Tolerance Policy in Schools: Rationale, Consequences, and Alternatives." *Teachers College Record* 105 (5): 872–92. https://doi.org/10.1111/1467-9620.00271.

CBC News. 2014. "Bra Straps Too Hot for Menihek High, Students Sent Home." May 29. www.cbc.ca/news/canada/newfoundland-labrador/bra-straps-too-hot-for-menihek-high-students-sent-home-1.2657903.

Chen, Greg. 2008. "Communities, Students, Schools, and School Crime: A Confirmatory Study of Crime in US High Schools." *Urban Education* 43 (3): 301–18. https://doi.org/10.1177/0042085907311791.

Connell, R.W. 2002. "On Hegemonic Masculinity and Violence: Response to Jefferson and Hall." *Theoretical Criminology* 6 (1): 89–99. https://doi.org/10.1177/136248060200600104.

Durkheim, Émile. 1938. *The Rules of Sociological Method.* 8th ed. Translated by Sir George Edward Gordon Catlin. Glencoe, IL: Free Press.

Foucault, Michel. 1977. *Discipline and Punish: The Birth of the Prison.* New York: Pantheon Books.

Frohmann, Lisa, and Elizabeth Mertz. 1994. "Legal Reform and Social Construction: Violence, Gender, and the Law." *Law & Social Inquiry* 19 (4): 829–52. https://doi.org/10.1111/j.1747-4469.1994.tb00941.x

Healy, William, and Augusta Fox Bronner. 1936. *New Light on Delinquency and its Treatment: Results on a Research Conducted for the Institute of Human Relations, Yale University.* New Haven: Yale University Press.

Heitzeg, Nancy A. 2009. "Education or Incarceration: Zero Tolerance Policies and the School to Prison Pipeline." *Forum on Public Policy Online* 2009 (2). ISSN-1938-9809. https://eric.ed.gov/?id=EJ870076.

Hirschi, Travis. 1969. *Causes of Delinquency.* Berkeley: University of California Press.

Jenkins, Patricia H. 1997. "School Deliquency and the School Social Bond." *Journal of Research in Crime and Delinquency* 34 (3): 337–67. https://doi.org/10.1177/0022427897034003003.

Kalish, Rachel, and Michael Kimmel. 2010. "Suicide by Mass Murder: Masculinity, Aggrieved Entitlement, and Rampage School Shootings." *Health Sociology Review* 19 (4): 451–64. https://doi.org/10.5172/hesr.2010.19.4.451.

Katz, Jackson. 2012. "Memo to Media: Manhood, Not Guns or Mental Illness, Should Be Central in Newtown Shooting." *Huffington Post–The Blog*, December 18 (updated February 17, 2013). http://www.huffingtonpost.com/jackson-katz/men-gender-gun-violence_b_2308522.html.

Kaukinen, Catherine. 2002. "The Help-Seeking Decisions of Violent Crime Victims: An Examination of the Direct and Conditional Effects of Gender and the Victim-Offender Relationship." *Journal of Interpersonal Violence* 17 (4): 432–56. https://doi.org/10.1177/0886260502017004006.

Kutateladze, Besiki L., Nancy R. Andiloro, Brian D. Johnson, and Cassia C. Spohn. 2014. "Cumulative Disadvantage: Examining Racial and Ethnic Disparity in Prosecution and Sentencing." *Criminology* 52 (3): 514–51. https://doi.org/10.1111/1745-9125.12047.

Lally, William, and Alfred DeMaris. 2012. "Gender and Relational-Distance Effects in Arrests for Domestic Violence." *Crime & Delinquency* 58 (1): 103–23. https://doi.org/10.1177/0011128711420102.

Lee, Talisha, Dewey Cornell, Anne Gregory, and Xitao Fan. 2011. "High Suspension Schools and Dropout Rates for Black and White Students." *Education and Treatment of Children* 34 (2): 167–92. https://doi.org/10.1353/etc.2011.0014.

Limber, Susan P., and Mark A. Small. 2003. "State Laws and Policies to Address Bullying in Schools." *School Psychology Review* 32 (3): 445–55.

Mayer, Matthew J., and Peter E. Leone. 1999. "A Structural Analysis of School Violence and Disruption: Implications for Creating Safer Schools." *Education and Treatment of Children* 22 (3): 333–56.

Merton, Robert K. 1967. *Social Theory and Social Structure*. New York: Free Press.

Miethe, Terance D. 1987. "Stereotypical Conceptions and Criminal Processing: The Case of the Victim-Offender Relationship." *Justice Quarterly* 4 (4): 571–93. https://doi.org/10.1080/07418828700089531.

Modecki, Kathryn L., Jeannie Minchin, Allen G. Harbaugh, Nancy G. Guerra, and Kevin C. Runions. 2014. "Bullying Prevalence Across Contexts: A Meta-Analysis Measuring Cyber and Traditional Bullying." *Journal of Adolescent Health* 55 (5): 602–11. https://doi.org/10.1016/j.jadohealth.2014.06.007.

Murray, Charles. 1990. *The Emerging Underclass*. London: Institute of Economic Affairs.

Newman, Katherine S. 2004. *Rampage: The Social Roots of School Shootings*. New York: Basic Books.

O'Grady, Bill, Stephen Gaetz, and Kristy Buccieri. 2013. "Tickets... and More Tickets: A Case Study of the Enforcement of the Ontario Safe Streets Act." *Canadian Public Policy* 39(4): 541–558. http://doi.org/10.3138/cpp.39.4.541.

O'Grady, William, Patrick F. Parnaby, and Justin Schikschneit. 2010. "Guns, Gangs, and the Underclass: A Constructionist Analysis of Gun Violence in a Toronto High School." *Canadian Journal of Criminology and Criminal Justice* 52 (1): 55–77. https://doi.org/10.3138/cjccj.52.1.55.

Ortega, Rosario, Paz Elipe, Joaquin A. Mora-Merchán, M. Luisa Genta, Antonella Brighi, Annalisa Guarini, Peter K. Smith, Fran Thompson, and Neil Tippett. 2012. "The Emotional

Impact of Bullying and Cyberbullying on Victims: A European Cross-National Study." *Aggressive Behavior* 38 (5): 342–56. https://doi.org/10.1002/ab.21440.

Pascoe, C.J. 2011. *Dude, You're a Fag: Masculinity and Sexuality in High School.* Berkeley: University of California Press.

Raby, Rebecca. 2005. "Polite, Well-Dressed and on Time: Secondary School Conduct Codes and the Production of Docile Citizens." *Canadian Review of Sociology* 42 (1): 71–91. https://doi.org/10.1111/j.1755-618X.2005.tb00791.x.

Rollwagen, Heather, and Joanna C. Jacob. 2018. "The Victim–Offender Relationship and Police Charging Decisions for Juvenile Delinquents: How Does Social Distance Moderate the Impact of Legal and Extralegal Factors?" *Youth Violence and Juvenile Justice* 16 (4): 378–94. https://doi.org/10.1177/1541204017710315.

Sacco, Vincent F., and Leslie W. Kennedy. 2012. *The Criminal Event.* Toronto: Nelson.

Salole, Abigail Tsionne, and Zakaria Abdulle. 2015. "Quick to Punish: An Examination of the School to Prison Pipeline for Marginalized Youth." *Canadian Review of Social Policy/Revue canadienne de politique sociale* 72/73: 124–68.

Sampson, Robert J., and John H. Laub. 1993. *Crime in the Making: Pathways and Turning Points through Life.* Cambridge: Harvard University Press.

Schept, Judah, Tyler Wall, and Avi Brisman. 2014. "Building, Staffing, and Insulating: An Architecture of Criminological Complicity in the School-To-Prison Pipeline." *Social Justice* 41(4): 96–115.

Skiba, Russel J., and Kimberly Nesting. 2001. "Zero Tolerance, Zero Evidence: An Analysis of School Disciplinary Practice." *New Directions for Youth Development* 2001 (92): 17–43. https://doi.org/10.1002/yd.23320019204.

Sprott, Jane B. 2004. "The Development of Early Delinquency: Can Classroom and School Climates Make a Difference?" *Canadian Journal of Criminology and Criminal Justice* 46 (5): 553–72. https://doi.org/10.3138/cjccj.46.5.553.

Sprott, Jane B., Jennifer M. Jenkins, and Anthony N. Doob. 2005. "The Importance of School: Protecting At-Risk Youth from Early Offending." *Youth Violence and Juvenile Justice* 3 (1): 59–77. https://doi.org/10.1177/1541204004270943.

Tanner, Julian, and Scot Wortley. 2002. *The Toronto Youth Crime and Victimization Survey: Overview Report.* Toronto: Centre of Criminology, University of Toronto.

Walton, Gerald. 2004. "Bullying and Homophobia in Canadian Schools: The Politics of Policies, Programs, and Educational Leadership." *Journal of Gay & Lesbian Issues in Education* 1 (4): 23–36. https://doi.org/10.1300/J367v01n04_03.

Ybarra, Michele L., Marie Diener-West, and Philip J. Leaf. 2007. "Examining the Overlap in Internet Harassment and School Bullying: Implications for School Intervention." *Journal of Adolescent Health* 41 (6): S42–50. https://doi.org/10.1016/j.jadohealth.2007.09.004.

Zingraff, Matthew T., Jeffrey Leiter, Matthew C. Johnsen, and Kristen A. Myers. 1994. "The Mediating Effect of Good School Performance on the Maltreatment-Delinquency Relationship." *Journal of Research in Crime and Delinquency* 31 (1): 62–91. https://doi.org /10.1177/0022427894031001003.

3 Pumpkin Spice Lattes: Marking the Seasons with Brands

SONIA BOOKMAN

LEARNING OUTCOMES

After reading this chapter, you should be able to:

- identify some of the ways in which seasons are culturally constructed through interlinked practices of branding and consumption
- recognize how seasonal branding is an important component of brands and branding, as well as understand its connection to longer histories of the commercialization of seasons, and its contemporary cultural significance
- describe some key sociological theories of brands and branding as well as some current sociological perspectives on consumption
- apply your understanding of how consumers actively use seasonal goods and branding to interpret how individuals and groups express aspects of identity and group belonging through the creation of shared experiences and seasonal consumption rituals
- apply the concept of a seasonal frame of action to your own autumn consumption practices

Introduction

Autumn is one of my favourite times of the year. The leaves begin to turn yellow, orange, and crimson. The cool morning air smells fresh and crisp. University campuses buzz with the excitement of new students at the start of the academic term. And as if on cue, Starbucks's pumpkin spice lattes appear on the coffee menu to mark the seasonal shift. There is something about the smell and taste of pumpkin spice that evokes a sense of fall, especially in the form of a warm, caffeinated beverage. Since its introduction in

2003, Starbucks's pumpkin spice latte has become, for many, a seasonal **ritual** that helps mark the transition to autumn and its principal Thanksgiving-Halloween holiday.

Brands and **seasonal consumption** are the focus of this chapter. All sorts of brands, from Cadbury to Coca-Cola, have become important elements in the making and marking of seasonal **traditions** and holidays. In the first half of the chapter, I discuss the commercialization of seasons and the development of **seasonal branding**. Taking the case of Starbucks and their pumpkin spice lattes, I suggest that brands, through seasonal marketing, not only extend but also establish elements of seasonal traditions. In the second half, I consider some of the ways in which individuals partake in seasonal consumption and use branded goods to celebrate seasonal holidays and transitions. This section traces how consumption practices such as imbibing and sharing photos of the pumpkin spice latte are used to express social identities and establish a sense of belonging. Overall, I argue that seasonal branding and consumption practices in the contemporary **marketplace** constitute key elements of seasonal activity, shaping how we mark and experience seasonal transitions and time.

This chapter will be mainly based on documentary research, especially drawing on existing case studies of seasonal consumption practices and the meanings people make of them. It also draws on material from empirical studies I conducted on major coffeehouse brands in the Canadian cities of Toronto, Vancouver, and Winnipeg. This material includes qualitative data from over 34 **interviews** with Starbucks consumers, as well as extensive **participant observation** of the branded cafés. In addition, the chapter incorporates material from Starbucks's branded sites on social media, such as Twitter.

Seasons, Culture, and Commercialization

Seasons and seasonal transitions are an important part of Canadian **culture** and everyday life. Seasonal cycles, which occur annually and are understood as forms of **cyclic time** (Lewis and Weigert, 1981), come with predictable, repeated changes in lifestyle "as we adopt the food, clothing, work, and recreational activities appropriate for the season," as well as changes in the holidays or traditions that mark each season (Lewis and Weigert 1981, 441; see further discussion of different types of time and transformations of time in chapters five and eleven). In Canada, autumn is a time when people start to wear cozy fall coats, return to a regular school and work schedule after the summer holidays, incorporate more root vegetables and warm comfort food into the daily fare, and decorate homes with the fall **symbols** of pumpkins, pinecones, sunflowers, and scarecrows. It is also a time when many Canadians attend harvest festivals, anticipate the smells and tastes of pumpkin, apple, and cranberry at Thanksgiving dinner, and plan Halloween outfits and outings. As sociologists J. David Lewis and Andrew Weigert (1981) note, such seasonal activity and sentiment is to a large extent shaped by corresponding festivals, holidays, and traditions: "The meaning and mood of each season are set by its principal holiday, and this aura penetrates our lives from season to season probably far more than we realize consciously" (442). Autumn is thus characterized by an *aura* – in other words, a particular atmosphere – established by the dominant "Halloween-Thanksgiving" holiday, which in turn shapes the kinds of foods, flavours, practices, and meanings associated to the season (Lewis and Weigert 1981, 442).

While seasons are grounded in transitions occurring in nature, they can also be understood as "culturally based time structures" (Lewis and Weigert 1981, 438). The seasonal changes in lifestyle we experience as cyclic time are not objective, naturally occurring phenomena; they are culturally constructed. The meanings associated with autumn and the Thanksgiving-Halloween holiday (reflecting the order in which they are celebrated in Canada) are established and instilled culturally through the stories we share, the practices we engage in, and the objects we use or consume. In this way, seasons are integrated into our lives, informing what we do to mark the seasons and why, as well as how we experience seasonal change. The ideas, practices, and material things associated with the seasons are, moreover, socially transmitted by families, schools, and the media, forming part of a shared culture and cultural identity among a certain group or **society**. This is demonstrated by Tara Milbrandt's discussion of winter culture in Edmonton in chapter seven, and Jen Wrye, Michael Graydon, and Patricia Thille's discussion of "resolution culture" in chapter eight.

Although some seasonal traditions such as Thanksgiving dinner seem relatively fixed, seasonal practices and the attributes of seasonal holidays are continually reworked as new rituals are introduced or established elements are revised. For example, Thanksgiving in Canada has expanded from a time of feasting and family gathering to encompass a day of shopping, with the introduction of Black Friday sales. Culture, in this sense, is not fixed but rather emerges from an ongoing process of interaction and negotiation between individuals, institutions, and broader **social structures**. One site where seasonal meanings and traditions are extensively and actively refashioned in contemporary society is the marketplace, where companies, brands, consumers, and culture converge.

To be sure, there is a long history of **commercial appropriation** of seasonal holidays and traditions, whereby department stores and companies have borrowed elements of holiday traditions such as Halloween trick-or-treating and adapted them to market products such as candy. Commercial interventions, including advertising for early mass brands, have inspired the continually evolving meanings and rituals associated with seasonal festivals and traditions (Whiteley 2008). For example, the Coca-Cola brand, through its advertising images of Santa dating back to the 1930s, helped "shape Americans' visual images of Santa Claus and have also helped reinforce the connection of Santa to contemporary Christmas celebrations" (Belk 1993, 76). The American Santa, promoted by Coca-Cola and associated with giving gifts to children, was then appropriated by department stores, which drew on Santa mythology to promote the phenomenon of Christmas shopping (see Miller 1993). **Myth** is a term used by Roland Barthes (1973) to refer to the underlying ideologies – sets of **values** and beliefs – of a cultural sign such as Santa, established through imagery and storytelling. In this sense, Coca-Cola and many department stores have worked to fashion an economically productive Santa myth, whereby Santa and gift giving (and shopping) are now part and parcel of the Christmas holiday in the United States, Canada, and elsewhere.

Although the Christmas festival attracts a great deal of attention as the focus of much commentary and criticism regarding its commercialization, the same process applies to all of the major holidays, from St. Patrick's Day in spring to Halloween in fall. For example, Levinson et al. (1992) highlight the progressively commercial nature of Halloween: the expansion of Halloween-themed products such as jack-o'-lantern leaf bags (decorative bags imprinted with an image of a jack-o'-lantern used for collecting fallen leaves); the rise of specialized, one-stop-shopping Halloween retail stores; and the expansion of pumpkin-themed events or corn mazes targeting families during the season. Indeed, there is no shortage of marketing advice for companies seeking to capitalize on seasonal holidays and rituals (for example, see Robertson 2012; Waldrop with Mogelonsky 1992).

Branding the Seasons

Brands, Brand Management, Brand Extension

Consumer brands have been at the forefront of seasonal marketing. Cadbury's Easter Creme Eggs are a staple of the Easter tradition, while the Life Savers Sweet Storybook has found its way into countless Canadian Christmas stockings. In many ways, the involvement of brands in seasonal holidays is not surprising. Over the past several decades, brands have become salient features of economic and cultural life (Arvidsson 2006). The rise of brands and their growing influence in society is related to broader cultural and economic shifts characteristic of **advanced capitalism**. These include (but are by no means limited to) the shift from industrial manufacturing as a key focus of economic activity to an emphasis on services and the symbolic economy (Zukin 1995; also see Lash and Urry 1994). The **symbolic economy** refers to the production, circulation, and **consumption** of goods or services that are primarily symbolic (or cultural) in nature, such as branded services or goods (e.g., Nike shoes), all forms of media, entertainment, fashion, finance, and artisanal food. As Naomi Klein (2000) points out in her renowned text *No Logo*, since the 1980s brands and their symbolism have become a central focus of companies, based on the business mantra that companies should produce brands, not material goods. The idea is that value no longer adheres in material goods themselves but in their cultural dimensions – the ideas, attitudes, and experiences conveyed by brands. As a result, brands have become, as branding scholar Celia Lury (2004) puts it, the **logos** of the contemporary economy, involved in the organization of markets, the coordination of production, and the mediation of consumption.

Brands are important elements of the symbolic economy, since they help to establish cultural meanings for a range of goods and services and are consumed as cultural resources. Whereas early mass brands served as markers of quality or the origin of a product, brands today are complex market cultural forms (Lury 2004) that provide individuals with "cultural contexts for everyday living, individual **identity**, and affective relationships" (Banet-Weiser 2012, 4). Critical brand theorist Adam Arvidsson (2006, 8) uses the term frame of action to describe how brands offer cultural contexts or ambiances for the use of branded goods: "[W]ith a particular brand I can act, feel and be in a particular way." (For more discussion on the concept of framing, see chapter eighteen.) Consumers are encouraged to use brands as sources of meaning and as a means to construct and express social relations, lifestyles, or identities; to productively engage in communicative processes and create what Arvidsson (2006, 10) refers to as a "surplus sociality." Surplus sociality denotes the ability of people to create a common world through communication, consisting of "a social relation, a shared meaning, or a sense of belonging that was not there before" (Arvidsson 2006, 10). **Brand management** provides the tools by which consumers can engage in immaterial labour (e.g., communication) and construct a surplus sociality, yet with the aim of appropriating this surplus and transforming it into brand value. This involves a process of co-creation, where consumers contribute to the realization of brand identity or image – a key source of which consists of what consumers "do *with the brand in mind*" (Arvidsson 2006, 7, italics in original).

In the case of seasonal branding, brands offer consumers seasonal frames of action or cultural contexts that suggest ways of marking the seasons with the brand. Brands use various forms of marketing to link goods and services to specific seasonal holidays or traditions. Since brands are not tied to one product, they can be used to introduce specially designated, time-limited seasonal goods through a marketing practice called "**brand extension**" (Lury 2011, 143). This practice involves extending a product range or developing a new line of goods and services under a brand. Alternatively, companies may embed existing branded goods within seasonal activity through conventional marketing practices such as advertising that displays brands being used during holiday events such as Thanksgiving dinner. Seasonal branding thus encourages consumers to use branded goods to create shared experiences and meanings centred on holidays, to establish seasonal traditions with brands, and, ultimately, to co-produce brand value-in-use.

The Pumpkin Spice Latte

Starbucks's pumpkin spice latte (see figure 3.1) is a poignant example of this trend of seasonal branding. Starbucks is a US-based specialty coffee brand that provides customized coffee in a café environment designed to encourage social **interactions** and invoke a sense of community. The popular brand also promotes a certain coffee connoisseurship, with an emphasis on coffee origins, style, and roast, along with the cultivation of a specific Euro-latte lingo (using terms like *venti* to indicate coffee size) among baristas and consumers alike (Bookman 2014). As an extension of its specialty coffee menu, Starbucks has introduced a range of seasonal coffees, which are served in holiday-themed take-away cups according to seasonal intervals. The pumpkin spice latte, for example, is

FIGURE 3.1 Suddenly, it's fall: Starbucks's pumpkin spice latte marks the start of the autumnal season. Photo credit: Sonia Bookman

a seasonal luxury coffee made with pumpkin-spice flavoured sauce (without any actual pumpkin until 2015) and offered in autumn (Powell and Engelhardt 2015). It evokes key elements of the Thanksgiving-Halloween holiday, such as the tradition of pumpkin carving at Halloween as well as the ritual of eating pumpkin pie at Thanksgiving. Interestingly, pumpkin consumption, unlike the consumption of many other fruits and vegetables that are increasingly made available year-round, is almost entirely limited to the festivals of Halloween and Thanksgiving in the United States (and in Canada, to an extent, as well) (Powell and Engelhardt 2015). There is a clear seasonal association between pumpkin, its spiced-up flavours, and fall (see Waldrop with Mogelonsky 1992).

Starbucks's pumpkin spice latte illustrates how brands tap into or appropriate existing seasonal conventions and traditions to position themselves as sites of seasonal celebration. Douglas Holt's (2004) theory of brands as cultural icons, or "**iconic brands**," provides insights into the relationship of brands to seasonal meanings and activity. For

Holt, cultural brands involve the performance of an identity myth – a set of cultural ideas and sentiments about masculinity, nationality, and so on – and are adapted by consumers for their expressive capacity (Holt 2004). The most successful brands, in this scheme, are those that offer a "compelling symbol of a set of ideas or values that a society deems important," and that translate into identity value for consumers who use such brands as a means of self-expression (Holt 2004, 1). Holt (2006) explains that cultural brands such as Starbucks operate as "**ideological parasites**" that draw on existing cultural ideas to establish brand symbolism and meaning (374). In this way, brands do not necessarily invent new ideas and manipulate culture as such; rather, they appropriate, modify, or extend established cultural ideas. In the case of seasonal branding, then, brands might not invent the ideas bound up with seasonal cycles, but they may reinforce, refine, or rework them by offering variations on key elements of a seasonal tradition, or they might expand the range of attributes (rituals, material objects) encompassed by a seasonal holiday (see Miller 1993). Starbucks, for instance, did not invent pumpkin-themed autumnal traditions, but it did adapt the pumpkin spice flavour associated with pumpkin pie to a portable luxury coffee drink – which bolsters its image as a purveyor of fine coffees and creates a source of community around which individuals can partake in seasonal festivities and create a common experience of fall. For many Starbucks consumers, the Thanksgiving–Halloween holiday now includes consuming a pumpkin spice latte in addition to the more established attributes of carving a pumpkin, eating pumpkin pie, and going trick-or-treating.

According to Holt (2006), strong cultural brands are especially effective at proselytizing the ideas they adapt. They are able to expand cultural ideas (and practices) that resonate with customers through "the sheer weight of their marketing spend" (Holt 2006, 375). The tremendous popularity of Starbucks's pumpkin spice latte can be seen in sales: over 200 million pumpkin spice lattes were sold in the first 10 years, from 2003 to 2013 (Maynard 2013). However, Starbucks can also be understood as a **hegemonic brandscape** that not only structures a particular market but correspondingly shapes consumption by acting as a "cultural model that consumers act, think, and feel through" (Thompson and Arsel 2004, 632). **Hegemony** is a concept that derives from the work of Antonio Gramsci and refers to the way a particular group (or, in this case, a brand) maintains power over subordinate groups through a process of negotiation and struggle, in which the dominance of the group (in this case, market share) is established by gaining widespread support (of consumers, in this instance) (O'Shaughnessy and Stadler 2012). For additional discussion of this concept see Ondine Park's discussion of hegemony and the **white wedding** in chapter sixteen. As a hegemonic brandscape, Starbucks exerts powerful influence on both local competitors and the socio-cultural milieus of local coffeehouse environments. Based on its dominant position as a global brand, when Starbucks introduces a trend such as the pumpkin spice latte, local coffeehouses tend to follow suit. Further, the hegemony of Starbucks is achieved through consumer involvement with the brand: persuaded by the pleasures of consuming Starbucks coffees and its branded environments, and how we use the brand as a cultural resource to celebrate autumn with a pumpkin spice latte, we acquiesce to its power. Influencing widespread shared seasonal practices, Starbucks is spun into the culture, shaping seasonal activity, experiences, and meaning.

Seasonal Consumption

So far, we have discussed how companies and their brands play an important role in the commercialization of seasons and seasonal branding. However, it is important to understand that brands do not simply foist consumption rituals and seasonal goods on consumers. McKechnie and Tynan (2006) note how, for instance, festive consumption practices such as preparing Thanksgiving dinner may be partly shaped by "the advertising and fashion systems promoting colour-coded décor through glossy magazines, television 'make-over' programmes and retail displays," yet consumers actively adapt elements and negotiate meanings based on their own values, tastes, family practices, and social expectations (137). Individuals thus play an important role in maintaining or reworking seasonal rituals, festivities, and the cultural meanings associated with winter, spring, summer, or fall through active consumer practices. Consequently, in order to understand the ways in which brands and seasonal branding are spun into seasonal activity, we need to consider the realm of consumption.

The Study of Consumption

Until the 1970s, sociological work on consumption was largely dominated by critical perspectives advanced by the **Frankfurt School** – a group of post-Marxist scholars who fled from Frankfurt to the United States in the early 1930s to escape the Nazis. Focusing attention on mass consumption and mass culture under **capitalism**, they forwarded a model of consumers as passive, conformist dupes who bought into forms of mindless, debased culture (such as Hollywood films or popular music) produced by capitalist firms with the aim of generating profits (Horkheimer and Adorno 2002). This view of consumers, however, was critiqued for its neglect of consumer **agency**, especially by scholars in the **cultural studies** tradition. These scholars illustrated how groups such as youth **subcultures** used consumer goods to develop shared identities, and they actively resisted dominant culture through their consumption practices (for example, see Hebdige 1979; Hall 2006; for more on cultural studies, see chapters ten and nineteen).

Contemporary accounts of consumption emphasize the dynamic and productive nature of consumption activity, paying attention to its complexities (Lury 2011). Consumption is understood as an active process in which consumers negotiate meanings, values, and, of course, the cost of goods (Miller 1998; Lury 2011). Even ordinary consumption such as grocery shopping involves negotiating consumption based on factors related to price, the performance of familial roles and identities, as well as values such as healthy living or ethical consumption. Consumption is also perceived as a creative practice in which individuals select and use products to construct and express identities and lifestyles (Featherstone 2007; Lury 2011) or to fashion unique items from mass-produced goods in the form of **craft consumption** (Campbell 2005). Craft consumption is a term coined by Colin Campbell (2005) to describe a creative form of consumption in which the craft consumer uses mass-produced goods as raw materials to create something unique – a new product – for personal consumption, deploying their skills to enable self-expression. For example, someone might "hack" Ikea products using do-it-yourself skills to create a personalized piece of modern, Scandinavian furniture. In addition, consumption in general is seen to be productive, since it can be used to construct experiences, social relations, and common social worlds (Bourdieu 1984; Cova, Kozinets, and Shankar 2007). For example, Muñiz and O'Guinn (2001) discuss how individuals form and maintain **brand communities**, such as Starbucks pumpkin spice latte enthusiasts, that centre on shared experiences and relationships to a brand. While there are many ways of thinking about consumption as an active process, in the following sections I focus on practice theoretical approaches as well as **cultural consumption** perspectives to explore how consumers encounter, use, and adapt seasonal goods and brands.

Marking the Seasons with Brands: Routines, Rituals, Rhythms

Leading sociologist of consumption Alan Warde (2005, 2014) has proposed a **theory of practice** approach to consumption that helps to explain how the pumpkin spice latte has become a marker of the fall season for many Starbucks consumers. The theory of practice approach to consumption emphasizes the routine nature of consumption activity, which is bound up with various, everyday practices such as getting a coffee on the way to work. Of particular note, this approach suggests that consumption preferences and patterns are not only established as a matter of individual choice, but that they are especially shaped through the ways in which consumption practices are organized or framed. Thus, consumption routines such as getting a morning coffee are organized by elements such as the availability of take-away coffee, drive-through service for commuters, and the location of coffee shops.

Routines

In the case of Starbucks, consumption is framed through the coordination of a branded environment, designed as a **third place** that people can go to between home and work and that functions as a social space of interaction (see Oldenberg 1989). The café environment, moreover, is structured according to daily rhythms, with devices such as opening and closing times that intersect with consumers' routines of work and leisure. As well, there are changes in food display and lighting at different times of day to coordinate with consumer activity and mood. In my research on Starbucks consumption, I found that consumers negotiate consumption practices in conjunction with the spatial and temporal frames afforded by the brand (Bookman 2014). Consumers develop daily or weekly routines of stopping at Starbucks while taking the kids to daycare, meeting up with friends for an intimate conversation in the evening, or reading the newspaper in a Starbucks café on a Saturday morning. Such practices, repeated on a regular basis, crystallize into rituals and customs along a range of temporal registers (daily or weekly cycles), and co-construct meanings about elements of cyclic time such as the day or the weekend (Lewis and Weigert 1981).

Rhythms

Along these lines, Starbucks shapes seasonal practices, such as consuming the pumpkin spice latte, by aligning with seasonal rhythms and cycles – the time of fall – by offering the drink toward the beginning of September for a limited time. Such practices, which may be repeated annually and in conjunction with existing daily or weekly routines, become established seasonal consumption rituals for some patrons. Many regular pumpkin spice latte consumers, like myself, eagerly anticipate the arrival of pumpkin spice at the start of every autumn. In fact, there are over 110,000 followers of @TheRealPSL, described as "THE OFFICIAL TWITTER FOR FALL'S OFFICIAL BEVERAGE From @ Starbucks" (twitter.com), which announces the rollout date for Starbucks's pumpkin spice latte, posts creative photos of the pumpkin spice latte on Instagram, and retweets customer commentary linked to #PSL and similarly themed hashtags. Indeed, consumer anticipation and demand for the drink toward the end of summer is so great that Starbucks has launched the product earlier over the years, contributing to what one writer refers to as "PSL creep" (Kowitt 2016).

Ritual

Integrated into seasonal rituals and traditions through consumption practices organized according to daily and seasonal cyclic time, Starbucks establishes connections with consumers that are not only temporal but also **embodied** and emotional. The practice of consuming a pumpkin spice latte is a sensorial experience, engaging the senses with the smells and tastes of pumpkin pie and the feeling of warmth radiating from the hot beverage. When consumed in the relaxed atmosphere of the café environment characterized by fireplaces, jazzy music, and comfy chairs, it helps create the sensation of coziness associated with fall. The practice also involves an emotional experience that draws on feelings of **nostalgia**, evoking memories linked to fall traditions of Thanksgiving dinner with family or visiting a pumpkin patch in childhood (Overmyer 2016; see chapter five for more on Thanksgiving). Such experiences orient our sense of fall – how it feels, smells, and tastes – and construct cultural meanings about the season. As mentioned, seasons are culturally constituted time structures that shape what we do and how we feel or think at a specific time (Lewis and Weigert 1981). Adapted by individuals as a seasonal consumption practice, Starbucks and its pumpkin spice latte thus co-shape a specific experience of autumn – an experience that many people look forward to reliving each year. It is a seasonal ritual for some: Autumn is not only a time for new pencils, apple pie, and Halloween pop-up stores, it is also a time for drinking pumpkin spice lattes.

Seasonal Socialities: Identity, Belonging, and Distinction through Seasonal Brand Consumption

Cultural consumption involves consuming goods for their expressive qualities in addition to (or instead of) their utility. As Lury (2011) writes, in contemporary **consumer culture**, goods and services are imbued with cultural meaning through the extensive use of design, advertising images, branding strategies, experts who discuss their value on lifestyle television shows, and other symbolic devices. This is reflective of the growing significance of the symbolic economy, as mentioned earlier, and the emphasis on establishing cultural value for goods (through brand symbolism, for example). Consumers selectively use the symbolic meanings attached to products to "create or maintain a given impression, identity or lifestyle" (Campbell, 2005: 24). In short, cultural consumption is bound up with complex cultural and social processes of meaning-making, involving the construction of identities, the establishment and maintenance of social relations, and the configuration of cultures (see, for example, Arvidsson, 2006; Bourdieu, 1984; Chaney 1996; Featherstone, 2007; Lury 2011; Warde, 1994).

Identities as Constructed and Demonstrated through Consumption

As noted earlier, brands serve as cultural resources that consumers are encouraged to use to express aspects of their identity, to create shared meanings and experiences, and to form certain kinds of relations to others. Identity here can be understood as "a temporary stabilization of meaning or description of ourselves with which we emotionally identify" (Barker 2003, 442). It involves both **self-identity**, how we think about ourselves personally (e.g., as someone who is creative or athletic), as well as our **social and cultural identity** developed through our position within categories of class, **gender**, or **race**, for example, and through our connections with others based in shared interests, neighbourhoods, experiences, and so on (e.g., as someone who is middle-class or working-class, a hipster or a coffee connoisseur). Our identities, which are multiple, are not inherent; they take shape over time through complex processes of **socialization**, negotiation, and active self-reflection. Furthermore, identities are not fixed; they are continually worked at as we learn, encounter new situations, become part of new social groupings, and as we age, for instance. In contemporary society, consumer culture is a key site where identities are expressed and our relations to others are reinforced.

As McCracken (2005) puts it, consumers are constantly "rummaging" the world of consumer goods for cultural meanings (values, ideas, styles) they can use to construct and express various aspects of their identities – what it means to be a woman, working class, or a Canadian, for instance. This includes seasonal goods and consumption rituals, which can strengthen social and cultural identities and mark our belonging to various groups.

Community and Belonging

For Starbucks consumers, sharing in a common experience of consuming a pumpkin spice latte in the fall, or sharing images of pumpkin spice lattes on Twitter and Instagram, can create a sense of community and belonging for those involved. As one marketing guru notes, "Of course, in the age of social media, simply drinking the PSL isn't enough – you have to post about it, too. The more people that post a PSL photo to Instagram, the more PSLs seem like a societal norm. We join the crowd because it makes us feel a little happier and more secure to be part of the group" (Overmyer 2016, par. 13). Still, this raises the question of *which crowd, which group?* To whom are we connected through seasonal consumption activity? Indeed, seasonal rituals and variations in the ways in which these are performed serve to mark *belonging to* certain groups as well as *distinction from* others. In other words, rituals such as consuming a pumpkin spice latte conveys aspects of our social and cultural identities, connecting us to some groups of people while distancing and differentiating us from others.

Class Distinction

For example, Edensor and Millington (2009) illustrate how the seasonal ritual of exterior lighting displays in winter, especially around Christmas, express differences between working-class and middle-class groups in the United Kingdom, based on different sets of values and **tastes** (Bourdieu 1984). They explain how middle-class preferences for simple displays, such as a string of white lights across the roofline of a house, reflect **aesthetic values** (a concern with style), and are oriented toward demonstrating *good taste*. In contrast, lighting displays in working-class neighbourhoods, characterized by an abundance of lights in multiple colours and items such as lit-up Santas, express moral values such as giving back to the community since they provide a light show for all to enjoy (also see Back 2015). These working-class displays are devalued by middle-class individuals, who describe them as excessive and therefore in *bad taste*. By making a distinction between their differing consumption practices and tastes, members of the middle class are able to distance themselves from the working class and vice versa. In this case, seasonal practices of purchasing and displaying Christmas lights are bound up with class distinction. **Class distinction** can be defined as the process by which members of a **social class** differentiate themselves from members of another social class. Bourdieu (1984) has shown that class distinction occurs in a number of ways, including through cultural means such as practices of consumption and taste. For Bourdieu (1984), taste – encompassing preferences for certain foods, music, clothing, and cultural activity, for instance – is shaped through what we learn to value or appreciate in processes of socialization, which are circumscribed according to social class position. (For other engagements with Bourdieu, see chapter ten on sports culture and chapter twenty on parenting culture.)

The consumption of Starbucks's pumpkin spice latte is similarly entwined with processes of social group belonging and distinction. The Starbucks brand is associated with middle-class tastes and practices through an emphasis on coffee connoisseurship as well as an upscale café design (see Bookman 2013; Elliot 2006). As mentioned, the brand evokes coffee expertise by sharing and cultivating knowledge about the origins of coffee and distinctions in coffee style. Further, the cafés are styled according to a soft modernist aesthetic – the same style found in the pages of middle-class lifestyle magazines, design blogs, and home makeover shows (Arsel and Bean 2013). Seasonal offerings such as the pumpkin spice latte target middle-class consumers (or those who aspire to be middle class), providing them with a means to celebrate fall *and* to express middle-class identities and belonging. This class distinction is performed on the platform of the brand, which enables customers to exhibit "refined" and "discriminating" tastes through aesthetic values, coffee connoisseurship, and symbolic display. In this context, the pumpkin spice latte can be understood as a middle-class mode of celebrating seasonal change: middle-class urbanites and professionals walk the streets of Toronto or Vancouver with a Starbucks pumpkin spice latte in hand, while working-class folks munch on pumpkin spice Timbits from the popular coffee and donut chain, Tim Hortons (see Cormack 2008 for a discussion of the "ordinary" Canadian image of Tim Hortons).

Gender Distinction

In addition to class distinction, Powell and Engelhardt (2015) observe that Starbucks's pumpkin spice latte is commonly represented as a feminine drink and has been associated with white femininity in popular media. Social media commentary has described the beverage's *perceived* demographic using terms such as "yoga pant wearing moms," "white girls wearing Uggs," and, more generally, women who are defined as "basic." Mainstream media coverage of this controversial issue has further helped to conflate pumpkin spice lattes and pumpkin-themed consumption more broadly with white femininity, perpetuating a myth of the pumpkin spice latte as a feminine drink. Cultural critics, however, have argued that the classification of the pumpkin spice latte as "basic" in popular culture implies a broader devaluation of a kind of feminized consumption characterized as predictable, branded, and banal (Powell and Engelhardt 2015). The idea is that "basic" as a judgment of taste can be used to describe (and stereotype) the consumption of **white**, female, middle-class consumers by those who seek to distinguish themselves as somehow better, more unique, and further refined. Expressly, the use of the term "basic" to judge someone's taste allows those who are doing the judging to distance themselves from those deemed basic; it is a cultural means of performing distinction (Bourdieu 1984). The **gendered** nature of the term "basic" and its application to all things pumpkin spice, moreover, implies a "casual misogyny" in such judgments of taste (Peterson 2014, cited in Powell and Engelhardt 2015, 418). In addition to casual misogyny, however, the use of the term "basic" to refer to white women's taste implies that whiteness is somehow normal/ordinary in contrast with non-whiteness, defined in this oppositional scheme as exotic/other. As such, the categorization of pumpkin spice latte as "basic" and in terms of white female consumption produces social divisions and boundaries along intersecting lines of gender, class, and race.

Conclusion

Seasons are an important part of everyday life and culture, shaping our daily routines and lifestyles. In this chapter, we considered how seasonal meanings, experiences, and rituals are increasingly mediated by brands, which are prominent market cultural forms and salient features of contemporary economic and cultural life.

The chapter considered how seasonal branding is part of a much longer trend toward the commercialization of seasons and seasonal holidays such as Christmas or Thanksgiving. Focusing on the season of fall and taking the case of the brand Starbucks, this chapter considered how pumpkin spice lattes have become a much-anticipated seasonal consumption ritual for many Starbucks consumers. It considered how pumpkin spice lattes draw from existing elements of the Thanksgiving-Halloween holiday period, yet rework these in the form of a specialty coffee beverage that promotes the values and image of the Starbucks brand. This is concerning, since hegemonic brands such as Starbucks not only appropriate culture but rework seasonal traditions, activities, and sentiments in Canadian society through their seasonal branding. What does this mean for Canadians, that our seasonal holidays and traditions are so mediated by brands?

The chapter also considered some of the complex ways by which seasonal branding is spun into social and cultural life via consumer activity. It traced how brand techniques of framing space and time enable an alignment of seasonal rhythms and cycles with the routines and daily customs of consumers, through which brands co-shape seasonal consumption rituals, establish emotional connections with consumers, and co-generate seasonal experiences. It is in this dynamic that consumers and brands co-create meanings of fall, with a prominent place for the pumpkin spice latte.

We also considered how seasonal branding and consumption rituals are used by consumers as a means to express identities and co-generate "common social worlds" (Arvidsson 2006). Here, we looked at the ways in which brand-based seasonal consumption not only links individuals to certain social groups, establishing a sense of belonging, but also serves to mark distinction as part of a process of social and cultural boundary-making. In this way, seasonal branding may contribute to evermore differentiated seasonal practices, meanings, and conventions, which express a range of social and cultural identities, belonging, and distinction in the arena of Canadian consumer culture.

Questions for Critical Thought

1. Think of an example of seasonal branding. In what ways has it shaped seasonal traditions and holidays in the Canadian context?
2. How has the commodification of seasonal traditions impacted other seasonal rituals and the social relations they help to establish?
3. How are brands spun into seasonal traditions, rituals, and meanings? Reflect on theories of brands and branding in your discussion.
4. Are the seasonal meanings and practices promoted by brands straightforwardly adopted by consumers? What are some of the ways in which consumers engage with seasonal branding and consumer goods?
5. Think of your own seasonal consumption activity. How do you use branded goods to mark the seasons and, in particular, to convey aspects of your identity and connect with others?

References

Arsel, Zeynep, and Jonathan Bean. 2013. "Taste Regimes and Market-Mediated Practice." *Journal of Consumer Research* 39 (5): 899–917. https://doi.org/10.1086/666595.

Arvidsson, Adam. 2006. *Brands: Meaning and Value in Media Culture.* London: Routledge.

Back, Les. 2015. "Why Everyday Life Matters: Class, Community and Making Life Livable." *Sociology* 49 (5): 820–36. https://doi.org/10.1177/0038038515589292.

Banet-Weiser, Sarah. 2012. *Authentic™: The Politics of Ambivalence in a Brand Culture.* New York: New York University Press.

Barker, Chris. 2003. *Cultural Studies: Theory and Practice.* 2nd ed. London: Sage.

Barthes, Roland. 1973. *Mythologies.* Paladin: London.

Belk, Russell W. 1993. "Materialism and the Making of the Modern American Christmas." In *Unwrapping Christmas,* edited by Daniel Miller, 75–104. Oxford: Clarendon Press.

Bookman, Sonia. 2013. "Coffee Brands, Class and Culture in a Canadian City." *European Journal of Cultural Studies* 16 (4): 405–23. https://doi.org/10.1177/1367549413484298.

———. 2014. "Brands and Urban Life: Specialty Coffee, Consumers and the Co-Creation of Urban Café Sociality." *Space and Culture* 17 (1): 85–99. https://doi.org/10.1177/1206331213493853.

Bourdieu, Pierre. 1984. *Distinction: A Social Critique of the Judgment of Taste.* Translated by Richard Nice. London: Routledge.

Campbell, Colin. 2005. "The Craft Consumer." *Journal of Consumer Culture* 5 (1): 23–42. https://doi.org/10.1177/1469540505049843.

Chaney, David. 1996. *Lifestyles*. London: Routledge.

Cormack, Patricia. 2008. "'True Stories' of Canada: Tim Hortons and the Branding of National Identity." *Cultural Sociology* 2 (3): 369–84. https://doi.org/10.1177/1749975508095617.

Cova, Bernard, Robert V. Kozinets, and Avi Shankar. 2007. "Tribes, Inc.: The New World of Tribalism." In *Consumer Tribes*, edited by Bernard Cova, Rovert V. Kozinets, and Avi Shankar, 3–26. Oxford: Butterworth-Heinemann.

Edensor, Tim, and Steve Millington. 2009. "Illuminations, Class Identities and the Contested Landscapes of Christmas." *Sociology* 43 (1): 103–21. https://doi.org/10.1177/0038038508099100.

Elliot, Charlene. 2006. "Sipping Starbucks: (Re)considering Communicative Media." In *Mediascapes: New Patterns in Canadian Communication*, 2nd ed., edited by Paul Attallah and Leslie Regan Shade, 62–76. Toronto: Nelson, Thompson.

Featherstone, Mike. 2007. *Consumer Culture and Postmodernism*. 2nd ed. London: Sage.

Hall, Stuart. 2006 [1973]. "Encoding/decoding." In *Media and Cultural Studies: KeyWorks*, edited by Douglas Kellner and Meenakshi Gigi Durham, 163–73. Oxford: Blackwell Publishing.

Hebdige, Dick. 1979. *Subculture: The Meaning of Style*. London: Routledge.

Holt, Douglas B. 2004. *How Brands Become Icons*. Boston: Harvard Business School Press.

———. 2006. "Jack Daniel's America: Iconic Brands as Ideological Parasites and Proselytizers." *Journal of Consumer Culture* 6 (3): 355–77. https://doi.org/10.1177/1469540506068683.

Horkheimer, Max, and Theodor W. Adorno. 2002 [1947]. *Dialectic of Enlightenment*. Edited by Gunzelin Schmid Noerr. Translated by Edmund Jephcott. Stanford: Stanford University Press.

Klein, Naomi. 2000. *No Logo*. Toronto: Knopf Canada.

Kowitt, Beth. 2016. "Why Pumpkin Spice Lattes Show Up Earlier Each Summer." *Fortune*, September 1. http://fortune.com/26016/09/01/pumpkin-spice-lattes-summer-starbucks/.

Lash, Scott, and John Urry. 1994. *Economies of Signs and Space*. London: Sage.

Levinson, Stacey, Stacey Mack, Dan Reinhardt, Helen Suarez, and Grace Yeh. 1992. "Halloween as a Consumption Experience." *Advances in Consumer Research* 19 (1): 219–28.

Lewis, J. David, and Andrew J. Weigert. 1981. "The Structures and Meanings of Social Time." *Social Forces* 60 (2): 432–62. https://doi.org/10.2307/2578444.

Lury, Celia. 2004. *Brands: The Logos of the Global Economy.* London: Routledge.

———. 2011. *Consumer Culture*. 2nd ed. New Brunswick, New Jersey: Rutgers University Press.

Maynard, Micheline. 2013. "How Starbucks Turned Pumpkin Spice into a Marketing Bonanza." *Forbes*, September 22. https://www.forbes.com/sites/michelinemaynard/2013/09/22/how-starbucks-turned-pumpkin-spice-into-a-marketing-bonanza/#3e.

McCracken, Grant David. 2005. *Culture and Consumption II: Markets, Meaning and Brand Management.* Bloomington: Indiana University Press.

McKechnie, Sally, and Caroline Tynan. 2006. "Social Meanings in Christmas Consumption: An Exploratory Study of UK Celebrants' Consumption Rituals." *Journal of Consumer Behaviour* 5 (2): 130–44. https://doi.org/10.1002/cb.40.

Miller, Daniel. 1993. "A Theory of Christmas." In *Unwrapping Christmas*, edited by Daniel Miller, 3–37. Oxford: Clarendon Press.
———. 1998. *A Theory of Shopping*. Ithaca: Cornell University Press.
Muñiz, Albert M., Jr., and Thomas C. O'Guinn. 2001. "Brand Community." *Journal of Consumer Research* 27 (4): 412–32. https://doi.org/10.1086/319618.
Oldenburg, Ray. 1989. *The Great Good Place*. New York: Marlowe & Company.
O'Shaughnessy, Michael, and Jane Stadler. 2012. *Media and Society*. 5th ed. Oxford: Oxford University Press.
Overmyer, Krystal. 2016. "The Consumer Psychology behind the Pumpkin Spice Latte." *Content Standard*, October 3.
Peterson, Anne Helen. 2014. "'Basic' Is Just Another Word for Class Anxiety." *Buzzfeed*, October 20.
Powell, Lisa Jordan, and Elizabeth S.D. Engelhardt. 2015. "The Perilous Whiteness of Pumpkins." *Geohumanities* 1 (2): 414–32. https://doi.org/10.1080/2373566X.2015.1099421.
Robertson, Lynne. 2012. "Pinch the Grinch." *Retail Merchandiser* 52 (Sept/Oct): 10–12.
Thompson, Craig J., and Zeynep Arsel. 2004. "The Starbucks Brandscape and Consumers' (Anticorporate) Experiences of Glocalization." *Journal of Consumer Research* 31 (3): 631–42. https://doi.org/10.1086/425098.
Waldrop, Judith, with Marcia Mogelonsky. 1992. *The Seasons of Business: The Marketer's Guide to Consumer Behavior*. Ithaca: American Demographic Books.
Warde, Alan. 1994. "Consumption, Identity-Formation and Uncertainty." *Sociology* 28 (4): 877–98. https://doi.org/10.1177/0038038594028004005.
———. 2005. "Consumption and Theories of Practice." *Journal of Consumer Culture* 5 (2): 131–53. https://doi.org/10.1177/1469540505053090.
———. 2014. "After Taste: Culture, Consumption and Theories of Practice." *Journal of Consumer Culture* 14 (3): 279–303. https://doi.org/10.1177/1469540514547828.
Whiteley, Sheila. 2008. *Christmas, Ideology, and Popular Culture*. Edinburgh: Edinburgh University Press.
Zukin, Sharon. 1995. *The Cultures of Cities*. Oxford: Blackwell Publishing.

4 "Neither Here Nor There": Migrant Rights and Realities in Canada's Seasonal Agricultural Worker Program

JENNA HENNEBRY, DAVID CELIS PARRA, and RACHELLE DALEY

LEARNING OUTCOMES

After reading this chapter, you should be able to:

- describe the labour conditions and rights of seasonal migrant workers in Canada
- describe the health and housing conditions of seasonal migrant workers
- explain how seasonal migrant labour reflects an international division of labour
- describe how the cycles of seasonal migrant workers' lives have been organized by international government agreements to meet the needs of the Canadian consumer market
- analyze how the Seasonal Agricultural Worker Program produces the conditions of structural precarity for the migrant workers

Introduction

> We think that when we are separated, in this way, during eight months, from our family, well ... in reality, we are living our lives in halves. This is how I see it, because we can't live completely when we don't have either place.
>
> – Migrant worker 13 (Hennebry 2006)

Fall signals the end of the growing period for many crops in Canada. Canadian farmers secure their livelihoods through the production of food sold in local and national supermarkets across the country, as well as for export (for sale or in products sold around the globe, such as wine). In Ontario, fruits and vegetables like apples, squash, rhubarb, potatoes, corn, grapes, and cucumbers are locally grown and sold across the province and around the world. Yet for many Canadian consumers, the label "locally grown" does not recognize the labour or hardship of the tens of thousands of migrant workers who seed, plant, and harvest our food. A government migration program to bring international farm workers to Canada has created a realm of employment in which employers enjoy the benefits of unparalleled control over the migrant workers, who have little recourse but to tolerate these unreasonable working conditions to keep their jobs.

The Seasonal Agricultural Worker Program (SAWP) is a 50-year-old federal **seasonal migrant worker** program that annually brings in approximately 40,000 people from Mexico and the Caribbean to work on farms across the country (Stuckey 2013) as **migrant farm workers** (MFWs). Every year, migrant farm workers are allowed to work in Canada but not to stay. With no access to permanent residency status, MFWs can only stay in Canada up to eight months per year on a work permit tied to one employer (ESDC 2017), but they can return year after year, with some workers coming to Canada for more than 30 years for every growing and harvesting season.

This chapter explores what seasonality means for the migrant farm workers who come to Canada annually to work in Canada's long-standing SAWP. This chapter is based on decades of primary research involving transnational ethnography that uses a **mobile sociology** approach. This method involved two main research activities. The first author of this chapter (J. Hennebry) has carried out **participant observation** by living and working among migrant farm workers in the SAWP program in Ontario (this involved 250 hours on the field as well as 100 hours out of the field in Ontario); and then returning to Mexico with the migrants to live among their families (for three months). Over the last 15 years, Dr. Hennebry has carried out hundreds of semi-structured interviews with Canadian farm employers, migrant farm workers, health care practitioners, government officials, and many others, as well as a **survey** with nearly 600 migrant farm workers in Ontario. We also reviewed secondary sources, including policy documents and findings from other researchers who have conducted surveys of migrant farm workers and have referenced them throughout the chapter.

We draw on theories including mobile sociology (Urry 2010), world systems theory (Wallerstein 2001), and theories of **racialization** (Preibisch 2004; Satzewich 1991, 1998). Mobile sociology incorporates definitions of **society** and methodological approaches that reflect the globalized world we live in to enable transnational research in more than one country and research site. Mobile sociology is the acknowledgement that we live in a globalized world and that "global networks criss-cross the regional borders of society" (see Urry 2010); in other words, this theory implies that doing research on international migration is more valid when we include participants that are in different countries because they are part of the same network. **World systems theory** is useful to make links between precarious legal status and the insecure livelihoods of migrant farm workers; this theory allows us to look at the macro levels (the bigger picture; the "forest") and micro levels (the more detailed experiences of the migrant worker; the "tree" in a forest) (see figure 4.1). World systems theory emphasizes the international, regional,

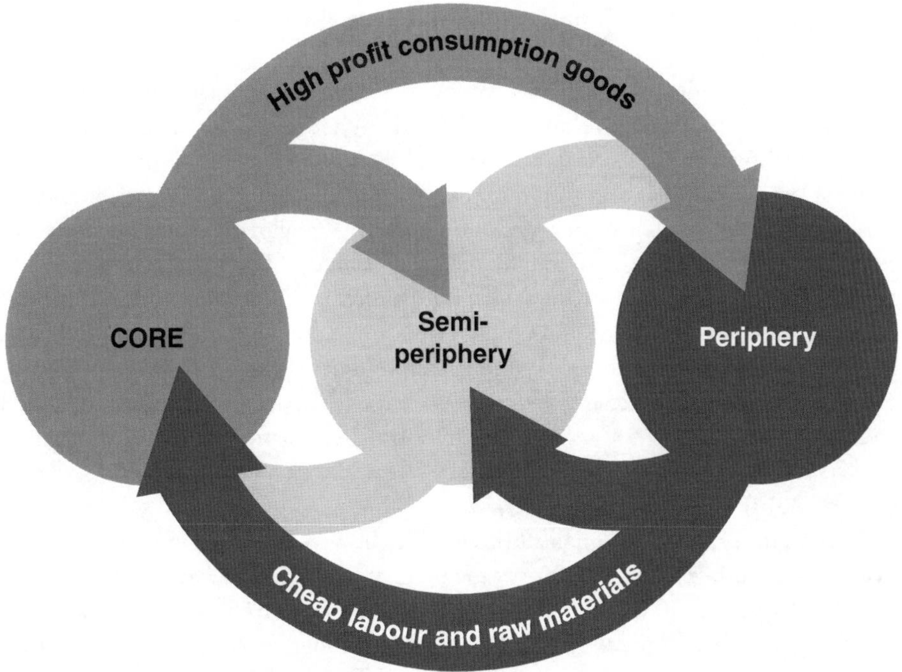

FIGURE 4.1 Wallerstein's world systems theory model. Model source: Wallerstein (2004)

and transnational **division of labour** as the unit of analysis; in this theory, the world is divided into core countries, semi-peripheral countries, and peripheral countries (Barfield 1997). Some regions (core countries) focus on higher-skill, capital-intensive production and some others (peripheral; semi-peripheral) focus on labour-intensive activities such as mineral extraction and agriculture. This reinforces the dominance of some regions over others (Lechner 2001). The SAWP similarly reinforces an international division of labour, and this theory helps us to position SAWP workers in relation to the power dynamics between regions and their implication for the limits imposed on the lives of workers as temporary guests in Canada.

In this chapter, racialization theory makes **race** a visible dimension for analysis by allowing us to ask questions about, first, the perceptions that employers have of temporary workers based on their place of origin and physical characteristics and, second, how these perceptions inform the treatment, working, and living conditions of these workers. Racialization theory helps us to recognize **social inequality** in treatment, unequal power relations, and biases that condition the lived experience of people of colour or communities that have been racialized. To racialize means to impose an interpretation of a person or context based on the ethnic background and/or skin colour of the person (as discussed in chapter two).

Context and History: Canadians Won't Pick Canadian Crops

The federal government started the SAWP in 1966 as a temporary solution for farm owners who lobbied the government to help them address an acute and immediate shortage of labour in the Canadian agricultural sector. Employers and the federal government determined that they would find a labour force willing to work in the agricultural sector in less developed countries. Originally, SAWP allowed Canadian farmers to recruit farm workers from Jamaica to fill their labour needs. However, employer demand for the program grew and the program was expanded in 1974 to allow recruitment of Mexican workers and citizens of multiple Commonwealth Caribbean states (countries in the Caribbean that had formerly been British colonies) (Satzewich 1991). Since that time, the number of Mexican workers has surpassed Jamaican workers. United Food and Commercial Workers Canada (UFCW) estimates that from the 21,499 Mexican workers hired in Canada under the SAWP in 2015, 20,791 were men and 708 women (UFCW 2014).

Though the program was originally designed to be a temporary solution to an immediate labour shortage, the popularity of the program among Canadian employers made the SAWP a permanent fixture and it reached its fiftieth anniversary in 2016 with very few changes made over the years (Hennebry and McLaughlin 2012). Canada's agricultural industry has come to depend on this source of labour: currently, employers from all 13 provinces and territories access the SAWP, with roughly 60 per cent of all SAWP workers employed in Ontario (ESDC 2016). See figure 4.2.

The program ensures that employers can access a flexible workforce of temporary migrants in response to expanding demands in the face of globalization and so that they can compete in the global agri-food marketplace (McLaughlin et al. 2017; see also chapter thirteen by Laywine and Sears). This flexibility enables employers to adapt quickly to changing market requirements and production demands but does little to ensure the safety, health, or well-being of these workers in the program, which promotes **structural precarity**. Structural precarity refers to the manner in which job insecurity becomes institutionalized within employment structures.

Under the program, impoverished racialized workers are recruited by a Canadian employer to work for up to eight months in Canada before they are required to return home as a condition for their participation the following year. Workers typically arrive in planting season (early spring), work throughout the growing season (summer), and return to their country of origin following the harvest season (fall). However, with the expansion of the greenhouse industry and increasing number of large factory farms, there is growing demand for migrant farm workers year-round. In order to be eligible for the SAWP, potential workers must be: married or in a common-law relationship, preferably with children; have a schooling level of minimum third grade and maximum eighth grade; be between 22 and 45 years of age; live in a rural area; and be a farm worker or demonstrate that they have worked primarily in agricultural jobs or have family farms (Consulado General de México en

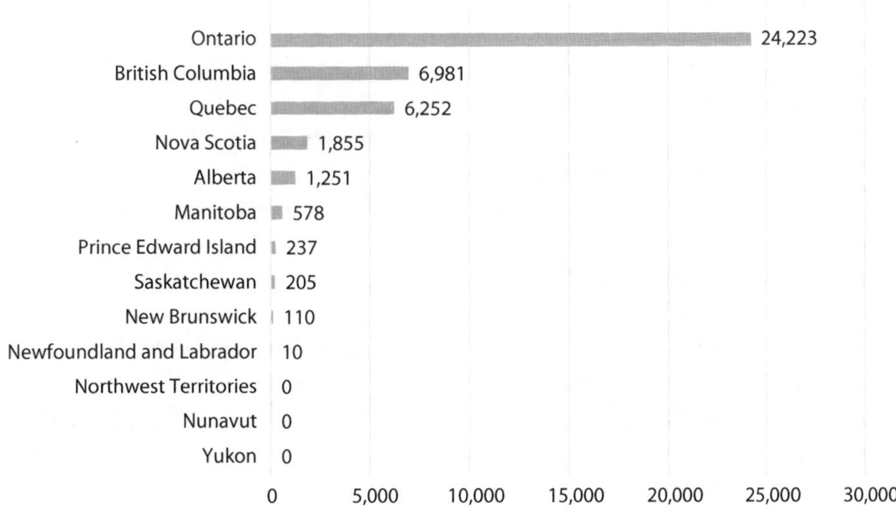

FIGURE 4.2 Number of SAWP migrant farm worker positions by province, 2015. Data source: ESDC 2016

Montréal 2018). All of these requirements ensure that migrant workers are motivated to return to their country of origin after working in Canada; it likewise contributes to the creation of a workforce that is willing to accept any work under any conditions, because they have few other options and their families are dependent on them for the money they send home (which are referred to as *remittances*) (Hennebry, Holliday, and Moniruzzaman 2017).

The structures that govern the SAWP shape the everyday realities of MFWs. The SAWP operates within a patchwork of regulations that are dictated and enforced by different transnational, federal, provincial, and local governmental and non-governmental entities. At the international level, the SAWP is governed by a memorandum of understanding (MOU) between Canada and migrant countries of origin, and this is where employment contracts between employers, migrant workers, and government agents are negotiated. Canadian federal departments, including Immigration, Refugees and Citizenship Canada (IRCC) and Employment and Skills Development Canada (ESDC), oversee the overall functioning of the program, determine who qualifies for a SAWP visa, and evaluate employer applications to hire migrant workers. Provincial and local government departments share responsibility for enforcing employment standards and occupational health and safety requirements. This patchwork of regulation heightens migrant vulnerability to risk and exploitation: it allows different government agencies to offload responsibility onto other departments, which tends to absolve governments from protecting the rights of migrant workers, who must navigate the complex systems to work and live in Canada.

Working Conditions and Labour Rights

Imagine if you, as a Canadian citizen, permanent resident, or international student with a work permit, were hired to a job where the work, the conditions, and the pay were not what you were expecting and you did not feel comfortable working there. If you needed the money, would you quit? Perhaps walk away and find a new job? Now imagine if you were far from home, that people were depending on you to send money back to them, and that quitting your job suddenly meant that you were understood to be staying in Canada illegally; you could not legally work for another employer and you were at risk of being deported from this country. This is the reality of the work permits held by migrant workers working in the SAWP. As a Jamaican worker explained, "That boss in Canada is the worst one I've ever had, because in Jamaica when I meet someone like him, I just don't stay with him, so I don't have to cope with his foolishness. Up there [Canada], I just ha[d] to cope with what he [was] doing, so it was the worst experience for me" (McLaughlin 2009).

Working Conditions

MFWs work extra hours without remuneration, experience inadequate housing, are exposed to dangerous or hazardous chemicals without proper protection, and are more likely than Canadian workers not to refuse unsafe work due to fear of loss of current or future employment (Hennebry, McLaughlin, and Preibisch 2016). These exploitative working conditions negatively impact the health and well-being of migrant workers, which ripples into negative long-term effects on the migrant workers' families and home communities. This is not to say that exploitative labour practices are characteristic of every agricultural employer in Canada; rather, the structures of the program enable such conditions and relations of exploitation.

Under the program, a migrant farm worker's legal status in Canada is bound to a single employer (through tied work permits), which is something that many argue is a violation of human rights and akin to indentured labour relationships between employers and workers under slavery (Depatie-Pelletier 2008; Marchitelli 2016). To change employers, the MFW must receive permission from their current and prospective employers, a government representative from their country of origin, and written approval from ESDC, a complicated and lengthy process for migrant workers to navigate. The MFW risks being identified as a troublemaker by the employer and must complete this process while continuing to meet their employer's labour demands.

From the employer's perspective, worker transfers can be done and coordinated among employers through Foreign Agricultural Resource Management Services (FARMS) in Ontario and other comparable growers' groups in other provinces, as well as through the country of origin's consulate or liaison office. This transfer mechanism of the SAWP is thus most often used by employers (and not migrant workers themselves) to shift migrants between farms based on the needs of farmers during the season. For example, the harvesting of potatoes happens later in the fall and farmers must get them out of the ground before rain and frost threaten the crops (for more on the potato season, see Machum, chapter eleven). They will ask for additional workers during such peak harvest times.

Year after year, migrant farm workers must meet their employer's labour demands if they wish to be chosen to return to the program the next year. Research on the SAWP Jamaican workers (Knowles 1997) and Mexican workers (Basok 2002) found that many migrant workers accepted poor employment conditions in the program in part because of economic necessity, **poverty**, and the limited chances of **social mobility** available to them in their countries of origin (Hennebry 2012).

Labour Rights

The structural precarity embedded in the SAWP erodes the labour rights for which **unions** have fought in Canada for the last 200 years. The closed-work permit system in the SAWP means that workers have an incentive to please the employer with very little effective protection from the law. Further, the naming system of the SAWP functions to give employers the power to request workers by name for subsequent seasons. This means that the worker then knows they have secured their place in the program for the following year.

MFWs do not have job security: they can be fired at any time by employers and sent back to their countries of origin for any reason (if there is not enough work, the worker is ill or injured and cannot work, the worker refuses to do the work, etc.).

MFWs face barriers to claiming labour rights, in large part because **collective bargaining** is prohibited among agricultural workers in Ontario – even though the province hosts nearly half of all migrant agricultural workers (Hennebry, McLaughlin, and Preibisch 2016). A decade-long legal challenge for MFWs right to collective bargain in Ontario was struck down by the Supreme Court of Canada in 2011; it was in their opinion that MFWs in Ontario had the constitutional right to free association, which somehow guarantees that "meaningful negotiations" can take place between workers and employers and, furthermore, that "[t]he Ontario legislature is not required to provide a particular form of collective bargaining rights to agricultural workers, in order to secure the effective exercise of their associational rights" (Makin 2011).

MFWs face intimidation not to join unions or act collectively, including the risk of exclusion from future migratory opportunities by their own governments (Watson 2014). Farm work is excluded from the Labour Relations Act in Ontario, and while it is included under the Agricultural Employees Protection Act (AEPA), this legislation does not include the right to collective bargaining – the ability for workers to work together to persuade employers to improve their working conditions – and does not adequately safeguard the ability of workers to organize and advocate for their rights. The International Labour Organization ruled in 2010 that the AEPA is in violation of human rights under two UN conventions (McLaughlin and Hennebry 2015).

MFWs' **precarious employment** status – including their exclusion from union protection, lack of job security, and immigration status – makes safeguarding all other rights (whether related to health, labour, and so on) practically impossible (McLaughlin and Hennebry 2015). Workers in the SAWP have access to consular representation to help mediate labour disputes and issues; however, advocates and researchers have continually noted that these officials are not viewed by workers as trusted, impartial, or effective sources of advocacy, nor do they always represent MFW interests. In fact, MFWs and their advocates have reported that consular officials sometimes become hostile or uncooperative in the face of complaints. Some MFWs who have spoken up or sought external assistance have even been blacklisted from re-entering the SAWP (Hennebry and McLaughlin 2012), and on several occasions, the Mexican government has attempted to blacklist Mexican MFWs due to the workers' alleged involvement with unions (UFCW 2014; CBC News 2011).

Housing

> The tap water smells and tastes bad ... I don't know if it's contaminated with pesticides ... when we can, we try to buy water from the store. There are no locks on the doors, and there are no beds, just some mattress on top of each other.
>
> – Mexican worker in Simcoe (Hennebry and McLaughlin 2012)

The SAWP requires workers to live in a residence of their employer's choosing. Rights of freedom of movement and residence, and to change jobs, are effectively denied under the SAWP (McLaughlin and Hennebry 2015). Typically, MFWs share trailers, portables, or modified farm buildings, commonly placed behind or next to their employers' properties. Commonly reported problems include insufficient access to clean water or safe food storage, inadequate food preparation and cleaning amenities, proximity to pesticides and fertilizers, and deficient bathroom facilities (Hennebry, Preibisch, and McLaughlin 2010; Otero and Preibisch 2010). In a survey (2008–9)[1] of approximately 600 migrant farm workers in Ontario led by Dr. Hennebry, nearly 50 per cent claimed that their housing was inadequate – many claimed their accommodations were overcrowded, poorly ventilated, and lacked privacy and security (Hennebry, Preibisch, and McLaughlin 2010).

While we know that inadequate housing can lead to health problems and heighten susceptibility to communicable diseases, similar areas of concern were reported in a British Columbia–based survey of 100 Mexican workers, in which 37 per cent felt that their housing was detrimental to their health (Otero and Preibisch 2010). Farm worker housing is inconsistently regulated in Canada; federal guidelines are not comprehensive enough to address many of the workers' concerns (for example, no maximum

1 This survey was funded by CERIS (Centre of Excellence for Research on Immigration and Settlement) and carried out by Hennebry, Preibisch, McLaughlin, Alcalá, Restrepo, Zuñiga, Encalada Grez, and Milkins. See Hennebry, Preibisch, and McLaughlin 2010.

temperature is provided, allowing for excessively hot conditions in summer, and workers are dissatisfied with the number of people allowed in dwellings). As a condition for receiving permission to hire SAWP workers, employers are required to have a housing inspection carried out prior to workers arriving in Canada. However, inspections are typically performed pre-season by the local public health department; they are not normally repeated once workers have arrived, after which conditions can change. The guidelines are likewise not always or evenly enforced across regions (Hennebry 2007).

Despite many workers' experiences with poor housing conditions, very few raise their concerns with employers or consular officials. As employers are typically MFWs' landlords, many workers fear making complaints about their accommodations.

Health

> The doctor told me that the surgery was very delicate and that I have to take great care of myself. But since I already had problems with my employer, he didn't allow any [doctors] visits ... I witnessed how a girlfriend of mine was sent back to Mexico as soon as she left the hospital.
>
> – Mexican SAWP worker (Hennebry and McLaughlin 2012)

This experience, shared by one Mexican worker, illustrates the difficulty of getting medical treatment under the SAWP, despite the significant toll that farm work can take on MFWs' bodies. Agricultural work can be dirty, difficult, and dangerous, and when work pace increases due to environmental or production demands (e.g., crops are threatened by weather), risks of workplace accidents can increase. With each *temporada* (the Spanish word used by MFWs to refer to the work periods) that MFWs are in Canada, they face a range of health and safety risks, including chemical and climatic exposures, ergonomic strains from repeated motions, work with large machinery, and unsafe transportation (McLaughlin, Hennebry, and Haines 2014). Our survey (undertaken 2008–9) of approximately 600 migrant farm workers in Ontario suggested that the average number of weekly hours worked ranged between 64 and 74; 51 per cent of workers likewise worked without breaks, of which 20 per cent reported that working without breaks happened "often" or "all the time" (Hennebry, Preibisch, and McLaughlin 2010). Our research also found that health and safety training has been inconsistent and insufficient for migrant farm workers. Nearly 60 per cent of workers surveyed in Ontario and 74 per cent in British Columbia said that they had not received any information or training relating to their health and safety (Hennebry, Preibisch, and McLaughlin 2010; Otero and Preibisch 2010). Of those workers who had received training, it was not always accessible; language and literacy barriers often caused problems of comprehension (McLaughlin, Hennebry, and Haines 2014). Workers furthermore do not feel comfortable raising health and safety concerns because of the risk of repatriation or job loss (McLaughlin, Hennebry, and Haines 2014).

The unequal power relationships and incentives for obedience inherent in the SAWP influence the type and amount of health treatment and protection that MFWs can access. The experiences of MFWs with health and health care demonstrate how access to health is inequitably distributed across society, a phenomenon that sociologists of health are interested in understanding. In this book, Heidi Bickis (chapter five), Alissa Overend (chapter six), and Jen Wrye, Michael Graydon, and Patty Thille (chapter eight) all demonstrate the ways in which access to health is framed by social as well as physical realities. Under the current SAWP system, MFWs can be repatriated to their countries of origin when they are no longer able to complete their duties due to illness and injuries, which often result from poor working conditions. Fear of medical repatriation disciplines MFWs, who often hesitate to claim or request access to health care services. Since most MFWs live and work in isolated areas, workers must request time off work as well as transportation to health facilities when necessary. In addition, in the case of Mexican workers, language and translation issues are significant barriers to health care provision and access; employers sometimes act as interpreters (Hennebry, Grass, and McLaughlin 2017). This is a serious violation of patient-doctor confidentiality, in addition to a contravention of health and labour rights.

Moreover, requesting access to health care can reflect badly on the MFW, who might be regarded as a troublemaker or at least as less productive then other workers. It also signals to employers that there is an existent health concern that might affect the MFW's ability to do their job. Under the program, an employer can replace injured workers with healthy workers. This incentivizes workers to work through injury and illness to stay in the program. Migrant workers also face challenges in accessing sexual and reproductive health care, with employer control, lack of privacy, and **stigma** compounding barriers. This is particularly problematic for female migrant workers, who, though smaller in number (representing only roughly 3 per cent of workers in the SAWP), have poor access to gynecological, prenatal, and reproductive care. If a woman migrant worker becomes pregnant while in the SAWP, she will face heightened risks of miscarriage and other complications due to exposure to chemicals and intense physical labour; additionally, faced with loss of employment and deportation, many women attempt to hide pregnancies from employers (Hennebry, Grass, and McLaughlin 2017).

Employers in the SAWP, who are responsible for arranging for workers' health coverage, often fail to do so in a timely manner or withhold health cards from workers (Hennebry and Williams 2015). Some employers are reluctant to allow workers to seek care or compensation because of concerns over work productivity, loss of crops, or delays in work (McLaughlin, Hennebry, and Haines 2014; McLaughlin et al. 2014). Almost 20 per cent of nearly 600 Ontario migrant farm workers surveyed (2008–9) did not have a health card; 45 per cent reported that their colleagues work despite illness or injury, for fear of telling their employers, and 55 per cent reported working while ill or injured themselves to avoid losing paid hours (Hennebry, Preibisch, and McLaughlin 2010). Since MFWs may only remain in Canada for a maximum of eight months, even when a claim is made or health care is sought, the MFW often cannot remain in Canada long enough for a diagnosed issue to be fully treated or the claim to be resolved. The result is that many MFWs return home with health conditions that are not fully diagnosed or managed, or claims that are left pending (Hennebry 2007, 2009; McLaughlin 2007, 2009; Preibisch and Hennebry 2011).

Emotional and Social Dimensions

> Every year I miss something big – a birthday, a death, a celebration. I grow further away from them each year, even though I return at the end of the season.
>
> – SAWP Mexican worker (Hennebry 2007)

Like you and us, migrant workers require social and emotional connections and form bonds with the others with whom they live and work, and their transnational lives under the SAWP influence their social and emotional well-being.

MFWs are not typically granted the right to leave and re-enter Canada, as they are only issued single-entry visas for the fulfilment of a contract. It is thus difficult for MFWs' family members to obtain visitors' visas to Canada, essentially denying them family reunification.

In Canada, MFWs live isolated on farms, with poor communication and transportation access, having left behind their families, communities, and **culture**. Social isolation is heightened by language barriers and by intensive workplace regimes and schedules, which limit interaction with Canadians and separate them from many networks and organizations. MFWs struggle to establish connections or develop a sense of belonging in Canada. They remain invisible guest workers in Canada even though they straddle nations, and many live here temporarily for decades. What little information Canadians learn about MFWs is often based on racial **stereotypes** (Bauder et al. 2002; Hennebry 2006; Preibisch 2004). This can generate fear or frustration directed at MFWs. Town locals have expressed distress at the "hordes of Mexicans taking over our town" (Alliston resident, Hennebry 2006), and store owners have expressed their frustration at the migrant workers "crowding their stores so that local customers stay away" (Alliston store owner, Hennebry 2006). MFWs face verbal harassment, disrespect, and violence from Canadians in local communities.

> I was in town and these kids started yelling at us near the grocery store. I understood them, but I did not want any problems. So, I just kept walking and did not answer. I think they thought I could not understand English. (Alliston-based Mexican SAWP worker in 2004, Hennebry 2006)

Upon returning to their countries of origin, MFWs must reintegrate into families who have developed priorities, routines, and schedules that exclude the worker during their eight-month absence. Wives, husbands, children, and families deal with trust issues and must become reaccustomed to each other's presence, needs, and demands. The temporariness of migrant workers also highlights the experiences of the **dual burden** that many female spouses deal with back home. These experiences could mean raising children while managing remittances and resources at home, cultivating land, and selling products or services (Hennebry 2014b). Women and children who have taken on more responsibilities and exercised more power during a father's absence must renegotiate their positions in the family for the four months that the MFW returns. There are elements of social exclusion both in Canada and upon return to countries of origin. For MFWs and their families, leading permanently temporary lives is emotionally taxing. The Canadian government's 50-year policy has ultimately worked to disrupt generations of families in the **Global South**.

Social Protections

All legal workers in Canada contribute to the Canada Pension Plan (CPP), Employment Insurance benefits (EI), and Old Age Security. The average SAWP worker participates in the program for seven to nine years and the Canadian government withholds portions of their earnings to pay into these social protection programs. Yet SAWP does not provide a pathway to permanent residency, and so MFWs are largely excluded from Canada's national framework of protections (Hennebry 2014a). While Canada and Mexico have negotiated bilateral agreements pertaining to some social protections, the issues surrounding residency requirements, lack of access to information and resources, language barriers, and illiteracy prevent many MFWs from claiming these protections.

EI benefits, which are normally paid to workers during times of unemployment, parental leave, or sickness, are not available to migrant workers; yet, migrant workers contribute an estimated $3.4 million in EI premiums per year. Although they could never access regular EI benefits, before 2012 migrant farm workers were able to access special EI benefits (such as maternity and parental benefits). In 2012, the federal government revoked this right. The removal of access to parental benefits under the EI program has been highly criticized by workers and their advocates.

Since MFWs spend so much time working and living outside of their countries of origin (and contributing financially to the Canadian social security system), they can be denied eligibility for social protection systems in their country of origin (McLaughlin 2009), and in Canada they are likewise at risk of "slipping through the cracks" (Hennebry 2014a).

Conclusion

For migrant workers, the spring marks the hard work to come, as workers anticipate tired bodies, social exclusion, prolonged family separation, and the precarious hold on their daily lives in Canada. When the weather begins to cool toward the end of harvest and the winds announce the coming of winter, Canadians celebrate the harvest through fall fairs, Thanksgiving, and harvest festivals. Migrant farm workers are generally not welcomed into these celebrations, and most Canadians are not even aware of the presence of thousands of temporary foreign workers who have planted, tended to, and harvested much of the abundance that is celebrated. While Canadians enjoy the bounty, migrant farm workers pack up their bags and clean the bunkbed or cot that they have called home for the past eight months. Their thoughts begin to drift to enjoying Christmas with their families, meeting their new child who was born while they were away, eating the traditional foods of their homelands, and the anxieties of returning to families and communities from which they have been away for so long. Migrant workers are often uncertain about both their return home and their return to Canada in subsequent years, since so much depends on whether their employer will name them to return to work again the next year. What does it mean for a family to be separated for virtually two-thirds of the year? What does it mean to work while knowing that you may not work next year depending on the whims of your boss or the decreasing health of your body? Moreover, how are local farming communities' understanding of MFWs as temporary in Canada determining their respect and solidarity toward migrant workers?

They say their goodbyes to the 20 other migrant farm workers with whom they have shared their bunkhouse, kitchen, and washroom for the last eight months, and they board a rickety old school bus that will take them to the airport to return to their communities. Why is Canada not their community?

This chapter has shown how seasonality is linked to the social inequality experienced by migrant farm workers in the SAWP, evident in their high exposure to health risks and unequal access to health care, social protection, and other human rights. Canada's SAWP has created permanently temporary lives for transnational migrant farm workers (living "neither here nor there"), who face economic uncertainty, often live in substandard housing conditions in Canada, work dirty, dangerous difficult jobs with poorly enforced labour standards, lack access to social and health protections, and face **discrimination** and isolation in Canada, all of which has lasting effects on the health and well-being of their families. These are the scars of an international division of labour that perpetuates the dominance of some countries over others, and the consequences are felt directly – both mentally and physically – over the course of workers' lives.

Despite these issues, many consider the SAWP a model program, an "example of a successful, organized labour mobility program, allowing for the organized entry of agricultural workers from the Caribbean and Mexico to meet the temporary seasonal need for labour in the agriculture sector when Canadian workers are not available" (GFMD 2014). However, this understanding of the program does not consider the lives and experiences of the migrant workers. In many ways, their lives are defined by the seasons, and within the structure of the SAWP they have very little control over when, where, and how they work and live in Canada.

The intention of this chapter is to provide a means for readers to question the current state of affairs for those who already do essential work for Canadians. We do not advocate for the elimination of the SAWP per se. What is needed is a radical shift in thinking; we need a system where workers can work seasonally and access permanent residency – regardless of program or status; a system where their human and labour rights are protected at all times. These migrant workers also boost small towns' economies with local purchases, contribute to the tax base and social protection system (through pension and EI contributions), and provide Canada with the essential labour necessary for ensuring the survival of our country's agricultural sector. Through the SAWP, migrants access work opportunities to earn money that assists with the economic needs of their families and communities in countries of origin. MFWs and Canadians therefore both benefit from the SAWP, yet the structure of the SAWP places the burden of risk and precarity onto MFWs without recognizing and protecting their human rights.

September, the month that marks the beginning of fall, is also the same month when Canadians observe Labour Day celebrations. Arguably, this season should also be the one in which Canadians recognize the contributions and sacrifices of migrant farm workers and call on governments to secure the livelihoods and protect the labour and human rights of those who labour for the food on our table.

Questions for Critical Thought

1. How did the authors of this chapter draw on both qualitative and quantitative data to understand the experiences of migrant farm workers?
2. How do the structures of the SAWP create conditions of precarity and ill treatment for migrant farm workers?
3. How does this research help us understand the relationship between an international division of labour and racialization?
4. How could a mobile sociological approach be valuable to researching other types of workers?
5. Does this research on migrant farm workers make you think differently about the celebrations of fall harvest, including Thanksgiving, and fall agricultural fairs, which so many Canadians enjoy every year?

References

Barfield, Thomas, ed. 1997. *The Dictionary of Anthropology*. Oxford: Wiley-Blackwell.

Basok, Tanya. 2002. *Tortillas and Tomatoes*. Montreal: McGill-Queens University Press.

Bauder, Harald, Kerry Preibisch, Siobhan Sutherland, and Kerry Nash. 2002. *Impacts of Foreign Farm Workers in Ontario Communities*. Guelph: University of Guelph. http://www.geography.ryerson.ca/hbauder/Immigrant%20Labour/impacts.pdf.

CBC News. 2011. "BC Labour Activists Rally for Mexican Migrant Workers." December 19. http://www.cbc.ca/news/canada/british-columbia/b-c-labour-activists-rally-for-mexicanmigrant-workers-1.993516.

Consulado General de México en Montreal. 2018. *Programa de Trabajadores Agrícolas Temporales*. https://consulmex.sre.gob.mx/montreal/index.php/es/ptat.

Depatie-Pelletier, E. 2008. "Under Legal Practices Similar to Slavery According to the UN Convention: Canada 'Not White' 'Temporary' Foreign Workers in 'Low-Skilled' Occupations." Presented at the *10th National Metropolis Conference*, Halifax, April 5. http://www.migrantworkersrights.net/fr/resources/under-legal-practices-similar-to-slavery-according-.

ESDC (Employment and Social Development Canada). 2016. *Annual Labour Market Impact Assessment Statistics: 2008–2015 Primary Agriculture stream.*

———. 2017. *Temporary Foreign Worker Program 2017 Q2*. http://open.canada.ca/data/en/dataset/e8745429-21e7-4a73-b3f5-90a779b78d1e.

Global Forum on Migration and Development (GFMD). 2014. *Canadian Seasonal Agricultural Worker's Program (SAWP)*. http://www.gfmd.org/pfp/ppd/1753.

Hennebry, Jenna. 2006. *Globalization and the Mexican-Canadian Seasonal Agricultural Worker Program: Power, Racialization and Transnationalism in Temporary Migration*. Unpublished PhD dissertation, University of Western Ontario.

———. 2007. *Public Health Risks and Infectious Disease Exposure for Migrant Workers in Rural Ontario*. Ottawa: Public Health Agency of Canada.

———. 2009. *Migrant Farm Worker Health and the Public Health Implications of International Agricultural Labour Migration—Phase II Focus Groups with Health Care Providers and Public Health Units*. Ottawa: Public Health Agency of Canada.

———. 2012. *Permanently Temporary? Agricultural Migrant Workers and Their Integration in Canada*. IRPP Study. Montreal: Institute for Research on Public Policy.

———. 2014a. "Falling through the Cracks? Migrant Workers and the Global Social Protection Floor." *Global Social Policy* 14 (3): 369–88. https://doi.org/10.1177/1468018114544765.

———. 2014b. "Transnational Precarity: Women's Migration Work and Mexican Seasonal Agricultural Migration to Canada." *International Journal of Sociology* 44 (3): 42–59. https://doi.org/10.2753/IJS0020-7659440303.

Hennebry, Jenna, William Grass, and Janet McLaughlin. 2017. *Women Migrant Workers' Journey Through the Margins: Labour, Migration and Trafficking*. New York: United Nations Entity for Gender Equality and the Empowerment of Women (UN Women). http://www.unwomen.org/en/digital-library/publications/2017/2/women-migrant-workers-journey-through-the-margins.

Hennebry, Jenna, Jenna Holliday, and Mohammad Moniruzzaman. 2017. "At What Cost? Women Migrant Workers, Remittances and Development." United Nations Entity for Gender Equality and the Empowerment of Women (UN Women).

Hennebry, Jenna, and Janet McLaughlin. 2012. "The Exception That Proves the Rule: Structural Vulnerability, Health Risks and Consequences for Temporary Migrant Farmworkers in Canada." In *Legislating Inequality: Canada's Temporary Migrant Worker Program*, edited by C. Hughes and P. Lenard (117–38). Montreal: McGill-Queen's University Press.

Hennebry, Jenna, Janet McLaughlin, and Kerry Preibisch. 2016. "Out of the Loop: (In) Access to Health Care for Migrant Workers in Canada." *Journal of International Migration and Integration* 17 (2): 521–38. https://doi.org/10.1007/s12134-015-0417-1.

Hennebry, Jenna, Kerry Preibisch, and Janet McLaughlin. 2010. *Health across Borders – Health Status, Risks and Care among Transnational Migrant Farm Workers in Ontario*. Toronto: CERIS Ontario Metropolis Centre.

Hennebry, Jenna, and Gabriel Williams. 2015. "Making Vulnerability Visible: Medical Repatriation and Canada's Migrant Agricultural Workers." *Canadian Medical Association Journal* 187 (6): 391–92. https://doi.org/10.1503/cmaj.141189.

Knowles, Kimberly. 1997. *The Seasonal Agricultural Workers' Program in Ontario: From the Perspective of Jamaican Migrants*. Unpublished MA thesis, University of Guelph.

Lechner, Frank. 2001. "Globalization Theories: World System Theory." *The Globalization Website*. http://www.sociology.emory.edu/globalization/theories01.html.

Makin, Kirk. 2011. "Farm Workers Have No Right to Unionize, Top Court Rules." *Globe and Mail*, April 29. https://www.theglobeandmail.com/news/national/farm-workers-have-no-right-to-unionize-top-court-rules/article578141/.

Marchitelli, Rosa. 2016. "Migrant Worker Program Called 'Worse Than Slavery' after Injured Participants Sent Home Without Treatment." *CBC News*, May 16. http://www.cbc.ca/news/canada/jamaican-farm-worker-sent-home-in-a-casket-1.3577643.

McLaughlin, Janet. 2007. "Falling through the Cracks: Seasonal Foreign Farm Workers' Health and Compensation across Borders." *Health Studies* 2. https://scholars.wlu.ca/brantford_hs/2.

———. 2009. *Trouble in Our Fields: Health and Human Rights among Mexican and Caribbean Migrant Farm Workers in Canada*. Unpublished doctoral dissertation, University of Toronto.

McLaughlin, Janet, and Jenna Hennebry. 2015. "Managed into the Margins: Examining Citizenship and Human Rights of Migrant Workers in Canada." In *The Human Right to Citizenship: A Slippery Concept*, edited by Rhoda E. Howard-Hassmann and Margaret Walton-Roberts, 176–90. Philadelphia: University of Pennsylvania Press.

McLaughlin, Janet, Jenna Hennebry, Donald Cole, and Gabriel Williams. 2014. *The Migrant Farmworker Health Journey: Stages and Strategies*. IMRC Policy Points, International Migration Research Centre, Waterloo, ON.

McLaughlin, Janet, Jenna Hennebry, and Ted Haines. 2014. "Paper versus Practice: Occupational Health and Safety Protections and Realities for Temporary Foreign Agricultural Workers in Ontario." *Perspectives interdisciplinaires sur le travail et la santé* 16 (2). http://journals.openedition.org/pistes/3844.

McLaughlin, Janet, Don Wells, Aaraón Mendiburo, André Lyn, and Biljana Vasilevska. 2017. "'Temporary Workers,' Temporary Fathers: Transnational Family Impacts of Canada's Seasonal Agricultural Worker Program." *Relations industrielles/Industrial Relations* 72 (4): 682–709. https://doi.org/10.7202/1043172ar.

Otero, Gerardo, and Kerry Preibisch. 2010. "Farmworker Health and Safety: Challenges for British Columbia." *WorkSafeBC*, August (RS2006-OG11).

Preibisch, Kerry. 2004. "Migrant Agricultural Workers and Processes of Social Inclusion in Rural Canada: Encuentros and Desencuentros." *Canadian Journal of Latin American and Caribbean Studies* 29: 57–58. https://doi.org/10.1080/08263663.2004.10816857.

Preibisch, Kerry, and Jenna Hennebry. 2011. "Temporary Migration, Chronic Effects: The Health of International Migrant Workers in Canada." *Canadian Medical Association Journal* 183 (9): 1033–8. https://doi.org/10.1503/cmaj.090736.

Satzewich, Vic. 1991. *Racism and the Incorporation of Foreign Labour*. New York: Routledge.
———. 1998. *Racism and Social Inequality in Canada: Concepts, Controversies, and Strategies of Resistance*. Toronto: Thompson Educational Publishing.
Stuckey, James. 2013. "Canadian Farmers Prove Size Doesn't Matter." *Globe and Mail*, July 1. https://www.theglobeandmail.com/report-on-business/economy/economy-lab/canadas-farmers-prove-size-doesnt-matter/article13262631/.
United Food and Commercial Workers Canada (UFCW). 2014. "UFCW Canada Denounces Gender-Based Discrimination against Migrant Women under Seasonal Agricultural Workers Program." *UFCW Canada*, July 31. http://www.ufcw.ca/index.php?option=com_content&view=article&id=30175:ufcw-canada20denounces-gender-based-discrimination-against-migrant-women-under-seasonal-agriculturalworkers-program&catid=9536:directions-14-59&Itemid=6&lang=en.
Urry, John. 2010. "Mobile Sociology." *The British Journal of Sociology* 61: 347–66. https://doi.org/10.1111/j.1468-4446.2009.01249.x.
Wallerstein, Immanuel. 2001. *Unthinking Social Science: The Limits of Nineteenth-Century Paradigms*. Philadelphia: Temple University Press.
———. 2004. *World-Systems Analysis: An Introduction*. Durham: Duke University Press.
Watson, H.G. 2014. "Mexico Accused of Blacklisting Seasonal Workers Who Unionize in Canada." *Rabble*, February 21. http://rabble.ca/news/2014/02/mexico-accused-blacklisting-seasonal-workers-who-unionize-canada.

5 A Long Weekend of Rest and Labour: Thanksgiving, Holiday Body Work, and the Holiday Body

HEIDI BICKIS

LEARNING OUTCOMES

After reading this chapter, you should be able to:

- describe how the body is social and how social life is embodied
- explain how industrialization impacted contemporary understandings of work and leisure
- differentiate the four different kinds of body work and their relevance for holidays
- analyze how body work is gendered
- apply the concept of the holiday body to reflect on the paradox of holidays as leisure time

Introduction

Have you ever had that feeling of needing a holiday after a holiday? Perhaps you've been looking forward to a summer camping trip, Christmas break, or the Thanksgiving long weekend? The holiday period arrives, you may or may not enjoy yourself, but at the end you don't find yourself feeling rested or rejuvenated, as you had hoped you would. In fact, you might even be more exhausted and find yourself thinking *I need a holiday to recover from my holiday*. Arguably, the idea of needing a holiday after a holiday has become part of our everyday exchanges when we return to school, work, and the mundanity of the routine. "We need a third week!" a colleague of mine said recently after the Christmas break. These feelings of being rested or tired remind us that, as social beings, we are all **embodied**. In other words, we cannot separate our thoughts, feelings, and actions from the bodies we inhabit and the bodies of others with whom we interact. The significance of bodies for analyses of social life is one of the key tenets of the **sociology of the body**, a subdiscipline that examines the embodied nature of social life – that is, how we live in and through our bodies, as well as how the body is social.

In this chapter, I consider the body as social by examining how the Thanksgiving long weekend and holidays more generally are deeply embodied. I focus specifically on what I call the ***holiday body***. I use this sociological concept to draw attention to the **paradox of holidays** – that is, the way holidays are legislated and imagined as periods of rest from work and yet are also a time that requires a considerable amount of paid and unpaid labour. In other words, holidays promise rest but require work in order to enable rest to occur. The holiday body describes how this paradox is lived in and through our bodies. To begin, I provide some general background on the sociology of the body. I then discuss the history of Thanksgiving in Canada, locating the Thanksgiving long weekend as part of broad social changes in the organization of labour and leisure since the **Industrial Revolution**. Next, I introduce the concept of **body work** and what I call *holiday body work*. I then include a feminist analysis of holiday body work to highlight how some bodies have to do more body work than – and for – other bodies. Together, these two sections will present an image of the Thanksgiving long weekend as simultaneously a period of leisure and rest as well as one of labour.

The holiday body has relevance for the many holidays that occur throughout the year. Thanksgiving, however, offers a good case study because, more than any other holiday, Thanksgiving focuses on family and friends gathering for a shared meal and thus highlights the forms of body work I examine – planning and preparing a meal, creating a festive atmosphere, and ensuring dinner guests are enjoying themselves. Moreover, because of the centrality of the meal, the body is already foregrounded: Thanksgiving is a time of eating too much turkey, feeling full, wanting more, and experiencing many other tastes and sensations.

Sociology and the Body

The focus on the body in sociology is relatively new. Although feminist theorists have long foregrounded the importance of the body, within mainstream sociology, it is only in the last 30 to 40 years that the body has been established as an important sociological topic. In part, this increased attention can be explained by social changes. As Chris Shilling (2012) argues, the technological capacity to directly intervene into and control the body (e.g., *in vitro* fertilization, organ transplants, plastic surgery) and the increased availability and social importance of body-related objects and lifestyles that can be purchased (e.g., through gym memberships, makeup, waxing, fashion) means that now more than ever, we are attentive to how our bodies look, how they can be altered, how they can become sick, and what we can do to keep them healthy. Shilling is not suggesting that bodies were previously unimportant to social life. Rather, the meaning and importance of the body for individuals and **society** has changed, and it is this change that has prompted a growing sociological interest.

As a subdiscipline of sociology, the relatively new sociology of the body is a diverse, rich, and often interdisciplinary area of study. Some approaches to studying the body, however, have been particularly influential. One way that bodies have been examined sociologically is from the perspective of **social constructionism**, an approach that encompasses a range of ways of examining how society shapes, conditions, and constructs bodies from the micro level (small-scale **interactions** between people) to the macro level (large-scale structural forces). Social constructionist views of the body aim to counter **biological determinism**. From the perspective of biological determinism, or biologism, human behaviour can be explained by the biological make-up of individuals (Blackman 2008). For example, popular television science programs that suggest heterosexual women are attracted to strong men because they are instinctively looking for someone to protect their offspring is a form of biologism. The problem with this perspective is that it fails to consider the role social **norms** play in establishing the meanings we give to our bodies and our assumptions about the ideal body. For instance, the gestures and facial expressions you might make on a date to indicate that you're having fun or to try to politely signal that you're not having fun are not natural, instinctual habits. They are determined by a society's **values** and norms, which we learn from our families, peers, and various forms of media. (For more on socialization, see the introduction and chapters ten, sixteen, and twenty.) Similarly, our assumptions about what counts as the ideal body in terms of size, shape, and health are also not natural; they are influenced by the media, the government (e.g., through public awareness campaigns that promote ideal body weights and diets), and medicine (by strictly defining what is considered healthy and unhealthy through waist size, body mass index, etc.). (For more on the effects of these norms about the body, see chapters six and eight.) The strength of social constructionist approaches to the body is that they emphasize how bodies are affected by the society within which they live. However, the problem with these approaches is that they may replace biological determinism with a **social determinism**: That is, they suggest that individual bodies are completely and only determined by social conditions (Blackman 2008; Shilling 2012).

To avoid this social determinism, sociologists and other body studies scholars have been working within what Lisa Blackman describes as the **embodiment paradigm**. As Blackman (2008, 37) explains, "this perspective refuses the idea that the biological and the social, the natural and the cultural, exist as separate entities." In other words, these sociologists recognize that bodies are fleshy substances that change as we get older, that are altered as hormones fluctuate, and so forth; at the same time, they recognize that our engagements with media, work, friends, family, education, and so on affect our bodies. Bodies, then, are not purely biological (unaffected by society), but nor are they purely social (that is, only social constructions). Rather, the biological and social are intricately intertwined and each affects the other (Shilling 2012). For example, the work that you do directly transforms your body; if you are a construction worker, then the pain you might experience, the postures you hold, the strengths you develop, the health issues you're likely to experience, and so forth will be drastically different than if you are an accountant or a nurse or a bartender. Additionally, your body and its age, health, ability, size, and so on will affect how you interact with others, your experiences at work or school, and even influence your worldview. This approach can still be understood as showing how the body is social (as opposed to only biological). It just does so without assuming that we can easily distinguish between biology and society, nature and **culture**.

Holiday Time and Thanksgiving Long Weekend

Canadian Thanksgiving as a Holiday

Canadian Thanksgiving began in the nineteenth century as a religious holiday with a strongly nationalist character. Religious leaders in Ontario borrowed the idea of American Thanksgiving to create a religious holiday. They saw the Canadian version of Thanksgiving as a way to foster Christianity and a sense of **national identity** in this newly formed nation by celebrating what they saw as the superiority of Canada and Canadians. For many of these religious leaders, the ideal Canadian identity was one that was **white** and Protestant (Sismondo 2017; Stevens 2016; for more on early Canadian history and **ideology**, see chapters nine and ten). Despite its religious beginnings, Thanksgiving became increasingly secular as celebrations moved away from church-associated **rituals** and activities. The holiday offered a day of leisure and relaxation for workers and, for the middle and upper classes, it was a time for sports, hunting, and concerts (Stevens 2016, 73). The most notable feature of this holiday was the increasing popularity of the family Thanksgiving meal. The popular press played a key role promoting the idea of this holiday **tradition**, instructing readers as early as 1874 that "'Thanksgiving dinner will be the grand social event of the day'" (cited in Stevens 2016, 71).

The Thanksgiving long weekend familiar to Canadians today was not established until 1908. In fact, prior to this, the date changed year to year, and was originally held on Thursdays (sometimes on Wednesdays). It became a nationally recognized holiday in 1878, but it remained a weekday celebration until 1908, when it was permanently moved to a Monday, thus officially instituting Thanksgiving as part of a long weekend (Stevens 2016). Thanksgiving is one of many long weekends legislated by the Canadian government that ensures workers have time off from work. Federal law stipulates that employees are entitled to days of rest and holidays as part of a working contract. Industries regulated by the federal government must follow the regulations set out in the Canada Labour Code, including standard hours of work. In addition to eight-hour working days and 40-hour weeks, federally regulated employees are also entitled to a day of rest (usually a Sunday) and "a minimum of two weeks of vacation annually" (once they've completed a year employment with the same employer). There are also nine paid holidays every year, including New Year's Day, Good Friday, Victoria Day, Canada Day, Labour Day, Thanksgiving Day, Remembrance Day, Christmas Day, and Boxing Day (ESDC 2018).

Industrialization and Changes to Time

Today, in Canada, we are very accustomed to thinking about the organization of our time in standard, coordinated terms of time on and off from work. However, as social historians have shown, this separation of work from leisure is a relatively recent phenomenon linked to changes that occurred in nineteenth-century Europe. During this period, Europe was going through a process of **industrialization**, shifting from a largely local, agricultural, and rural society to an increasingly widespread urban and industrial society. These changes contributed to, and were shaped by, the development of **clock time**, a form of socio-temporal organization based on the strict measurement of discrete units of time (minutes, hours) as represented in various means of measuring time (through clocks, timetables, time cards) (Urry 2000). Although it is something we take as normal and even natural today, clock time is markedly different from other ways of organizing life, such as according to the natural rhythms of the sun, the completion of a task, or bodily feelings such as hunger. (See chapters three and eleven for more on the different ways of conceiving time.) A key part of clock time is the scheduling of the workday, and the routinization of the day and week into periods of work and leisure. Before **industrial capitalism** took full force in England, work and leisure were not distinguished. Instead, irregular labour patterns were common and labour tended to be task-oriented – that is, based on completing what was seen as immediately necessary (e.g., this report needs writing or the field needs to be plowed instead of "I will work from 9 a.m. to 5 p.m."). Before industrialization, labour was strongly bound to the family home. Labourers did not experience the distinction so familiar to us today between being at work and not being at work (Cross 1990).

As workers were forced into the factory, work time became separate from family time, and the home and the family became associated with leisure. The result of these complex changes was that work and leisure became opposites and were marked by different places, times, and relationships. Additionally, workers started to see their time at work as taking away from their leisure opportunities (Cross 1990). Partly in response to this loss (among other concerns, such as poor wages and working conditions), North American, British, and European workers and **unions** fought for the limitation of the working day and the working week (Cross 1990). Despite victories here and there, overall, widespread change was slow coming, and it wasn't until after World War I that working-hour legislation stuck in Europe, with partial changes being instituted in the United States (Cross 1990).

The scheduling of work and leisure has important implications for bodies. Indeed, a crucial distinction between work and leisure is how the body is engaged. The assumption is that during work time, the body is labouring and only labouring. By contrast, during leisure time, the body ought to be engaged only in various types of leisure activities or resting. In other words, the emergence of clock time and the subsequent changes to legislation and customary practice organize bodies as either labouring or relaxing, regardless of whether this strict organization is clearly delineated in reality. However, as we will see, the holiday body stems in part from a blurring of these temporal-social categories. Although Thanksgiving is legislated as a long weekend, and it is imagined as time for bodies to be engaged in leisure as opposed to labour, in reality, Thanksgiving requires a significant amount of body work.

Body Work

A number of sociologists have proposed the concept of "body work" to emphasize the importance of bodies and embodiment for sociological analyses of paid work and the unpaid work of domestic labour (Gimlin 2007; Wolkowitz 2006). Body work describes various ways that work is embodied and, according to Debra Gimlin (2007), can be categorized in terms of four key types: **appearance work**, **emotional labour**, **inter-corporeal body work**, and **body-making through work**. Although forms of body work are evident outside the realm of what we might strictly describe as work (e.g., we all manage our bodily appearance as part of our day-to-day lives), the concept is intended to highlight how paid and, in some cases, unpaid working bodies can be examined.

Appearance Work

The first type of body work, appearance work, refers to how the maintenance of a particular bodily appearance (e.g., putting on makeup, shaving, cutting our nails, wearing certain types of clothes, and so on) is becoming a crucial part of many jobs and individuals' work experiences. In an economy dominated by service-sector jobs, in which workers have to sell products in retail or make customers feel happy, relaxed, and comfortable in the hospitality industry, job expectations include the way you look, and employers seek workers they consider to be attractive (Warhurst and Nickson 2001; Shilling 2012). For example, a personnel manager at Elba, a hotel chain in the United Kingdom, explained that the hotel wants to employ "pretty attractive looking people ... with a nice smile, nice teeth, neat hair and in decent proportion" (cited in Warhurst and Nickson, 2001, 15). Similarly, CBC's *Marketplace* found that a number of restaurant chains in Canada, including Joey's, Earl's, and Moxie's, required their female staff to wear tight skirts, high heels, and heavy makeup (Sample 2016). As Linda McDowell (1997) shows in her study of stockbrokers in London, this appearance work is also evident in jobs outside the service industry. She found that stockbrokers saw their dress and style as a key part of their ability to succeed at their job. This type of appearance work made headline news in May 2016 after a receptionist in London, England, was sent home when she refused to wear high heels to work (BBC 2016).

Emotional Labour

The second type of body work is emotional labour, a concept developed by sociologist Arlie Hochschild (1983) in her now-classic study of flight attendants at Delta Airlines. Emotional labour involves the management of one's feelings by suppressing how one actually feels, or making oneself feel differently than one actually does. This kind of body work can surface when you pretend to be feeling something you are not for the purposes of carrying out your job, or altering what you honestly feel (Shilling 2012, 124). For flight attendants, this emotional labour might involve creating a feeling of calm or happiness in their customers by smiling and acting friendly (Hochschild 1983; Schilling 2012) or feeling sympathy for rude or aggressive passengers instead of feeling angry (Shilling 2012). The requirement to manage emotions is evident in many other jobs, too. At Pret A Manger, a UK-based fresh-fast-food chain, creating a particular emotional atmosphere is a clear expectation of the job. As journalist Timothy Noah (2013) explains, "[a] 'mystery shopper' visits every Pret outlet once a week. If the employee who rings up the sale is appropriately ebullient, then everyone in the shop gets a bonus. If not, nobody does."

Inter-corporeal Body Work

The third type of body work is inter-corporeal body work. This idea refers to the labour of nurses, dentists, hairdressers, and funeral directors, among others, whose jobs involve working on or for other human bodies. The work might involve dealing with human bodily fluids or waste (e.g., by garbage collectors, medical lab technicians, hospital orderlies) or direct bodily contact (e.g., by doctors, aestheticians, caregivers, sex workers), and it potentially encompasses a vast range of jobs, including unpaid work caring for sick or elderly family members, typically performed by women (Gimlin 2007; Twigg 2000).

Finally, linking the aforementioned types of body work is the idea that bodies are produced through the work they do. In other words, body work highlights how biology can be altered in the way that "the work environment is literally 'written on' the body" (Gimlin 2007, 363) insofar as it alters a body physically and physiologically. Consider, for example, how manual labour will put physical strain on a person's bones and muscles; how stressful work environments contribute to high blood pressure, weight gain, and so on; how wearing high heels while waiting tables all day can create physical pain and change the structure of the feet and the rest of the body; or how shift work can create extreme fatigue and alter the body's biological rhythms and chemical balance of the brain.

Although the concept of body work primarily highlights how paid work is embodied, the concept has relevance for other areas of social life and, as noted previously, can be productive for thinking through the embodied nature of holidays and the Thanksgiving long weekend in particular. I propose a new, related concept – **holiday body work** – to capture the intersection of the various types of body work activated during a particular time (e.g., a long weekend) and in relation to a particular ritual (here, Thanksgiving).

Thanksgiving Holiday Body Work: Feminist Perspectives

The Thanksgiving meal – roast turkey, cranberry sauce, mashed potatoes, and pumpkin pie – is one of the central features of Thanksgiving and requires a considerable amount of body work. First, the work involved in planning, shopping, cooking, and serving food can be understood as a kind of inter-corporeal work. Preparing food is strongly connected to the consumption of food: the food prepared by one body is consumed by another. Consuming the meal is itself a deeply embodied practice: encountering smells upon entering the home, feeling hungry, experiencing the tastes and textures on our tongues, the sensation of being full, wanting more, and other, less appealing effects such as burping, farting, feeling too full and sleepy, and so on. Also important for this holiday consumption are bodily memories of past meals and the associated tastes and sensations. Making food for others, then, is inter-corporeal insofar as it involves the preparation of something that is subsumed into the deep recesses of a complex digestive system, and it directly affects others' bodies by producing particular sensations.

Hosting a Thanksgiving meal requires another kind of body work: emotional labour. Hosts are expected to produce a festive environment – in other words, a holiday feeling. Although we might tend to assume we just naturally feel festive during certain holidays, if we take a step back for a moment, we can think about what makes the mood feel festive: smells, decorations, gatherings of people, music – all of which someone has to organize. The production of a holiday feeling involves the evocation and management of particular emotions in one's self, as the host, and in others, whether family, friends, or other guests. A host must create a welcoming environment and ensure all guests feel comfortable by directing conversation, laughing off inappropriate comments, or offering food and drink. Regardless of how they might feel themselves – worried about the turkey in the oven, unhappy about one of the guests, tired – the hosts must act as if they are enjoying themselves and ensure their guests are feeling happy, calm, and at ease. Although the specifics of the holiday feeling will differ from event to event and family to family, even as levels of familiarity vary, the role of the host tends to remain the same.

The host isn't the only one who must engage in emotional labour, however. This type of body work at Thanksgiving is also required of guests. In some cases, guests are expected to participate in the event by contributing a food item. In this way, they are also engaged in a kind of inter-corporeal work similar to the host. More notably, they must manage their emotions and enjoy themselves. To counter the festive feeling by expressing distaste or reluctance about the event might be interpreted as a rejection of the host and their efforts, a failure to properly perform emotional labour and a rejection of the emotional labour of the host. Failure to participate in the holiday feeling is seen as a rejection of the ritual and the ungrateful guest becomes responsible for ruining the event for others.

Importantly, not all bodies are equally involved in this work. Some bodies are expected to do more or different work than other bodies for Thanksgiving (as well as during other holidays); and the success of the event relies on this differentiated work. One way to examine these differences is to take a feminist approach. In sociology, feminism is a theoretical perspective that provides a distinctive way to analyze society and social relations by emphasizing how the social world is **gendered** – that is, how behaviours, feelings, jobs, dress, roles, and so on are defined as either feminine or masculine and seen as appropriate for men or women. Importantly, this gendering of social life is not natural; it is socially produced and something we learn in complex ways through socialization. Not only is social life gendered, it is also patriarchal – it is organized hierarchically where men, as a group, have more power than women as a group (Seidman 2013). **Gender** difference helps maintain a patriarchal society, a society dominated by men.

Analyzing holiday body work from a feminist perspective can provide a deeper and more nuanced understanding of this concept by bringing attention to how holiday body work is gendered. The emotional labour and inter-corporeal body work discussed previously is often taken on by women and, furthermore, is also seen as the responsibility of women. Indeed, studies show that women do most of the domestic labour (unpaid child care and housework). Statistics Canada's most recent time-use survey (2015) showed that despite improvements from 2010, women do an average of 3.6 hours a day of unpaid domestic work compared to 2.4 hours done by men (Fletcher 2017). Although this difference might be explained in part by the fact that, due to social expectations around raising children, women are often in part-time work and therefore have more time for housework, it still highlights how domestic labour (including child care) is deeply gendered. Recent findings of the European Social Survey, published in 2013, similarly showed that women do the majority of housework. In the United Kingdom, for example, the **survey** found that 70 per cent of housework is done by women (ESRC 2013). Globally, trends are the same. Research collected by the United Nations found that around the world, women do more unpaid domestic work than men (United Nations Statistics Division and Chen 2015). As Hochschild with Machung (1989) argue, women often have a "**second shift**" of unpaid domestic labour after finishing a day of paid work. In addition, women often play – or are expected to play – a key role in maintaining and fostering emotional bonds with partners and children, and this is not an expectation that is imposed on men. Duncombe and Marsden (1993) use the term "**triple shift**" to describe this added burden of work, highlighting women's third job on top of paid employment and domestic labour.

During holidays such as Thanksgiving, this gendered **division of labour** persists and even intensifies, and the holiday body work central for Thanksgiving will typically fall on the shoulders of women. Idealized notions of femininity – social expectations for how women should ideally act, dress, and feel, as well as the roles they should perform – circulate in magazines and television, where women are offered holiday planning advice or targeted for sales on turkeys. Family rituals centred on the mother or grandmother hosting the Thanksgiving meal also teach other family members that this work is the responsibility of the women in the family. These personal histories and media images inform how women, and others around them, see their role. As a result, women become the holiday planners and are expected to fulfill the role of host and chef, along with the labour required for both. Additionally, they are expected to enjoy this work as if it was a labour of love and not a gendered social expectation. As a result, Thanksgiving holiday body work becomes **feminized** – that is, it becomes strictly the domain of women and is strongly associated with femininity. Additionally, the feminization of holiday body work means that it is seen as less important than other types of work or not as work at all.

There is more to the long weekend, however, than hosting or attending a meal. Thanksgiving dinner, in particular, relies on the labour of others: farmers, butchers, truck drivers, supermarket cashiers, and the labour of public transportation workers who enable people to travel to see family and friends. Not everyone has a long weekend and, for many, the long weekend often means longer and harder hours. **Social class** is another way holiday body work is differentiated. There are differences in labour and leisure practices for the working classes, middle classes, and upper classes. Holiday body work will also be differentiated by ability, **race**, and sexual orientation. In other words, the body work required during holidays is not the same for everyone. As a concept, it can be applied broadly, but it also requires a careful consideration of differences between bodies and the implications of these differences for how holidays are embodied.

The Holiday Body

As the prior discussion shows, holidays require all kinds of body work that is unevenly distributed and practised. Indeed, holidays are much more than time off work or celebratory gatherings of family and friends. Although legally designated as a day of rest and customarily part of a social ritual of giving thanks, Thanksgiving could not happen without a considerable amount and variety of labouring on the part of various bodies. This contrast is important because it shows how holidays are embodied in unequal and paradoxical ways. It is this complexity that the concept of the holiday body captures. Even though we might be aware of the work that goes into Thanksgiving, or that some people have to work through it, we still tend to have a particular expectation of long weekends. We *imagine* that our bodies will be in a particular condition: a state of being rested or resting, engaged in leisure, or consuming a particular kind of meal and feeling sated. The holiday body, then, is in part about the promise of an embodied future characterized by rest and leisure – but it must also encompass the body work needed for the holiday to succeed. In other words, it highlights the paradox at the heart of holidays: the future promise of rest from work requires a significant amount of work that makes rest impossible.

At this point, we can recall the discussion at the beginning of the chapter about the embodied perspective. The concept of the holiday body enables us to recognize the body as social *and* biological, never solely one nor the other. This means, on the one hand, that the holiday body is a product of social factors: labour practices, body work, and holiday rituals are shaped by social norms and expectations. On the other hand, the holiday body is strongly linked to the body's physiological requirement for rest. Legislation and imaginings of restful or leisurely periods are, in some ways, informed by the biological functioning of bodies. Beyond our individual bodily experiences, our collective understandings of work and leisure, and our shared engagements with Thanksgiving rituals, are based both on a bodily existence and its social organization.

Conclusion

Social life is deeply embodied, and bodies are both shaped by and shape social life. This chapter has invited you to reflect on and examine this fact by looking at what bodies might do and hope to do during the Thanksgiving long weekend. I introduced the concept of the holiday body to draw attention to what I have described as the paradox of this holiday. Although imagined and legislated as a time of leisure or rest, Thanksgiving can only happen through the labouring of bodies, a labouring that is unevenly distributed and whereby some bodies work more than others. This paradox is also evident in other holidays such as a week at the cottage, a trip to a resort, or Christmas. Similar to Thanksgiving, many of us have expectations that these holidays will give our bodies time to rest or participate in leisure activities. However, all three require many kinds of body work in order for this promise of rest to be realized. Important to this argument is the contemporary distinction between work and leisure. As the chapter explained, this distinction developed with the emergence of clock time during industrialization. An important aspect of clock time is the organization of the working day and week into periods of work and leisure. By extension, this division of time also separates the working body from the resting body. Our contemporary understanding of holidays is, furthermore, premised on this clear separation. However, by taking a closer look at the multiple ways the Thanksgiving long weekend is embodied, this chapter has demonstrated that what it means to be on holiday is not as straightforward as we might think. Indeed, holidays are embodied in complex and contradictory ways.

Questions for Critical Thought

1. Reflect on the holidays discussed in other chapters and consider how they are also embodied. Can you think of other examples of holiday body work, how bodies either shape or are shaped by these holidays, how social norms and expectations affect how bodies must look, or how bodies experience these holidays?
2. Do you think the paradox of holidays can be applied to other holidays and seasonal rituals discussed in the book? In what ways? What are your own experiences

of holidays? Does the concept of the holiday body apply to your holidays? Why or why not?

3. The chapter focused on the importance of clock time for our contemporary understandings of work and leisure. Do you think clock time still dominates social life? Why? Are there other kinds of temporal organizing that have become important?
4. The chapter outlined four types of body work. Select an example of paid or unpaid work and analyze how one or several forms of body work might be evident.
5. The chapter examined how holiday body work is gendered. What other social differences are important for holiday body work? For example, how might holiday body work differ based on social class, race, ability, or sexual orientation?

References

BBC. 2016. "London Receptionist 'Sent Home for Not Wearing Heels.'" *BBC News*, May 11. http://www.bbc.co.uk/news/uk-england-london-36264229.

Blackman, Lisa. 2008. *The Body: The Key Concepts*. Oxford: Berg Publishers.

Cross, Gary S. 1990. *A Social History of Leisure Since 1600*. State College: Venture Publishing, Inc.

Duncombe, Jean, and Dennis Marsden. 1993. "Love and Intimacy: The Gender Division of Emotion and 'Emotion Work: A Neglected Aspect of Sociological Discussion of Heterosexual Relationships.'" *Sociology* 27 (2): 221–41. https://doi.org/10.1177/0038038593027002003.

Economic and Social Research Council (ESRC). 2013. "A Woman's Work Is Never Done?" *ScienceDaily*, July 22. www.sciencedaily.com/releases/2013/07/130722202820.htm.

Employment and Social Development Canada (ESDC). 2018. "Vacation and General Holidays." March 27 (last updated). Ottawa: Employment and Social Development Canada. https://laws-lois.justice.gc.ca/eng/acts/L-2/page-1.html.

Fletcher, Robson. 2017. "Women Spend 50% More Time Doing Unpaid Work than Men: Statistics Canada." *CBC News*, June 1. http://www.cbc.ca/news/canada/calgary/men-women-housework-unpaid-statistics-canada-1.4141367.

Gimlin, Debra. 2007. "What is 'Body Work'? A Review of the Literature." *Sociology Compass* 1 (1): 353–70. https://doi.org/10.1111/j.1751-9020.2007.00015.x.

Hochschild, Arlie Russell. 1983. *The Managed Heart: Commercialization of Human Feeling*. Berkeley: University of California Press.

Hochschild, Arlie, with Anne Machung. 1989. *Second Shift: Working Parents and the Revolution at Home*. New York: Viking Penguin.

McDowell, Linda. 1997. *Capital Culture: Gender at Work in the City*. Oxford: Blackwell.

Noah, Timothy. 2013. "Labor of Love: The Enforced Happiness of Pret A Manger." *New Republic*, February 1. https://newrepublic.com/article/112204/pret-manger-when-corporations-enforce-happiness.

Sample, Lindsay. 2016. "Restaurant Dress Codes: Sexy Outfits for Female Staff May Be Discriminatory." *CBC News*, March 4 (updated March 6). http://www.cbc.ca/news/business/marketplace-gender-specific-dress-codes-1.3474289.

Seidman, Steven. 2013. *Contested Knowledge: Social Theory Today*. 5th ed. Malden: Wiley-Blackwell.

Shilling, Chris. 2012. *The Body and Social Theory*. London: Sage.

Sismondo, Christine. 2017. "The Odd, Complicated History of Canadian Thanksgiving." *Maclean's*, October 5. https://www.macleans.ca/opinion/the-odd-complicated-history-of-canadian-thanksgiving/.

Stevens, Peter A. 2016. "'Righteousness Exalteth the Nation': Religion, Nationalism, and Thanksgiving Day in Ontario, 1859–1914." In *Celebrating Canada: Holidays, National Days, and the Crafting of Identities*, edited by Matthew Hayday and Raymond Blake, 54–82. Toronto: University of Toronto Press.

Twigg, Julia. 2000. "Carework as a Form of Bodywork." *Ageing and Society* 20 (4): 389–411. https://doi.org/10.1017/S0144686X99007801.

United Nations Statistics Division, and Haoyi Chen. 2015. "Work – Chapter 4." *The World's Women 2015: Trends and Statistics by United Nations Statistics Division*, October 21. https://unstats.un.org/unsd/gender/chapter4/chapter4.html.

Urry, John. 2000. *Sociology Beyond Societies: Mobilities for the Twenty-first Century.* London: Routledge.

Warhurst, Christine L., and Dennis Nickson. 2001. *"Looking Good and Sounding Right": Style Counselling and the Aesthetics of the New Economy*. London: Industrial Society.

Wolkowitcz, Carol. 2006. *Bodies at Work*. London: Sage.

Winter

Canada is a winter nation. In many parts of the country, winter – and its various associated elements, including snow, ice, frost, cold, and darkness – is the dominant season. For example, in Edmonton, home of one of the co-editors of this volume, snow is a distinct likelihood from September through April but looms as a realistic possibility twelve months of the year. Indeed, Canada's iconic North (or, more broadly, Canada as an Arctic nation) is envisioned as wintery year-round. When Canadian athletes do not dominate at international winter sport competitions, it can produce national angst. Winter is central to both collective experiences of living in Canada and the Canadian imagination – how Canadians and others think of Canada and Canadianness. Yet winter is also experienced as deeply individual, even intimate, and, for many months of the year, winter can feel very much like a personal problem as external elements creep right into your flesh. In the -10° to -40° Celsius range, winter across Canada cools your breath, chills your bones, and seems to settle down in your heart. Snow, ice, and wind can make it quite perilous (or exhilarating) to try to venture outside, but the lack of social stimulation by staying inside can likewise make it feel perilous (or safer) to not head out into the cold. In this section, authors discuss the many ways in which, although the conditions of winter are felt through deeply **embodied** individual experiences, they are also both highly mediated by **social structures**, ideas, and **rituals**, and influence the enactment of **institutions** and **ideologies**.

In chapter six, Alissa Overend details how, for those with seasonal affective disorder (SAD), winter can feel very personal. SAD is a condition marked by changes in physiological and psychological well-being, including symptoms of depression, anxiety, and irritability. SAD can also be sociologically interpreted, Overend argues, as the **medicalization** of winter sadness, categorizing something that can better be understood as a social issue (e.g., the social meanings and expectations attached to mood and energy levels) into a pathological personal trouble.

As Tara Milbrandt describes in chapter seven, winter requires all sorts of physical interventions as well as its own distinct **socialization**, requiring the newly initiated to learn how to dress for, drive in, and manage themselves in winter. In her study of the WinterCity initiatives in Edmonton, Milbrandt notes that although the idea of celebrating Edmonton as a "winter city" is an idea largely fuelled by top-down city branding initiatives, the winter festivals they encourage nevertheless offer powerful moments for city dwellers to come together as a community. Moreover, these festivals counter understandings of the winter as something that needs to be individually endured and reimagines winter in the city as a collective, joyful experience.

In chapter eight, Jen Wrye, Michael Graydon, and Patricia Thille detail another embodied engagement with winter that is simultaneously highly individual and shaped by society: the pervasive New Year's resolution to lose weight. Rather than bulking up for a long winter hibernation, as some of our woodland animal friends do, North Americans instead often resolve to go on diets or hit the gym to sculpt their bodies. As Wrye, Graydon, and Thille assert, seasonal attempts to reshape the body are themselves influenced by a **neoliberal** logic of personal responsibility for achieving well-being and by socially dominant **norms** around appearance. Thus, the myriad seemingly individual projects of self-improvement reflect and are motivated by larger cultural values and logics.

Matthew P. Unger, in chapter nine, details how, in the early days of the Canadian **nation-state**, colonial law and what Unger calls the "colonial legal imaginary" were deeply dependent on both socially determined ideas of biological nature and the natural environmental conditions of the land. Socially constructed racist beliefs about which individuals or communities might be considered biologically prone to criminality strongly influenced the definition and enactment of justice in colonial law. At the same time, winter's snow, blizzards, and seasonally related illnesses and deaths in the large expanses over which colonial law attempted to preside limited the ability of the emerging colonial **state** to pursue and enact its own laws.

In chapter ten, Nicole Neverson analyzes how key winter sporting events – including the International Ice Hockey Federation's World Juniors Championships on Boxing Day, the National Hockey League's New Year's Day outdoor match, and the National Football League's Superbowl Sunday – can be understood as rituals that inspire specific forms of **social solidarity**. Although each of these sports events are celebrated as reflecting the universal values of their respective societies, they actually are highly political, organized around able-bodied, white masculinity and reflecting the power, influence, values, and **cultural capital** of those of the few but dominant.

In this section, the authors explore how winter is experienced, understood, and imagined, demonstrating the seeming paradoxes of this season: both oppressive and magical; a personal burden to bear yet the manifestation of social values and interactions; a set of constraining material conditions while also the possibility for **collective effervescence**.

6 Seasonal Affective Disorder (SAD): The Medicalization of Winter Sadness

ALISSA OVEREND

LEARNING OUTCOMES

After reading this chapter, you should be able to:

- explain the idea of illness as a social construct, influenced by contextual, social, and environmental factors
- summarize the symptoms, diagnosis, and causes of seasonal affective disorder (SAD), as well as explain how these symptoms, diagnosis, and causes reflect the social construction of illness
- explain both the push for demedicalization and the reasons it is important to retain sadness and winter sadness as part of a wide range of human behaviour
- define the biomedical gaze and explains how it fits within a poststructural theoretical approach to health and illness
- apply the concept of medicalization to sadness and winter sadness

Introduction

Fittingly, I write the first lines of this chapter at first snow (see figure 6.1). It's Thanksgiving weekend in Alberta, and just east of the **city** of Edmonton, the sky is overcast grey, the ground is covered with about two inches of wet snow, and the air is cold and damp – a chilly reminder of what's to come in the next *five months* (or more!) of winter. For many Canadians, winter is a time when we may notice our mood drop as we transition from the bright warmth of summer to the cold darkness of winter. Northern cities experience shortened daylight hours and receive little vitamin D (the vitamin known to help mood regulation). During the shortest day of the year in

FIGURE 6.1 A wintery October, just outside of Edmonton, Alberta. Photo credit: Alissa Overend

the northern hemisphere, known as winter solstice (which can occur between December 20 and 23), those in northern Canadian cities receive between five and seven hours of daylight, compared to their southern city counterparts, who receive between seven and nine hours of daylight (National Research Council of Canada 2017). When combining shortened daylight hours with freezing temperatures, blizzards, ice storms, and cold winds, it is no surprise that our winter environments (just as our summer environments) can affect our mood, sometimes significantly so.

In this chapter, I question to what degree we should medicalize seasonal sadness. That is, should we think of winter sadness as a medical condition that needs to be fixed, treated, or otherwise avoided? Or should we retain winter sadness as part of a range of normal and acceptable human emotions and as a reasonable response to harsh physical conditions? What purpose(s) or benefits might winter sadness serve? Under the broad umbrella of the **sociology of health**, a subdiscipline of sociology that examines the interaction between health, illness, and **society** (Clarke 2016), I analyze seasonal affective disorder (SAD) from a poststructural theoretical framework using the concept of **medicalization**. I move away from the common assumption of illness as a biological entity and toward a critical understanding of illness as a *social* process. This perspective does not negate or deny that mental and physical illnesses have material effects on the body – a cold congests, depression makes it hard to get out of bed, and cancer and heart disease claim far too many lives. However, if we only see illness as a physical entity, we fail to see the ways in which illness – its definitions, diagnoses, causes, and treatments – are also social, environmental, and contextual. For example, why do some woman and men respond to colds or depression differently? Or why do people of colour, and specifically black people, get under-diagnosed for many medical conditions? The answers lie in the social conditions that dictate and regulate **gendered** norms and racial **stereotypes**, not in individual biology. With regard to cancer or heart disease, these are disproportionately **Western** illnesses found in the conditions in which we live. Counter to the dominant biological accounts of illness, which regard illness as an objective fact measured on or in the body, poststructural accounts of illness look at the wider social conditions that affect how we come to define and diagnose illness. One effective technique for understanding illness as a social phenomenon is to look at how diagnoses change historically and cross-culturally. As I will document in the case of SAD, this is another illness that is predominantly westernized and thus not found in other cultural contexts, even in those with harsher winters than Canada.

Theorizing Illness

The critique of illness as an overwhelmingly physical entity draws on the theoretical foundations of poststructural theorist Michel Foucault (1973), who documents the ways that science comes to shape and understand illness through what he calls the **biomedical gaze** (sometimes referred to as the medical or clinical gaze). Foucault (1973) uses this term to refer to the changing ways of viewing illness that emerged alongside the **Enlightenment** and that continue to dominate scientific approaches to illness today. As medicine was able to pierce the previously unknown depths of the physical body, it gained a new understanding of illness – one that approached the study of illness and the human body "with the purity of an unprejudiced gaze" (Foucault 1973, 195). Guided by **positivist** ways of knowing (the dominant epistemological orientation described and critiqued by Zoe Todd in chapter one), illness came to be seen as a visible, locatable pathology within the confines of the human body as well as an objectively knowable entity disconnected from **culture**. Foucault's (1973) work remains foundational for critically examining how illness comes to be defined and diagnosed in contemporary culture and for showing that seemingly objective or scientific accounts illness are also shaped by historical and culturally relative ways of knowing. By over- or hyper-focusing on the biology of illness, we have tended to negate and overlook the social and cultural causes and effects of disease, and this is where the value of health sociology remains important. For health sociologists working with poststructural accounts of illness, what defines an illness and what does not is as much a social designation as it is a medical one. In applying these theoretical orientations to the case of SAD, I question the medicalization and thus pathologization of winter sadness. Due to Canada's winter climate, the pathologization of winter sadness is an issue in which Canadians have much at stake.

As a health sociologist who has taught extensively in the areas of medicalization, I gathered data for this chapter using **secondary data analysis**. I first conducted a literature review, collecting and summarizing available and relevant literature on SAD and seasonal sadness. The vast majority of this literature has been published post-2000; it overwhelmingly invokes biomedical and psychological perspectives, and it is based in industrialized, high-income, and northern climates such as Canada, Denmark, the northern United States, and Sweden. I then organized and amalgamated resources that outline the definition, diagnosis, prevalence, causes, and treatments of SAD as well as resources that offer critiques of SAD as a medical diagnosis. My next step was to theorize SAD using the concept of medicalization (Conrad 1992, 2007; Zola 1991). To theorize is an analytic and speculative way of thinking that actively rethinks concepts that are usually taken as "common" or "natural" (Sears and Cairns 2015). As Bertold Brecht (1964) famously stated, "before familiarity can turn into awareness the familiar must be stripped of its inconspicuousness; we must give up assuming that the object in question needs no explanation" (quoted in Sears and Cairns 2015, 15). In other words, before we can start to question why the social world is organized as it is (indeed, the very work of sociology and sociologists), we must first unpack what is considered normal and **normalized**. Rather than accepting the diagnostic category of SAD at face value (i.e., as an illness that simply exists), poststructural theorizing using the medicalization framework highlights the cultural ways of seeing, knowing, classifying, labelling, and even experiencing illness.

My argument on the medicalization of winter sadness sits within and contributes to an extensive literature on the broader medicalization of sadness. As Horwitz and Wakefield (2007) have effectively argued, the expansion of pathological (i.e., abnormal) sadness in the Diagnostic and Statistical Manual of Mental Disorders (DSM) – the standard manual used by a range of medical and paramedical practitioners to identify and diagnose mental illness – has grown since the first iteration of the manual in 1952. As the definitions and diagnoses of pathological sadness continue to widen, not only do more people come under a medical and medicalized gaze, but in doing so, the discipline of psychiatry also effectively transforms and normalizes multiple variations of human sadness into individualized depressive disorders. Sociologically, this raises concerns for me and I use the medicalization of winter sadness – thus far overlooked in the wider medicalization literature – to question the effects of the loss of normal sadness.

In what follows, I first outline the medical case of SAD – its definitions, diagnosis, and prevalence; its causes and treatments; and its controversy and critiques. Next, I detail the emergence, definition, and application of the concept of medicalization. Third, I make the case that winter sadness (as an example of seasonal sadness) is a part of a normal range of human emotions and argue for the **demedicalization** of some forms of SAD. And finally, I situate these arguments in broader discussions of the loss of sadness, where I explore whether, as a culture, we are losing our ability to be sad outside of medical definitions and understandings.

Seasonal Affective Disorder (SAD)

Definition, Diagnosis, and Prevalence

SAD was first classified as a medical condition in 1984 as a form of recurrent depressive or bipolar disorder that manifests in late autumn and winter[1] (Rosenthal 2009). The Canadian Mental Health Association (2013) estimates that 2 to 3 per cent of the general **population** suffers SAD, while another 15 per cent may experience low-lying but sub-threshold symptoms. SAD is common among Canadians and among other northern populations. It seems that with increased distance from the equator, there is greater prevalence of SAD in the population (Partonen and Magnusson 2009; Rosenthal 2009). Reports indicate that the condition is more common in women, which holds true for broader cases of depression as well. However, given the gendered expectations of masculinity and femininity, where men are encouraged to bottle up emotion and women are taught to speak more freely about it, we can understand why women would report seasonal and non-seasonal depressions more often than men. Reports further indicate that SAD is more common in shift workers and people living in urban areas who experience reduced levels of daylight due to their working and living environments (Partonen and Lönnqvist 1998). Common symptoms of SAD include changes in appetite, cravings for sweet or starchy foods, weight gain, decreased energy, fatigue, tendency to oversleep, difficulty concentrating, irritability, avoidance of social situations, and feelings of anxiety and despair (Canadian Mental Health Association, 2013). SAD is difficult to diagnose partly because of the commonness of the symptoms in the winter months and the similarity of these symptoms to other mental disorders. Typically, for a diagnosis of SAD to be given, these symptoms need to recur for at least two consecutive

1 Some people suffer summer SAD, usually beginning in late spring or early summer, but it is much less common (Canadian Mental Health Association 2013).

winters, without any other explanation for the changes in mood and behaviour, and go into remission when spring arrives (Hansen, Skre, and Lund 2008; Jacobsen et al. 1987; Meisler 2001).

Presumed Biological Causes

While the exact causes of SAD are not yet known, the timing of symptoms seems to point strongly to seasonal variations in light. One biological explanation posits that the occurrence of SAD has to do with our internal circadian clocks that evolved over many thousands of years according to seasonal cycles of light and dark (Hannibal 2009). From this perspective, circadian clocks are important systems that enable organisms to detect relevant environmental changes (Sahar and Sassone-Corsi 2009); to help regulate temperature, hormone secretion, and sleep-wake cycles (Hannibal 2009); and to aid cognition, attention, and mood (Mukherjee and McClung 2009). Since it takes organisms a long time to adapt to changes in environmental conditions, this explanation proposes that our circadian clocks are now out of sync with our modern environments, which typically include the ubiquitous use of electricity. As such, our slow-to-adapt circadian clocks are making us tired and lethargic in the winter months. They may also be responsible for the weight changes and carbohydrate cravings common in SAD, where historically people in northern, cold climates relied on winter weight to survive long winters (Wirz-Justice 2009, v). The circadian clock theory may account for why those living in northern climates (as well as those working night shifts) are more commonly affected by SAD, but it doesn't explain why only a fraction of the population is affected.

Another biological theory proposes that SAD manifests in those who experience a dysfunctional production of serotonin and melatonin. Serotonin is one of the neurotransmitters – sometimes referred to as the "happy messengers" of the brain – that help to regulate sleep, mood, and appetite, notably the areas of functioning affected in SAD (Canadian Mental Health Association 2013). A recent study showed that people with SAD produce significantly less serotonin during the winter months than do their healthy peers (Brauser 2014). Melatonin, which is produced by the body to help us sleep, is also affected in SAD. It is thought that the change in seasons, jet lag, and shift work can disrupt the balance of the body's melatonin levels, which in turn affect a person's pattern of sleep and mood (Brown et al. 2009).

While the circadian clock and dysfunctional production of hormones are two of the going biological accounts for the cause of SAD, more research is needed to understand the exact mechanisms by which hormones are switched on and off by circadian rhythms and clocks (Mukherjee and McClung 2009). More importantly, these theories fail to account for the sociological factors that influence the hypothesized causes of SAD and for the very classification of SAD as a disease in the first place, since it is not found in all northern cultural contexts.

Diagnostic Controversy

Within the existing literature on SAD, there is general consensus that many people are a little more lethargic and/or sad in the winter months. Controversy arises, however, around the degree to which the clinical version of SAD really exists. The main line of controversy in this debate is that there isn't reliable empirical evidence that shows SAD always correlates with shortened daylight hours and distance from the equator, demonstrated by the evidence that SAD is not consistently diagnosed across all northern populations. A large American study, for instance, could not confirm incidences of depression that correlated with variations in season, latitude, and/or sunlight exposure (Middleton 2016). A recent Norwegian study was also unable to confirm the presence of SAD in a population of residents who live with as little as four hours of sunlight for two months of the year (Hansen, Skre, and Lund 2008). Further confusing the SAD hypothesis is that Norway, Denmark, Iceland, Switzerland, and Finland – all cold, northern climates – routinely fill out the top five in the World Happiness Report (Sustainable Development Solutions Network 2017). Examples such as these raise important critical questions about the cultural relativity of SAD. Differing diagnostic rates point to important cultural distinctions in definitions and classification systems. A poststructural theoretical approach highlights the ways that definitions, diagnoses, and rates of illness are also contingent on the social environments in which they come to be known. In focusing on a cultural perspective of illness, we can critically question why winter sadness may be a norm in one social context and medicalized in another. To understand the contingent and culturally contextual status of SAD, we have to critically examine the broader cultural factors that come to shape how we think (or have been taught to think) about seasonal sadness, which, historically (prior to Western medicalization), used to be referred to colloquially as the winter blues.

Medicalization

The aim in adopting a medicalization lens is not to refute illnesses as real. Some people do suffer serious and sometimes debilitating mental health disorders that require medical attention. The aim in adopting a medicalization lens is to critically question what constitutes "normal" and "pathological" human behaviour, where we draw the line between "wellness" and "illness," and in whose interest. In doing so, we can understand the ways in which medicalized conditions such as SAD come to be treated as medical phenomena, how their interpretation has become detached from the social and political factors of illness, and how they have come to be treated as individualized problems removed from their external environments.

Emerging as a concept in the sociology of health and illness in the 1970s, medicalization, as medical sociologist Peter Conrad (1992) explains, "consists of defining a problem in medical terms, using medical language to describe a problem, adopting a medical framework to understand a problem, or using a medical intervention to 'treat' it" (211).

Table 6.1 Increasing number of disorders documented in the DSM

Version	Year	Number of disorders
DSM-I	1952	106
DSM-II	1968	182
DSM-III	1980	265
DSM-IV	1994	297
DSM-5[a]	2013	313

[a] The DSM-5 changed to the Arabic numerical system because the former Roman numerical system was, according to the American Psychological Association, more difficult to code online and caused more confusion among readers (Rosenteel 2012).

Medical sociologist Irving Zola (1991) similarly defines medicalization as "a process whereby ... everyday life has come under medical dominion, influence, and supervision" (295). Since the 1970s, the concept has been applied to a growing range of physical and mental health conditions, including but not limited to personality, conduct, sleep, sexual, attachment, eating, mood, and behavioural disorders (Conrad 2007; Horwitz 2002). Instead of retaining a wide breadth of human behaviour, the process of medicalization tends to squeeze people into narrower, individualized definitions of "normality," which, in Christopher Lane's (2010, 105) words, is "already a vague, tendentious category." As sociologists have long argued, **norms** – standards or patterns of social behaviour – are culturally relative (Symbaluk and Bereska 2015). What is considered appropriate in one cultural context may be forbidden or taboo in another. Thus, to understand human behaviour, we must first understand its social context. Likewise, to understand winter sadness, we must question how the line between normal and pathological sadness is drawn and who makes this distinction.

Established in 1952 and updated roughly every decade since, the Diagnostic and Statistical Manual of Mental Disorders (DSM) is the American authoritative guide to diagnosing mental health disorders. Known to many as psychiatry's bible (Horwitz 2002), it is used by a wide range of mental health and health care professionals worldwide. In the first iteration of the manual, there were 106 disorders described in 103 pages. By 2013, when the guide was last updated, there were 313 disorders described across 947 pages. (See table 6.1.)

In the 61 years since the first iteration of the manual, the total number of diagnosable mental disorders has more than tripled, illustrating the expansion of diagnostic psychiatry. The increase in the number of disorders leads many to wonder some or more of the following questions: Are we more mentally ill than previous generations? Are we getting better at diagnosing new disorders? Or are we diagnosing illness too liberally? Remember that the concept of medicalization urges us to consider how ways of seeing and defining illness have changed, thus leading to changed (and expanding) definitions of mental illness and, specific to our discussion here, of sadness. Definitions of mental illness and sadness have grown more encompassing with each new version of the DSM.

Not only do we see greater numbers of people being diagnosed, but we also see what health sociologist Robert Crawford (1980) calls the medicalization of everyday life: the growing reach of the medical profession (including psychiatry) to define and ultimately regulate a range of normal human functioning, which includes sadness but also sleeping, eating, conduct, and sexual disorders (to name just a few).

We can further track the increasing medicalization of culture through the commonplace use of clinical and psychiatry terms such as *syndrome* and *disorder* in everyday language. In his study on the medicalization of passive-aggressive disorder (PAD), Christopher Lane (2010, 106) remarks that "sixty years ago, the phrase 'passive-aggressive' didn't exist; now, like 'bipolar' and 'obsessive compulsive' it is almost ubiquitous." Similarly, a study conducting **content analysis** of British newspapers found that in 1993, there were 278 references to the word *syndrome*, compared to the year 2000, where that number had jumped to 6,670 (Füredi 2004). This jump is indicative of the degree to which psychiatry's language of mental illness has permeated day-to-day discourse. Consider for a moment how often we use or hear medicalized language to describe relatively mundane forms of disappointment, frustration, or behaviour: "I'm *depressed* that my soccer team didn't win city finals," "I'm *addicted* to the television show *Game of Thrones*," "that test gave me serious *anxiety*." In not-that-distant historical models of mental illness, terms like *depression*, *addiction*, and *anxiety* were used only in extreme cases of psychiatric illness (Shorter 2008). Today, terms such as these (and many more) have become so commonplace that many of us may not even realize the degree to which we've adopted, accepted, and circulate medicalized understandings of illness.

In tracing the medicalization of everyday life, health sociologists also consistently point to the powerful, often-invisible role of pharmaceutical companies in the purposeful expansion of pathologized understandings of human behaviour. If increasing numbers of people come under the expanding net of mental illness and pathological sadness, then increasing numbers of people can also be prescribed expensive psychoactive medications to treat what many now consider an internal and individualized illness. As Lane (2010, 105) describes, medicalization is "borne out of the pharmaceutical industry's vested interest in turning ordinary behaviours into treatable conditions." In looking at the trends in major classes of psychiatric drugs, between the years 1998 and 2010, antidepressant prescriptions increased by 10 per cent per year on average and remain the most commonly prescribed psychiatric medications (Ilyas and Moncrieff 2012). While there is heightened awareness of depression and mental health issues in contemporary culture, expanding definitions of sadness also undoubtedly contribute to this increase in antidepressant prescriptions and to the broader medicalization of culture common to Western societies.

Demedicalization

As a response to the growing medicalization of society, individuals, advocacy groups, and academics have advanced the idea of demedicalization – the removal of and resistance to medical authority in everyday life. In Lin's (2016, 304) words, "demedicalization ... denotes the opposite process [of medicalization] where a condition escapes the shackles of medical labeling and control." Unlike trends toward medicalization, which typically stem from socially powerful groups like psychiatry, medicine, and pharmaceutical companies, demedicalization trends tend to emerge from grassroots, social, and academic advocacy. Since the 1970s, feminist groups and scholars have sought to demedicalize childbirth, abortion, and premenstrual syndrome (Conrad 1992; Lee 2003); LGBTQ scholars and activists have sought to demedicalize homosexuality and **gender** dysphoria/gender identity disorder (Narrain and Chadran 2016); and sexuality scholars have fought to demedicalize masturbation, erectile dysfunction, and paraphylia[2] (Lin 2017). Mainstream psychology and the DSM have a long history of medicalizing women's bodies as well as a range of non-**normative** social behaviours. Diagnostic categories such as the ones outlined function to suppress a range of relatively common human behaviours and to deviantize social variance. Rather than seeing these behaviours as part of a spectrum of normal human functioning, or even as purposeful, fulfilling ways of being human, the labelling of these behaviours as mental illness renders them individual pathologies that need to be fixed or cured.

In other recent attempts to demedicalize difference, disability scholars and activists have advocated for the concept of **neurodiversity**. Neurodiversity refers to the range of cognitive and behavioural functioning within human populations. Embracing neurodiversity is the idea that differences in behavioural and cognitive functioning are not something to be cured or fixed, but rather natural, normal, and common variations among humans (Jaarsma and Welin 2011). Neurodiversity is likened to biodiversity as well as social diversity movements, where plurality and difference actually contribute to the strength of an ecosystem and community. The concept was first coined in the late 1990s among high-functioning autists, who pointed out that while many high-functioning autists may have deficiencies in some areas of functioning, such as social skills or maintaining eye contact, they can also possess huge strengths in other areas of functioning, such as mathematical and musical intelligence (Jaarsma and Welin 2011). Neurodiversity has also recently been adopted by those with ADHD, anxiety, and depression as a way to **de-stigmatize** and normalize behavioural difference in humans (Armstrong 2010). As part of the broader push toward demedicalization, neurodiversity reframes pathological differences as individual strengths and enables a questioning of what constitutes illness. In this configuration, sadness (including SAD) need not be seen as that which needs to be removed or remedied, but rather as part of the diverse range of human behaviour understood in relation to external environments.

---

2 Broadly classified as a wide range of sexual deviation including BDSM and other "kink" practices (Lin 2017).

Demedicalizing Winter Sadness

Using the lenses of demedicalization and neurodiversity, another way to look at winter sadness is to see it is as an expected response to an external situation (in this case, climatic). Winter marks a seasonal shift that encourages us to slow down, to reflect, to turn inward, to release or let go, to sleep, and ultimately to embrace the darkness that's part of natural (and personal) cycles. Human cultures have long observed the changing seasons, and many cultures and **religions** ritualize and celebrate the seasonal turn to darkness.

North American **Indigenous** groups, for example, have long integrated winter solstice in spiritual and community **rituals**, marking an important time of cosmic change and renewal. As Indigenous writer Derek Nepinak (2012, n.p.) explains,

> [t]o acknowledge the vast complexity of the earth's cycles, our people celebrate through ceremony what is considered the longest night – the Winter Solstice. It has always been a time when we have given of ourselves spiritually and prepared ourselves to greet the New Sun, with intentions of living a vision that is anchored to spirit and a new light.

Similarly, in the next chapter, Tara Milbrandt describes in detail how new and traditional Indigenous, French-Canadian, and European winter festivals are being embraced as a part of the "WinterCity" branding initiatives of Edmonton.

Anthropologist Simon Harrison (2004, 594) documents that in many Euro-American historical contexts, peoples' changing moods in the winter were a mundane aspect of their relationship to nature. As he explains, "to many ... the 'dark time' had always been a season for reflection, for a certain pensiveness tinged with sadness, and in this respect, they deemed it a part of their way of life, indeed even part of their **national identity**." Likewise, ancient Greek philosopher Hippocrates (ca. 460–377 BCE) articulated the correlation between seasonal changes and mood. He argued that *melancholia* (i.e., sadness) occurred primarily in the fall and winter, whereas *mania* (i.e., agitation or excitation) occurred in the spring and summer and were a result of responses to seasonal climatic change (Magnusson and Partonen 2009).

While the current North American language on seasonal and winter sadness has been medicalized, there exists historical and cross-cultural examples of terms and phrases that uphold winter sadness as colloquial and thus as a non-medical aspect of human experiences of winter. The Icelandic word *skammdegisthunglyndi* means the heavy mood of short days (Magnusson and Partonen 2009, 215). The Finns also have a similar word, *ruskavastavaikutus*, referring to the sadness experienced in autumn (Magnusson and Partonen 2009, 217). In a North American context, prior to the medicalization of SAD, winter sadness was referred to casually as "the winter blues." Another North American phrase that refers to the irritability and restlessness resulting from living in isolation or within a confined indoor area for a prolonged period of time is "cabin fever" (Magnusson and Partonen 2009, 217). With average winter temperatures across Canada between -10° and -30° Celsius (Government of Canada 2018), many Canadians are unable to stay outside for prolonged periods, especially given that capitalist economies require many people to work indoors during the lightest and warmest parts of the day. If we combine this with heavy snowfalls and high winds also common to winter, then the heavy mood of short days and cabin fever are reasonable responses to these environmental contexts. In upholding a version of winter sadness that is demedicalized and therefore removed from the assumption of pathological sadness, winter sadness can be reframed as normal, common, and an expected response to a harsh and sometimes unrelenting winter climate.

In arguing for a cultural demedicalization of winter sadness I want to be clear that I am not contending that all winter sadness should be considered a normal and natural reaction to sub-zero temperatures and reduced daylight hours. Sociologist Allan Horwitz and psychiatrist Jerome Wakefield (2007) make an important distinction between normal and pathological sadness – a distinction that is often negated or erased in the context of medicalization. They contend that sadness that is *reactive* (i.e., triggered by some external event) is part of a normal grieving or mourning process. It is expected that we would be sad after the end of a romantic relationship or the loss of a job. Sadness that is *endogenous* (i.e., having no external trigger) is disordered. They make the case that normal sadness is of a proportional intensity and ends when the situation ends. Of course, what counts as proportional is historically and culturally subjective and based on an individual's specific context. In determining normal versus pathological functioning, winter sadness that involves disproportional or extreme changes in sleep, eating, and mood patterns, or that doesn't ameliorate when spring arrives, is disordered. Winter sadness that involves moderate (reasonable or expected) changes of appetite, energy, and sleep is normal, and should thus be removed from the growing grip of medicalization as a problem to be fixed, cured, or treated.

The Loss of Sadness[3]

Diagnostic psychiatry has expanded the definitions of depression partially to ensure that false negatives (i.e., those suffering major depressive episodes who are not currently seeking treatment) are not missed and are thus able to access helpful, sometimes life-saving medical and psychiatric services. However, at least two unintended consequences arise from the medicalization of sadness: First is the creation of many false positives (i.e., people who may be suffering from relatively normal and situational forms of sadness) who think they have a major depressive disorder and may be treating

3 I adopt this subheading from Horwitz and Wakefield's (2007) book *The Loss of Sadness: How Psychiatry Transformed Normal Sadness into Depressive Disorder.*

it with unnecessary psychoactive medications. A second unintended consequence of medicalization is that we have a changed and skewed cultural understanding of normal sadness. In their book *The Loss of Sadness*, Horwitz and Wakefield (2007) detail how diagnostic psychiatry increasingly fails to distinguish between reactive sadness (i.e., with cause) and endogenous sadness (i.e., without cause) by omitting the social, cultural, and environmental contexts in and through which a major depressive episode (MDE) or major depressive disorder (MDD) diagnosis is made. Outlined in the DSM-5, a diagnosis for a MDD or MDE requires five of nine of the following symptoms be present during a two-week period: (1) depressed mood, (2) diminished interest or pleasure in activities, (3) weight gain/loss/change in appetite, (4) insomnia or hypersomnia, (5) psychomotor agitation or retardation, (6) fatigue or loss of energy, (7) feelings of worthlessness or guilt, (8) decreased ability to concentrate or make decisions, and (9) recurrent thoughts of death/suicide attempts. Except for the latter symptom, which is never normal or common, many of these symptoms can be read as reasonable responses to external situations and as normal reactions to stressful circumstances. How many of us have experienced a depressed mood after the end of relationship, a diminished interest in activities after the death of a loved one,[4] or insomnia before a big test or job interview? Many behavioural changes involved with common life stressors endure longer than the prescribed two-week period of the DSM. By omitting the social contexts in which sadness, grief, loss, and anxiety arise, the DSM effectively turns normal (i.e., reactive) sadness into MDD and MDE, thus affecting our ability to be sad outside of a medicalized perspective.

While sadness is not always an enjoyable emotion, it is integral to the experiences of being alive. There is growing awareness that animals grieve and exhibit sadness (Bekoff 2009). Humans of all ages and cultural and ethnic backgrounds experience sadness along with the other core emotions of happiness, disgust, and fear. And while we cannot necessarily know the evolutionary purpose of sadness (that is, how it renders us better adapted to our environments), or if there even is one, there is a case to be made that it is a human emotion worth retaining. Sadness helps us to appreciate joy, provides perspective, enables us to grieve loss, gives us the ability to empathize and connect with others, and, as many writers, painters, and musicians have attested, is often a pathway to creativity (Armstrong 2010; Horwitz and Wakefield 2007). A seasoned person is someone with a range of lived experiences and this is part of what we gain by going through and experiencing life's difficulties. In the 2015 Pixar movie *Inside Out*, it is the character Sadness, not Joy, who is the hero of the movie as she guides Riley, the young protagonist, back to fulfillment after a period of emotional confusion and strife. For those who may remember the movie, Sadness touches one of Riley's long-term memories and, in doing so, reminds Riley of her feelings of loss and pain that are

4 While the DSM-IV included a bereavement exclusion (i.e., a diagnosis of MDE or MDD could not be made if an individual was grieving the loss of a loved one), this exclusion was removed from the DSM-5 (Horwitz and Wakefield 2007).

intricately connected to strong memories of love and family as well as the foundations upon which these memories were made possible. Culminating in this near-final scene, the story goes on to show that while "[s]adness was often 'pushed out' of the circle of emotion-friends inside Riley's mind, Sadness helped Riley develop resilience through the seasons of life, providing plenty of opportunities for relationships to grow strong, the support she needed for times of change and tumult, disappointments and defeat" (Harkness 2015). Sadness, in short, is part of who we are and an emotion that reminds us of our attachments to joy, love, and connection.

If we lose our ability to be sad due to an increased medicalization of sadness, including seasonal sadness, we risk losing an important and necessary aspect of being human – one in which a range of human emotions and neurodiversities are acknowledged, accepted, *and* deemed worthwhile. What do we lose if increasingly sadness is considered an illness to be cured or treated? I think we lose a great deal, including the opportunity to grow, to reflect, and to change. Thus, to retain a definition of normal, reactive sadness is to fiercely defend it from increasingly invasive biomedical and medicalized terms that disconnect humans from our social, cultural, and contextual environments. As sociologists have long maintained, we are deeply shaped by our external worlds and, as I have argued in this chapter, winter sadness is no exception. How we come to name, classify, know, and experience winter sadness is foundationally shaped by our cultural – and increasingly medicalized – contexts.

Conclusion

While the concept of medicalization is not new, it has yet to be applied to the case of winter sadness. As the biomedical gaze moves to adopt ever-broadening illness criteria in an increasing age of medicalization, I urge us to consider what we risk losing in the process and what we're willing to fight to hold onto. What do we gain by holding onto a non-medicalization version of seasonal sadness? Following the work of Horwtiz and Wakefield (2007), who argue more broadly for retaining sadness in the face of medicalization, I contend that a moderate – that is, *reactive and proportional* – degree of winter sadness is part of the common cycle of seasons in northern climates like Canada. In individualistic, medicalized cultures like Canada, it becomes too easy to pathologize a wide range of human behaviours and to treat these behaviours as something to be changed, rather than accepted or appreciated, and to be avoided rather than endured or valued. In doing so, we risk altering an integral part of what it means to be human. By minimizing the range of human sadness we are capable of experiencing, we risk negating the depth of human emotion required for personal, community, and cultural well-being, as well as for continued connection to others. Perhaps, like Riley, we can learn to see sadness as an opportunity for growth, not merely an unpleasant emotion to be eschewed.

In outlining a poststructural critique of the medicalization of SAD, this chapter has shifted dominant conceptualizations of "normal" and "disordered" winter sadness.

In addition to rethinking dominant and widespread biomedical accounts of illness, a demedicalized understanding of SAD can improve diagnosis and treatment, avoid unnecessary medication, provide more accurate epidemiological estimates, and reclaim sadness as a common and necessary human emotion in an age of often-unquestioned medicalization. Given that human societies have long been influenced by seasons of life and death, our social and physical environments remain anchors both to ourselves and to something greater than ourselves. Just as the Grammy Hall of Fame band The Byrds once famously sang, "to everything there is a season."[5] The same, I contend, holds true for sadness.

Questions for Critical Thought

1. Have you ever noticed your mood drop or change in the often cold and dark months of winter, and/or after all the excitement of the holiday season? What do you find difficult about winter? Do you consider these symptoms a disorder or not? At what point would you seek treatment for SAD?
2. Aside from the medicalization of sadness and winter outlined in the chapter, what other examples of medicalization do you notice in contemporary culture?
3. How can we understand illness as a social construct? How does the concept of medicalization encourage us to move beyond strictly biological and biomedical accounts of disease?
4. What life events might invoke a sadness response? How might sadness be useful in these situations? What is the push for the demedicalization of sadness and what do we gain by retaining sadness as a normal and common human emotion?
5. What do poststructuralists mean by the concept of the medical gaze? Can you think of examples in contemporary culture where the focus on the biology of illness overshadows its social, environmental, and contextual factors?

References

Armstrong, Thomas. 2010. *Neurodiversity: Discovering the Extraordinary Gifts of Autism, ADHD, Dyslexia, and Other Brain Differences.* Cambridge: Da Capo Press.

Bekoff, Marc. 2009. "Grief in Animals: It's Arrogant to Think We're the Only Animals Who Mourn." *Psychology Today,* October 29. https://www.psychologytoday.com/blog/animal-emotions/200910/grief-in-animals-its-arrogant-think-were-the-only-animals-who-mourn.

5 The song was written by Pete Seeger, a folk singer and social activist of the 1950s, popularized by The Byrds in 1965. With the exception of the song's title and its final two lines, the lyrics are adapted from the Ecclesiastes section of the Hebrew Bible (what Christians refer to as the Old Testament), originally written between 450–150 BCE (Keller 2012). The spiritual inflections of the song are apparent, as are the age-old cultural beliefs of cyclical change.

Brauser, Deborah. 2014. "Seasonal Fluctuations in Serotonin Responsible for SAD?" *Medscape*, October 29. http://www.medscape.com/viewarticle/834066.

Brown, Gregory M., Seithikurippu R. Pandi-Perumal, Ilya Trakht, and Daniel P. Cardinali. 2009. "The Role of Melatonin in Seasonal Affective Disorder." In *Seasonal Affective Disorder: Practice and Research*, edited by Timo Partonen and Seithikurippu R. Pandi-Perumal, 149–62. New York: Oxford University Press.

Canadian Mental Health Association. 2013. *Seasonal Affective Disorder*. http://www.heretohelp.bc.ca/sites/default/files/seasonal-affective-disorder_0.pdf.

Clarke, Juanne N. 2016. *Health, Illness, and Medicine in Canada*. 7th ed. Toronto: Oxford University Press.

Conrad, Peter. 1992. "Medicalization and Social Control." *Annual Review of Sociology* 18 (1): 209–32. https://doi.org/10.1146/annurev.so.18.080192.001233.

———. 2007. *The Medicalization of Society: On the Transformation of Human Conditions into Treatable Disorders*. Baltimore: John Hopkins University Press.

Crawford, Robert. 1980. "Healthism and the Medicalization of Everyday Life." *International Journal of Health Services* 10 (3): 365–88. https://doi.org/10.2190/3H2H-3XJN-3KAY-G9NY.

Foucault, Michel. 1973. *The Birth of the Clinic: An Archaeology of Medical Perception*. New York: Random House.

Füredi, Frank. 2004. *Therapy Culture: Cultivating Vulnerability in an Uncertain Age*. New York: Routledge.

Government of Canada. 2018. "Temperature Climatology – Map – Average – Dec-Jan-Feb (Winter)." https://weather.gc.ca/saisons/image_e.html?format=clim_stn&season=djf&type=temp.

Hannibal, Jens. 2009. "Input Pathways to the Biological Clock." In *Seasonal Affective Disorder: Practice and Research*, edited by Timo Partonen and Seithikurippu R. Pandi-Perumal, 13–28. New York: Oxford University Press.

Hansen, Vidje, Ingunn Skre, and Eiliv Lund. 2008. "What Is This Thing Called 'SAD'? A Critique of the Concept of Seasonal Affective Disorder." *Epidemiologia e Psichiatria Sociale* 17 (2): 120–27. https://doi.org/10.1017/S1121189X00002815.

Harkness, Joyce. 2015. "When Sadness Saves the Day (Reflections on Life and the Movie "Inside Out")." https://joyceharkness.com/2015/08/26/when-sadness-saves-the-day-reflections-on-life-and-the-movie-inside-out/.

Harrison, Simon. 2004. "Emotional Climates: Ritual, Seasonality, and Affective Disorders." *Royal Anthropology Institute* 10 (3): 583–602. https://doi.org/10.1111/j.1467-9655.2004.00203.x.

Horwitz, Allan V. 2002. *Creating Mental Illness*. Chicago.: University of Chicago Press.

Horwitz, Allan V., and Jerome C. Wakefield. 2007. *The Loss of Sadness: How Psychiatry Transformed Normal Sorry into Depressive Disorder*. New York: Oxford University Press.

Ilyas, Stephen, and Joanna Moncrieff. 2012. "Trends in Prescriptions and Costs of Drugs for Mental Disorders in England, 1998–2010." *British Journal of Psychiatry* 200 (5): 393–98. https://doi.org/10.1192/bjp.bp.111.104257.

Jaarsma, Pier, and Stellan Welin. 2011. "Autism as a Natural Human Variation: Reflections on the Claims of the Neurodiversity Movement." *Health Care Analysis* 20 (1): 20–30. https://doi.org/10.1007/s10728-011-0169-9.

Jacobsen, Frederick M., Thomas A. Wehr, David A. Sack, Steven P. James, and Norman E. Rosenthal. 1987. "Seasonal Affective Disorder: A Review of the Syndrome and Its Public Health Implications." *American Journal of Public Health* 77 (1): 57–60. https://doi.org/10.2105/AJPH.77.1.57.

Keller, Marti. 2012. "Turn, Turn, Turn." https://www.questformeaning.org/spiritual-themes/healing-forgiveness-spiritual-topic/turn-turn-turn/.

Lane, Christopher. 2010. "The Strangely Passive-Aggressive History of Passive-Aggressive Personality Disorder." In *Against Health: How Health Became the New Morality*, edited by Anna R. Kirkland and Jonathan Metzl, 105–20. New York: New York University Press.

Lee, Ellie. 2003. *Abortion, Motherhood, and Mental Health: Medicalizing Reproduction in the United States and Great Britain.* Hawthorne: Aldine de Gruyter.

Lin, Kai. 2017. "The Medicalization and Demedicalization Of Kink: Shifting Contexts of Sexual Politics." *Sexualities* 20 (3): 302–23. https://doi.org/10.1177/1363460716651420.

Magnusson, Andres, and Timo Partonen. 2009. "History." In *Seasonal Affective Disorder: Practice and Research*, edited by Timo Partonen and Seithikurippu R. Pandi-Perumal, 213–19. New York: Oxford University Press.

Meisler, Jodi. G. 2001. "Toward Optimal Health: The Experts Discuss Seasonal Affective Disorder." *Journal of Women's Health and Gender-Based Medicine* 10 (9): 831–37. https://doi.org/10.1089/152460901753285714.

Middleton, Hugh. 2016. "Is Seasonal Affective Disorder a Myth?" *The Crux*. http://blogs.discovermagazine.com/crux/2016/02/09/seasonal-affective-disorder-sad/#.WeQnIq3Myb8.

Mukherjee, Shibani, and Colleen A. McClung. 2009. "Circadian Rhythms and Mood Regulations." In *Seasonal Affective Disorder: Practice and Research*, edited by Timo Partonen and Seithikurippu R. Pandi-Perumal, 73–91. New York: Oxford University Press.

Narrain, Arvind, and Vinay Chadran. 2016. *Nothing to Fix: Medicalisation of Sexual Orientation and Gender Identity.* Thousand Oaks: Sage.

National Research Council of Canada. 2017. "Sunrise/Sunset Calculator." http://www.nrc-cnrc.gc.ca/eng/services/sunrise/.

Nepinak, Derek J. 2012. "A Time for Positive Renewal." *First Nations Voice*, December 2.

Partonen, Timo, and Jouko Lönnqvist. 1998. "Season Affective Disorder." *Lancet* 352 (9137): 1369–74. https://doi.org/10.1016/S0140-6736(98)01015-0.

Partonen, Timo, and Andres Magnusson. 2009. "Northern Exposure." In *Seasonal Affective Disorder: Practice and Research*, edited by Timo Partonen and Seithikurippu R. Pandi-Perumal, 235–54. New York: Oxford University Press.

Rosenteel, Susanna. 2012. "DSM-5: Why '5' and not 'V'?" *Medscape*. June 1. https://www.medscape.com/viewarticle/764833.

Rosenthal, Norman E. 2009. "Issues for DSM-V: Seasonal Affective Disorder and Seasonality." *American Journal of Psychiatry* 166 (8): 852. https://doi.org/10.1176/appi.ajp.2009.09020188.

Sahar, Sarabh, and Paolo Sassone-Corsi. 2009. "Circadian Clocks and Their Molecular Organization." In *Seasonal Affective Disorder: Practice and Research*, edited by Timo Partonen and Seithikurippu R. Pandi-Perumal, 5–12. New York: Oxford University Press.

Sears, Alan, and James Irvine Cairns. 2015. *A Good Book, in Theory: Making Sense through Inquiry*. Toronto: University of Toronto Press.

Shorter, Edward. 2008. *Before Prozac: The Troubled History of Mood Disorders in Psychiatry*. New York: Oxford University Press.

Symbaluk, Diane, and Bereska, Tami (2015). *Sociology in Action: A Canadian Perspective*. 2nd ed. Toronto: Nelson Publishing.

Wirz-Justice, Anna. 2009. "Foreword." In *Seasonal Affective Disorder: Practice and Research*, edited by Timo Partonen and Seithikurippu R. Pandi-Perumal, v–vi. New York: Oxford University Press.

Sustainable Development Solutions Network. 2017. *World Happiness Report*. http://worldhappiness.report/ed/2017/.

Zola, Irving Kenneth. 1991. "The Medicalization of Age and Disability." *Advances in Medical Sociology* 2, 299–315.

7 Season of Dreaded Joys: Adaptation, Enchantment, and Solidarity in a "Winter" City

TARA MILBRANDT

LEARNING OUTCOMES

After reading this chapter, you should be able to:

- explain Durkheim's understanding of social solidarity and Weber's understanding of disenchantment
- reflect upon how the human encounter in the winter season is a complex socio-cultural phenomenon, which includes material and non-material (symbolic) dimensions
- describe how public spaces, events, and festivals can encourage seasonal identification in a city
- reflect upon how specific municipal policies, such as residential snow clearance, shape how individuals define, experience, and respond to winter conditions.
- analyze how municipal snow clearance policies might contribute to forms of social exclusion, thereby raising critical questions about social justice in a diverse city

Introduction

Canada's Season

> This is Canada, we have winter, life sucks, get a toque, and embrace it.
>
> – Rick Mercer, Canadian Weather Rant (2007)

Love it or dread it, across most of Canada, winter brings prolonged freezing temperatures, frost, snow, and ice, as well as shorter days and longer nights. Throughout the

Canadian prairies, which are the primary reference point for this chapter, winter endures for five to six months every year, bringing a snow-covered landscape, with temperatures well below zero Celsius for most of this time. That its conditions are not permanent, that winter comes and winter goes, is an important – if under-recognized – factor in how we experience the season. Winter's arrival and departure compel significant changes in daily life, foregrounding its socially meaningful and not merely climatically distinctive nature.

This chapter is a sociological exploration of the social landscape of winter in urban Canada, focusing on the prairie **city** of Edmonton, Alberta. I examine local municipal efforts underway to transform Edmonton into what it calls a "great winter city," from a place where winter's conditions are typically dreaded or merely endured into a place where they are creatively embraced and collectively celebrated. I analyze Edmonton's current residential snow clearing policy within this context and argue for a more radically inclusive and collectivist vision. Thinking sociologically generates questions about what is and what might be, opening up a critically reflective approach to taken-for-granted understandings and social arrangements (Berger 1963). Highlighting the humanly produced and institutionally reinforced environment through which winter is interpreted and experienced, as well as opening up alternative possibilities, this case offers a point of comparison with other cities as they too grapple with winter's unique challenges and possibilities.

Sociological Approach

I am guided by a sociological approach that explores the social foundations of human existence and shared meanings that shape people's experiences in everyday life. I bring what C. Wright Mills called a **sociological imagination** (1959) to the human encounter with the winter season, emphasizing the dynamic intersections between individual experiences and wider **society**. Theoretically, I develop my ideas within the context of key themes and concepts derived from sociology's classical tradition, especially Émile Durkheim, Karl Marx, and Max Weber. Although much has changed in the world between their time and ours, each of these nineteenth-and early twentieth-century thinkers addressed some of the defining features and challenges of modern **Western** capitalist societies that persist in our time.

While each person experiences the season in their unique way, circumstances are always mediated within a socially ordered and organized world. To bring this into view, I approach the everyday world as a fruitful site for sociological inquiry and critical engagement, combining qualitative methods of **textual analysis** and **participant observation**. In sociological terms, "everyday life" encompasses the shared meanings, patterns, and routines that organize day-to-day living. In this chapter, I collect and analyze publicly circulating stories and images from Canada, and especially Edmonton, that communicate and reinforce different, sometimes conflicting, understandings of winter. I draw from diverse textual sources, including everyday talk, news media representations, weather reports, city websites, festival pamphlets, policy documents, and travel guides.

I also incorporate sociological observations derived from my participant observation during winter festivals in Edmonton (2016–17). In participant observation, a researcher partakes in the activities of the group being studied as both participant and observer, aiming to grasp the shared meanings that are "at work" and being enacted in social settings. Such methods underscore what sociologist Peter Berger calls the "dual citizenship" of the sociologist, who lives as both a member and an analyst of society.

The Sign of Winter

> "Still snowing out there?" "*Yup.*" "The *nerve.*"
>
> – Conversational fragment at Edmonton's Old Strathcona Farmers' Market, October 8, 2016

Winter's official beginning is marked on calendars and ritualized on the solstice, the longest night of the year. In everyday life, winter's unofficial beginning is typically defined in relation to the first snowfall. Snow is generally regarded as winter's most tangible sign; its material reality dramatically changes the world it settles upon. As if mild weather is the norm and cold weather a deviation, snow's sudden presence can look and feel like an unwelcome imposition. While it may not last, its manifestation generates diverse human responses, as people must begin to (re)orient themselves to the impending season.

Often prompted by a snowfall, the period between the end of fall and beginning of winter is a time of practical adaptation as people must begin to prepare for the relatively cold, dark, and frozen season. For bodies and households, this requires significant adjustments for prolonged periods of time. One must retrieve or acquire necessary accoutrements for everyday winter living, including toques, mittens, boots, shovels, and snow tires. These are elements of **material culture**, tangible objects that reflect the ways and means of the group. Summer things are stored away, drafty windows are sealed. Newcomers to Canadian winters must learn how to acclimatize for the season. Knowing what constitutes a sufficiently warm coat, after all, is not as self-evident as seasoned Canadians typically imagine. Even mundane forms of winter play, such as the making of a snowman, have their own cultural conventions, often vigorously reinforced by seasoned children (e.g., snowmen are always three balls of snow, never four, never two!). For everybody, to winterize is a complex, extensive, and costly process. It entails a variety of seasonally specific cultural objects, skills, and practices that come to be integrated into daily life for the relatively cold, dark, and snowy months ahead.

Winter in the City

A snow-covered street is a familiar sight to behold during the winter across much of Canada (figure 7.1). The effects of a major snowfall can be taken up as an occasion to notice some of the typically taken-for-granted features of everyday urban life. Urban sociologist Louis Wirth defined the **city** as "a relatively large, dense, and permanent settlement of socially heterogeneous individuals" (Wirth 1938, 8), most of whom are personally unacquainted. While it can seem as though city dwellers inhabit different worlds, snow's effects in the world often elicit exchanges and expressions of mutual concern between strangers, neighbours, acquaintances, and friends, such as "take care, it's brutal out there." True, discussing the weather is sometimes derided as a banal subject of conversation, and "complaining about the cold" has even been cited as a sign that Canadians have become "a nation of winter wusses" (Hutchins 2016). Considered sociologically, brief weather talk exchanges constitute ceremonial **interaction rituals** (Goffman 1963), mundane but meaningful methods by which people honour and communicate their regard for one another. While they may be performed in perfunctory ways, they can renew a sense of solidarity in relation to conditions and a shared world out there that we must navigate alone and together.

Snowy and icy weather creates hazards for physical movement and coordination, amplifying the interdependencies that we normally take for granted – including the complex communication systems, occupational specializations, and forms of infrastructure that tie us together, upon which we all depend. For instance, roads must be built, maintained, and cleared to enable farmers to get their produce to the city market for the vast majority of urbanites who do not produce their own food. As Durkheim (1984) theorized – and the effects of a snowstorm can magnify – at the same time as we have become more individuated (i.e., distinguished from one another) in modern, urban, industrial societies, so too have we become more interdependent. The type of social integration associated with this is what he called **organic solidarity**, and it is qualitatively different from what Durkheim called **mechanical solidarity**, a type of social integration based on "likeness" and characteristic of more socially homogenous groups, rural life, and traditional societies. Whereas mechanical solidarity is strengthened by a "common faith," Durkheim theorized that the kind of cohesion that is associated with organic solidarity is strengthened by "justice," by the degree to which social members are able to develop and flourish, contribute to, and be enhanced by the larger society of which they are a part (Durkheim 1984 [1933], 322).

By drawing attention to the conditions necessary for people to safely navigate winter conditions, thinking sociologically challenges the ideology of **individualism** that supports a modern capitalist society (Marx and Engels 1978). Rooted in the image of the private-property-accumulating individual, this refers to the mythical idea that we are – or should be – self-sufficient "masters and mistresses of our own destinies." We might consider the enduring **myth** of the "self-determining" individual who "lifts him/herself" up by his/her own bootstraps, or perhaps who "tows his/her way out" of a snowbank. Not one of us would get very far if left entirely to our own devices during a winter blizzard!

Falling snow is also a potent reminder that we are subject to natural forces that lie outside of human control, in spite of our technologically sophisticated societies. Sometimes this is taken up as a joyful event, but often it is tinged with trepidation.

FIGURE 7.1 An Edmonton residential street after a snowfall. Photo credit: Tara Milbrandt

While winter weather reports often highlight precarious traffic conditions and vehicle collisions in ways that reinforce particular subjective experiences of the season, such as the feeling of winter dread, it is sociologically interesting to consider how existing organizational expectations, such as compelling people to get to work and treating "time as money" (Weber 1958), may be the more significant – if invisible – factor. Icy roads, on their own, don't cause accidents.

Winter (Dis)enchantment

Our late, modern lives have become increasingly organized around means-end calculation and technical procedures aimed at maximizing efficiency. This is associated with the rise of Western science and **capitalism**, and by a corresponding decline of a sense of mystery, magic, and meaning in everyday life. According to Weber, a defining feature in modern Western societies is a growing **rationalization** and corresponding **disenchantment** of the world (Weber 1946, 155). For Weber, this means that "principally there are no mysterious incalculable forces that come into play, but rather that one can, in principle, master all things by calculation" (Weber 1946, 139).

Perhaps more than other seasons, our orientations to winter reveal a mixture of rationalization *and* magic in contemporary life. We simultaneously put trust in weather experts and advanced prediction methods – tuning in to reports from Environment Canada or reading the *Farmer's Almanac* – and commonly invest winter's manifestations from the sky with **agency** and even gall ("the *nerve*"), as if they embody trickery, will, and intention. We talk about the "spirit" of the season as though it is a mysterious force from above, and we sometimes playfully shush a person for saying the word *snow* out of season, as if this will jinx the universe and summon up a blizzard. Winter's defining element is also commonly **anthropomorphized** – attributed with human characteristics and spirit – in stories, **ritual**, and play, from the mischief-maker "Jack Frost" and "Old Man Winter" to the formation of figures we call snowmen and snow angels. In scientifically informed weather reporting, even meteorologists commonly attribute human characteristics to extreme weather systems, giving human names to blizzards, hurricanes and tornados. While winter's elements demand our attention, lest we perish from exposure, we also and always make and remake winter in our own image. Sociologically, we can ask: what image (or images) of ourselves can be found reflected back through the diverse and (possibly) contradictory ways that we make winter meaningful and tangible in the city today?

Edmonton's WinterCity Initiative

Changing Perceptions of Winter

> ... Some of us fear its arrival. Others escape it altogether, fleeing to Arizona or Mexico for half the year. A good portion of the population has built a life in opposition to it: house to garage to underground parking lot and back again. Most of us complain about it....Still, even when we pretend we aren't winter people, we are....
>
> – Babiak 2011

A dominant orientation to Canadian winter is characterized by Edmonton writer Todd Babiak in an article published in the *Edmonton Journal* in October 2011: winter as the dreaded season that elicits fear, complaining, avoidance, and escape plans. Such emotions and strategies constitute aspects of (non-material) symbolic culture, intangible aspects of society that reflect shared ideas, values, and beliefs. These are reinforced in different ways through the built environment. Taken together, they express what Weber would call an ethos – a particular and overarching spirit of engagement that expresses a complex configuration of social and historical factors and forces.

Like in other prairie cities, Edmonton's primary seasonal association has been that of a cold, harsh, and challenging place to be, due to foreboding winters; "frigidly cold for much of the year," according to a recent entry in the *Lonely Planet* travel guide. While empirically true, to highlight this *above all else* reinforces winter dread. Recounting her move from Toronto to Edmonton in a *Globe and Mail* article, city planner and winter advocate Susan Holdsworth recalled how "[o]ver and over, I was told how horrible winter [in Edmonton] was" (in Bozokovic 2015, n.p.). In sociological terms, "horrible winter" has operated as a seasonal **master status** for Edmonton's **identity**: the demographic category or label that is typically perceived by observers as "overpower[ing]" any other in significance (Hughes 1945, 357). Like the image of Canada as a perpetually cold and snowy country, there is some truth to this perception but also elements of exaggeration that contribute to a stereotype. While normally sociologists talk about master status in reference to a person or group, the concept can also be applied to a city. Anti-winter **culture** was identified as a national problem of sorts – not unique to Edmonton, for, as Holdsworth put it, "For Canadians, not just Edmontonians, the [dominant] approach [to winter] has been to hide inside and use things like pedways" (Holdsworth, cited in Bozokovic 2015, n.p.).

It was against this dominant anti-winter cultural backdrop that Edmontonians were invited to imagine new possibilities of winter, share stories, and enter discussions concerning what it would take to enjoy, and not merely accommodate or metaphorically hibernate through, the season. In late 2011, Edmonton's municipal government began to contemplate the urban winter experience, and the city's seasonal identity, in a focused way. Inspired by a growing international network of self-identified "winter cities" and encouraged by local city councillor Ben Henderson, earlier that year, a small delegation of Edmonton politicians travelled to different cities in Norway and Finland to study successful models of winter cities. Following a period of public consultation, the city council announced a plan to transform Edmonton into a "great" and even "world-leading" winter city (City of Edmonton 2013). Since this time, Edmontonians have been encouraged to embrace the season and even "fall in love with winter" as part of this ongoing winter city strategy (Soles 2012). In part, this strategy reflects a type of **place branding** and was likely inspired by a mixture of different interests, economic and otherwise. My primary sociological interest here is to consider how this explicitly positive approach to the challenging season could be meaningful and potentially transformative for everyday Edmontonians, not merely those animated by business and/or tourist-promotion interests.

The city council endorsed a document called *For the Love of Winter: Strategy for Transforming Edmonton into a World-Leading Winter City* (City of Edmonton 2012), which outlined different elements of its winter-positive initiative. Sounding at times like a manifesto, it stated that "[w]inter challenges us all to break our summer states of mind.... It is high time that Edmonton took full advantage of its northernness." This was followed by an "implementation" guide (2013) and design plan organized around an explicitly winter "lens" (City of Edmonton 2016). Edmonton's mayor, Don Iveson, summed up its guiding orientation in a public blog post: "While we've spent decades pretending (and planning) like we lived somewhere else, the Winter City Strategy is about celebrating and embracing the very season that defines us" (Iveson 2015, n.p.).

Anchoring Seasonal Engagement

Edmonton's WinterCity implementation guide outlines diverse ways to encourage and support forms of positive winter engagement, especially out-of-doors. Many components of the implementation plan are aimed at simply encouraging more people to get out and have fun with others during a season in which the temptation to remain indoors is strong. Early examples, such as organizing "hot chocolate squads" to deliver free treats to tobogganers at select hills on designated days, or to ice skating during a Valentine's Day "disco skate" at Edmonton's city hall, aim to create simple enticements to get people out. A "reverse striptease" in Edmonton's central public square in December leads newcomers through a process of bundling up in warm seasonal attire. This activity reverses the potentially intimidating component of winterizing one's body into a playfully subversive and socially integrative event. The city also orchestrates an annual "winterscaping" contest, where residents are encouraged to construct winter "gardens" on lawns or balconies through creative arrangements of light, ice, trees, and other materials. Mirroring seasonal lighting that appears throughout the city, illuminating the night sky in cinematic ways on utility poles and civic buildings, such contests encourage people to perceive and engage with winter elements – ice and snow, short days and dark nights – as sources of beauty, wonder, and (re)enchantment. Future-stated plans include installing heated bus stops and expanding cross-country ski paths throughout the city, creating more heated outdoor patios, and changing zoning bylaws to facilitate a more winter-positive and heated outdoor-friendly urban environment throughout the year.

Since the inception of its winter positive initiative, Edmonton has been supporting and promoting local winter stories, special events, and ordinary activities, often using selectively cheerful visuals of people partaking in different offerings of this "winter" city on its website. The cover of Edmonton's Winter Design Guidelines (figure 7.2) offers such an example through a staged picture of quotidian winter city life: on a snowy, sunny day when it is cold enough to wear a parka, diverse people are matter-of-factly meeting, consuming, and socializing at tables on outdoor patios downtown. The implicit hope is that a positive seasonal "buzz" is being generated, tempting more people to get out to recreate the meaning and experience of winter in Edmonton. Over time, it is possible that the idea that winter is a loveable season, and that Edmonton is a great winter city, will crystallize and become **social facts** (Durkheim 1982), and not merely be seen as a singularly municipal initiative or strange proclivity of a small population segment. Sociologically, this would mean that new manners of "acting, thinking, and feeling" about winter have become solidified, with an historical existence that transcends individual manifestations and offers resistance to deviants (e.g., "Stop grumbling about the snow, this is a winter city!"). The possibility of such transformation reveals that seasons are social and not simply the sum total of climatic conditions. The ways we embrace and engage, interpret and inhabit these conditions are components of a forever unfinished, collectively ordered reality (Berger and Luckmann 1966).

FIGURE 7.2 WinterCity Edmonton design plan. With permission from the City of Edmonton.

Winter Festivals: Seasonal Concentration, Cultural Activities, and Collective Effervescence

Like tens of thousands of Edmontonians, I attended several winter-themed festivals and events that were promoted as part of Edmonton's winter city festival calendar in 2016–17. Engaging in participant observation, I took notes before and after, read flyers and websites, made and studied photographs, engaged in activities, observed patterns, and spoke with other participants in casual conversations. I attended the opening of Edmonton's newly defined winter patio season at Café Bicyclette in the city's French-Canadian quarter, spent an afternoon and evening at the Byzantine Deep Freeze festival on 118 Street, went to Ice on Whyte in Old Strathcona, and attended the Flying Canoe Volant Festival in Mill Creek Ravine. I also visited the Ice Castle and spent an afternoon and evening at the Silver City Skate festival in Hawrelak Park. In all these engagements, I kept in mind my primary sociological research questions: What ideas of embracing winter are being enacted and what is being socially produced through these collective occasions?

First, as the bundled-up bodies demonstrated, embracing winter is not just thinking about winter differently, but doing things differently. This is suggested in figure 7.3, which shows friends and strangers milling about while listening to musicians play on a cold winter night in an Edmonton ravine. While one normally dresses for brief encounters with winter, winter festival dressing must take into account prolonged immersion in the cold, an acquired skill that is developed through repeated practice. In casual conversations, savvy festival participants referenced past experiences and lessons learned.

FIGURE 7.3 Milling around, square dancing in the snow (Flying Canoe Volant Winter Festival, February 2017). Photo credit: Tara Milbrandt

Getting creative with winter elements was an organizing theme at all events. Winter's hardest physical manifestation – ice – was often used to elicit different kinds of interaction, bringing together adults and children, sometimes combining risk with play. It was transformed from frozen water into skilfully carved sculptures to admire and touch, an ice castle in which to wander, ice slides equipped with "crazy carpets" to zip down, a frozen lake to skate upon, and a race involving people inside of deep freezers being pushed along a small track of ice on a temporarily pedestrianized city street, while onlookers cheered. Contrasts between dark and light were used to transform cold, snowy spaces where one would ordinarily not venture on a winter night – e.g., a trail in a park or a clearing in a valley – into inviting social places. During the day, ice formations amplified the prairie sunlight. At night, the dark sky became a canvas against which to illuminate otherwise mundane objects, sometimes integrating imaginative elements that defied rational explanation, and opening up spaces for casual conversation between strangers. Strange and seemingly magical things could be seen, such as a visual display of red lights illuminating white snow and floating fish, set against dormant trees (figure 7.4). Suggesting that Edmonton's festivals were a way of re-enchanting the natural world, and infusing it with a sense of childhood wonder, I overheard people commenting on a feeling of magic in the air as they spectated upon these constructed winter sights.

Different kinds of activities – both focused and unstructured – punctuated the festivals and integrated diverse people of varying ages: music and dancing, storytelling and craft

FIGURE 7.4 Winter art installation at Mill Creek Ravine, February 2017. Photo credit: Tara Milbrandt

tables, performances and contests, skating and sleigh rides, hot chocolate sipping and bannock roasting. Such activities created temporary moments of conversation and contact among otherwise dispersed participants, as people drifted in and out of spaces gently filled with the sounds of voices, bells, drums, and fiddles. While the rich details of each particular festival exceed the scope of this chapter, it is important to note that diverse cultural **traditions** associated with communities that have deep historical connections to this land, season, region, and (now) city – both prior to and after European colonization – were an important presence during most of the festivals I attended. This included **Indigenous**, Métis, and French-Canadian cultural traditions and practices, as well as Ukrainian, Dutch, Norwegian, Acadian, and Afro-Albertan cultures, to name but a selection.

Edmonton's winter festivals were not religious in the conventional sense, but from a sociological perspective, especially a Durkheimian perspective, there were observable dimensions of secular religiosity. Notably, these occasions drew otherwise dispersed people together in ways that seemed to generate powerful, if only momentary, experiences of self-awareness in being part of a larger entity – Edmonton, the winter city – that is special and valuable. As Durkheim (1995) stressed in his writing on **religion** (and as is demonstrated in the next chapter by Wrye, Graydon, and Thille, as well as by Buffam in chapter fifteen), collective practices are essential for the generation and renewal of shared identity. When people commune together and celebrate representations of the group, ideas about that group become real and energizing for its members. In what has become a highly anticipated annual event in Edmonton on selected nights during the annual Silverskate Festival, a Dutch-themed ten-day festival that began in 1990, a "fire sculpture" unites participants together in a dramatic ritual display (see Fleischer-Brown 2017). A folkloric tale about wolves and princesses was narrated by a guide during a lantern-filled walk I attended in the wooded area of the park one night in 2017. This culminated in participants – young and old – howling at a full moon, then cheering as a wolf-like structure was burned to the ground, with the assembled crowd encircling the flames.This exemplifies what Durkheim (1995) calls **collective effervescence**, a ritualistic occasion where people congregate together in ways that generate "a sort of electricity ... [that] quickly launches them to an extraordinary height of exaltation" (217). Impossible to produce on one's own, such experiences can be important memory-generating events that strengthen a sense of being part of a collectivity – here, as shared membership in a socially heterogeneous and self-consciously "winter city."

While being cold posed a continuous tension, sources of heat drew strangers together, from temporary structures such as a tent or a teepee to fire pits of varying shapes and sizes interspersed across outdoor areas. People generally accommodated each other in a solidarity of coldness, making space around a fire for shivering newcomers, giving up seats to children, or offering a warm blanket at an outdoor patio. While the bodily experience of *being cold* is physiological, *warming up* with others gives it a communal dimension. Locating people temporarily outside of **privatized spaces** with central heating, these islands of warmth created possibilities for intensified, and even egalitarian, integration among strangers. Social statuses, differences that divide people based on their relative ranking according to economic, cultural, and institutional positions, seemed to have no place at such warming circles.

Troubling Shared Conditions "Out There"

Participation in winter-themed activities and events, especially when this becomes generalized, can gradually contribute to a new seasonal identity for Edmontonians. While all Edmontonians may be implicitly invited, some are unwittingly excluded from accepting the city's invitation to fall in love with winter. The mundane but significant issue of snow clearing on residential sidewalks, and the ability for Edmonton pedestrians – in all of their **embodied** diversity – to get around in the city, whether out to festivals or simply out of their homes – is what we next consider. Highlighting the embodied challenges that snow and ice-covered sidewalks pose for safe mobility throughout the season, I argue for a more inclusive and radically solidaristic vision of the winter city.

Conditions of Existence for Embracing Winter

> If you are in favour of winter, tell us why; if you (are loathe) tell us what you want to do about it.
>
> – CBC Radio One, *Alberta at Noon*, October 11, 2016

Prompted by an early snowfall in October 2016, the popular CBC radio call-in program *Alberta at Noon* set up a debate inviting listeners to make the case for or against winter. The tone was playful, and a question was posed to an Edmonton caller named Phyllis, introduced as being in her eighties: "So does winter get easier, or do you loathe it?" Her response disrupted the jokingly macho tenor of the preceding talk: "I don't like it very much. Most of the time I didn't mind winter at all but now I can't even go out because I can't push my walker on a snowy sidewalk; and I ... I'm afraid of falling on the ice; so, it's a bit of a problem." The host interjected, "You find yourself a bit of a shut-in during the winter...." And Phyllis replied, "Yeah, you feel quite isolated." The exchange ended with the host's closing remark: "Yeah, that can be a bit of a bummer for sure. Thanks for calling. We appreciate you weighing in on this ever-contentious debate."

The caller reminds listeners that shared conditions "out there" are experienced in vastly different ways and that to love or loathe winter goes beyond an individual's attitude and personal preferences. Phyllis feels "quite isolated" because now that she uses a walker, she is excluded from getting out and about during the snowy sidewalk-covered winter season. Isolation is a social experience, meaningful only within a comparative context. Her story is a reminder that there is no universal human body and that winter's climatic conditions are physically encountered in different ways. Her subjective experiences of winter are shaped by forces beyond that lead to her being relatively "shut in" on a snowy day. Phyllis might as well live as the sole inhabitant of a remote snowy island. Exhibiting the pervasive ideology of individualism**,** the host reduces her story of seasonal restriction, fear, and isolation to an unfortunate occurrence. In sociological terms, he reduces her story to what C. Wright Mills would call a personal trouble, essentially a private matter, resolvable at the individual level. The host gives voice to the dominant – and decidedly un-sociological – view of society as the "sum total of individuals," which, as Durkheim would remind us, both contradicts and denies our essential interdependency. While acknowledging that it is a "bummer" to be a bit of a "shut-in" during the winter, his comments imply that it is *her* bummer to bear (i.e., it's too bad for Phyllis) and not, for instance, part of a shared (moral) responsibility and thus also an Edmonton problem. An alternative and sociological approach would be to locate Phyllis's isolation within a socially structured context and identify it as a possible public issue (Mills 1959). This would mean that its meaningful solution is best addressed at a collective and institutional level.

Phyllis's story aligns with recent **survey** research findings, which show that as they become older, Canadian urbanites perceive and experience winter as significantly more challenging than other seasons (Toupin 2014), partly due to the experience of feeling and being trapped inside. Is winter isolation inevitable? While "difficult winter," and being more "shut in" might seem natural and inevitable in light of the aging body, the urban-rural difference found in Toupin's study suggests that the ways aging bodies experience the winter season are influenced by social-infrastructural realities, not simply physiological factors.

Snow clearing on residential sidewalks is an important place where winter danger and isolating restriction could be minimized and where a winter-positive city could be more robustly realized. It is consistently cited as a pressing issue for urban Canadians; Edmonton, in spite of its self-representation as an aspiring "great winter city," is no exception. In early 2017, local news media reported on treacherous sidewalk conditions, decreased tickets for snow clearing violations, and increased incidents of slips and falls in Edmonton's university area of Garneau. A coordinator for Edmonton's community standards bylaw enforcement unit largely attributed the problem of uncleared sidewalks to student tenant turnover, citing their alleged lack of stewardship and community-mindedness (Courtoreille, quoted in Riebe 2017). In addition to **scapegoating** student tenants, problematically singling them out for blame and potentially negative treatment, such a response pre-empts collective analysis of a complex issue.

In my own walks around the city during winter, I encountered significant inconsistency with respect to snow and ice clearing on residential sidewalks. An ordinary example of this can be seen in figure 7.5. While there was evidence of effective snow and ice shovelling along many sidewalks, there were often segments of dangerously slippery snow and ice between cleared parts. Uncleared sidewalks were not merely the occasional aftermath of falling snow or freeze-melt cycles; they often endured over time, even near winter festival sites. Dangerously restrictive snowy sidewalks are more than an occasional problem in Edmonton, neither reducible to nor resolvable at the individual level.

Institutionalized Individualism: Residential Snow Clearing Policy

Like most Canadian cities, it is taken for granted in Edmonton that heavy snow on roads will be cleared by the city. Edmonton's current residential sidewalk snow-clearing policy positions pedestrians as subordinate to automobile drivers, as "second class citizens" (Wellar, cited in Macleans 2011). This has not been meaningfully modified in light of Edmonton's winter city rebranding ambitions, and it is (still) primarily the responsibility of individual property owners and residents. Constituting a form of institutionalized individualism, it is formally structured through private property relations rather than being supported as a vital public service. An alternative would be to treat sidewalk snow clearing as a matter of significant societal responsibility, as a component of what some Marxist urban geographers and sociologists call a "right to the city" (Harvey 2012; Lefebvre 1996; see also Brown and Kristiansen 2009). Such an approach can be found in more collectively oriented Scandinavian counties. Some Swedish cities, for example, have recently implemented a "**gender**-equal" snow-clearing policy, intended to benefit pedestrians and cyclists, who are disproportionately women, by giving snow clearing priority to sidewalks, bike lanes, and bus lanes. In addition to being aligned with social justice principles, such an approach creates the conditions for greater social diversity in the urban public realm.

At present, Edmonton's community standards bylaw prescribes that "residents must shovel adjacent walkways – sidewalks and driveways – within 48 hours of snowfall" (City of Edmonton 2018, under "Sidewalks and Sand"). Violators face a fine of $100 plus removal costs seven days after a first warning. This process is primarily initiated

FIGURE 7.5 Snowy residential sidewalks, Edmonton, February 2017. Photo credit: Tara Milbrandt

on an individual-complaint basis, unlike the regularly monitored and enforced parking violation system operating throughout the city. This bylaw suggests that inaccessible, uncleared residential sidewalks are not a high priority in Edmonton, conflicting with the city's call to embrace the winter season in ways that also reinforce winter dread.

The City of Edmonton promotes a program called Snow Angels, which finds volunteers to assist physically vulnerable persons with winter snow shovelling. This encourages a socially integrative type of civic altruism. However, it also positions sidewalk safety and accessibility as something that depends upon the generosity of individual volunteers. Imagine if adequate road clearance was left to the benevolence of individual volunteers!

Snowy and icy sidewalks pose risks for every *body*, but they magnify different kinds of physical vulnerabilities that exist across the social landscape, especially for those more susceptible to risks of slipping and falling, using mobility devices, or caring for vulnerable persons. This illustrates the ordinary ways that the built environment, and policies that concern its maintenance, can create forms of differential precarity and social exclusion (Butler 2015). Critical disability scholars and activists draw attention to the potentially disabling effects of the social environment through what is called the **social model of disability**. Challenging the dominant medical view, which locates disability within the body of the individual person, this approach draws critical attention to ways in which the built environment creates barriers and exclusions, even if unintentionally. It offers a valuable perspective through which to consider the important issue of residential snow clearing, as well as urban planning more generally (see Freund 2010; Imrie 2012; Prince 2008), challenging politicians, planners, and citizens to create more radically inclusive urban landscapes that recognize and honour human diversity in all of its forms, in line with modern principles of dignity and justice (see Mazumder, cited in Wilkie 2017).

Toward a (More) Sociological Imagination of a Winter City for Every Body

To self-identify as a great and potentially world-leading winter city at the same time that many ordinary people cannot safely navigate sidewalks represents a contradictory state of affairs requiring resolution. An important component of thinking sociologically, argued by classical theorist Harriet Martineau in the mid-nineteenth century, is to identify contradictions between cultural ideals (such as inclusivity) and actual social practices (and policies) (Martineau 1837). Striving to become a leader and exemplar of inclusive winter mobility would arguably be more consistent with Edmonton's stated goals of becoming a "great" and "world-leading" winter city than leaving vulnerable people to their own devices. It would also align with Edmonton's own findings of successful winter-city living from Norway and Finland, which emphasize the need to place greater focus on "clearing bike paths, walking paths, and public transportation routes" and less prioritizing of cars (Fricson and Ranson 2011, 5).

The current state of residential sidewalk snow and ice clearing signals the need for a more self-consciously inclusive and solidaristic vision of winter in the city. By encouraging Edmontonians to creatively embrace and even "fall in love with" winter, the city begins to make itself more accountable to what is dream-able and possible, as it opens itself up to comparison with other "winter cities" around the northern world. There are some grounds for optimism. Although its residential snow and ice clearing policy has not been updated since 2011, in the wake of significant criticism about its current inadequacies from members of the public, Edmonton's city council announced in March 2019 that it will be reviewing this issue and policy in the months ahead. Meaningful change will require considered rethinking of current budget priorities and resource distribution generally. More deeply, it will require a shift away from a privatized vision of accessibility and toward a more collectivist understanding, one better rooted in a vision of everybody's "right" to meaningfully engage in the (winter) city. Going back to Durkheim's theorization of modern society, not only would such a revised policy – and its implementation – bring about greater justice and strengthen solidarity in a diverse city, it would also imply that those who are presently excluded from getting out and about during the winter season have interesting and valuable things to share and contribute – that we are *all* enhanced and made stronger when the city is made to be more inclusive.

Conclusion

Snow drifting down from the sky lands on our bodies, windows, windshields, streets, and sidewalks, pays no heed to borders of municipality or property, human needs or intentions. Its discernible patterns expose traces of the forms of life that inhabit and interact on the ground, implying encounters between them: boot tracks and animal footprints, automobile and bicycle tracks, divided here and criss-crossing there, sometimes precariously so. In the city, snow falls, lands, melts, and freezes again onto a complex built world, having forms that can be modified to absorb these elements in innumerable ways.

Winter's unique challenges intermingle in our collective imaginations, social experiences, and embodied experiences with its possibilities and pleasures. Indeed, what can be joyful about this season, its sublime forms of beauty, and the outdoor activities that a snow-covered landscape makes possible comingle with what is dreaded and dangerous about it. If winter's quiet yet forceful reminder, magnified by a snowfall, is that we share conditions and a world "out there," whether we go outside or stay under cover, sociology's reminder is that the world "out there" is also always the world "in here." Our subjective and embodied experiences in the world, which are influenced by the change of seasons, are shaped in countless ways by the social forms of existence that surround us, from taken-for-granted ideas and images to physical structures, fleeting events, and the implementation of policies. To encourage people to say "yes" to winter and resist the temptation to remain indoors is laudable; while it has to some extent been successful in Edmonton in recent years, such an orientation is not merely attitudinal, as it has material conditions of existence.

Winter in Canada tests us to create social conditions – a world – that support not only what is necessary for survival, comfort, and coordination, but which might also nurture creativity, solidarity, and diversity *throughout the year*. The question of what constitutes a good winter city, I suggest, is inseparable from the question of what constitutes a good city. We can go further to suggest that the question of what constitutes a good city is inseparable from the question of what constitutes a good society and even a good life (Harvey 2012; Park 1952). When we say to a friend, stranger, neighbour, or acquaintance to "take care, it's brutal out there," we want to know that conditions "out there" support what is required for this for every body; that such words and sentiments can be found mirrored back in the built world, in ways that enable us to presume that if we were to switch positions, we would be equally supported. Since human nature is social and interdependent, to engage with this question requires going beyond the picture of society as a collection of essentially separate individuals. It leads us to deep and fundamental human questions, including about the kind of world we seek to create, what kind of people we want to be, and what will enable such people to flourish.

Questions for Critical Thought

1. What are your attitudes and feelings toward winter? Reflect sociologically on where these ideas emerged from and how they are reinforced in the social world around you.
2. What assumptions are being made about the social world in Edmonton's municipal residential snow clearing policy? How does this compare with similar policies in the city or town where you presently live?
3. What are some of the dominant and taken-for-granted understandings of winter in your city, town, or neighbourhood? How are they reinforced, modified, or challenged – for instance, through specific phrases, building forms, tourism ads, public events, or social policies?
4. How do different public events reinforce a winter (or other) seasonal identification in your city, town, or community? How successful do you think they are in meaningfully integrating the diverse inhabitants of your town or city?
5. What research methods would you use to begin to understand how your community makes sense of winter?

References

Babiak, Todd. 2011. "Massey Lecture Series on Winter Blows into Town." *Edmonton Journal*, October 12, A5.

Berger, Peter L. 1963. *Invitation to Sociology*. New York: Doubleday.

Berger, Peter L., and Thomas Luckmann. 1966. *The Social Construction of Reality: A Treatise in the Sociology of Knowledge*. New York: Penguin Books.

Bozokovic, Alex. 2015. "How Urban Designers Are Getting Canadians Outside – Even in the Deepest Freeze." *Globe and Mail*, January 28. http://www.theglobeandmail.com/life/home-and-garden/architecture/how-urban-designers-are-getting-canadians-outside--even-in-the-deepest-freeze/article22676397/.

Brown, Alison, and Annali Kristiansen. 2009. "Urban Policies and the Right to the City." *MOST-2, Management of Social Transformations, Policy papers series: UNESCO Un-habitat*. http://unesdoc.unesco.org/images/0017/001780/178090e.pdf.

Butler, Judith. 2015. *Notes Towards a Performative Theory of Assembly*. Cambridge: Harvard University Press.

City of Edmonton. 2012. "For the Love of Winter: Strategy for Transforming Edmonton into a World Leading Winter City." https://www.edmonton.ca/city_government/documents/PDF/COE-WinterCity-Love-Winter-Summary-Report.pdf.

———. 2013. "For the Love of Winter: WinterCity Strategy Implementation Plan." https://www.edmonton.ca/city_government/documents/PDF/TheLoveofWinter-ImplementationPlan.pdf.

———. 2016. "Winter Design Guidelines: Transforming Edmonton into a Great Winter City." https://www.edmonton.ca/city_government/documents/PDF/WinterCityDesignGuidelines_draft.pdf.

———. 2018. "Sidewalks and Sand." https://www.edmonton.ca/transportation/on_your_streets/sidewalk-snow-removal.aspx.

Durkheim, Émile. 1982. *The Rules of Sociological Method and Selected Texts on Sociology and its Method.* Edited by Steven Lukes. Translated by W.D. Halls. New York: Free Press.

———. 1984. *The Division of Labor in Society*. Translated by W.D. Halls. New York: Free Press.

———. 1995. *The Elementary Forms of Religious Life*. Translated by Karen E. Fields. New York: Free Press.

Fleischer-Brown, Rosalind. 2017. "Silver Skate Festival Celebrates Edmonton's Winter Spirit, as well as Its Cultures and Communities." *The Gateway*, February 14. https://thegatewayonline.ca/2017/02/silver-skate-fest-2017/.

Freund, Peter. 2010. "Bodies, Disability and Spaces: The Social Model and Disabling Spatial Organisations." *Disability & Society* 16 (5): 689–706. https://doi.org/10.1080/09687590120070079.

Fricson, Bea, and Kenna Ranson. 2011 "Winter City Strategy: Executive Research Study Findings: Norway and Finland, February 16 to 24, 2011." https://www.edmonton.ca/city_government/documents/PDF/WinterCity-Executive-Research-Tour.pdf.

Goffman, Erving. 1963. *Behaviour in Public Spaces*. New York: Free Press.

Harvey, David. 2012. *Rebel Cities: From the Right to the City to the Urban Revolution*. London and New York: Verso.

Hughes, Everett. 1945. "Dilemmas and Contradictions of Status." *American Journal of Sociology* 50 (5): 353–59. https://doi.org/10.1086/219652.

Hutchins, Aaron. 2016. "Canada: A Nation of Winter Wusses." *Macleans*, January 1. http://www.macleans.ca/society/life/canada-a-nation-of-winter-wusses/.

Imrie, Rob. 2012. "Auto-disabilities: The Case of Shared Space Environments." *Environment and Planning A* 44 (9): 2260–77. https://doi.org/10.1068/a44595.

Iveson, Don. 2015. "For the Love of Winter (blog)." January 27. http://doniveson.ca/2015/01/27/for-the-love-of-winter/.

Lefebvre, Henri. 1996. *Henri Lefebvre: Writings on Cities*. Translated and edited by Eleonore Kofman and Elizabeth Lebas. Malden: Blackwell Publishers.

Macleans. 2011. "Down Shovels: The City Should Clear the Sidewalks." *Macleans*, March 17. http://www.macleans.ca/news/canada/down-shovels-the-city-should-clear-the-sidewalks/.

Martineau, Harriet. 1837. *Society in America*. New York: Saunders and Otley.

Marx, Karl, and Friedrich Engels. 1978. "The German Ideology, Part I." In *The Marx-Engels Reader*, 2nd ed., edited by Robert C. Tucker, 146–200. New York: W.W. Norton & Company.

Mercer, Rick. 2007. "Canadian Weather Rant." https://www.youtube.com/watch?v=0EQdXyKiFY4.

Mills, C. Wright. 1959. *The Sociological Imagination*. New York: Oxford.

Park, Robert. 1952. *Human Communities: The City and Human Ecology*. Glencoe: Free Press.

Prince, Michael J. 2008. "Inclusive City Life: Persons with Disabilities and the Politics of Difference." *Disability Studies Quarterly* 28 (1). https://doi.org/10.18061/dsq.v28i1.65.

Riebe, Natasha. 2017. "Garneau Gets Most Fines of Any Edmonton Neighbourhood for Snowy Sidewalks." *CBC News Online*, January 16. http://www.cbc.ca/news/canada/edmonton/garneau-gets-most-fines-of-any-edmonton-neighbourhood-for-snowy-sidewalks-1.3935931.

Soles, Katie. 2012. "Edmonton Winter City Strategy Consultation Summary." https://www.edmonton.ca/city_government/documents/PDF/WinterCity_Consultation_Summary_FINAL.pdf.

Toupin, Jerry. 2014. *Winter in Canada: Weird Facts, Records, Nostalgia, Hockey, Stats, Childhood Memories and More.* Canada: Folklore Publishing.

Weber, Max. 1946. "Science as a Vocation." In *From Max Weber: Essays in Sociology*, translated and edited by H. Gerth and C. Wright Mills, 129–56. New York: Oxford University Press.

———. 1958. *The Protestant Ethic and the Spirit of Capitalism.* Translated by Talcott Parsons. New York: Charles Scribner's Sons.

Wilkie, Trent. 2017. "Winter Cities Shake-Up Conference Addresses Edmonton's Northern Winter Experience." *Vue Weekly*, February 16. http://www.vueweekly.com/winter-cities-shake-up-conference-addresses-edmontons-northern-urban-experience/.

Wirth, Lewis. 1938. "Urbanism as a Way of Life." *American Journal of Sociology* 44 (1): 1–24. https://doi.org/10.1086/217913.

8 The Winter of Our Discontent: New Year's Resolutions and the Ideal Body

JEN WRYE, MICHAEL GRAYDON, and PATRICIA THILLE

LEARNING OUTCOMES

After reading this chapter, you should be able to:

- describe the relationship between ritual, religion, and New Year's resolutions
- describe how weight loss resolutions are often a reflection of neoliberalism and individualism
- explain how food systems shape people's diet and health
- outline how media representations of fat bodies contribute to fat shaming and stigma
- evaluate dominant attitudes towards weight loss and obesity

Introduction

The ball drops over Times Square in New York City. As the clock strikes midnight and the new year arrives, revellers, bundled in winter coats, shriek enthusiastically and embrace joyfully while the snow falls upon them. This **ritual** of friends and family celebrating the promise of new beginnings and possibilities happens in many places around the world. The new year also brings with it another common ritual: the act of making New Year's resolutions. New Year's resolutions are commitments people make to change behaviours or attitudes in ways intended improve their lives. Many people perceive this symbolically meaningful moment as an ideal time to change something about themselves (Norcross, Myrkalo, and Blagys 2002). By making resolutions, people commit to letting go of some undesirable quality and leaving it in the past in order to reinvent themselves. These pledges cover an array of activities, including learning a new skill, getting out of debt, spending more time with loved ones, eliminating cigarettes, alcohol, caffeine, or other drugs, travelling more, and so on. By far the most common resolutions concern techniques for managing our bodies and health, such as eating better or losing weight (Nielsen 2015). Why do so many people make New Year's resolutions focused on the body? While we might look at the individual desires and motivations that propel such decisions, applying our **sociological imagination** (Mills 1959; reviewed in chapter seven) can help to reveal the *social* dimensions of New Year's resolutions. We will explain how New Year's resolutions create shared meanings about weight and ideal bodies in **society**. A sociological imagination links people's individual experiences with broader societal contexts and can help us to understand where resolutions come from, why so many people make them, how they reflect some core values within Canadian mainstream **culture**, and why they are difficult to achieve (McManus, 2004).

This chapter considers the processes by which New Year's resolutions have become a favoured approach for making personal change, particularly a change related to diet and physical activity. We begin by examining the cross-cultural, 2,000-year history of resolution making. Resolutions had their early origins in **religion**. Drawing on the work of sociologist Émile Durkheim, we outline how resolutions provided people opportunities to express religious piety, and in so doing, strengthen **social bonds** between people. Over time, resolutions lost their spiritual undertones, becoming more secular and linked to individual discipline and worth. In the next section, we talk about dominant views concerning food, diet, and bodies in Canada. The contemporary food system – which encompasses all of the processes by which societies produce, distribute, consume, and dispose of food – creates poor-quality food and makes it easy for people to consume excessive calories. Although this is a larger policy problem, eating is treated as an individual choice such that what one eats, how much one eats, and how often one does so become matters characterized as exclusively within an individual's personal control. Accordingly, people who are fat – people imagined to eat bad food or too much food – are blamed for their bodies and perceived as irresponsible and lacking in self-control. Fat bodies are interpreted as **deviant** and are stigmatized as a result. While previously New Year's resolutions brought holiness, and failing at them occurred in front of God, today such resolutions entrench ideas of personal responsibility and failure.

Scope, Theory, and Method

Scope

New Year's resolutions take a number of forms. This chapter deals with the common resolution to change one's diet to improve one's appearance or health. Our main argument is that New Year's resolutions rely on **narratives** that emphasize personal responsibility for eating, body shape, and health. We argue that such resolutions rarely create change, but they do have other effects, including celebrating "disciplined" bodies and demonizing fat bodies as deviant. We likewise situate resolutions within broader forces of **neoliberalism**, an **ideology** that holds that free markets should shape society. As Laywine and Sears (this volume, chapter thirteen) explain, neoliberal philosophies celebrate **state** practices that encourage entrepreneurialism and minimize the role of the state in social interactions. As such, neoliberalism applauds individualistic ideas that enterprising people can succeed with grit, bold action, and hard work in an opportunity-laden capitalist free market. The impact of neoliberalism encompasses modern societies and is a critical component of sociological theorizing.

Theoretical Orientation

Our analysis draws on three areas of sociological investigation: **historical sociology**, the **sociology of food**, and the **sociology of the body**, specifically work by fat/critical weight scholars. Each of these fields of sociological research emerge mainly from critical and feminist theorists who take an interdisciplinary approach to understanding society, although some will employ a theoretical perspective known as symbolic interactionism. Food studies and **fat/critical weight studies** scholars question some of the main assumptions about how we look at health and the human body, and they offer alternative understandings rooted in greater consideration for justice.

Historical sociology examines how societies develop over time. It mainly uses macro-level perspectives to examine the shape and character of different social **institutions** and **social structures**. Historical sociologists do much of their work by analyzing texts and documents to understand how the past has shaped the present. In this chapter, historical sociology allows us to situate present-day resolution practices within their long history to better understand how they have changed or remained the same.

Sociology of food scholars look at food systems – how food is grown/produced, distributed, eaten, and disposed of – and how these systems shape human existence. Food systems scholars believe that food is the central organizing object of all societies (Koc, Sumner, and Winson 2016). Because food-related issues vary considerably, scholars who work in this area use a variety of theoretical approaches and conduct micro-, macro-, and global-level analyses. They look at contemporary and historical food systems as a reflection of both individual **agency** and broader social structures. Questions that food systems scholars might ask include: Why do we eat certain things or not others? What type of food system would be best for the environment? Why do hunger and malnutrition persist globally, even in wealthy countries like Canada? How can we make our food system fairer? In this case, we use food studies ideas to explore influences on what we eat and why we think we need to change it – ideas embedded in New Year's resolutions.

Fat studies and critical weight studies scholars examine how body types are understood across societies and within **subcultures** (Ellison, McPhail and Mitchinson 2016; Lupton 2013). In wealthy countries such as Canada, fat studies scholars explore how fatness is thought of as unhealthy, as a threat to the country. Fat and critical weight scholars study the micro to macro range, including experiences of living in fat bodies and collective resistance movements – such as fat acceptance, fat pride, and body positivity – to institutional forms of stigmatization and **discrimination**. Reducing weight – more specifically, body fat – is a very common resolution; fat studies help unpack that.

Methods

Our work synthesizes approaches from these sociological fields to consider why New Year's resolutions take the form they do. We explore why the practice of making resolutions holds such influence in modern society and why body change appears to be an especially popular concern. Our method mainly involved analyzing existing writing on these matters to describe the resolution making done every year in late December and early January. We selected some of the most influential pieces in the literature concerning New Year's resolutions, food systems, and anti-fatness. We also included some **secondary data analysis** in our investigation. Secondary data analysis involves using primary data collected from other sources, including researchers, government organizations, or private companies. We used these sources to support our broader arguments rather than as the foundational materials to conduct our analysis. Readers will find our analysis interprets and reconsiders existing texts to think about resolutions in our everyday lives.

New Year's Resolutions: Historical Context

In 1912, sociologist Émile Durkheim published *The Elementary Forms of Religious Life,* in which he argued that religion was a purely social phenomenon, one that had a clear social function – namely the strengthening of **social solidarity** (see chapters seven and fifteen). By taking part in religious observances and rituals within groups, people reaffirmed shared beliefs, values, and an understanding of their place in the world, thereby reinforcing social cohesion and integration (Durkheim 1968). Similarly, we can understand holidays and celebrations as occasions where people come together and take part in activities and rituals that reaffirm collective beliefs and connect people to each other (Etzioni 2004). At both individual and public New Year's celebrations, we see rituals that reinforce the idea that the New Year is a time of new beginnings.

Today we celebrate New Year's Day shortly after the winter solstice, the shortest day of the year, which usually falls around December 21. The New Year marks an ascent out of winter's darkness; the days are becoming longer and brightening toward a spring awakening. Celebrated in January, New Years' festivities acknowledge a coming renewal, waking up from the "dead of winter." On New Year's Day, we mark the passing (away) of one year and the birth of another (Aveni 2003).

For the ancient Romans, the beginning of the New Year heralded the transition out of winter, and they marked this by eating and drinking to excess. In their holy temples, people hung and left offerings of honey to the gods to *sweeten* the coming year. The god Janus was celebrated for three days and given offerings of food and coins so that he would bring the people good luck in the new year (Aveni 2003).

Christianity marked the new year differently, echoes of which are still present in the now secular resolutions common on New Year's Day. In the earlier Medieval era, Christian saints, holy fathers, monks, and nuns denied themselves physical comforts. Some, like Catherine of Sienna, denied herself food at times to an extreme degree, such as eating only a Eucharist wafer (Gardner 2013). In part, this suffering was intended to echo Christ's trials. Some believed that what one denied the self was given to the body of Christ (Bynum 1987). Christians regarded the body as a vessel for one's immortal soul. The physical body, however, was always at risk of giving into pleasure and sinful desires. A body that gave in to pleasure threatened to bring damnation upon one's immortal soul. Keeping one's body under control was essential, though the methods used to do so could weaken people.

We can trace our current understanding of self-improvement to the emergence of Protestantism in the early sixteenth century (Thorner 1951). Early Protestant doctrine emphasized the importance of maintaining a disciplined, emotionally controlled personality. Such views gave rise to a way of life in which individuals avoided drinking excessively, eating indulgently and partaking in other frivolous activities. Protestantism, with its emphasis on discipline, also influenced a new spiritual understanding of the physical body. As Roy Porter (2004, 227–9) notes, Protestants viewed the body differently than Catholics had: "for Protestants, the preferred discipline of the body did not take the form of pious infirmity but of regular labour in one's calling." The body was to be celebrated, maintained, and made robust, to honour God's creation. As nineteenth-century sociologist Max Weber (1992) explained, Protestants believed the way they lived life was essential to ensuring their souls' salvation. In Weber's words, "In practice this means that God helps those who help themselves" (69–70). Personal salvation, and remaining in good graces, required the individual to maintain "systematic self-control which at every moment stands before the inexorable alternative, chosen [for salvation] or damned" (69–70). According to Isidor Thorner (1951), New Year's became a time to reaffirm your status as one of God's chosen, as someone who would avoid damnation. Thorner noted that for Protestants, avoiding frivolity, maintaining self-control, working diligently, and practising self-denial were necessary if "the godly man" was to lead a "rationally organized life devoted to bring about the Kingdom of God on Earth" (102–3). Therefore, an observant Protestant would resist the temptation to eat or drink to excess, controlling their bodily appetites. While contemporary resolutions do not tend to emphasize spirituality, they still value self-control. In a secular context, self-improvement is no longer about proximity to God, but about being a disciplined, responsible individual. Over time, neoliberal society, rather than God, has come to adjudicate what this looks like. New Year's resolutions represent the practice of recommitting to an imagined proper diet, body, or state of health.

New Year's Resolutions in Modern Society

If New Year's resolutions were previously intended to situate people in greater proximity to God, today's secular version is about folks identifying and fixing deficiencies to achieve an elusive form of what we might broadly call "wellness." Making New Year's resolutions is a popular activity, yet few scholarly researchers analyze these behaviours in relation to the cultural forces that encourage them or the collective effect of making them. For instance, instead of scrutinizing why resolutions exist, or who gains the most socially or economically from New Year's resolutions – sociological types of questions – academic studies tend to focus on how people can construct better resolutions, be more successful, and how resolutions affect people's attitudes about themselves. People may find value in this type of research, but as sociologists, we believe there is value in examining how contemporary "resolution culture" constructs narratives about what is desirable and undesirable in modern society.

Although the pressure to change at the New Year may be strong, it does not necessarily mean people succeed. If you have been to a gym in January and again in April, you can probably attest that resolutions rarely lead to long-term personal action or transformation. But they do have other personal and social effects. In their research on New Year's resolutions, Polivy and Herman (2000, 2002) claim that aspirations for change are often unrealistic, noting that resolvers make the same New Year's resolutions an average of 10 times over the course of a lifetime (often before giving up on them). In earlier research, Norcross and Vangarelli (1988–9) determined that the majority of people who falter in their resolutions do so within the first three months. Polivy and Herman (2002) believe that many health resolvers have unrealistic expectations about the ease, amount, or speed of self-change, and that their repeated stumbling brings considerable psychological consequences, such as worsening self-esteem and feelings of guilt and self-loathing. Weiner (2017) argues that resolutions sell hope that things can get better. But she also points out that this hope undermines self-worth, drains individuals' energy, and directs their attention away from broader social issues. People who inevitably abandon their resolutions may come to feel worse than they did before the experience, thinking they have failed twice – in their current existence and their ability to *do* something about it. Repeated failure creates images of one's self as undisciplined, lazy, and failing; it also allows resolvers to ignore barriers to change, including high costs, challenges keeping up with regular responsibilities, or difficulties that follow introducing drastic changes within a family. Resolution culture depicts simplistic and unrealistic forms of success and failure in the absence of social, environmental, or cultural contexts. As Sarah Knight (2017) puts it: "nine out of 10 magazines on newsstands' on Jan. 1 will be touting some version of 'Five Steps to a New You!' … if you're only doing it because you've been conditioned to believe that the month of January signals An End to Everything You Ever Were and the Beginning of a New You, then maybe slow your roll" (n.p.). Perhaps New Year's resolutions typically fail because they create a seemingly mandatory personal growth plan born of a combination of self-loathing and peer pressure. Still, individuals persist in making, and faltering with, New Year's resolutions.

In his review of New Year's resolutions, McManus (2004) outlines the way people approach personal change, noting a difference between intentions, desires, and actions. He points out that some intentions produce action while others result in none. This is key for McManus, who claims that intentions, rather than actions, are the *outcome* of most New Year's resolutions. In other words, New Year's resolutions mainly foster conditions for generating goals rather than supporting the actual changes. Resolutions are not a realistic means to achieve a goal, but they are a way to entrench mainstream notions about what is ideal or appropriate.

Resolution making can be understood as a pernicious activity that fuels narrow expectations of faultless existence. Resolvers marginalize characteristics that fall outside the idealized norm while establishing resolutions as standard activity (Cederström and Spicer 2015). Failing to live or want a disciplined life is considered an individual and moral failure. Instead of carrying religious meaning, self-improvement resolutions and failures reinforce the idea that people are in charge of their own destinies. As previously mentioned, the most prevalent New Year's resolutions are about diet, exercise, and weight loss. Why are so many resolutions about these forms of health, and particularly, about eating and bodily transformation? What do these resolutions say about body norms?

Health, Bodies, and Diet in Contemporary Society

For sociologists, it makes sense that diet, exercise, weight loss, and a general focus on enhancing one's health are the most common New Year's resolutions (Nielsen 2015; Spector 2017). In rich countries such as Canada, healthiness is often treated as a sign of moral living (Lupton 1995; Mayes 2016). In countries where so-called "lifestyle diseases" dominate, people are encouraged to work on themselves and their everyday routines to help prevent or manage chronic diseases, such as diabetes and heart disease. In this section, we explore the systems that influence what we eat, and how corporations profit from emphasizing personal responsibility for healthy eating over systemic issues. We then examine how New Year's resolutions reinforce anti-fatness and idealize individually responsible citizens.

Diet Resolutions and Food Systems

The contemporary food environment in which New Year's resolutions emerge is complex. Innovations in agriculture, as well as innovations in food preservation, distribution, and preparation have changed nutrition patterns in affluent nations significantly in the twentieth century (Beardsworth and Keil 1997). The use of fertilizers, herbicides, pesticides, antibiotics, and genetic modification have greatly increased crop yield but have reduced the quality of the both the foods and the environments in which they are produced (Lappé 2010). People regularly eat foods grown across the world within days of harvest because food distribution networks are fast and efficient. The consequence is that most food-related human health problems in affluent countries are caused not by food scarcity, as has been the case for most of human history, but from the consumption of too much food and of food that has poorer nutritional quality than in the past (Schlosser 2001). How did we get here?

First, people are increasingly detached from the foods they consume. Fewer people today grow food or know how it gets to their plate than in previous generations. Rather, diet and nutrition matters have become problems to be solved by science and managed by individuals. This means that cooking, eating with others, and enjoying meals are less a priority than nutrition (Pollan 2006). We can see the impact of such a cultural shift in orientation to food. Today, at least half of all food consumption in the United States happens outside the home while supermarkets dedicate more and more shelf space to ready-made foods and meals, squeezing out fresh produce and other raw ingredients (Lang and Heasman 2004). These ready-made meals provide a solution for the problem of limited time, but contain chemicals and additives for artificial preservation, disproportionately high levels of calories, sodium, fat, and/or sugar per serving, but low levels in vitamins and other minerals. Anthony Winson (2004) calls such poorer food options "**pseudofoods.**" Winson notes that pseudofoods have become ubiquitous and **normalized**; we can find them in variety stores, gas stations, malls, theme parks, schools, and even hospitals. Virtually every space imaginable has become a pseudofood retail space that encourages the consumption of excess and imbalanced calories, fat(s), sugar, and preservatives. The food system has been reshaping people's dietary habits to include more food with less nutrition, supporting conditions for poorer health. This is the food environment within which people make resolutions.

Second, the food industry has found a way to capitalize on the problem of worsening health while denying any responsibility for it. The problem, food companies tell us, is that people make poor choices. Food makers profit from this definition of the problem by regularly introducing and marketing "healthier" and "diet" versions of their popular food products in "low-calorie, low-sodium, low-cholesterol, low-fat, caffeine-free, high-fructose, high-protein, high-calcium, and high-fiber forms" (Levenstein 1988, 205; quoted in Retzinger 2008, 153). Such foods get positioned as addressing the causes of obesity or ill health. Individuals are guided toward increasing their consumption of certain nutritional components and away from others, but not toward a better relationship with food or a better understanding of the food system as a whole. Assessing nutrients has become the pre-eminent mode of evaluating the healthfulness of a diet. This has the effect of reshaping foods into mysterious nutritional component parts (protein, fat, carbohydrates, folate, vitamin B12, etc.), leading consumers to value nutrients over actual food (Pollan 2008; Scrinis 2015). Food companies cement a broader social understanding of what counts as "good" food while also acting as the purveyors of it. Packaged, prepared, and processed foods identify calorie counts and micronutrient levels. They outline what people should eat and should avoid. In doing so, food companies situate their foods, representing nutrient measures, within a "healthy" eating framework, echoing only one facet of the message found in public health. In sum, food companies sell *products* that offer people relatively easy-looking, consumer-based solutions to eat a good diet while offering conflicting information about what folks need to realize that objective. This food environment sets people up to try to achieve body aspirations, such as reducing body fat or getting fit, on an individual basis, shielding the food industry from critique without addressing overconsumption or poorer food quality. Reinforcing individually focused ideas about eating tends to take people away from the practices that lead to the best diets: eating simple food prepared with good quality ingredients and consuming meals with other people (Pollan 2008).

Despite these larger social and structural conditions of food, the food industry approach gains traction within dominant cultural perspectives that view individuals as responsible for their own food consumption and, by extension, the impact of these decisions. Neoliberal philosophy, which promotes the belief that individuals are solely responsible for their place in life, shapes this idea of the responsibilized person or responsibilization more generally. As Crotty (1995) explains, this so-called responsibilized person is accountable for his or her own achievements and failures regardless of influence from the social environment. Neoliberalism echoes earlier religious sentiments about personal responsibility and discipline without the religious tie to salvation after death. It has shaped our ideas about morality, health, and bodies. Ultimately, the responsible subject fits neatly within the form of **capitalism** that is currently globally dominant (see Laywine and Sears, chapter thirteen).

The Medicalization of Fatness

Popular understandings of fatness are a prime example of how morality is tied to lifestyle. A religious privileging of thinness preceded and informed current social ideas about fatness (Jutel 2005; Lupton 2013). At present, fat bodies are interpreted as unfit and deviant (that is, not conforming to dominant norms) while bodies that are small, lean, or fit are seen as ideal, healthy, and reflecting a controlled inner self. Under neoliberalism, fat is read as evidence of an individual moral and economic failure by the individual: a failure to take enough responsibility to make oneself aesthetically and medically "normal" and a failure to contribute productively to society more generally. Such judgments overlook the way in which socially preferred physical appearance, including what is considered normal, varies over time and across cultures (Jutel 2005). Thus, a person is seen as "over" weight or fat when they surpass this socially preferred body size in one society, but they might be considered physically ideal or "under" weight in another cultural or historical context.

While religion contributed to ideas about body size in the past, today **mass media** and health care are two societal institutions that promote the view that weight simply reflects "lifestyle choices," despite the many mediators of weight. Fatness, like seasonal affective disorder discussed by Alissa Overend in chapter six, is medicalized, meaning what is understood as a social or moral problem is reinterpreted as a medical one. **Medicalization** means that the medical understanding of the phenomenon becomes normalized, so much so that medical language is what is commonly used (e.g., using the terms *obese* and *epidemic*, the latter formerly reserved for infectious disease). Abigail Saguy (2013) argues that the use of a medicalized interpretation of body size makes it appear as if fatphobia is based on scientific objectivity and that fatness is simply the outcome of an individual's undisciplined lifestyle. A medicalized frame of fatness is often used to justify anti-fat attitudes, fatphobia, and **fat shaming** (belittling individuals for being fat).

Fat bodies are not necessarily indicative of poor diet, little exercise, or poorer health (Brown et al. 2016; Kuk et al. 2018). Decades of research have found that improving eating and physical activity produces only small impacts on weight in most people (Wadden et al. 2014). People can rarely sustain drastic weight loss, as a recent follow-up study of participants in *The Biggest Loser* found: the participants' metabolism had slowed, and their bodies regained the weight (Doyle 2018). Based on data collected over decades in the American **population**, Brown and colleagues (2016) found that when people today eat and exercise the same amount as those 30 years ago, their bodies are substantially heavier and fatter. Scientists now recognize many influences on body composition and metabolism beyond eating and exercise: Julie Guthman's (2011) research, for example, highlights the scientific studies of the metabolic impact of chemicals (specifically, endocrine disruptors), to which we are now commonly exposed (especially those living in **poverty**). She argues such exposures are the result, in part, of the strength of neoliberalism, which limits environmental regulations to protect what are called "free markets." Like with understandings of the food system, these larger physiological, social, and environmental factors get underplayed in discussions of weight and of well-being more generally. Instead, the focus is on individuals' diet and exercise.

Medicalizing Fatness in Media

Diet, exercise, and weight loss advice flourishes on the internet, in magazines, on television, and in film. In this media, fat bodies are consistently presented as both aesthetically inferior and medically unfit (LeBesco 2004; Lupton 2013). While the processes by which media ostracize fatness vary, reality TV, scripted shows, and news reporting all reinforce anti-fat, stigmatizing messages about heavier bodies. Roost (2016) found that weight-loss TV shows such as *The Biggest Loser* promote **stereotypes** about fat people as lazy and out of control. At the same time, these shows encourage unhealthy weight loss techniques characterized by punishingly strenuous exercise and extreme calorie reductions. Roxane Gay (2017) notes that the contestants endure constant ridicule in the form of shirtless weigh-ins and medical professionals who stress how near death these participants are. For Gay, the show is not about health, but teaching the indignity of unruly, obese bodies.

Similarly, in their research on scripted television characters, Greenberg et al. (2003) found several negative biases against fat bodies. Their research on 10 top-rated prime-time fictional television programs on six broadcast networks during the 1999–2000 season reveals that only 14 per cent of women and 25 per cent of men among the 1,018 television characters represented during their study period were fat, which is less than half of the ratio in the general population. Moreover, fat characters are less likely to be depicted with romantic partners or displaying physical affection. The absence of fat people in popular television positions skinnier bodies as both the ideal and the norm. The poor representation of love and intimacy among fat characters further suggests that fat people are disinterested in, or undeserving of, love, romance, or sexual activity. Such treatment belittles fat characters to suggest that mainstream acceptance requires people to exorcise fatness permanently.

Even the frequent use of the term the "obesity epidemic" in the media, as well as the health sector, has strengthened the idea that fat is a dangerous public health threat (Saguy 2013). Epidemic is a term typically reserved for describing outbreaks of infectious disease or high levels of chronic diseases, both of which prove dangerous to the public. This phrasing fosters a sense of urgency and positions fat bodies as problems to solve.

Saguy's study of over 650 American and French news articles about fatness demonstrates that American media, using extreme examples to make the point, routinely framed fatness as a consequence of bad choices, reflecting a moral failure to be responsible. French news media, in contrast, mention socio-cultural, environmental, and biological influences on weight much more often. She argues that this difference across countries is predictable, given the heavy promotion of self-reliance in the United States, a reflection of powerful neoliberal economic and political interests that aim to shift costs from the state to individuals. Christopher Mayes's (2016) extensive study of health policy, health promotion/public health, and consumer appeals in the United Kingdom, United States, and Australia makes similar arguments about the centrality of neoliberalism to understanding how we speak and act on fatness.

Fat-Shaming in Policy and Health Care

The threat of obesity, we are told, is not just to health. The "problem" of obesity gets communicated as an economic one by pressuring public health budgets and threatening financial stability (Mayes 2016). Health policy documents routinely detail how much obesity costs the country. For example, a recent report written by a committee of the Canadian Senate argues for acting on obesity because of its economic toll: "Obesity costs Canada between $4.6 billion and $7.1 billion annually in health care and lost productivity" (Standing Senate Committee on Social Affairs, Science and Technology 2016). Transforming fatness into a threat to the security of the population, one that reflects poor "individual choices," has consequences. In particular, there has been an intensification of governmental policies and public health activities to address fatness – and both sectors tend to focus on changing eating and exercise to the exclusion of other determinants of weight (Mayes 2016).

How does the intensification of anti-obesity rhetoric affect people's lives? In a comprehensive review across societal institutions, Puhl and Heuer (2009) found strong evidence of discrimination on the basis of fatness in employment – in particular, a wage penalty and negative effects on job evaluations and hiring decisions. Discrimination in other sectors is less well studied, but there are indications of discrimination in health care and education. In health care, anti-fat attitudes can result in clinicians fat shaming patients, such as by attributing all of their health problems to their weight, giving simplistic advice, or not completing appropriate clinical assessments (Malterud and Ulriksen 2011; Phelan et al. 2015). Similar concerns about anti-fat messaging, and its impacts, have been made by sociologists about public health campaigns, which typically focus on promoting individual change rather than addressing big-impact environmental or societal threats to health (Lupton 2013; Mayes 2016).

Taken overall, mainstream beliefs about body size create shame and marginalization in many institutions. It is in this context that individuals reassert their willpower in search of health and weight-loss solutions. New Year's resolutions and the resolution culture from which they emerge give people the opportunity to appropriately endeavour to shed their nasty old diets and habits and reinvent themselves as appropriate and responsible subjects.

Conclusion

For centuries, the passing of one year and the arrival of the next has been socially recognized as unique – a time to pause, to embrace the opportunity a "new year" provided. In many cultures, the New Year highlighted that the worst of winter's cold and dark was behind us, a spring renewal was coming; something welcomed by all. For the Romans, paying respects to the gods through New Year's rituals strengthened social cohesion by reaffirming shared beliefs and ensuring a prosperous coming year (reflecting beliefs that angering the gods brought bad luck or worse). In the sixteenth century, European Protestants also saw a connection between resolutions and a higher power. In their case, resolutions reflected and reaffirmed a commitment to leading a sober, disciplined life, one free of sinful excess. Doing so demonstrated that as a Protestant you led a "godly life" and were therefore worthy of salvation. This shifted the focus of resolutions. It was here that resolutions began to emphasize *physical* self-discipline, self-improvement, living and behaving *better*. Initially, Protestants celebrated and maintained a disciplined body to honour God's wondrous creation. Over time, we came to improve our bodily selves not to please God, but because it was simply the proper, *responsible* thing to do. As good, responsible members of society we resolve to stay healthy, eat healthily, work out more and the like. Resolutions demonstrate a commitment to being a good citizen, one who wisely maintains their health and does not make too many demands on the state. In wealthy countries in particular, society champions individual responsibility and self-control. In turn, resolutions reflect the social concerns of the day, namely an emphasis on maintaining fitness and health, and judging harshly those who eat to excess or have fatter bodies. In contrast to psychologists who ask, "why can't people stick to their resolutions?," sociologists question the very nature of resolutions – namely, "why are we obsessed with healthy bodies?" By looking back at the roots of our resolutions, we can partly answer the question.

Sociologically, we recognize New Year resolutions as a social creation, a social ritual that reflects existing concerns, influences, and ways of thinking. There is nothing inherently wrong with making a commitment to improve one's own life. But as sociologists, we need to ask critical questions about what resolutions mean for individual social actors and society in general. Feeling good, worthy, and fulfilled is an important aspect of the human condition. Sometimes people need to make significant life changes to grow and become happier, and the New Year is one such time when this may occur. In this chapter, we have argued that most New Year's resolutions fail to provide those experiences for people and instead undermine self-worth. New Year's resolutions impair self-acceptance and push resolvers to think about their individual deficiencies instead of the larger social, economic, or political circumstances that may have helped fuel their problems, or indeed, whether the circumstances are in fact even problematic. Resolution culture creates simplistic solutions to complex and contradictory personal and emotional circumstances, often ostracizing individuals and normalizing feelings of self-loathing and individual accountability while reflecting reductive social beliefs about wellness. There may be a place for New Year's resolutions in society. But as they exist now – underpinned by requirements that people identify and remedy deficiencies – resolutions remain untenable as a meaningful approach to genuine happiness.

Questions for Critical Thought

1. How can the cultural ritual of creating and sharing New Year's resolutions be understood with a sociological imagination?
2. Can you identify ways in which the various religious orientations to the body, as discussed in this chapter, can be seen reflected in other aspects of culture?
3. This chapter has explored the impact of neoliberalism and capitalism on the way we think about health-related New Year's resolutions. How might these factors shape how we think about other types of popular New Year's resolutions (e.g., debt reduction and financial stability)?
4. Do you know the sources of the food you eat? How does your relationship with food producers and food preparation affect your attitudes toward weight-loss resolutions?
5. We have criticized mainstream attitudes about the way media, health care systems, and other social institutions frame fatness. Can you identify examples of fatphobia that you have noticed in any of these social institutions in your everyday life?

References

Aveni, Anthony. 2003. *The Book of the Year: A Brief History of our Seasonal Holidays*. New York: Oxford University Press.

Beardsworth, Alan, and Teresa Keil. 1997. *Sociology on the Menu: An Invitation to the Study of Food and Society*. London: Routledge.

Brown, Ruth E., Sharma, Arya M., Ardern, Chris I., Mirdamadi, Pedi, Mirdamadi, Paul, and Jennifer L. Kuk. 2016. "Secular Differences in the Association between Caloric Intake, Macronutrient Intake, and Physical Activity with Obesity." *Obesity Research & Clinical Practice* 10 (3): 243–55. https://doi.org/10.1016/j.orcp.2015.08.007.

Bynum, Carolyn Walker. 1987. *Holy Feast and Holy Fast: The Religious Significance of Food to Medieval Women*. Berkeley: University of California Press.

Cederström, Carl, and André Spicer. 2015. *The Wellness Syndrome*. Cambridge: Polity Press.

Crotty, Patricia. 1995. *Good Nutrition?: Fact and Fashion in Dietary Advice*. Melbourne: Allen and Unwin.

Doyle, Kathryn. 2018. "6 Years after *The Biggest Loser*, Metabolism is Slower and Weight Is Back Up" *Reuters Wellness/Scientific American*. https://www.scientificamerican.com/article/6-years-after-the-biggest-loser-metabolism-is-slower-and-weight-is-back-up/.

Durkheim, Emile. 1968. *The Elementary Forms of the Religious Life*. Translated by Joseph Ward Swain. London: George Allen & Unwin, Ltd.

Ellison, Jenny, Deborah McPhail, and Wendy Mitchinson. 2016. "Introduction: Obesity in Canada." In *Obesity in Canada: Critical Perspectives*, edited by Jenny Ellison, Deborah McPhail and Wendy Mitchinson, 3–31, Toronto: University of Toronto Press.

Etzioni, Amitai. 2004. "Holidays and Rituals: Neglected Seedbeds of Virtue." In *We Are What We Celebrate: Understanding Holidays and Rituals*, edited by Amitai Etzioni and Jared Bloom, 3–40. New York: New York University Press.

Gardner, Edmund. 2013. "St. Catherine of Siena." *The Catholic Encyclopedia*, vol. 3. New York: Robert Appleton Company.

Gay, Roxanne. 2017. *Hunger: A Memoir of (My) Body*. New York: Harper Collins.

Greenberg, Bradley, Matthew Eastin, Linda Hofschire, Ken Lachlan, and Kelly D. Brownell. 2003. "Portrayals of Overweight and Obese Individuals on Commercial Television." *American Journal of Public Health* 93 (8): 1342–48. https://doi.org/10.2105/AJPH.93.8.1342.

Guthman, Julie. 2011. *Weighing In: Obesity, Food Justice, and the Limits of Capitalism*. Berkeley: University of California Press.

Jutel, Annemarie. 2005. "Weighing Health: The Moral Burden of Obesity." *Social Semiotics* 15 (2): 113–25. https://doi.org/10.1080/10350330500154717.

Knight, Sarah. 2017. "There's Nothing Wrong with You, So Skip the New Year's Resolutions." *Globe and Mail*, December 30. https://www.theglobeandmail.com/opinion/theres-nothing-wrong-with-you-so-skip-the-new-years-resolutions/article37457686/.

Koc, Mustafa, Jennifer Sumner, and Anthony Winson, editors. 2016. *Critical Perspectives in Food Studies*. 2nd ed. Toronto: Oxford University Press.

Kuk, J.L., M. Rotondi, X. Sui, S.N. Blair, and C.I. Ardern. 2018. "Individuals with Obesity but No Other Metabolic Risk Factors Are Not at Significantly Elevated All Cause

Mortality Risk in Men and Women." *Clinical Obesity* 8 (5): 305–12. https://doi.org/10.1111/cob.12263.

Lang, Tim, and Michael Heasman. 2004. *Food Wars: The Global Battle for Mouths, Minds, and Markets*. London: Earthscan.

Lappé, Anna. 2010. *Diet for a Hot Planet: The Climate Crisis at the End of Your Fork and What You Can Do About It*. New York: Bloomsbury.

Lebesco, Kathleen. 2004. *Revolting Bodies?: The Struggle to Redefine Fat Identity*. Amherst: University of Massachusetts Press.

Levenstein, Harvey. 1988. *Revolution at the Table: The Transformation of the American Diet*. New York: Oxford University Press.

Lupton, Deborah. 2013. *Fat*. London: Routledge.

Malterud, Kirsti, and Kjersti Ulriksen. 2011. "Obesity, Stigma, and Responsibility in Health Care: A Synthesis of Qualitative Studies" *International Journal of Qualitative Studies on Health and Well-being* 6 (4): 8404. https://doi.org/10.3402/qhw.v6i4.8404.

Mayes, Christopher. 2016. *The Biopolitics of Lifestyle: Foucault, Ethics and Healthy Choices*. London: Routledge.

Mills, C. Wright. 1959. *The Sociological Imagination*. Oxford University Press: Oxford.

McManus, Chris. 2004. "New Year's Resolutions: Mind the Gap between Intention and Behaviour." *British Medical Journal* 329. 1413–14. https://doi.org/10.1136/bmj.329.7480.1413.

Nielsen. 2015. "This Year's Top New Year's Resolution?: Fitness!!" January 8. https://www.nielsen.com/us/en/insights/article/2015/2015s-top-new-years-resolution-fitness/.

Norcross, John, Marci Mrykalo, and Matthew Blagys. 2002. "Auld Lang Syne: Success Predictors, Change Processes, and Self-Reported Outcomes of New Year's Resolvers and Nonresolvers." *Journal of Clinical Psychology* 58 (4): 397–405. https://doi.org/10.1002/jclp.1151.

Norcross, John, and Dominic Vangarelli. 1998–1999. "The Resolution Solution: Longitudinal Examination of New Year's Change Attempts." *Journal of Substance Abuse* 1 (2): 127–34. https://doi.org/10.1016/S0899-3289(88)80016-6.

Phelan, Sean, Diane Burgess, Mark Yeazel, Wendy Hellerstedt, Joan Griffin, and Michelle van Ryn. 2015. "Impact of Weight Bias and Stigma on Quality of Care and Outcomes for Patients with Obesity" *Obesity Reviews* 16 (4): 319–26. https://doi.org/10.1111/obr.12266.

Polivy, Janet and Peter Herman. 2000. "The False-Hope Syndrome: Unfulfilled Expectations of Self-Change." *Current Directions in Psychological Science* 9 (4): 128–31. https://doi.org/10.1111/1467-8721.00076.

———. 2002. "If at First You Don't Succeed: False Hopes of Self-Change." *American Psychologist* 57 (9): 677–89. https://doi.org/10.1037/0003-066X.57.9.677.

Pollan, Michael. 2006. *The Omnivore's Dilemma: A Natural History of Four Meals*. London: Penguin Books.

———. 2008. *In Defense of Food: An Eater's Manifesto*. New York: Penguin Press.

Porter, Roy. 2004. *Flesh in the Age of Reason*. New York: W.W. Norton & Company.

Puhl, Rebecca, and Chelsea A. Heuer. 2009. "The Stigma of Obesity: A Review and Update." *Obesity: A Research Journal*. 17 (5): 941–64. https://doi.org/10.1038/oby.2008.636.

Retzinger, Jean. 2008. "The Embodied Rhetoric of 'Health' from Farm Fields to Salad Bowls." In *Edible Ideologies: Representing Food and Marketing*, edited by Kathleen LeBesco and Peter Naccarato, 149–78. New York: State University of New York Press.

Roost, Alisa. 2016. "Losing It: The Construction and Stigmatization of Obesity on Reality Television in the United States." *The Journal of Popular Culture* 49 (1): 174–95. https://doi.org/10.1111/jpcu.12377.

Saguy, Abigail. 2013. *What's Wrong with Fat?* Oxford: Oxford University Press.

Schlosser, Eric. 2001. *Fast Food Nation: The Dark Side of the All-American Meal.* Boston: Houghton-Mifflin.

Scrinis, Gyorgy. 2015. *Nutritionism: The Science and Politics of Dietary Advice.* New York: Columbia University Press.

Spector, Nicole. 2017. "New Year's Resolutions: The Most Popular and How to Stick to Them." *NBC News,* January 1, 2017. https://www.nbcnews.com/business/consumer/2017-new-year-s-resolutions-most-popular-how-stick-them-n701891.

Standing Senate Committee on Social Affairs, Science and Technology. 2016. *Obesity in Canada: A Whole-of-Society Approach for a Healthier Canada.* Government of Canada, February 25. www.parl.gc.ca/content/sen/committee/421/SOCI/Reports/2016-02-25_Revised_report_Obesity_in_Canada_e.pdf.

Thorner, Isidor. 1951. "The New Year's Resolution and Ascetic Protestantism." *Social Forces* 30 (1): 102–7. https://doi.org/10.2307/2571748.

Wadden, Thomas A., Meghan L. Butryn, Patricia S. Hong, and Adam G. Tsai. 2014. "Behavioral Treatment of Obesity in Patients Encountered in Primary Care Settings: A Systematic Review." *JAMA* 312 (17): 1779–91. https://doi.org/10.1001/jama.2014.14173.

Weber, Max. 1992. *The Protestant Ethic and the Spirit of Capitalism.* London: Routledge.

Weiner, Jennifer. 2017. "Try a New Year's Revolution." *New York Times,* December 31. https://www.nytimes.com/2016/12/31/opinion/sunday/try-a-new-years-revolution.html?_r=0.

Winson, Anthony. 2004. "Bringing Political Economy into the Debate on the Obesity Epidemic." *Agriculture and Human Values* 21: 299–312. https://doi.org/10.1007/s10460-003-1206-6.

9 Extending Law's Reach: Winter, Accusations, and the Colonial Encounter

MATTHEW P. UNGER

LEARNING OUTCOMES

After reading this chapter, you should be able to:

- distinguish between positivist and constructionist understandings of criminal behaviour
- recognize the different traditions of establishing a relationship between nature and law
- describe the history of the Canadian legal relationship with Indigenous peoples, and the colonial legal imaginary
- explain Michel Foucault's approach toward crime and punishment
- evaluate the merits of doing archival research

Introduction

On April 25, 1879, members of the Anderson Lake **Indigenous** community (St'át'imc peoples), travelling along the Douglas wagon road, saw smoke billowing behind the trees from the direction of what they knew to be the residence of Thomas Poole. A prominent settler who tended a roadhouse in the Pemberton region of British Columbia, Poole had maintained good relations with the St'át'imc community, and he had married and had two children with a St'át'imc Indigenous woman. The rising plume of smoke caught the travellers' concern and they changed their course to check on the family. They approached to find the house a smoldering ruin. They found the badly burnt bodies of Thomas Poole and his daughter in the potato cellar. Immediately, this group of Indigenous people sent one of the younger members to the nearby Anderson Lake community to raise the alarm and summon the nearest police officer, Constable

Livingston. When the boys reached the community, they were told to cross the lake in a canoe to where the constable was stationed. What happened after this point was a long, drawn-out series of trials that consisted of many people being accused of murdering the family and setting fire to the house. The trials caught the attention of the provincial and national media, and, although they lasted approximately 12 years and consisted of many accusations, no one was ever finally charged with the **crime**. Yet this event is significant because it reflects a number of important themes within early Canadian **law** and its development, including 1) the importance of law to the colonial period of Canadian history, 2) how Canada established **sovereignty** (complete legal rule over a geographical and political region) over a vast area consisting of many different Indigenous communities and nations, and 3) what the settler colonial society thought about the project of establishing Canada. I call this complex of themes the colonial legal imaginary, which includes the images, ideas, philosophies, hopes, and dreams that the colonial regime had about their developing nation and Indigenous peoples. (For other discussion of **settler colonialism**, see chapters one and seventeen.)

This case, although buried deep in the British Columbia provincial archives and all but lost to history, nevertheless had some important effects on the region. First, the few settlers who were in the Pemberton region during the 1870s left after this crime. Second, the subsequent investigations stretched the limits of law enforcement in a **territory** that was difficult to navigate: the police traversed treacherous and mountainous terrain, and the manhunts were called off as the weather turned colder. Indeed, we can see the challenges that colonial authorities faced given the shortage of labour, navigating the weather, geography and space, and in their complex relationships with Indigenous people. In order to explore the relationship between law and the Canadian colonial past through the trope of nature and winter, this chapter will first examine the relationship between crime and **society,** as well as the intellectual history of how scholars understood the relationship between nature and law. Second, I argue that this understanding of nature is a social construction that developed out of **Enlightenment** philosophical discourses, and these still influence our thinking today. By returning to the case in the third section, I outline how winter affected the outcome of the Poole trials. In the final section, I examine how early colonial legal cases such as the Poole case and the adventure writings by Sir William Francis Butler show the importance of the colonial legal imaginary for how Indigenous people were treated and continue to be treated in the legal system today. This chapter, then, by tracing the pathways that law has taken after a crime took place at an important moment in the development of Canadian law, will take us through several predominant **sociological theories of crime** and **deviance**. I argue that looking critically to the past reveals how society constructs and addresses crime and also discloses how we understand people, **norms**, and difference in society. Fundamentally, the reason that Indigenous people are marginalized in contemporary law is because of continuing historical patterns of control and exclusion. (For other discussions of crime and criminality, see chapters two and eighteen; chapter six addresses other forms of deviance.)

Crime and Society

Law and Order Perspective

Scholars have suggested that we live in a crime-obsessed **culture**: Images of crime, the criminal, the justice system, punishment, and prison increasingly permeate our everyday lives (Melossi 2008; Pavlich 2016). The call for increasing law and order, with tougher sentences for those who commit crime, is common in political speeches and politically conservative platforms (Flamm 2005; Platt 1994; Reiner 2007). This **law and order perspective** that is currently dominant in North America argues that our culture should go in the direction of harsher sentences for criminals, increasing incarceration, and an increasing culture of fear in which the criminal justice system plays a prominent role. In popular culture, the striking number of crime procedurals on television and the rise of the true crime genre in documentary and podcast form reflects its prevalence in North American life. These images can serve to reinforce the common understanding that criminality needs to be strictly and punitively controlled, but the consequence of strict criminal sentencing and **zero-tolerance** policies is the creation of social boundaries that declare whether or not people can function as citizens in society. Despite the dominance of this law and order perspective, not everyone agrees with it (Garland 2002). Much recent scholarship suggests that the cultural and political focus on the punitive aspects of crime and punishment disproportionately disadvantages those segments of the population that are already more vulnerable, including people of different socio-economic backgrounds, people of colour, and young people (see Rollwagen, chapter two). Incarceration, in the way that it is practised in the United States and Canada, has profound effects on one's life by often reinforcing criminality (continued criminal activity) and **recidivism** (the tendency for convicted criminals to reoffend) through increasing social **stigma**, continuing impoverishment, and **disenfranchisement** (the removal of rights such as the ability to vote) (Wacquant 2009). Scholars have suggested that North American government policy is increasingly geared toward the **criminalization** of people and actions, including finding, apprehending, and incarcerating criminals (Simon 2007) rather than being focused on understanding the origins of social problems and developing preventative solutions.

Critical Theorizing

In order to understand the changing face of the criminal justice system, a critical theorizing of **criminal entryways** (how people enter that system) is needed to attempt to shed light on how people find themselves excluded and marginalized in society (Bernstein, Benhabib, and Fraser 2004; Pavlich and Unger 2016). By critical theorizing, I mean a mode of interpretation that allows us to see that what seems to be natural and inevitable is actually the result of history and various social forces. The work of Michel Foucault, a prominent French social theorist and philosopher, demonstrates this kind of critical theorizing. From his writings in the 1970s, we learn how the contemporary understanding of crime and punishment comes from a specific history of social exclusion that forms the backdrop for why imprisonment has become the predominant mode of dealing with people who transgress social norms (Foucault 1977a). Critical theorizing allows us to uncover this history in order to understand what social discourses (predominant yet often implicit ways of thinking) shape the way that our society privileges certain people over others.

The kind of critical theorizing in this chapter takes the form of a **genealogy**. A genealogical study examines perceptions, **stereotypes**, and predominant social discourses that are solidified by informing how social **institutions** (legal, political, economic) see people (Foucault 1977b, 1980, 2014, 2015; Foucault and Lotringer 1996; Mahon 1992). Part of the purpose of this genealogy is to examine implicit aspects of a colonial legal imaginary, such as dominant metaphors and perceptions that structure what we can call a **politics of recognition** – for example, how legal institutions viewed Indigenous people and treated them in law, media, and politics. I argue that embedded in the way that policing occurred during the early era of British Columbia's entry to Confederation (1871–92) was a pattern of exclusion and criminalization of Indigenous people that has implications for contemporary policing practices. Many images within archival records show how encounters between European settlers and Indigenous **populations** was shaped by the English colonial project to conquer what they saw as uninhabited wilderness. These images and perceptions of nature are significant when evaluating how colonial law was introduced into British Columbia. In this chapter, I examine how these images, experiences, and writings about nature, landscapes, seasons, and weather form the background of early Canadian lawmaking practices.

Methodology

For this research, I conducted **archival research** at the British Columbia provincial archives in Victoria, British Columbia, in October 2015. I spent a week in the archives, looking through court documents and colonial correspondence for significant cases during the 1870s to understand common processes of criminal accusation as well as who and how people were arrested and accused of crimes in Canada before the legal system was formalized. As the legal framework in British Columbia during this time was nascent and gradually solidifying, this was a great exercise to understand how law was changing and how these changes reflected recurrent patterns that still affect us today. **Archival analysis** is important because it allows researchers not only to understand the past, but also to gain a critical perspective on the present by showing the lineage of contemporary practices, perceptions, and social patterns. For instance, if we are to understand how and why Indigenous people are marginalized in law and politics, it is instructive to dig into the past to see the beginnings of this mistreatment.

In the following sections of this chapter, I detail a short history of the relationship between seasons and law enforcement by focusing on two distinct sociological approaches to understanding crime: **positivist** (analysis based on natural scientific methods) and **anti-positivist** perspectives (analysis based on social constructionist methods).

The theoretical perspective that we take to understand crime affects how we govern, develop policy, and understand differences between people in society. I argue that by taking an anti-positivist approach, we can see the history of how differences between people have been understood, and we can even begin to challenge how law and politics have historically excluded people from society.

Early Understandings of Crime

Sociological thinking requires understanding that how questions about society are asked can significantly impact the answer. For instance, if we are to ask what caused an event, we are immediately predisposed to look for variables to explain the event. On the other hand, if we ask "what does this mean?," we are forced to look into very different aspects of the phenomenon we are studying. The significance of this distinction has been foundational in social theoretical thinking since the Enlightenment, an intellectual movement between the sixteenth and eighteenth centuries that was marked by intense philosophical, scientific, technological, social, and historical change. Different frameworks will produce different interpretations because each framework has different starting assumptions about the nature of reality and how we can know that reality. (See chapter one for a discussion of other ways of knowing.)

Deviance

The sociological concept of deviance is one attempt to describe the relationship between human action, society, and history. Deviance, most basically, is a divergence from **normative** behaviour (that is, behaviour that is seen to be normal, moral, and proper). Why do some people follow rules while others do not? Is it something inherent in the individual or is it something outside of the individual that makes people step out of line? Enlightenment attempts to understand deviance relied on positivist (natural and physiological) explanations to search for a universal law that might explain why people transgress social norms and even become criminals. Many of the tumultuous social changes (such as **urbanization** and **industrialization**) to **Western** social life between the seventeenth and nineteenth centuries led to the appearance of visible social problems, such as crime, homelessness, and **poverty**, and these prompted many Enlightenment thinkers to try to solve social and political ills.

Crime and Nature: Positivist Perspective

Cesare Lombroso (1835–1909) is often called the father of **criminology**. Lombroso attempted to show that criminal behaviour is directly linked to nature – both the physiological qualities of people and the natural environment. For Lombroso, criminality is reflected in the anatomy of the individual (Lombroso 2006). The size and shape of skulls, bodies, and congenital differences could all be interpreted as factors that indicated individuals' propensity toward criminality. While this theory has long been discredited, it is significant for two reasons: first, there is still a dominant orientation to this type of causal, positivist understanding that genetics reflect a certain capacity for criminality; second, this model was dominant during the early colonial period and informed much of the legal discourse around developing a specifically Canadian society and people. Like many other social scientists of his time, Lombroso believed in **social Darwinism**, a school of thought that suggested that natural selection occurred not just in nature but also in human societies. For social Darwinists, this process of natural selection meant that human societies inevitably improve (that is, become more civilized) over time as less desirable traits recede for more sociable ones. In that vein, Lombroso believed that criminals were genetic throwbacks to a more savage time (Lombroso and Horton 1968). Hence, in *Criminal Man* he writes: "Born criminals, programmed to do harm, are atavistic reproductions of not only savage men but also the most ferocious carnivores and rodents" (Lombroso 2006, 348). Clearly, Lombroso did not think well of people who committed crimes, but, more significantly, he espoused racist views that were in line with a form of social Darwinism and the **eugenics** (a set of beliefs and practices relying on ideas of racial and genetic superiority to "improve" the genetic stock of a people) movements around the turn of the twentieth century.

Lombroso was also interested in the relationship between the natural environment and crime. In early criminological literature (beginning in the mid-nineteenth century), there is a persistent understanding that there is a causal relationship between seasons and crimes. Lombroso studied the effects of geography and climate on crime rates, suggesting that there is a relationship between crime, temperature, and seasons. For instance, he found that murder, political crimes, and revolutions occur with greater frequency during the hottest months. He explained this trend occurred because of the greater "sensuality" of the warmer seasons (Falk 1952, 202). Essentially, Lombroso and others who took an organic or a biological perspective of crime argued that seasons impact people's biology, causing a variation in the kinds of crimes and in their intensity. For these positivist criminologists, criminality is located in the body and in the nature of the individual, so some individuals have bodies that more naturally cause them to respond in deviant, criminal ways to environmental conditions. (In contrast, for contemporary, sociologically valid perspectives of the body, see chapters five, six, and eight.)

Crime: Anti-positivist Perspective

Another way of understanding the relationship between law and nature is to understand them both as social creations. But isn't it paradoxical to say that nature is social? From an anti-positivist perspective of crime, lived experience should be understood to be fundamentally social. In other words, nature functions as discourse that is shaped historically through the different fields of knowledge, or disciplines, that I mentioned earlier. That is, in order to understand the relationship between the seasons and crime sociologically, it is important to understand the manner in which both are produced through social and political ideas that are situated in history and generated through social interaction. In other words, positivist approaches attempt to find universal laws to explain phenomena, whereas anti-positivist approaches understand that these laws do not exist in the realm of human action. Genealogy, the methodology with which I approach this material, is one anti-positivist approach that helps analyze the importance of social and historical contingency.

Winter and the Enactment of Law in Early British Columbia

A first step in capturing the significance, or meaning, of seasons in relation to law and crime, and particularly of winter and its relation to law and crime in Canada specifically, is to examine historical events to see how the experience of seasons contributed to the colonial legal imaginary. Dominant metaphors, images, and ideas about the seasons, winter, and nature shaped the way law was practised. Rather than looking at the relationship between nature and law in a causal relationship (that the natural environment or human biology leads to criminal behaviour), I am interested in what meaning seasons, and in particular winter, had for the colonial regime and how that meaning motivated particular governing practices that form the foundation of the contemporary justice system.

The Thomas Poole Murder Case

Let's return to the murder case from the beginning of this chapter and the initial coroner's inquest. A coroner's inquest would have been similar to a contemporary grand jury, where a judicial committee evaluates evidence to come to a decision on how to proceed with the investigation and trial, but the committee would have been more informal and composed of community members. At the inquest were men who were considered to be of good standing from nearby communities, as well as the coroner for New Westminster, who had been brought out to lead the inquest. Witness depositions were taken from people in the community and the first accusations were established. In this case, the inquest consisted only of **white** settlers, while the majority of the people accused were Indigenous. From what I've been able to discover, not enough evidence was available to convict any person in the end. Nemiah, an Indigenous person implicated in the Poole murders and associated with other crimes, was exonerated in 1891.[1] An important indicator of social inequalities is the ability of certain people to accuse others of criminality and others who are more prone to having the label of criminality attached to them (Pavlich 2006, 2007, 2016). In this case, it is very clear that settlers can accuse in a way that is legible to the criminal justice system, whereas Indigenous people are more believably accused of crimes.

1 Pemberton museum correspondence, October 28, 2015.

FIGURE 9.1 The Second Halfway House on Pemberton Portage, which was built after the Poole house burnt down. Source: Pemberton and District Museum & Archives, item #p21.14

From my research, it appears the case lasted for more than ten years for various reasons, including the multiplicity of legal **traditions** operating at the same time, the general informality of colonial law, and the conditions of the territory, which made it difficult to enforce laws. First, at the time, law was plural: there was not just one legal system, but across the emerging nation, there were various well-established Indigenous legal traditions and different colonial legal traditions. The **interactions** between Indigenous and colonial legal traditions were characterized by relatively informal arrangements developed through various concessions to each other's tradition (Foster 1994, 2001; Loo 1994a, 1994b; Webber 1995), and thus the system at that time was primarily informal, **frontier law**: legal relations were shaped spontaneously through interactions between colonial powers (English and French), corporations (the Hudson's Bay Company and the North-West Company), and the various Indigenous nations throughout Canada (Webber 1995).

A second reason the Thomas Poole murder case lasted so long was that colonial law was not formally established in many of the communities throughout British Columbia at this time due to the sparsity of the population across many regions, including the Pemberton area. It wasn't until 1858 that a police force was established in British Columbia in response to a gold rush, which began in that summer (see figure 9.1). The Fraser River area was flooded with 30,000 people from the American South, Britain, and the rest of Canada who hoped to find gold; this influx prompted the colonial regime to establish a police force (British Columbia Provincial Police [BCPP]) to help keep the peace (Barman 2004; Downs 2015). It was also in 1858 that British Columbia was established as a crown colony (a colonial administrative region that consisted of a governor appointed by the British monarch), and its first constabulary (military-style police force) was developed by a royally appointed man named Chartres Brew. This small force of 12 men faced considerable challenges, as they policed an immense wilderness area with few roads from the Pacific coast to the Rocky Mountains (Foster 1984).

Finally, since there were so few lawmakers in the region even after the establishment of the BCPP, it could not operate completely formally due to the local geographical conditions. Because of this, different community members had to be commissioned to act on the law's behest, carrying out enforcement and arrests, and acting as a judiciary (grand juries and investigative bodies). Judges and the only coroner in BC had to travel long distances; thus, courts in BC were only convened periodically (periodic courts are called *assizes*) and often trials could not be held until months after the crime had been committed.

The Legal Experience of Winter

Under these conditions, the environment, the weather, and the seasons greatly determined how the law was enacted. In particular, based on my reading of archival material, I have found that there was a distinctive legal experience of winter. Of particular significance is how the weather and terrain affected the manhunts that ensued at different points during the trials. There are two important moments that I found in the archives that expressed the difficulty of finding the accused because of the weather. In 1882, Constable Livingston, the officer in charge of the Poole investigation, wrote to the Attorney General about Charlie, a new suspect, and the hunt for him. Charlie had also been implicated in a different murder some years previously. In Livingston's letter, we see that the hunt for Charlie is complicated by weather, terrain, and lack of people and resources. He writes:

> That in our arrival there found that he [Charlie] had crossed the mountains some time previous and was there encamped on one of the two streams emptying in to the head of the Bute Inlet. Owing to the great quantity of loose snow which had fallen in the lowest layer of mountains the Indians deemed the crossing of them impractical and would not make the attempt.

Continuing, he expresses frustration "after having traveled a distance of one hundred and fifty miles and without having accomplished anything" (GR-0429-01-10). This manhunt continued the next summer and into the fall (see figure 9.2).

The second moment of difficulty in the manhunt in winter is from 1883, when Mr. English, another commissioned individual tasked with finding Charlie, sent a telegraph detailing a different manhunt through the mountains and topography of the western interior of British Columbia that took roughly two years. After a year of tracking Charlie and searching the mountains in the Tsilhqot'in region, they called off the hunt until the following spring, when the snow had melted. The hunt was

FIGURE 9.2 Overlooking Pemberton Portage. Pemberton Portage is where Thomas Poole and his children were found. Image I-57562 courtesy of the Royal BC Museum and Archives.

terminated by the St'át'imc guides because of the threat of winter in what Mr. English referred to as "a very miserable and mountainous part of the country" (GR-0429-01-10). In this way, finding Poole's killer was impaired by the difficulty of the terrain and the changing of the seasons.

In her archival research of nineteenth-century legal cases in the Northwest Territories (then covering much of Manitoba, Saskatchewan, Alberta, the current Northwest Territories, Nunavut, and the Yukon), historical legal scholar Shelly Gavigan (2012, 13) argues that "the land, the distance, the space, the weather, the terrain, the seasons, the location – a 'distinct sense of place' – significantly form and inform the stories" embedded within the experience of the legal cases. The seasons, weather, and topography certainly mark the direction of the Poole trials. The environment, and specifically winter weather, greatly affected how law was practised, understood, and enacted within the young colony of British Columbia. At the same time, the experience of winter in this case reveals several deeper aspects of the relations between Indigenous peoples and the burgeoning settler society in the area. Specifically, by examining how lawmakers experienced seasons, especially winter, in the Poole case, we see how the enactment of laws during this time was fundamentally *colonial*: the inquisitions and investigations notably reflected the ways in which the new colonial laws increasingly marginalized Indigenous peoples. The emerging colonial law made decisions about who was able to accuse and who was accusable, and this decision-making capacity was an important marker of power relations at the time.

In the Poole case, Indigenous individuals and even entire communities were accused of the murders, and it is this "accusability" that shows how **colonialism** formalized patterns of violence and domination through law.

Colonial Law and Adventure Literature

Scholars suggest that the development of colonial law in Canada is closely tied to ideas about nature (Blomley 2004; Harris 2002, 2004). For instance, examining early Canadian expressions of **nationalism**, we can see the romanticizing of a so-called untouched landscape, the harsh beauty of the Canadian wilderness, and of the kind of people who would constitute what was defined as the proper inhabitants of that land (Berg 2011; Mawani 2007; Shields 1991; Valverde 1991). In legal conceptions of nature, there are significant assertions of what constitutes the proper citizen, how they live, and how they work the land. Since the fifteenth century, the Christian church and European royal families shaped how the western legal imaginary understood the land by attempting to express Western European dominance around the world. These understandings are embedded within two distinct legal doctrines that motivated colonial expansion around the world. The first is the **doctrine of discovery**: a claim embedded within the 1494 Treaty of Tordesillas stipulating that governments can lay claim to lands that are uninhabited by Christian peoples; this was soon used in the **dispossession** of lands inhabited by Indigenous peoples. The second legal doctrine is ***terra nullius***, which means "empty land." According to this doctrine, if a territory had not previously been claimed by a (European) sovereign **state**, it could be claimed by another government. Together, these doctrines comprise a "framework of dominance" (Frichner 2010) that allowed for widespread occupation, dispossession, and genocide of Indigenous populations around the world. In other words, the colonial legal imaginary created the legal justification to take land away from Indigenous peoples throughout Canada (Harris 2004). (See also chapter seventeen for a discussion of *terra nullius* and its implications.)

We can see this colonial understanding of nature in adventure writing from that era. A form of literature that was common from the eighteenth until the mid-twentieth century, with *Robinson Crusoe* from 1719 considered the first, this kind of writing provided images of masculinity, romanticized **narratives** of foreign lands, and derogatory judgments of Indigenous people and people of colour (Dixon 1995). In very poignant ways, colonial adventure literature illustrated how **Eurocentric** perspectives of Western superiority helped to justify the prejudices, stereotypes, and negative perceptions of others on whom the colonial project depended. Postcolonial scholars have noted that this kind of writing helped resolve the ambivalences of the colonial project (feelings of unease – not everyone who participated in colonization agreed with how it was accomplished, and they may have sympathized with the colonized).

Canadian Colonial Adventure Literature

An important example of Canadian adventure literature are the writings of British military officer Sir William Francis Butler. Butler was an intelligence officer in two expeditions to the Red River Fort. The task of these trips was to report on the conditions along the Saskatchewan River and to help bring Canadian law and sovereignty into what Butler describes as a solitary, wild, northern climate populated by wild people, **myths**, and irrational customs (Butler 1872). He recounts his travels in the form of autobiographical adventure literature in *The Great Lone Land* (1872) and *The Wild North Land* (1873). In these narratives, Butler romanticizes the landscape and describes Indigenous people disparagingly, as was common in these types of books. In denigrating stereotypical terms, Butler describes the Indigenous people as "savage" and irrational and that these qualities were inevitability subject to the progress of civilization. Butler describes winter as a particularly brutal, but romantic, time. Similarly, he describes the inhospitable wildlife and landscape, even in its harshness, as full of commercial potential. In this, he again reflected a common colonial imaginary of the emerging Canada as a wild land that could not only be tamed but would yield commercial wealth (Willems Braun 1997). Overlooking the forks of the Saskatchewan River in January, Butler envisions a future of trade and development:

> As I stood in the twilight looking down on the silent rivers merging in the great single stream which here enters the forest region, the mind had little difficulty in seeing another picture, when the river forks would be a busy scene of commerce, and man's labour would waken echoes now answering only to the wild things of plain and forest. (1872, 331)

But in the meantime, after hearing news of various wars in the rest of the world, Butler continues to describe his own "war" with the winter:

> It was the close of January the very depth of winter. With heads bent down to meet the crushing blast, we plodded on, ofttimes as silent as the river and the forest, from whose bosom no sound ever came, no ripple ever broke, no bird, no beast, no human face, but ever the same great forest-fringed river whose majestic turn bent always to the northwest. (1872, 335)

Much like Butler's experience of the land as barren, empty and needing civilization's shaping hand, colonialism misrecognized a rich tapestry of Indigenous cultures and the lands they inhabited because they did not resemble the colonialists' way of life (see figure 9.3). Butler's narratives reflect that the images of nature, law, and rationality found in these forms of literature are indelibly intertwined with "colonial forms of power" (Willems Braun 1997, 11). A colonial imaginary has real implications for the law and for people. Legal scholar Bruce Willems Braun writes that when images like the depictions of Canada in adventure literature are "wedded to a western metaphysics of truth, such

FIGURE 9.3 Poole Creek Canyon, British Columbia. Image E-08510 courtesy of the Royal BC Museum and Archives.

representations [of nature and law] could be seen as revealing the 'real' structure of the landscape, and could give rise, in turn, to forms of administration that accepted this as a matter of course" (11). That is, when these images of nature and people inform disciplines of law, they reproduce the power relations of the colonial regime by establishing laws that negatively impact others. Critical Indigenous scholars suggest that an important method of critique is to examine the politics of recognition, as is practised in previously colonized societies, to allow the voices of Indigenous experience and law to finally be heard (Coulthard 2014; Borrows 2010; Tomiak 2011; Turner 2006).

Conclusion

Sociology of law scholar Renisa Mawani (2007) suggests that Canadian law, as it entered into places like British Columbia, was informed by English legal theory, which drew explicitly on specific understandings of nature to position itself as the pinnacle of rationality. This discourse informed the manner in which Canadian/English legal sovereignty stretched its dominion throughout Canada. We can see through travel narratives from people such as Sir William Francis Butler that the Canadian north and the inhospitality of the land contrasts distinctly with the project of bringing law and order into territories that previously were governed by fur trade frontier forms of justice and economic relations. Canada's **identity** as civilized and lawful developed partly in contrast to conceptions of nature, where Canadian legality was believed to be rooted in the new nation's climate and landscape (Foster 1984; Mawani 2007). But from the Poole case, we can also see how the difficulty of the experience of seasons and nature for lawmakers is contoured by the colonial legal imaginary. Employing a constructionist and anti-positivist perspective allows us to see that often very informal discourses and **prejudices** enter into formal law, which sediments and justifies the marginalization, dispossession, and legal control of Indigenous people in Canada. In order to understand the relationship between the law and the seasons, it is necessary to examine the dominant assumptions about nature and the ongoing tendency to naturalize crime and criminality.

Questions for Critical Thought

1. In the Thomas Poole case, how did nature, topography, and the seasons impact the experience and interpretation of law?
2. What are the difficulties of viewing crime through a positivist perspective?
3. What does it mean to take an anti-positivist perspective on law? Can you illustrate this with a detailed example, perhaps from a news story you have come across?
4. Drawing on examples from this chapter, why and how do scholars use archival methods to study the present?
5. Does the colonial legal imaginary continue to inform contemporary relations between Indigenous and non-Indigenous peoples? Can you give examples?

References

Barman, Jean. 2004. *The West Beyond the West: A History of British Columbia.* Toronto: University of Toronto Press.

Berg, Lawrence. 2011. "Banal Naming, Neoliberalism, and Landscapes of Dispossession." *ACME: An International E-Journal for Critical Geographies* 10 (1): 13–22.

Bernstein, Richard J., Seyla Benhabib, and Nancy Fraser, eds. 2004. *Pragmatism, Critique, Judgment: Essays for Richard J. Bernstein.* Cambridge: MIT Press.

Blomley, Nicholas. 2004. *Unsettling the City: Urban Land and the Politics of Property.* New York and London: Routledge.

Borrows, John. *Canada's Indigenous Constitution.* Toronto: University of Toronto Press, 2010.

Butler, William Francis (Sir). 1872. *The Great Lone Land: A Narrative of Travel and Adventure in the North-West of America.* London: Sampson Low, Marston, Low and Searle.

Coulthard, Glen Sean. 2014. *Red Skin, White Masks: Rejecting the Colonial Politics of Recognition.* Minneapolis: University of Minnesota Press.

Dixon, Robert. 1995. *Writing the Colonial Adventure: Race, Gender and Nation in Anglo-Australian Popular Fiction, 1875–1914.* Cambridge: Cambridge University Press.

Downs, Art. 2015. *The Law and the Lawless: Frontier Justice on the Canadian Prairies 1896–1935.* Vancouver: Heritage Publishing House.

Falk, Gerhard J. 1952. "The Influence of the Seasons on the Crime Rate." *Journal of Criminal Law and Criminology* 32(2): 199–213.

Flamm, Michael W. 2005. *Law and Order: Street Crime, Civil Unrest, and the Crisis of Liberalism in the 1960s.* New York: Columbia University Press.

Foster, Hamar. 1984. "Law Enforcement in Nineteenth-Century British Columbia: A Brief and Comparative Review." *BC Studies* 63 (Autumn): 1–24. https://doi.org/10.14288/bcs.v0i63.1189.

———. 1994. "'The Queen's Law Is Better Than Yours': International Homicide in Early British Columbia." In *Essays in the History of Canadian Law: Crime and Criminal Justice,* edited by Jim Phillips, Tina Loo, and Susan Lewthwaite, 41–111. Toronto: University of Toronto Press.

———. 2001. "British Columbia: Legal Institutions in the Far West, from Contact to 1871." *Manitoba Law Journal* 23 (1): 293–340.

Foucault, Michel. 1977a. *Discipline And Punish: The Birth of the Prison.* New York: Pantheon Books.

———. 1977b. "The Political Function of the Intellectual." *Radical Philosophy* 17 (13): 126–33.

———. 1980. *Power/Knowledge.* Edited by Colin Gordon. New York: Pantheon Books.

———. 2014. *Wrong-Doing, Truth-Telling: The Function of Avowal in Justice.* Translated by Fabienne Brion, Bernard E. Harcourt, and Stephen W. Sawyer. Chicago: University of Chicago Press.

———. 2015. *On the Punitive Society: Lectures at the Collège de France, 1972–1973.* Translated by Graham Burchell. London: Palgrave Macmillan.

Foucault, Michel, and Sylvere Lotringer. 1996. *Foucault Live: Collected Interviews, 1961–1984.* Los Angeles: Semiotext(e).

Frichner, Tonya Gonnella. 2010. "The 'Preliminary Study' on the Doctrine of Discovery." *Pace Environmental Law Review* 28 (1): 339. https://digitalcommons.pace.edu/pelr/vol28/iss1/11.

Garland, David. 2002. *The Culture of Control: Crime and Social Order in Contemporary Society.* Chicago: University of Chicago Press.

Gavigan, Shelley A. M. 2012. *Hunger, Horses, and Government Men: Criminal Law on the Aboriginal Plains, 1870–1905.* Vancouver: Published by UBC Press for the Osgoode Society of Canadian Legal History.

Harris, Cole. 2002. *Making Native Space: Colonialism, Resistance, and Reserves in British Columbia.* Vancouver: UBC Press.

———. 2004. "How Did Colonialism Dispossess? Comments from an Edge of Empire." *Annals of the Association of American Geography* 94: 1: 165–82. https://doi.org/10.1111/j.1467-8306.2004.09401009.x.

Lombroso, Cesare. 2006. *Criminal Man. Translated* by Mary Gibson and Nicole Hahn Rafter. Durham, NC: Duke University Press.

Lombroso, Cesare, and Henry P. Horton. 1968. *Crime, Its Causes and Remedies.* Montclair: Patterson Smith.

Loo, Tina Merrill. 1994a. *Making Law, Order and Authority in British Columbia, 1821–1871: Social History of Canada Volume 50.* Toronto: University of Toronto Press.

———. 1994b. "The Road from Bute Inlet: Crime and Colonial Identity in British Columbia." In *Essays in the History of Canadian Law: Crime and Criminal Justice Vol. 5,* edited by Jim Phillips, Tina Loo, and Susan Lewthwaite, 112–42. Toronto: University of Toronto Press.

Mahon, Michael. 1992. *Foucault's Nietzschean Genealogy: Truth, Power and the Subject.* Albany: State University of New York.

Mawani, Renisa. 2007. "Legalities of Nature: Law, Empire, and Wilderness Landscapes in Canada." *Social Identities* 13 (6): 715–34. https://doi.org/10.1080/13504630701696351.

Melossi, Dario. 2008. *Controlling Crime, Controlling Society: Thinking about Crime in Europe and America.* Cambridge: Polity.

Pavlich, George. 2006. "Accusation: Landscapes of Exclusion." In *The Geography of Law: Landscape, Identity and Regulation,* edited by William Taylor, 85–100. Oxford: Hart Publishing.

———. 2007. "The Lore of Criminal Accusation." *Criminal Law and Philosophy* 1 (1): 79–97. https://doi.org/10.1007/s11572-006-9004-z.

———. 2016. "Avowal and Criminal Accusation." *Law and Critique* 27 (1): 229–45. https://doi.org/10.1007/s10978-016-9179-y.

Pavlich, George and Matthew P. Unger. 2016. "Introduction: Framing Criminal Accusation." In *Accusation: Creating Criminals,* edited by George Pavlich and Matthew P. Unger, 1–21. Vancouver: UBC Press.

Platt, Anthony M. 1994. "The Politics of Law and Order." *Social Justice* 21 (3[57]): 3–13. https://www.jstor.org/stable/29766821.

Reiner, Robert. 2007. *Citizen's Guide to Crime and Control.* Hoboken: Blackwell-Wiley.

Shields, Rob. 1991. *Places on the Margin: Alternative Geographies of Modernity.* London: Routledge.

Simon, Jonathan. 2007. *Governing through Crime: How the War on Crime Transformed American Democracy and Created a Culture of Fear.* New York: Oxford University Press.

Tomiak, Julie. 2011. "Indigeneity and the City: Representations, Resistance, and the Right to the City." In *Lumpen-City: Discourses of Marginality/Marginalizing Discourses,* edited by Alan Bourke, Tia Dafnos and Markus Kip, 163–92. Ottawa: Red Quill Books.

Turner, Dale. 2006. *This is Not a Peace Pipe: Towards a Critical Indigenous Philosophy.* Toronto: University of Toronto Press.

Valverde, Mariana. 1991. *The Age of Light, Soap, and Water: Moral Reform in English Canada, 1885–1925*. Toronto: McClelland and Stewart Inc.

Wacquant, Loic. 2009. *Punishing the Poor: The Neoliberal Government of Social Insecurity*. Durham, NC: Duke University Press.

Webber, Jeremy. 1995. "Relations of Force and Relations of Justice: The Emergence of Normative Community Between Colonists and Aboriginal Peoples." *Osgoode Hall Law Journal* 33 (4): 623–60. https://digitalcommons.osgoode.yorku.ca/ohlj/vol33/iss4/1.

Willems Braun, Bruce. 1997. "Buried Epistemologies: The Politics of Nature in (Post) Colonial British Columbia." *Annals of the Association of American Geographers* 87 (1): 3–31. https://doi.org/10.1111/0004-5608.00039.

10 Cracked Ice: Winter, Canada, Whiteness, and the Politics of Sports

NICOLE NEVERSON

LEARNING OUTCOMES

After reading this chapter, you should be able to:

- use a critical approach to examine winter sports culture in Canada
- describe how some forms of cultural capital in sports are more powerful and meaningful than others
- explain how sports are contested activities that are struggled over, challenged, resisted, and transformed
- understand how sports culture is rarely free of politics
- analyze the mass media's role in constructing, maintaining, and sometimes resisting dominant narratives associated with sports culture

Introduction

I played on almost every girls' and some co-ed sports teams in high school (1990–5). I remember waking up early to walk to school in the darkness of winter mornings to attend practices and the misfortune of playing in gymnasiums, where very few spectators could be found. I didn't understand why people didn't come to games to cheer us on. The teams I played on had successful seasons and often earned playoff berths. Many of the girls' games were part of a double-header feature where boys' teams played after. On double-header days for the winter season sports of basketball or volleyball, spectators would begin streaming into the gym halfway through the last quarter or third game of girls' matches. This seemed odd to me but I quickly learned that most came to our games late to arrive early for the boys' matches. Not just that, but often, the girls' games were scheduled for start times that coincided with the final periods of class, thereby discouraging many student spectators from attending. The boys' matches had more favourable start times and were simply more visible.

I didn't know how to explain this consistent pattern of playing in front of near-empty bleachers for both home and away games. I knew the pattern wasn't an isolated one; it reminded me of how bummed I was that I couldn't watch women's hockey or basketball on television, hear about them on the radio, or read about them in the newspaper outside of the Olympic Games and a handful of other events. Broadcasts and news articles on the National Hockey League (NHL), a men's league, were abundantly available – I even collected some players' trading cards with their pictures and career statistics. I wondered why there weren't trading cards for women athletes and sports. When I think back, I knew I was starting to develop my **sociological imagination** (Mills 1959) – an awareness of how my personal experiences were connected to larger structural and cultural issues that were bigger than the games I played. I was experiencing the seemingly innocuous consequences of **sexism.**

Sports are a part of our **culture** that reveals, reinforces, and at times challenges social inequalities and oppression. This chapter uses a **critical approach** to understanding how commonsensical and widely accepted ideas about sports culture represented in the media can be examined and challenged. It uses winter sports like men's hockey and football to illustrate how taken-for-granted assumptions about sports help shape ideas about Canadian **identity**, nationhood, **gender**, **race**, and politics.

Methodological and Theoretical Framework

In this chapter I use critical media analysis to examine the meanings and **narratives** associated with sports culture that we consume during the winter in Canada. A critical media analysis focuses on the perspectives that are often ignored and marginalized in the representation and interpretation of issues and events in the mediated social world. Narratives (e.g., the underdog, the hero versus the villain, winners and losers, patriotism) are storytelling devices and frames of reference that are used to represent the sports that we consume via **mass media.** Examining media content is important because, in our social world, the **consumption** of sports culture is primarily made possible through television and social media reporting on it. Consuming media is also a large part of our daily routines – it has become second nature – and looking at the social world in a critical way involves questioning what seems natural.

In this chapter, I use **cultural studies** as a framework to examine ideas about hockey and its role in nationhood and belonging. This framework helps to explain how dominant culture, or what we consume everyday via mass and social media, reinforces **ideologies** or ways of seeing, representing, and thinking about reality. As parts of everyday culture, mass and social media play important roles in constructing narratives about some sports while ignoring others. Paying attention to what narratives are produced and when they are used (or not) is important because it allows us to understand how common representations of sports create meanings about who plays, who watches, and which sports are valued.

I also use *habitus*, a term popularized by Pierre Bourdieu (1987), to make sense of the winter sports culture. For Bourdieu, a critical theorist, habitus refers to the ideas, **values**, and worldview that we acquire in our experiences with the social world; it is what we use to understand our world and make decisions about how to act and behave in it (White and Wilson 1999). On one hand, sports are a part of popular culture that appeal to mass audiences, meaning that we consume them as entertainment in our leisure time. On the other hand, sports are part of official culture represented in government policies and documents. When we watch sports on television, we are consuming popular culture. When we read federal documents produced by government, like the handbook *Discover Canada*, used by potential new Canadians to prepare for the citizenship test, we learn that ice hockey and lacrosse are our nation's official winter and summer sports, respectively (Citizenship and Immigration Canada 2012). We use and develop habitus as we consume sports. Ice hockey is a large part of our imagined identity (though not uncontested) and there is a habitus or way of thinking about who we are as a people via the sport. Related to habitus is *capital*, a term introduced by Karl Marx that Bourdieu used to describe resources that individuals and groups acquire as they navigate the social world. Bourdieu believed that capital can be economic – the financial assets and materials individuals are born with or acquire. It can be social – the assets we are born with and acquire that connect us to people, places, and things. Finally, it can be cultural – the **tastes**, preferences, and behaviours that one learns through the process of **socialization** that can be used to advance **social mobility**. For example, in chapter twenty, Patrizia Albanese details how **cultural capital** impacts the different parenting practices of working class and middle-class parents. Bourdieu explained that our social networks (social capital), material resources (economic capital), and upbringing (cultural capital) have all informed how we have **embodied** certain dispositions (habitus). In Canada, hockey playing ability and fandom are, for some, deeply ingrained. How and why these things become central to a Canadian "habitus" is what requires analysis.

Jay Coakley's (2015) concept of the great sport myth (GSM) can help us make sense of sports culture. The GSM refers to the belief that sports are inherently good activities that have predominantly positive outcomes for all involved in their participation and consumption. Many of the examples and information in this chapter challenge this **normalized** perspective of sports culture by using a critical approach to make sense of the sports that we ritualistically consume via the media during the winter season. A critical approach thinks about the things that we ignore or fail to see when interpreting social phenomena; it often unsettles and challenges our knowledge about sports culture and broader **social inequality** because it problematizes what is deemed normal in the everyday. In addition, Coakley's work will help to illustrate how sports culture, even in Canada, is a site where social justice and politics are permanently intertwined and in need of our undivided attention.

Surviving Canadian Winter: The Power of Hockey

Hockey is closely associated with winter and has been dubbed "Canada's game" in popular **discourse** (Bennett and the Canadian Press 2017; Holman 2009; McKinley 2014). This connection is also evident in the media attention paid to men's and increasingly women's national ice hockey performances, whether they are successes (e.g., gold medals, finishing first) or failures (e.g., silver medals or not winning anything at all). In 1999, for instance, Hockey Canada (the national governing body for the sport) and Molson Breweries (a beer company, now known as Molson-Coors) co-hosted the Molson Open Ice Summit on Hockey. This summit was created in part to discuss and address the reasons that Team Canada's men's team performed poorly at international competitions and how other countries were outperforming Canada at its own game (CBC 1999; Deacon 1999). The team did not finish first in competitions like the 1996 World Cup (which was won by the United States), and the 1998 Nagano winter Olympic Games (where the team earned a fourth-place finish). That a three-day conference was organized to address the future of hockey in Canada – where the invitees included former players like Wayne Gretzky and Ken Dryden, as well as hockey moms and dads – speaks volumes about the cultural capital of and preoccupation with the sport. The sport also has its history and narratives curated at the Hockey Hall of Fame in downtown Toronto – again, demonstrating its power and cultural significance. Further, men's professional hockey – through the NHL and the amateur event of the men's World Junior Championships – forms a major part of many Canadians' experiences of wintertime television and digital media.

An End-of-Year Tradition: The NHL and the World Juniors Tournament

When it comes to ice hockey, substantial evidence shows that Canadians enjoy watching the sport on television during the winter months (McGran 2017). During the early 2017–18 season, *Hockey Night in Canada*, the flagship television program representing NHL hockey to Canadians and produced by Rogers, boasted an average audience of 18 million viewers (SportsNet 2017). The popularity of this program is important to note because it shows that large numbers of Canadians (nearly 50 per cent) invest a large portion of their time on Saturday nights watching NHL hockey. *Hockey Night in Canada* is a good example of dominant and popular culture as it is an entertainment product that appeals to mass audiences and is a large part of winter weekend leisure **rituals** for many Canadian viewers. Other annual hockey events, like the International Ice Hockey Federation's (IIHF) World Junior Championships (WJC) and the NHL's Winter Classic are also a part of sports culture (featuring male athletes) that many Canadians ritualistically consume during the winter.

The IIHF WJC is a 10-day tournament beginning on Boxing Day. From 2014–17, its matches – featuring amateur male players under the age of 20, many of whom are considered future NHL stars – have ranked number one in terms of television viewership ratings in Canada (Numeris 2014a, 2015a, 2016a, 2017a). The tournament bookmarks the end and beginning of the year by starting close to Christmas and ending just after the New Year. During this period, many families are able to spend time together as people take vacations from work and school. For many people, this tournament is associated with Christmas holidays and is even part of Christmas and New Year **traditions**. The tournament is also unique because it doesn't usually compete with new episodes of popular television drama or sitcom programs, which are often broadcast as reruns – viewers are able to consume something that is new, entertaining, and drama-filled while spending leisure time with family and friends during a time of year when consumption of food, drink, and television is celebrated and normalized. This context allows viewers to consume and participate in sports culture that is accepted as quintessentially Canadian.

The annual NHL New Year's Day outdoor match is another prominent feature of televised sports during winter in Canada. In January 2016, the heavily hyped Winter Classic game between the Montreal Canadiens and the Boston Bruins was viewed by 1.3 million Canadians via television (Numeris 2016a). In January 2017, the Toronto Maple Leafs and the Detroit Red Wings played in the Centennial Classic, which was watched by 1.5 million Canadians (Numeris 2017a). The common narratives used by television broadcasters and those who produce the match for viewers tend to construct a vision of hockey that connects the sport to a love of the land, the outdoors, and a celebration of cold-temperature resilience, all also characteristics of rugged Canadian identity. The event also conjures particular ideas about a nostalgic past – where hockey, in its imagined pure state, involved children and adults playing on frozen ponds and other bodies of water – an experience that is elusive for many Canadians in winter due to **climate change**, geographic location, and overall financial barriers in terms of accessing the resources required to play this equipment-filled organized sport (Johnson and Ali 2017). If we critically reflect on these factors, we should also pay attention to the people who are the characters in the narratives about hockey that we see on television events like the NHL's Winter Classic and the IIHF World Junior Championship.

The Maleness and Whiteness of Canadian Winter: Hockey Narratives

If we look critically at the narratives of ice hockey represented in the media, we can see that the primary protagonists are men – men from North America (Canada and the United States) and Europe (Russia, Sweden, Finland). The NHL has 31 teams, seven that are Canadian, and the remaining 24 American. Canadian players can be found on almost every team in the league. Until 2015, Canadian-born players accounted for at least 50 per cent of all players (Quanthockey.com 2018a). The 2017 numbers, however, show that Canadian-born players accounted for 45.3 per cent of all players in the league, while those from the United States, Europe, and other countries account for the remaining 54.7 per cent (Quanthockey.com 2018a). These players, who are the main characters in the narratives of hockey that we consume and who are so prominently featured in the Canadian winter sports landscape, are overwhelmingly male and **white**. The 2017–18 numbers show that of 982 active NHL players, 22 are black (Quanthockey.com 2018b; Bennett 2018). While reliable statistics on the number of players in the league who are not white or black (e.g., Asian, Middle Eastern, **Indigenous**) are hard to find, it was evident that only 2.2 per cent of players in the 2017–18 season were black. Further, not every team has a black player, and therefore the predominant narratives of NHL ice hockey available to us star white men.

Earlier in this chapter, I mentioned the study guide, *Discover Canada*, that is used by those preparing for the Canadian citizenship test. This official government document also represents ice hockey in the same limited ways as the NHL. In the guide, the NHL and Olympic men's ice hockey teams are discussed in the text and shown in prominent pictures (see figure 10.3). Readers learn that many Canadians watch hockey and that Canadian hockey players are some of the most talented in the world. Men's national teams, and male hockey icons like Paul Henderson and Wayne Gretzky, are discussed and pictured (see figures 10.1 and 10.2). The Stanley Cup, the championship trophy played for in the NHL, and the Montreal Canadiens are mentioned and pictured (see figure 10.3). Readers also learn that women play for the Clarkson Cup, but there is no mention of the Canadian Women's Hockey League (CWHL) associated with the women's game. No picture accompanies the description of the Clarkson Cup. There are no pictures of Canada's highly successful women's hockey players and teams, or sledge hockey teams that feature both male and female Paralympic athletes. In *Discover Canada*, the pictures of hockey only feature men and boys. Men, especially white men, take up space as the sole proprietors and faces of a hockey nation. How can we make sense of this in a critical way?

Such representations and celebrations of hockey in our culture tell us much about who plays, who is valued, and who has power. Power is essential to understanding the cultural significance of hockey in Canada. Many scholars who use a critical approach to examine sports have commented on the rich cultural capital associated with hockey and the ways that it is used to symbolize Canadian identity in the national habitus (Johnson and Ali 2017; MacNeill 1996; Vincent and Crossman 2015; Whitson and Gruneau 2006). These scholars also observe that the cultural capital of hockey, vis-à-vis our widely adopted and cultivated tastes and preferences for the sport, can be a useful site for critical reflection. One way to do so is to think about the different ways that hockey is used to symbolize Canadian identity – through the prevalence of televised ice hockey during the winter months, the ritualized events of the NHL and WJC, and the demographics of the NHL, the most-watched hockey league in Canada and the league most prominently represented as part of our official culture in *Discover Canada*.

Another way to think about hockey in a critical way is to consider these questions: Is hockey Canada's game? If so, whose bodies are playing the game in our collective imagination? Does hockey define who we are as Canadians and what unites us? If so, what does this say about Canada and what Canadians might look like?

FIGURE 10.1 Men's hockey player Paul Henderson. Source: Frank Lennon/Toronto Star via Getty Images

Mary Louise Adams, a sociologist who examines sports using a critical lens, helps us understand how the answers to these sorts of questions can tell us a lot about whose bodies and identities are predominantly associated with images and narratives of hockey. As she explains:

> If hockey is life in Canada, then life in Canada remains decidedly masculine and white. Despite increasing numbers of female players, hockey still makes a major contribution to the discourses of Canadian **national identity** that privilege

FIGURE 10.2 Men's hockey player Wayne Gretzky. Source: The Canadian Press/Mike Ridewood

FIGURE 10.3 The 1978 Montreal Canadiens of the NHL. Source: Denis Brodeur/National Hockey League via Getty Images

> native-born, white men. In its roles as national symbol and everyday pastime, hockey produces a very ordinary but pernicious sense of male entitlement: to space, to status, to national belonging. (Adams 2006, 71)

Adams's use of the word "pernicious" is another way of saying that it is dangerous and problematic to represent and associate the sport of hockey in Canada predominantly with the images, stories, and experiences of white men because these are limited and neglect the histories and roles of marginalized groups like women, racialized and Indigenous people, and those with variable (dis)abilities who also play the sport. Hockey isn't just a game many Canadians predominantly watch on television on Saturday nights, or during the Christmas season, or look forward to during the winter Olympic Games. It is a **symbol** of privilege and **white supremacy** – meaning that white people overwhelmingly have institutional control, influence, and power over resources in the sport. These advantages translate into pervasive institutional dominance over non-white people, as well as another type of dominance known as **patriarchy** – a hierarchal system where men (especially white men) hold social, economic, and cultural power.

I've deliberately qualified NHL and WJC competitions and events with the words "men," "men's," "male," or "males" to call attention to the focal point of each respective event. I've also done so to challenge the common status quo meaning of hockey: The men's game is understood to be the universal unless qualified with "women's" or "sledge." Also, the winter sports culture that is represented in Canadian mass media is overwhelmingly associated with able-bodied white men. If we account for the marker of race (discussed above), we can also observe that in the NHL, white men are overrepresented, as African-American and black athletes account for only about 2.2 per cent of all players and statistics on other racialized players are limited (Canadian Press 2017a). White men are also the predominant owners, general managers, and coaches of NHL franchises (McLaren 2018). In other words, a highly homogenous group of individuals controls the financial and labour resources, as well as on-ice decisions, for an entire league.

The NFL Super Bowl Ritual

The National Football League (NFL) enjoys healthy mid-winter ratings in Canada when playoff matches occur. Five years' worth of ratings show that, on average, 1 million Canadian viewers watch the January playoff games (Numeris 2014b, 2015a, 2016a, 2017a, 2018a). The results of these playoff matches determine the two teams that vie for the Super Bowl. The Super Bowl is the NFL's championship match that takes place on the first Sunday of February, fittingly called "Super Bowl Sunday." In Canada, the event and accompanying pre-game programming were ranked in the top three of all programming based on viewership, seen by approximately 4–8 million people from 2015–18 (Numeris 2015b, 2016b, 2017b, 2018b).

Like the NHL's Winter Classic game, the Super Bowl is also an event of ritual. This ritual often includes preparing to watch the event by buying food and drink for parties, making plans to meet at a local bar or restaurant, and making special dishes to share and eat during the match (Real and Wenner 2017). That the match has a fixed schedule and occurs on a day known as "Super Bowl Sunday" illustrates its similarity to a holiday (Hopsicker and Dyreson 2017) – holidays are ritualistic annual events where the activities of planning get-togethers, hosting and attending parties, and the consumption of food are common. Like other holidays, there is a habitus (Bourdieu 1987) associated with the Super Bowl. As discussed earlier, habitus refers to our worldview, which is based on our experiences and knowledge (e.g., what we know and do not know). The activities in which we might engage in the week leading up to the game – like buying food, drink, NFL merchandise, and other decorations, or finalizing potluck dishes and reservations for bars or restaurants in order to watch the match – are examples of our ability to understand the **norms** and cultural expectations surrounding the consumption of the event. Habitus includes this knowledge or awareness of the cultural significance of the Super Bowl, how to celebrate the ritual of watching it, and the importance of witnessing it. Other parts of the ritual include watching commercials that have been especially designed for the event and the halftime entertainment segment featuring a well-known musical act. The Super Bowl is another example of how power and capital are represented via sports culture. The annual event is not only a ritual; it is a ritual that encourages us to engage in the consumption of goods (i.e., spending money) and culture primarily associated with the exploits of male athletes.

Sports Are Political

Sport sociologists recognize that part of what explains people's reluctance to view sports as political has to do with what Coakley (2013) calls the "great sport myth" (GSM). The GSM encompasses three things: that there is a dominant and "unshakable belief in the inherent purity and goodness of sport"; that "the purity and goodness of sport is transmitted to those who participate in or consume it; and [that] sport inevitably leads to individual and community development" (Coakley 2013, 403). But who defines "inherent purity and goodness"? On whose terms does this exist? If the purity and goodness of sport can infuse or be injected into those who participate in and consume it, then why do competitors and consumers of sports culture sometimes have different experiences? If sport fosters greater individual and community development, why are some individuals and communities successfully thriving while others languish and remain invisible?

Bourdieu (1984 [1987]) believed that sports are **fields**. He used this word to refer to a sociological concept, not the actual fields upon which many sports are played. A social or cultural field is a space that is organized by relationships of power. These relationships of power shape the **interactions** of and products created by individuals and groups that exist in a given space. Those who hold more power also tend to have great influence over the dominant ideologies or perspectives used to organize fields. We could say that in sports fields, men's professional sports are dominant powers in the broader culture when compared to women's sports. We could also say that able-bodied athletes enjoy more prestige than disabled athletes. We could also say that in the field of Canadian sports culture, men's ice hockey is more prestigious and has more influence in defining Canadian identity than women's ice hockey, lacrosse, or wheelchair basketball. The field of sport also historically excludes, limits, and renders invisible intersex and **transgender** bodies.

The power struggles and social inequalities that exist in sports fields are reflections and representations of power struggles and social inequalities in the broader social world. It is for this reason that sports sociologists regard sports as contested activities. This means that sports are a product of the time and place in which they exist. If the non-sports world is characterized by social and political conflicts, these transfer to the world of sports. If we are to truly understand sports in a critical way, then we must understand that while consuming and participating in sports might not be a political act for some, it can be for others. For instance, medals and victories are not the only things that I remember about the 2010 Vancouver Winter Olympic Games. I remember consuming stories about many Indigenous peoples' refusal to accept the tenets of GSM celebrated at the Games. From the perspectives of many Indigenous peoples, the hosting of the Olympics on unceded land sacred to First Nations was a problem that clearly undermined the GSM (Adese 2012; Kaste 2010; O'Bonsawin 2010). Amid the pageantry of winning medals and other distractions, many Indigenous groups and their allies called attention to the disparity between the amount of financial resources and infrastructure invested in the Games and the amount of financial resources invested in Indigenous health, housing, and the environment. Similarly, prior to the opening of the 2014 Sochi Winter Games in Russia, Russian lawmakers made it illegal to spread and endorse propaganda associated with "nontraditional sexual relations amongst minors" (Travers and Shearman 2017). The passage of this law was met with anger and dissent among many in the Olympic movement, citing the incompatibility of the law (specifically, its inherent **homophobia**) with the historically inclusive principles of the Olympic Games.

To Protest or Not to Protest: Sports and the Politics of Speaking (or Not) about Race and Racism

In the 2016–17 NFL pre-season, African-American quarterback Colin Kaepernick began peacefully protesting the treatment of black people in the United States at the hands of the police, the (in)justice system, and broader social **institutions**. In the early days of his protests, Kaepernick sat on a bench while the American national anthem played before games. His protests evolved into kneeling on the sidelines as his San Francisco 49ers teammates stood. In a 2016 interview, Kaepernick explained the reason for his protest:

> I am not going to stand up to show pride in a flag for a country that oppresses black people and people of color.... To me, this is bigger than football and it would be selfish on my part to look the other way. There are bodies in the street and people getting paid leave and getting away with murder. (Wyche 2016)

The words "bodies in the street" and "people getting paid leave and getting away with murder" reference the killings of black men and women at the hands of police officers who rarely have their actions assessed in the courts, and when they are, rarely result in criminal conviction. While Kaepernick remains unemployed in the NFL, other NFL players, largely African-American, have taken up the practice of kneeling during the anthem. On one Sunday in the 2017–18 season, many teams and owners knelt or protested in some way in response to divisive, dismissive, and racist remarks from the US president, Donald Trump (Guardian Sport 2017). This protest was viewed as more wide ranging, as players of all races, owners, and some fans attending games knelt or linked arms in solidarity.

The case of Sidney Crosby and the NHL's Pittsburgh Penguins decision to visit the White House to celebrate their 2017 Stanley Cup victory also demonstrates how sports are political. Visiting the White House to celebrate sports championships is, for some, considered both a great honour and a benign ritualistic practice. The 2017–18 NFL season illustrated how the assumed agreed-upon meanings of ritualistic practices, like standing for the national anthem, could be rejected and contested. While NFL protests called attention to racism and police brutality, the US president responded by referring to NFL players kneeling in protest during the national anthem, who are predominantly black, as "sons of bitches" (Guardian Sport 2017). Both of these spoke to a heightened awareness of social and cultural tensions playing out within and outside of the sports world. Meanwhile, Crosby and the Penguins chose to visit the White House. Crosby claimed that the visit had nothing to do with politics, should not be viewed as an endorsement of the president's policies, and that politics and sports should remain separate. He further added: "I'm pretty aware of what's going on.... People have that right to not go, too. Nobody's saying they have to go. As a group, we decided to go. There hasn't really been a whole lot of discussion about it" (Mackey 2017). These sentiments earned Crosby and the Penguins respect from some (Cook 2017; Steigerwald 2017) because they were separating politics from sport and treating the White House invitation as an unproblematic honour. But Crosby's status quo perspective that sports aren't political and that athletes should ignore social injustice also earned pointed criticism from others because it disregarded the realities of racism and white supremacy in the United States *and* Canada (Ahmed 2017; Canadian Press 2017b). His perspective was challenged by El Jones, Mount Saint Vincent professor and former poet laureate of Halifax, in a viral commentary piece for *Vice Sports*. Jones's (2017) critical response to the issue involved reminding readers of the history of racism in the very place where Crosby was born and raised. Jones writes:

> Sidney Crosby, a 30-year-old man and hometown hero in Nova Scotia, has been defended by apologists who suggested that as a Canadian, he simply did not understand race issues in America. Canada, they argue, does not have the same issues with race.... Crosby himself grew up in a province where black hockey players, descendants of slaves, once pioneered the sport. In Cole Harbour, where he was born, in his own lifetime there were two "race riots" at the high school. If he is not aware of racism it is not because it does not exist, but because he has chosen not to see it.... Crosby's choice to prioritize a photo opportunity with Trump doesn't only harm those protesting in the United States. For black Canadians it is yet another reminder that we are not included in Canada, that white Canadians can safely ignore us and be excused for doing so. For black Canadians who love hockey, or who play hockey, it is yet another reminder that the sport does not welcome them. For all the African Nova Scotians who initially sided with Crosby, hoping he would speak out, it let them know that he does not side with them.

Jones draws attention to the great amount of cultural capital that visiting the White House has in comparison to that of standing in solidarity with those who experience and are disadvantaged by racism. This is another example of how sports are contested activities where cultural capital is at play because a championship sports team's visit to the White House could be considered a harmless celebration, on the one hand, or an example of how oppression (i.e., racism) is reinforced by those in high-profile positions of authority and status on the other. Not all forms of cultural capital are useful or valued in given situations and this is the point that Jones makes in her piece. The cultural capital or awareness of the realities of marginalized and oppressed people was regrettably overlooked for the more palatable and comfortable awareness of the ritualistic visit to the White House. This is also a point that Coakley (2013) makes when discussing the GSM: the GSM works to reinforce the idea that sports are good for all and apolitical. But it is important to remember that the GSM is simply equivalent to the uncritical status quo perspective of sports. In the NHL, whiteness (the status quo) is so entrenched and normalized as a system of knowing and belonging – and thus, sociologically, when we use a critical lens to explain the issue, the league's overwhelming whiteness makes it difficult for the lived experiences of racism and police brutality for non-white groups to be seen as relevant or even seen at all.

Conclusion

In their 2006 book, *Artificial Ice*, Whitson and Gruneau recognize that to say that hockey is Canada's game is to send a message about cultural **myths**, power, and influence, who has them, and why these things matter:

> Myths in any culture have a complex character. On the one hand, they often distil and dramatize the deepest truths about a society and its people.... On the other hand, myths are also often highly misleading, suggesting an abstract, even sacred, "truth" that has little grounding in historical reality.... The myth is true because "everybody" knows it to be true as a matter of belief or common sense.... Anyone who questions the core assertions that make up the mythological system can simply be written off as either a fool or a heretic. (4)

We know that ice surfaces made by us and not the forces of the environment are artificial. This chapter invited you to think about winter sports culture from a critical perspective and to understand that, like hockey, sports in general reveal cultural truths and myths to us simultaneously. This is also Coakley's (2013) point about the GSM. For some, sports reveal an "objective" reality that cannot be challenged. Yet reality is not objective and is experienced in different ways depending on the context of one's life. Sports, more accurately, present limited perspectives of reality that *can* be challenged and sometimes transformed. Sports, moreover, are highly politicized activities that implicitly and explicitly implicate race, gender, class, nationhood, ability, and social justice.

Questions for Critical Thought

1. You have been asked to revise the sports sections of *Discover Canada*, the study guide for the Canadian citizenship test. Using a critical approach, what type of information would you include in the revised edition for each section? How would you begin the process? The link for the Citizenship and Immigration handbook can be found in the References list for this chapter.

2. Consider sports other than ice hockey that you see represented in the media during winter. What is the cultural capital associated with these sports? How might the representations of these sports differ from the representations of ice hockey? What could explain these differences?
3. Think about a recent sports event in the media. How did the representation of the event challenge, resist, or uphold the status quo?
4. What are some meaningful ways that Canadian sports fans can challenge the status-quo belief that sports are not political? What are other examples of how sports are political beyond NHL hockey and NFL football?
5. Think about your sports experiences (as a bystander, consumer, or participant). In what ways were you privileged? In what ways did you encounter barriers? How does the idea of habitus apply to these experiences?

Acknowledgement

The preparation of this chapter was supported with a grant provided by the Office of the Dean of Arts, Ryerson University.

References

Adams, Mary Louise. 2006. "'The Game of Whose Lives?': Gender, Race, and Entitlement in Canada's 'National' Game." In *Artificial Ice: Hockey, Culture, and Commerce*, edited by David Whitson and Richard Gruneau, 71–84. Peterborough: Broadview Press.

Adese, Jennifer. 2012. "Colluding with the Enemy? Nationalism and Depictions of 'Aboriginality' in Canadian Olympic Moments." *American Indian Quarterly* 36 (4): 479–502. https://doi.org/10.5250/amerindiquar.36.4.0479.

Ahmed, Shireen. 2017. "Sidney Crosby's Penguins Are Blowing It by Visiting Trump White House." *Vice Sports*, September 26. https://sports.vice.com/en_ca/article/j5gjd4/sidney-crosbys-penguins-are-blowing-it-by-visiting-trump-white-house.

Bennett, Dean, and the Canadian Press. 2017. "Canada's Game: Everything You Ever Needed to Know about Canada's Love Affair with Hockey." *Hamilton Spectator*, June 23. https://www.thespec.com/sports-story/7346321-canada-s-game/.

Bennett, Donnovan. 2018. "Hope and Hard Work." *Sportsnet.ca* under "Big Reads." https://www.sportsnet.ca/hockey/nhl/meet-flames-assistant-paul-jerrard-black-coach-behind-nhl-bench/.

Bourdieu, Pierre. 1987. *Distinction: A Social Critique of the Judgement of Taste*. Boston: Harvard University Press.

The Canadian Press. 2017a. "Lightning's J.T. Brown Brings Anthem Protest to NHL." *Toronto Star*, October 7. https://www.thestar.com/sports/hockey/2017/10/07/lightnings-jt-brown-brings-anthem-protest-to-nhl.html.

———. 2017b. "Laraque Calls Penguins' Decision to Visit White House 'Embarrassing.'" *Sportsnet.ca*, September 25. http://www.sportsnet.ca/hockey/nhl/laraque-calls-penguins-decision-visit-white-house-embarrassing/.

CBC. 1999. "Summit Aims to Restore Canada's Hockey Supremacy." *CBC Digital Archives*, August 25. http://www.cbc.ca/player/play/1590415504.

Citizenship and Immigration Canada. 2012. *Study Guide: Discover Canada: The Rights and Responsibilities of Citizenship*. Ci1-11/2012E-PDF, ISBN 978-1-100-20117-7. Ottawa: Citizenship and Immigration Canada. http://www.cic.gc.ca/english/pdf/pub/discover.pdf.

Coakley, Jay. 2015. "Assessing the Sociology of Sport: On Cultural Sensibilities and the Great Sport Myth." *International Review for the Sociology of Sport* 50 (4–5): 402–06. https://doi.org/10.1177/1012690214538864.

Cook, Ron. 2017. "Ron Cook: Penguins' White House Trip is about Respect for the Office." *Pittsburgh Post-Gazette*, October 9. http://www.post-gazette.com/sports/ron-cook/2017/10/09/penguins-white-house-trip-2017-donald-trump-nfl-anthem-protests-mike-pence-colts/stories/201710100010.

Deacon, James. 1999. "Sports Special Report: No Quick Fix." *Maclean's*, August 30, 112 (35): 42–44. https://archive.macleans.ca/issue/19990830#!&pid=42.

Guardian Sport. 2017. "Donald Trump Accuses NFL Players of 'Total Disrespect' as Protests Continue." *Guardian*, October 23. https://www.theguardian.com/sport/2017/oct/23/donald-trump-nfl-protests.

Holman, Andrew C. 2009. *Canada's Game: Hockey and Identity*. Kingston: McGill-Queens University Press.

Hopsicker, Peter, and Mark Dyreson. 2017. "Super Bowl Sunday: A national holiday and global curiosity." *International Journal of the History of Sport* 34 (1–2): 1–6. https://doi.org/10.1080/09523367.2017.1348756.

Johnson, Jay, and Adam Ehsan Ali. 2017. "Skating on Thin Ice? An Interrogation of Canada's Melting Pastime." *World Leisure Journal* 59 (4): 259–71. https://doi.org/10.1080/16078055.2016.1216889.

Jones, El. 2017. "Sidney Crosby Should Have Done Better." *Vice Sports*, under "Views My Own," September 26. https://www.vice.com/en_ca/article/kz734y/sidney-crosby-should-have-done-better.

Kaste, Martin. 2010. "Olympics Met with Mixed Emotions by First Nations." *NPR*, heard on "Morning Edition," February 12. https://www.npr.org/templates/story/story.php?storyId=123603649.

Mackey, Jason. 2017. "Sidney Crosby Calls White House Trip 'an Opportunity.'" *Pittsburgh Post-Gazette*, September 14. http://www.post-gazette.com/sports/penguins/2017/09/24/Penguins-captain-Crosby-calls-White-House-trip-an-opportunity/stories/201709240158.

MacNeill, Margaret. 1996. "Networks: Producing Olympic Ice Hockey for a National Television Audience." *Sociology of Sport Journal* 13 (2): 103–24. https://doi.org/10.1123/ssj.13.2.103.

McGran, Kevin. 2017. "NHL TV Ratings Bounce Back with Success of Leafs, Other Canadian Teams." *Toronto Star*, June 14. https://www.thestar.com/sports/hockey/2017/06/14/nhl-tv-ratings-bounce-back-with-success-of-leafs-other-canadian-teams.html.

McKinley, Michael. 2014. *It's Our Game: Celebrating 100 Years of Hockey Canada*. Toronto: Penguin Canada.

McLaren, Ian. 2018. "Ranking the 31 NHL Owners." *The Score*. https://www.thescore.com/nhl/news/1064620-ranking-the-31-nhl-owners.

Mills, C. Wright. 1959. *The Sociological Imagination*. New York: Oxford University Press.

Numeris. 2014a. *Top Programs – Total Canada (English): December 30, 2013–January 5, 2014.* http://assets.numeris.ca/Downloads/December%2030%20-%20January%205,%20 2014%20(Week%2019).pdf.

———. 2014b. *Top Programs – Total Canada (English): January 6–January 12, 2014.* http:// assets.numeris.ca/Downloads/January%206-12,%202014%20(Week%2020).pdf.

———. 2015a. *Top Programs – Total Canada (English): December 29, 2014–January 4, 2015.* http://assets.numeris.ca/Downloads/December%2029,%202014%20-%20January%204, %202015%20(National).pdf.

———. 2015b. *Top Programs – Total Canada (English): January 26–February 1, 2015.* http:// assets.numeris.ca/Downloads/January%2026%20-%20February%201,%202015%20 (National).pdf.

———. 2016a. *Top Programs – Total Canada (English): December 28, 2015–January 3, 2016.* http://assets.numeris.ca/Downloads/December%2028,%202015%20-%20January%203, %202016%20(National).pdf.

———. 2016b. *Top Programs – Total Canada (English): February 1–February 7, 2016.* http:// assets.numeris.ca/Downloads/February%201,%202016%20-%20February%207,%202016 %20(National).pdf.

———. 2017a. *Top Programs – Total Canada (English): December 26, 2016–January 1, 2017.* http://assets.numeris.ca/Downloads/December%2026,%202016%20-%20January%201, %202017%20(National).pdf.

———. 2017b. *Top Programs – Total Canada (English): January 30–February 5, 2017.* http:// assets.numeris.ca/Downloads/January%2030,%202017%20-%20February%205,%202017 %20(National).pdf.

———. 2018a. *Top Programs – Total Canada (English): January 8–January 14, 2018.* http:// assets.numeris.ca/Downloads/January%208,%202018%20-%20January%2014,%202018 %20(National).pdf.

———. 2018b. *Top Programs – Total Canada (English): January 29–February 4, 2018.* http:// assets.numeris.ca/Downloads/January%2029,%202018%20-%20February%204,%202018 %20(National).pdf.

O'Bonsawin, Christine M. 2010. "'No Olympics on Stolen Native Land': Contesting Olympic Narratives and Asserting Indigenous Rights within the Discourse of the 2010 Vancouver Games." *Sport in Society* 13 (1): 143–56. https://doi.org/10.1080/17430430903377987.

Quanthockey.com. 2018a. *Active NHL Players Totals by Nationality – 2017–2018 Stats.* Last updated July 14. http://www.quanthockey.com/nhl/nationality-totals/active-nhl-players -2017-18-stats.html.

———. 2018b. *Active NHL Players Totals by Nationality—2017–2018 Stats.* Last updated July 14. http://www.quanthockey.com/nhl/seasons/2017-18-active-nhl-players-stats. html.

Real, Michael R., and Lawrence A. Wenner. 2017. "Super Bowl: Mythic Spectacle Revisited." In *Sport, Media and Mega Events*, edited by Lawrence A. Wenner and Andrew C. Billings, 199–217. New York: Routledge.

SportsNet Staff. 2017. "Rogers and CBC Sign New 7-Year Deal for Hockey Night in Canada." *Sportsnet.ca*, December 19. https://www.sportsnet.ca/hockey/nhl/rogers-cbc-sign-new-7 -year-deal-hockey-night-canada/.

Steigerwald, John. 2017. "Pens Visiting the White House the Right Decision." *PGH Hockey Now*, under "Opinion," October 11. http://pittsburghhockeynow.com/steigerwald-pens-visiting-white-house-right-decision/.

Travers, Ann, and Mary Shearman. 2017. "The Sochi Olympics: Celebration, Capitalism, and Homonationalist Pride." *Journal of Sport and Social Issues* 41 (1): 42–69. https://doi.org/10.1177/0193723516685273.

Vincent, John, and Jane Crossman. 2015. "'Our Game Our Gold': Newspaper Narratives about the Canadian Men's Ice Hockey Team at the 2010 Winter Olympic Games." *Journal of Sport Behavior* 38 (1): 97–117.

White, Philip, and Brian Wilson. 1999. "Distinctions in the Stands: An Investigation of Bourdieu's 'Habitus,' Socioeconomic Status and Sport Spectatorship in Canada." *International Review for the Sociology of Sport* 34 (3): 245–64. https://doi.org/10.1177/101269099034003002.

Whitson, David, and Richard S. Gruneau. 2006. *Artificial Ice: Hockey, Culture, and Commerce.* Peterborough: Broadview Press.

Wyche, Steve. 2016. "Colin Kaepernick Explains Why He Sat During National Anthem." *NFL.com*, August 28. http://www.nfl.com/news/story/0ap3000000691077/article/colin-kaepernick-explains-why-he-sat-during-national-anthem.

Spring

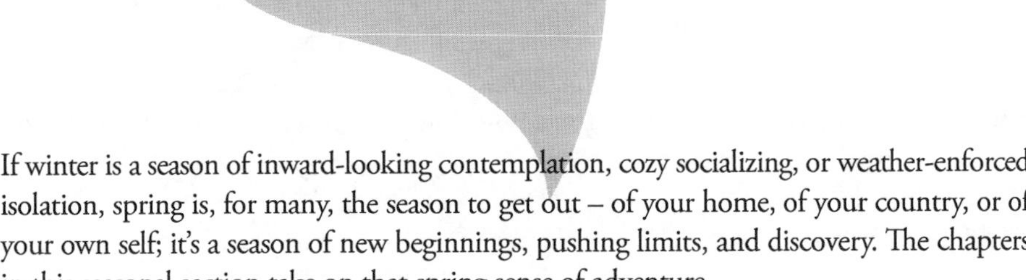

If winter is a season of inward-looking contemplation, cozy socializing, or weather-enforced isolation, spring is, for many, the season to get out – of your home, of your country, or of your own self; it's a season of new beginnings, pushing limits, and discovery. The chapters in this seasonal section take on that spring sense of adventure.

In Canadian agriculture, spring is the season of tilling soil and planting crops, and it's the season for delivering baby animals like lambs and calves. In chapter eleven, Susan Machum details how the natural seasonal rhythms of agricultural life – known as **agrarian time** – have had to be fit into other sets of demands placed on farmers by **social time**, which is the socially agreed-upon way in which we collectively mark time. As Machum shows, our relation to food has changed both spatially and temporally. Due to globalization, the **food supply chain** has expanded geographically while new technologies mean that many Canadians now have access to, and have come to expect the ability to buy, any food at any time of year. In this way, the meaning of time and place – the fundamental meaning of seasons and seasonality – are being reshaped.

Yet seasons continue to shape and describe human lives in ways that might seem surprising and unexpected. In chapter twelve, Rania Tfaily details how births, deaths, marriages, and divorces in human **populations** are impacted by the seasons. Thus, for example, there is an uptick, albeit slight, in human births in spring, and there is a more noticeable uptick in human deaths in winter. Every birthday we have, every wedding and funeral we attend, are data points for demographers who study not just local, but global human populations. As Tfaily shows, the stages of our individual **life course** – including our individual births and deaths – while felt to be very specific and intimately personal, follow larger, predictable, seasonal and social patterns.

In chapter thirteen, Nathaniel Laywine and Alan Sears analyze the **tradition** of spring break in the Canadian university year, and a newer practice of going on a voluntourism-based "**alternative spring break**" trip. Laywine and Sears's analysis of alternative spring break programs offered to Canadian university students introduces how globalization is imagined and experienced in the **Global North**. Imagining and embracing the logic of going to a country in the **Global South** for a short duration to presumably help the needy draws on what Laywine and Sears call "**systems of representation**" – these present countries in the Global South as full of abject **poverty** that students in the Global North could effectively aid during their week-long visit. Thus, spring offers Global North university students a time to simultaneously expand their experience of the world while reproducing existing narrow ideas of what the world is like.

If spring is the season of new opportunities and new life, it is also the season of celebrating those who made that life possible in one way or another. The spring traditions of fêting moms on Mother's Day and then dads on Father's Day are steeped in a set of cultural ideas about parenting. In chapter fourteen, Alison Thomas and Elizabeth Dennis tease out how we imagine and celebrate parenting, the **culture of parenthood**, and how this differs – and is often at odds – with the **conduct of parenthood**, how parenting actually happens and is valued.

In chapter fifteen, the final chapter of this season, Bonar Buffam considers **Vaisakhi**, a Sikh religious and cultural celebration that occurs every spring, marking the new year, harvest, and founding of the religion. Although it was 1971 when Canada adopted **multiculturalism** as official policy, Canada has de facto (whether willingly or not) included a multiplicity of cultures since its beginnings as a **nation-state**. In his analysis of Vaisakhi in Vancouver, Buffam details how politicians have embraced this spring festival as representative of a pluralist iteration of multiculturalism while problematizing how we are to understand Canada's history and current expressions of this ideal.

All seasons are marked with specific forms of social and cultural work aimed at creating, maintaining, reproducing, and celebrating collective life, and spring is no exception. While some of this work corresponds tightly with seasonal changes, other practices work at odds with seasonal changes, as we have collectively designed many aspects of social life to protect us or to release us from the vagaries of nature. In this section, authors consider how changes to our shared world expand and reshape natural and traditional seasonal rhythms, relations, and meanings.

11 Spring Sowing for Fall Harvest: An Exploration of Time in Farmers' Food Production and Marketing

SUSAN MACHUM

LEARNING OUTCOMES

After reading this chapter, you should be able to:

- describe how sequential time guides economic activity and food supply chains
- explain the difference between agrarian time and social time and describe how these two conceptions of time compete for attention in farmers' work lives
- describe how farm families negotiate multiple demands and conceptions of time as they work to balance family, farm, career, and community responsibilities
- apply the concepts of food miles and the perpetual harvest to your own grocery shopping practices
- analyze how technological and social innovations overcome nature and natural growing cycles

If you spend your working life in an office building, you may hardly notice day-to-day weather conditions or changing seasons. Since farmers work outdoors, their daily tasks and activities change when the weather and seasons change. Work is so guided by the seasons that this chapter could appear in any section of *Seasonal Sociology*. It is located in the spring because this is the season that marks the beginning of new life in the northern hemisphere. The soil thaws and gets tilled and furrowed in preparation for planting. Spring planting is essential for a fall harvest, and it is key to bountiful grocery store shelves. The process of moving food from farm to market to our individual family households is called the **food supply chain**. Food supply chains involve a significant number of linear, step-by-step activities, which sociologists like Elizabeth Shove (2009) call **sequential time** because to succeed, each activity must be done in a particular order. For example, it is impossible to cook a meal without collecting ingredients; it is also impossible to harvest a crop if you have not planted and cared for it. Sequential time captures the series of actions required to get food from farm to plate.

Farming's relationship to the three sectors of the economy also illustrates how the food supply chain embodies sequential time. As an occupation, farming is located in the **primary sector** of the economy. The primary sector accounts for jobs that rely on turning elements of nature into raw natural resources by extracting or harvesting these resources (and in the case of farming, also producing these resources). In addition to farming, primary-sector jobs include fishing, forestry, and mining. In contrast, **secondary-sector** jobs transform these raw, natural resources into consumable products. And the **tertiary sector** refers to service jobs and occupations. The food supply chain spans all three sectors in that it follows the production, processing, distribution, and **consumption** of food. Each sector builds on the successful completion of earlier stages. An example of how this works is that potatoes are grown on New Brunswick farms, processed in the McCain Foods International french fry plant in Florenceville, New Brunswick, and then transported, purchased, cooked and served in a plethora of restaurants, institutional cafeterias, and households throughout the world. Without potatoes being grown and harvested, none of the later steps could occur.

In this chapter, I demonstrate how **agrarian time** and **social time** draw farm families' work lives, specifically their growing and marketing of food, in competing directions; to do so, I use data collected from various research projects and **interviews** with farm men and women over the past three decades in rural New Brunswick. My interviews captured individual work-life histories and were aimed at understanding how farm production practices had changed in relation to changing social, cultural, economic, and political processes. Therefore, my **primary data** – original data collected through interviews – is interwoven with **secondary data analysis**. Secondary data analysis involves analyzing and collecting data gathered from other sources. A second form of primary data collection was through **participant observation**. Participant observation is a research technique where the researcher participates in the activities they are studying. In my case, I grew up on a small farm in New Brunswick's lower Saint John River Valley, so my research also includes my personal observations as a food shopper, food lover, and food security activist concerned with making the **global food system** more sustainable, equitable, and local.

This chapter is organized into three substantive sections. In the first section, I detail how agrarian time is a crucial determinant of a farm family's work life. In section two, I explore how social time impacts life on the farm. In the third section, I reflect on strategies farmers and the **marketplace** have used to respond to agrarian and social time constraints.

Farming and Agrarian Time

Whether it is a small market garden or a large corporate grain farm, growing food for the marketplace is the task of every commercial farming operation. Within agriculture, fruit production, grains, vegetables, dairy, beef, pork, poultry, and eggs all represent different industries with their own production requirements and marketing arrangements. Field crops include foods like potatoes, corn, wheat, and other grains. Fruit production can involve planting and maintaining fruit trees for apples, bushes for blueberries, canes for raspberries, or field crops like cultivated blueberries. Even within a food sector, there is a substantial amount of plant and animal variation; for example, there are over 100 varieties of potatoes grown and sold in Canada and more than 250 recognized breeds of cattle throughout the world (Canadian Food Inspection Agency 2015; Successful Farming 2018). This means that for farmers, the exact work tasks in which they engage and the length of time it takes to grow their product depends upon the particular foods they are producing.

To work successfully, farmers need to know and work with nature's biological (including seasonal) rhythms. This led Dutch sociologist Heide Inhetveen (1994) and psychological anthropologist Kevin Birth (2005) to argue that farmers work with agrarian time. According to Inhetveen (1994), agrarian time recognizes that farming involves natural, slow-paced processes. As he explains, "no matter why, what, when, where or how [farmers] work, they have to be aware at all times of the organic conditions ... [that is] the processes of growth and ripening, and the natural preconditions necessary for these processes" (261). Other social science researchers refer to agrarian time as "natural/cyclical time" (Dalsgaard and Nielsen 2013; Grønmo 1989; Negrey 2012; Newton 2003; O'Malley 1992; Shove 2009; Walford 2013). The rhythms and cycles of agrarian/natural time are tied to our everyday experiences of daily and annual rhythms, such as day and night, sunrise and sunset, and the different seasons of the year.

Our experiences of natural time are also affected by where we are physically located on the globe. For example, the closer we are to the north and south poles, the shorter our winter days and the longer our summer days will be. Changing patterns in length of day affect both farmers' daily work rhythms and seasonal growing patterns from one region to the next (Birth 2005). It is a farmer's need to adapt to local natural conditions and rhythms that makes them so acutely aware of their agrarian time cycles.

The importance of agrarian time cycles became very obvious when I asked farm men and women to describe a typical workday. Almost always their immediate response was: "It depends on the season." Why? Because plowing and planting cannot be done if there is 10 feet of snow on the ground. When the snow melts and the ground thaws in the spring, farmers can get out into their fields. Since 1792, the *Old Farmer's Almanac* has advised farmers and gardeners on when to sow particular fruits and vegetable crops according to local growing conditions. The almanac predicts when the soil will be warm enough for seeds to germinate ("Old Farmer's Almanac" 2018), because such information is crucial for crop success. As the National Gardening Association (2018) elaborates: "(spring) crops such as peas should be planted as soon as the ground thaws ... but summer vegetables like beans, corn, and cucumbers ... should be planted ... around May 24 [i.e., around Victoria Day], or if your soil is still very cold, once the soil is near 60° F in temperature" (n.p.).

It is farmers' experiences of relatively stable climate patterns from one season to the next that helps them plan and structure their work lives. While *weather* is highly variable, in that rain, snow, hot, and cold are momentary conditions that can change throughout the day, *climate* is much more stable (Quin 2017). Climate captures expected seasonal conditions, highs and lows, levels of precipitation, and so on. **Climate change** occurs when expected seasonal weather patterns are different from what they used to be and there are hotter, drier summers and warmer winters with more rain and ice than snow (Jolly et al. 2015). Since farmers work outdoors and interact with weather, soil, and biological processes, they are very aware of seasonal weather patterns.

Differences in weather and climate patterns can lead farmers across the country to talk about a late or early spring or fall, a particularly long winter, or a short drying season for hay. And as we might expect from an awareness of sequential time, accomplishments or setbacks in each prior season affect the daily activities of subsequent ones. A field still covered in snow or full of mud in late April cannot be plowed or seeded until everything melts and thaws. Likewise, farmers are not going to spray their field crops with herbicides or pesticides or cut hay if it is pouring rain. Farmers monitor weather forecasts to ascertain if enough sunny days are anticipated to dry the hay they cut or if cold and rain during fruit trees' spring blossoming will adversely affect fall harvests. They also watch the weather to determine if the soil is warm enough for the seeds they plant to germinate. Farmers make daily judgment calls on how to spend their time: if it is sunny today and rain is forecast for tomorrow, daily work activities will be adjusted to take advantage of good working conditions. But if farm fences are broken and cattle are escaping, farmers head outdoors regardless of the weather, even if it is not ideal. Frigid outside temperatures in winter tend to keep farmers indoors. Historian Marina Moskowitz (2009) provides fascinating insight into how seed companies turned this winter "lull" in farm production into a seasonal planning and purchasing period.

In practice, seasonal and daily tasks are integrated. As a rule, caring for animals is a full-time occupation whereas the work cycle of field crops is more cyclical. Dairy farming is perhaps the most onerous **commodity** sector as cows must be milked twice or even three times daily, seven days a week, for fifty-two weeks of the year. There is literally no time off from milking. On top of daily milking, dairy farmers will be spending the spring and summer tending to and harvesting grasses for hay and silage to feed the cows during the late fall and winter months. Seasonal birthing in spring or autumn is another dimension of the dairy farmer's job, but all year birthing is also an option, as it is for piglets, chicks, and even lambs (Akinwemoye 2018). In effect, many farmers no longer adhere to an annual reproductive cycle but rather stagger birthing so as to have a continual supply of their product. Variations in growing and harvesting seasons are a reality for fruit, grain, and vegetables, too. Every species thus has its own biological clock or natural rhythms that farm families need to work with if they want to have a crop to take to market.

Farming and Social Time

Farming, Globalization, and Synchronizing with Clock Time

Working with nature means biological processes are an integral part of every farmer's workday. But farmers are also working with other farmers, food processors, truckers, government inspectors, and many others to ensure their food products make it into local, regional, national, and global markets. Marketing and selling the food they grow ties farmers into social time in a way that would not be the case if they were simply growing food for themselves and their families. Social time is a concept developed by researchers to recognize and study how people have constructed, measured, used, and valued time in different times and places (Birth 2005; Dalsgaard and Nielsen 2013; Grønmo 1989; Negrey 2012; Newton 2003; O'Malley 1992; Shove 2009; Sorokin and Merton 1937; Walford 2013). In this context, time cannot be taken for granted; it requires sociological attention.

Researchers of social time study how mechanical measures of time such as calendars and clocks influence our perceptions and experiences of the passage of time. They argue that calendars, clocks, and watches allow us to mark the passing of months, weeks, days, hours, minutes, and seconds (Grønmo 1989; Negrey 2012; Shove 2009). Whereas researchers perceive agrarian time as cyclical, they see social time as a series of linear, step-by-step processes, wherein we move from time A to time Z, from Sunday to Saturday, January to December, 1850 to 2050, noon to midnight. Our preoccupation in the industrial and post-industrial eras (that is, since about the 1800s) with measuring time – especially in terms of clocking in and out of the factory at the beginning and ending of shifts – has led researchers to call social time "**clock time**" (Bickis, chapter five; Birth 2005; Dalsgaard and Nielsen 2013; Grønmo 1989; Negrey 2012; Newton 2003; Shove 2009). In studying the development of modern calendars, classical sociologists Pitirim Sorokin and Robert Merton (1937) documented how "natural phenomena were used to fix the limits of time periods" (621). Of particular interest here is how early calendars were organized around the harvesting and selling of crops and how market days were prominent as an organizing principle. Quoting Émile Durkheim, they write: "a calendar expresses the rhythm of collective activities, while at the same time its function is to assure their regularity" (Sorokin and Merton 1937, 620). As they note, farmers' daily and weekly work schedules, and especially market day, are organized in relation to other people's schedules. A calendar is thus a tool of social time that helps people coordinate their practices from day to day, week to week, month to month, and year to year.

Synchronizing agrarian harvesting schedules and storage with social time is one key example of how a farmer's work is governed by clocks and calendars. With the growth in supermarkets and the globalization of food sourcing came the distancing of the food consumer from the food producer, according to farmer and food systems researcher Brewster Kneen (1995). For example, it is estimated that the average meal in North America travels about 2,400 kilometres to get from farm to plate. However, recent efforts to shorten the food supply chain to create a more sustainable food system are once again making market day meaningful to Canadians. That is, food consumers and farmers are increasingly sharing a social time that is more closely synchronized with agrarian time. The exact market day will vary in a town or **city**, and some larger centres may have a market that is open daily. For instance, in Fredericton, New Brunswick, the Boyce Farmers' Market is open every Saturday from 6:00 a.m. until 1:00 p.m., while in Saint John, New Brunswick, the City Market is open Monday to Saturday from 6:00 a.m. to 6:00 p.m. Shopping at the farmers' markets, purchasing at the farm gate, or participating in community supported agriculture (CSA) initiatives all give consumers an opportunity to meet the farmers who grow their food. By promoting personal contact, these marketing strategies build rapport between growers and buyers (Marsden, Banks, and Bristow 2000; Renting, Marsden, and Banks 2003; Starr 2010).

Besides selling directly to food consumers, farmers also sell to food processing companies. Some food items – like milk and eggs – are harvested daily and stored on the farm for only a short period before being moved within the food system. Conversely, it takes approximately 100 days for a piglet to reach market weight, so pig farmers space litters to have a relatively stable market supply. Meanwhile it takes spring, summer, and part of the fall to grow potatoes, carrots, and other root vegetables. They tend to be stored on the farm in elaborate cold storage facilities that allow the farm family to control when they take their product to market. If farmers have contracts with local food processing companies, the company will determine when they want a shipment and the farmer will comply or lose a sale or be penalized according to the contract conditions. Food distribution systems are heavily wedded to clock time precisely because multiple actors and activities must be coordinated; the successful operation of subsequent steps depends upon synchronizing earlier ones.

Agrarian Time, School Time, and Tax Time

While farmers' work and agrarian time in many ways can (or can be made to) synchronize with social time, there are also ways in which these different times cannot or will not be reconciled. School bells do not ring according to when farm chores need to be done. School time socializes young children into the work expectations and rhythms of urban factory work rather than the rural, natural time-based rhythms of farm work. Sorokin and Merton's (1937) argument that "systems of time reckoning reflect the social activities of the group" (620) is evidenced in relatively recent changes to the school year in the "potato belt" of New Brunswick. The fall of 2011 was the last year that the school year began in early August so school children could have three weeks off in late September and early October to participate in the potato harvest. Children's labour contributions were critical to the harvest, and social **institutions** like the local school board were cognizant of and accommodated agrarian time. However, in the last few decades, tensions rose over this irregular school year between the rural-farm and the rural-non-farm populations. Those who did not farm wanted longer summer vacations. As the non-farm population grew, the dominant activities of the local population shifted and the political will was not there to continue the fall potato break. Thus, school-age children are no longer exposed to the seasonal rhythms of potato production.

Financial accounting is another example of how farm life is governed by social conventions that are decided by political and economic institutions. Farm finances are tracked on a yearly basis, but farmers must pay their employees on a weekly or biweekly basis, so they must stay constantly vigilant of social time expectations, even when natural, biological processes are the basis of their livelihoods. The need to pay farm bills is not always congruent with when farm products are sold. Bills might be due before crops sitting in cold storage make their way into the marketplace. This occurs often on potato farms where the crop is sold on an open market. Dairy farms have more financial stability because they are paid biweekly by the Milk Marketing Board based on their quota allotment and production; adjustments are made at the end of each month to reflect actual activity. Farm taxes need to be paid by March 1 of each year, but personal income tax needs to be filed by April 30. Tracking these dates and ensuring compliance imposes social, linear time on an industry that is driven by natural, cyclical time.

Gendered Time

Like Inhetveen (1994), because of the gendered **division of labour** in family farm households, I found farm women were particularly challenged to reconcile family expectations and family time with agrarian work time. The frustrations expressed by farm women demonstrate how, in this context (like during the preparation of Thanksgiving dinners discussed by Heidi Bickis in chapter five, and during summer cottage holidays discussed by Tonya K. Davidson in chapter seventeen), women do a disproportionate amount of the labour of social reproduction. For example, one farm woman told me, "I resented the way the barn took priority on all days, even Christmas. You'd even have to time Christmas dinner to coincide with milking the cows." This statement reinforces how biological processes like the gestation cycle, the need to feed animals, and, in this instance, milk the cows shape the home life of farm families. A woman living on a potato farm confided, "my husband has been making a real effort to not bring the business home with him. He works set hours and he is here for the family on Saturdays. He takes that day off from the farm." Conversely, a dairy farmer shared, "farming is a year to year, day by day thing." These two contrasting views of the passage of time – one trying to set clear boundaries between work and family and the other as seeing the two intertwined – reflect the commodity sectors in which these farmers work. "Time off" may be possible in field crop production but impossible when caring for animals.

Bridging Agrarian and Social Time

Ironically, even when farmers discuss the seasonality of their work, they are using a social time construct to discuss and explain the agrarian activities in which they engage. As historian Michael O'Malley (1992) points out, while nature is the source of time for the *Farmer's Almanac*, the almanac itself is a time-management tool that effectively bridges a farmer's agrarian time with their social time. The whole concept of the weekend and associating the weekend with leisure, family time, and time off as opposed to the so-called work week also reflects social and cultural expectations. Clearly, farm families who want this work structure are driven by social rather than agrarian conceptions of time, which suggests a conflict between social expectations and the realities of farm work. Such conflicts emerge because our everyday lives are lived within multiple layers of time – what Helga Notwotny (1992) calls **pluritemporalism**, wherein "many different times exist side by side" (cited by Walford 2013, 22). Kevin Birth (2005, 21) reinforces this idea when he writes, "the possibility of multiple times providing different, and even conflicting, temporal orientations" must be taken into account when building an understanding of how time is perceived, spent, and valued.

Farm and Marketplace Responses to Agrarian and Social Time Constraints

Food Technologies

Multiple conceptions of time are present in the production and distribution of food. The global food system is organized to transport food across time and space. Natural, biological processes place limits on farm production, but many technological innovations have been developed to overcome these constraints. For example, agricultural research and development programs have sought to shorten biological cycles to allow successful production in more limited time frames. This is the case for hybrid plants and rapid-growth seeds that can be germinated and grown in shorter periods of time: both involve adapting nature to meet local growing conditions. Another strategy for overcoming nature's limitations is to extend the working day by erecting large, temporary field lights during planting and harvesting season and/or to extend growing seasons by building greenhouses for early planting of seedlings, which can later either be transplanted under plastic tunnels for earlier spring and summer harvesting or directly into fields. (This strategy has largely shaped the working conditions of the seasonal migrant workers harvesting in greenhouses, as discussed in chapter four.) In a list of strategies to extend the growing season, Roos and Jones (2012) explain how wind tunnels allow farmers to create a warmer microclimate that effectively lengthens the growing season. Wind tunnels warm the soil and keep the air warmer so it is possible to plant earlier in the spring and keep the crops in the fields much later in the autumn. This strategy allows growers to maximize their yields by reducing the impact of cold weather conditions.

In a country like Canada, where seasons limit the length of the growing season, food storage is necessary. Technological innovations have also been used to lengthen the shelf life of foods. Cold storage facilities slow down the decomposition of food, especially root vegetables and fruits like apples, which are more easily stockpiled. Industrial canning, freezing food, and completely transforming food into ingredients for totally new products (some of which may not be food) are other ways that food's "best-before" date is extended. Another technique to extend shelf life is to change the food itself. The genetically modified tomato *Flavr Savr* was designed to have a longer shelf life by delaying ripening. **Genetically modified foods** (sometimes called genetically engineered foods) are foods that have been altered at the molecular level by adding genes from one species into another in a manner that does not occur in nature (Nottingham, 2003). Several food crops, including rice, soy, and corn, have been genetically modified, but the *Flavr Savr*, which came on the market in 1994, was withdrawn in 1997 as a result of public pressure from environmentalists and health experts (Bruening and Lyons 2000; Lang and Hallman 2005; Pollan 2008). However, as scientific researchers Chen Zhang, Robert Wohlhueter, and Han Zhang (2016) note, "Genetic modification is not limited to plants, but is also applied to animal products. Some researchers are exploring transgenic [i.e., genetically modified] fish with a view to enhancing the generation of growth hormones to accelerate growth and body mass ... of salmon ... [with the goal of it growing] to full size in 18 months, rather than 3 years" (121). In each instance, the goal is to have a marketable food product that arrives faster and lasts longer, thus overcoming nature's slow production cycles and rapid deterioration processes. However, the verdict is still out on how safe genetically engineered food is for our personal health and the health of the planet. Many environmental and food activists argue that the risks of genetically engineering the biological composition of plants and animals to speed production and increase financial gain outweigh any benefits, while industry experts and other camps of food activists argue the reverse (Gurău and Ranchhod 2016; Lang and Hallman 2005; Patel 2007; Pollan 2008; Zhang, Wohlhueter, and Zhang 2016).

Food Transit and the Perpetual Harvest

Food processing and genetically engineering food not only increases a food's shelf life, it makes it easier to store and transport food to multiple markets around the globe. This globalization of food production is one reason we do not need to rely on our region's local growing capacity to feed ourselves. Lengthening food storage and growing seasons overcomes the boundaries nature places on food production and allows the lengthening of the food supply chain. Thus, with technological innovations, farmers can push nature. But they are still limited by local growing conditions. The foods local farmers are able to send to market depend on the season or how effective storage facilities are for foods harvested earlier in time. Fresh fruits and vegetables from local sources in New Brunswick are thus either seasonal products or preserved root vegetables and apples that can be kept in cold storage. Yet our grocery store shelves are filled with much more than our local farmers have to offer, and this represents one way that parameters of social time are transforming the food supply chain.

Global food distributors scour the globe collecting, shipping, and distributing fresh products from their point of production to their point of consumption. Food sold in New Brunswick grocery stores is sourced from around the globe, from California to Guatemala to Spain and all places in between. This global harvest, and the incredible distance our food travels (known as **food miles**) makes our grocery store shelves look like we are surrounded by a food system that is in **perpetual harvest**, where every food is in season all of the time. While our global food system is in perpetual harvest, no local food system can ever be, because food production is constrained by local growing conditions and seasonal weather patterns.

Food consumers' constant access to fresh produce and meat that is locally out of season is the result of shipping food from distant locations, where these foods are currently in season. Bringing the harvest to every eater regardless of their geographic location undermines our knowledge of seasonal foods and diets. Consumers often don't realize the ecological cost of having out-of-season food shipped to be at their disposal at any time. New Brunswick farmers I interviewed are always amused when asked by customers at farmer's markets where they can source locally grown bananas or lemons or other crops that cannot be grown in our temperate climate.

As our food supply chain becomes more global, it shifts how we, as food consumers, perceive and understand time and seasonality. When grocery stores never close, there is no sense of day or night, boundaries, or limitations. A grocery store that never closes or slows down and stays open 24 hours a day, seven days a week creates both an illusion and expectation of perpetual harvest, obliterating consumers' awareness of and relationship to nature's biological time cycles. The perception emerges that nature and all the plants, animals, and people working within the food supply chain are constantly at work and specifically working to fulfill the consumers' desires. Of course, from a global perspective, work is occurring at all hours of the day and night. However, in local environs, this is only possible (and even then, only to a limited degree) by controlling and expanding growing and harvesting activities through technological innovation.

Inside the twenty-first century supermarket, seasonality disappears, but not on the farms where the food is produced. Imposing new social time frameworks and expectations that food is available around the clock does not change the fact that local farmers remain constrained by nature, despite their efforts to increase the growing season and improve storage options in an effort to keep their food crops and processed food items on the shelf alongside food imports, on a 24/7 basis.

Conclusion

This chapter has argued that each season brings a new set of farm activities for farm families, whose work is governed by climatic and weather conditions as well as the biological growing cycles of the food being produced (Devereux and Longhurst 2010;

Inhetveen 1994). In short, "agrarian time reflects each seasons' rhythm" (Inhetveen 1994, 264). But farming and the farm family's life are not just governed by agrarian time, they are also influenced by social time. The day-to-day practices and reproduction of the family farm and the movement of food through the food supply chain are socially determined acts. Farmers' "seasonal awareness," as Inge Daniels (2009) calls it, guides them through their annual cycle of events and helps explain why their first response to being asked to "describe a typical day" is "what season are we talking about?" (172).

Seasonal tasks are dependent upon the successful layering of natural processes – that is to say, fall harvest requires spring planting, spring planting requires preparing the soil and purchasing seeds. Seed purchasing often takes place in the winter. Each step is dependent upon the successful completion of a prior one. Even when farmers seek to overcome nature's limits, they remain to some extent constrained by nature. And, of course, farmers' work, family, and social lives cannot escape the social, economic, and political times within which they unfold.

In exploring how agrarian and social time intersect and compete for farm families' time, you have been introduced to pluritemporalism – that is, the existence of multiple conceptions of time simultaneously competing for farmers' and food consumers' attention. Every time you open your kitchen cupboards and fridge to contemplate what's for breakfast, lunch, or supper or in search of a snack, I invite you to think about how different conceptions of time and temporal orientations are reflected in your everyday food choices. Of course, there is an extensive network of people whose carefully coordinated work lives brought this food within your reach, and these people's work is organized and coordinated by the food supply chain. If the supply chain is local, farmers and consumers are embedded in similar socio-cultural rhythms and cycles of natural and social time. But the longer and more global the food supply chain, the more complex natural and social time become as our food traverses multiple time zones and cultural and **social practices**.

Moving food through the global food system requires the coordination of multiple activities, which relies on an awareness of sequential time. Each node of the food supply chain, from production to distribution to consumption, is built on sequentially completing one step after another. Sequential time provides a framework for linking the primary, secondary, and tertiary sectors of the economy; and also captures our social conventions surrounding meal time. For example, we are expected to eat our main course before dessert, and we need to cook the chicken before we can eat it. On a daily basis, time and food intersect in consumers' lives. In this chapter I have shown how this intersection is even more prevalent in the lives of farm families, where spring planting and birthing are critical steps for a successful fall harvest.

Questions for Critical Thought

1. What are three ways sequential time is woven into the food supply chain?
2. How do social time and agrarian time intersect in food production and how do they intersect in your food consumption practices?

3. How have farmers and supermarkets sought to overcome nature's limits?
4. To get food to market, farm families navigate multiple responsibilities. What responsibilities do you negotiate as part of your food consumption practices? Outline the advantages and disadvantages of the "perpetual harvest" on the lives of local farmers and the day-to-day food practices of consumers.
5. Do you think it would be feasible for you and your family to source your food from local farmers? Why or why not? How do your answers explain your relationship to the global food system?

References

Akinwemoye, Akinbobola. 2018. "Management: Pregnancy and Gestation Periods of Various Farm Animals." *Livestocking: Building Great Livestock Farmers*. https://www.livestocking.net/pregnancy-and-gestation-periods-of-various-farm-animals.

Birth, Kevin. 2005. "Time and Consciousness." In *A Companion to Psychological Anthropology*, edited by Robert Edgerton and Conerly Casey, 17–29. Oxford: Blackwell Publishers.

Bruening, G. and Lyons, J.M. 2000. "The Case of the FLAVR SAVR Tomato." *California Agriculture* 54 (4): 6–7. https://doi.org/10.3733/ca.v054n04p6.

Canadian Food Inspection Agency. 2015. "Canadian Potato Varieties – Descriptions." http://www.inspection.gc.ca/plants/potatoes/potatovarieties/eng/1299172436155/1299172577580.

Dalsgaard, Steffen, and Morton Nielsen. 2013. "Introduction: Time and the Field." *Social Analysis* 57 (1): 1–19. https://doi.org/10.3167/sa.2013.570101.

Daniels, Inge. 2009. "Seasonal and Commercial Rhythms of Domestic Consumption: A Japanese Case Study." In *Time, Consumption and Everyday Life: Practice, Materiality and Culture*, edited by Elizabeth Shove, Frank Trentmann, and Richard Wilk, 171–88. New York: Berg.

Devereux, Stephen, and Richard Longhurst. 2010. "Incorporating Seasonality into Agricultural Project Design and Learning." *IDS Bulletin* 41 (6): 88–95. https://doi.org/10.1111/j.1759-5436.2010.00186.x.

Grønmo, Sigmund. 1989. "Concepts of Time: Some Implications for Consumer Research." *Advances in Consumer Research* 16 (1): 339–45. https://www.acrwebsite.org/volumes/6925/volumes/v16/NA-16.

Gurau, Calin, and Ashok Ronchhod. 2016. "The Futures of Genetically-Modified Foods: Global Threat or Panacea?" *Futures* 83 (October): 24–36.

Inhetveen, Heide. 1994. "Farming Women, Time and the 'Re-agrarianization' of Consciousness." *Time and Society* 3 (3): 259–76. https://doi.org/10.1177/0961463X94003003001.

Jolly, W. Matt, Mark A. Cochrane, Patrick H. Freeborn, Zachary A. Holden, Timothy J. Brown, Grant J. Williamson, and David M.J.S. Bowman. 2015. "Climate-Induced Variations in Global Wildfire Danger from 1979 to 2013." *Nature Communications* 6 (7537): 1–11. https://doi.org/10.1038/ncomms8537.

Kneen, Brewster. 1995. *From Land to Mouth: Understanding the Food System*. 2nd ed. Toronto: NC Press Ltd.

Lang, John T., and William K. Hallman. 2005. "Who Does the Public Trust? The Case of Genetically Modified Food in the United States." *Risk Analysis* 25 (5): 1241–52. https://doi.org/10.1111/j.1539-6924.2005.00668.x.

Marsden, Terry, Jo Banks, and Gillian Bristow. 2000. "Food Supply Chain Approaches: Exploring Their Role in Rural Development." *Sociologia Ruralis* 40 (4): 424–38. https://doi.org/10.1111/1467-9523.00158.

Moskowitz, Marina. 2009. "Calendars and Clocks: Cycles of Horticultural Commerce in Nineteenth-Century America." In *Time, Consumption and Everyday Life: Practice, Materiality and Culture*, edited by Elizabeth Shove, Frank Trentmann, and Richard Wilk, 115–28. New York: Berg.

National Gardening Association. 2018. "When to Plant Vegetables in Moncton, NB." *National Gardening Association*. https://garden.org/apps/calendar/?q=Moncton%2C+NB.

Negrey, Cynthia. 2012. *Work Time: Conflict, Control, and Change*. Cambridge: Polity.

Newton, Tim. 2003. "Crossing the Great Divide: Time, Nature and the Social." *Sociology* 37 (3): 433–57. https://doi.org/10.1177/00380385030373003.

Nottingham, Stephen. 2003. *Eat Your Genes: How Genetically Modified Food is Entering Our Diet*. London: Zed Books.

Notwotny, Helga. 1992. "Time and Social Theory: Towards A Social Theory of Time." *Time and Society* 1(3): 421–54. https://doi.org/10.1177/0961463X92001003006.

"The Old Farmer's Almanac: Founded in 1792." 2018. *The Old Farmer's Almanac*. https://www.almanac.com.

O'Malley, Michael. 1992. "Time, Work and Task Orientation: A Critique of American Historiography." *Time and Society* 1 (3): 341–58. https://doi.org/10.1177/096146 3X92001003002.

Patel, Raj. 2007. *Stuffed and Starved: The Hidden Battle for the World Food System*. New York: Melville House Publishing.

Pollan, Michael. 2008. *In Defense of Food*. London: Penguin Books.

Quin, Weihong. 2017. "Weather and Climate." In *Temporal Climatology and Anomalous Weather Analysis*, edited by Weihong Quin, 1–30. New York: Springer Atmospheric Sciences.

Renting, Henk, Terry Marsden, and Jo Banks. 2003. "Understanding Alternative Food Networks: Exploring the Role of Short Supply Chains in Rural Development." *Environment and Planning* 35 (3): 393–411. https://doi.org/10.1068/a3510.

Roos, Debbie and Doug Jones. 2012. "Season Extension: Introduction and Basic Principles." NC Cooperative Extension. https://growingsmallfarms.ces.ncsu.edu/growingsmallfarms-seasonextension2012/.

Shove, Elizabeth. 2009. "Everyday Practice and the Production and Consumption of Time." In *Time, Consumption and Everyday Life: Practice, Materiality and Culture*, edited by Elizabeth Shove, Frank Trentmann, and Richard Wilk, 17–34. New York: Berg.

Sorokin, Pitirim, and Robert Merton. 1937. "Social Time: A Methodological and Functional Analysis." *American Journal of Sociology* 42 (5): 615–29. https://doi.org/10.1086/217540.

Starr, Amory. 2010. "Local Food: A Social Movement?" *Cultural Studies ↔ Critical Methodologies* 10 (6): 479–90. https://doi.org/10.1177/1532708610372769.

Successful Farming. 2018. "16 Common Cattle Breeds." *Successful Farming*, April 13. https://www.agriculture.com/family/living-the-country-life/16-common-cattle-breeds.

Walford, Antonia. 2013. "Limits and Limitlessness: Exploring Time in Scientific Practice." *Social Analysis* 57 (1): 20–33. https://doi.org/10.3167/sa.2013.570102.

Zhang, Chen, Robert Wohlhueter, and Han Zhang. 2016. "Genetically Modified Foods: A Critical Review of Their Promise and Problems." *Food Science and Wellness* 5 (3):116–23. https://doi.org/10.1016/j.fshw.2016.04.002.

12 Spring Babies, Summer Weddings, Fall Divorces, and Winter Deaths: Seasons and Population

RANIA TFAILY

LEARNING OUTCOMES

After reading this chapter, you should be able to:

- define demography and describe demographic research
- identify the main sources of demographic data
- explain and identify the critiques of the Malthusian theory of population growth
- describe how fertility rates, family formation, and life expectancy vary across time and space
- evaluate the differences between neo-Malthusian and neo-Marxist understandings of global population growth

Introduction

> Four Seasons fill the measure of the year; There are four seasons in the mind of man
>
> – "The Human Seasons," Keats (1819)

Many poets and songwriters juxtapose the seasons of the year with the various phases of the human life cycle – what John Keats called the "human seasons." Spring is regarded as the season of birth and innocence. Summer is the season of love and weddings (as Ondine Park demonstrates in chapter sixteen). Autumn is like middle age, a time of reflection and reckoning. Winter is the phase of vulnerability, deterioration, and death. While poets write down their reflections on the seasons of life, demographers conduct empirical studies of the various stages of the human life cycle. Analyses show that the frequency of demographic phenomena such as births, marriages, divorces, and deaths vary from one season to another. The seasonality of demographic phenomena is shaped by socio-cultural (e.g., religious observances; holidays), economic (e.g., agricultural cycles; seasonal migration; vacation months), environmental (e.g., climate; temperature; light intensity), and biological (e.g., physiological responses to temperature; light) factors (Keatinge 2002; Lam and Miron 1994; Rault and Régnier-Loilier 2016). While this chapter is situated in the spring section of this book, I offer an understanding of the human **life course** through the seasons – both the metaphorical seasons of life and the actual seasons. Demographic studies have demonstrated that birth, marriage, divorce, and death have seasonal associations.

Demography comes from the Greek words *demos* (meaning "people") and *graphia* (meaning writing about, or the description of). It focuses on the study of **population** growth, **fertility** (births), nuptiality (cohabitation, marriage, and divorce), mortality (deaths) and migration in human populations. Demographers examine how trends, patterns, causes and consequences of demographic phenomena differ over time and across populations. In this chapter, I begin by defining key concepts and sources of data in demography. I discuss how sociologists and demographers have theorized the causes and implications of global population growth. I then examine the various demographic stages in the life cycle from birth to marriage, divorce, and death in tandem with the changes in seasons from spring to summer, fall, and winter. I focus on changes in demographic trends over time and examine variations in these trends across populations.

Doing Demography

Defining and Depicting Populations

In demography, a population is a group of people defined in terms of specific characteristics (such as age and sex) as well as space and time. For example, we can refer to the population of old people aged 65 years and over in Canada in 2017. Population can also refer to a collectivity of people in a specific location even though the size and the composition of the population are continuously changing (Trovato 2015). For example, Canada's population grew from about 3.5 million in 1867 to around 35 million in 2016 (Statistics Canada 2017c). The numbers of births, deaths, immigrants, and outmigrants (people who leave a specific geographic **territory**/location) determine whether a population increases or decreases, as well as the relative size of different age groups (e.g., young children versus elderly). A graphic representation of the distribution of various age groups in a population by sex at a specific time period is called a **population pyramid**. When the population is growing due to high fertility (which demographers define as the number of children per woman), the population pyramid has a typical pyramid shape with a broad base and a narrow top. When fertility is low, the population pyramid no longer has a pyramid shape. Figure 12.1 shows the population pyramid of Canada

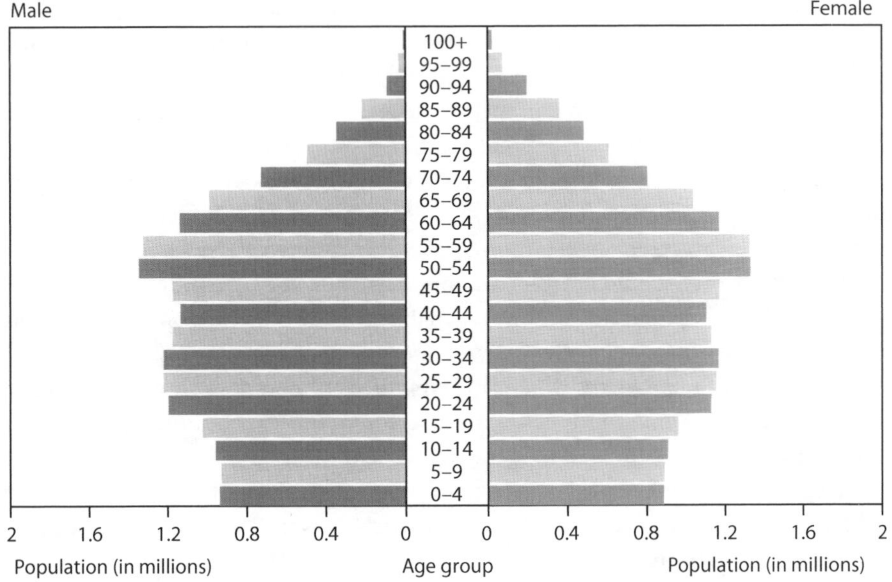

FIGURE 12.1 Canada's population pyramid, 2016. Source: US Census Bureau International Database (2017)

in 2016. The right side shows the number of women in Canada in 2016 by five-year age groups, while the left side shows the corresponding numbers for men. One of the most striking features is that the number of children aged 0–4 years is smaller than the number of people aged 20–24 years. The same is true regarding ages 5–9, 10–14, and 15–19. This is due to the decline in the number of births in recent years compared to previous time periods due to Canada's low fertility.

Demographic Data

Demographers' main sources of data are censuses, vital statistics, and **sample surveys**. Censuses are undertaken to count all people in a given population at a particular time. They are generally conducted by national governments every five or ten years. **Census** questionnaires often include questions about demographic, socio-cultural, socio-economic, and geographic characteristics of a population. Another important source of demographic data is **vital registration** (also known as vital statistics), the system by which governments continuously collect and process information on key demographic events such as births, adoptions, marriages, divorces, and deaths in a population. Some Asian and European countries also track changes in residence which, like vital events such as births and deaths, must be reported to authorities. These registration systems are called population registers. Demographers also rely on sample surveys, which are generally conducted by national statistical organizations or agencies (e.g., Statistics Canada; the US National Institutes of Health), international organizations, or academics. Demographic sample surveys generally collect information from a representative sample of the population and include detailed questions and topics not covered in the census or vital statistics. In recent years, there has been an increase in the use of administrative data in demographic studies. **Administrative data** refer to information collected for administrative purposes (e.g., tax records or medical files), which can be used for research purposes.

Demographers generally rely on data routinely collected by national governments or on sample surveys conducted by national statistical organizations, international agencies, or academics. Nationally representative demographic sample surveys generally have thousands of respondents who answer hundreds of questions. It generally takes a couple of years and significant financial resources to conduct such surveys (this involves designing the questionnaire, selecting a sample, recruiting and training staff, pretesting and finalizing the questionnaire, collecting, coding, and entering the data into statistical software, evaluating the quality of the data, preparing documentation, and making the data available for research purposes).

Theorizing Population Growth

In the song, "What a Wonderful World," musician Louis Armstrong (1968) marvels at spring, roses blooming, babies crying, life expanding. Many share Armstrong's feelings of awe as they celebrate birth and life, especially during the spring season. However, such romanticism stands in sharp contrast to the theorization of one of the most influential modern thinkers on population growth: Thomas Robert Malthus. Malthus advocated for restraint from behaviours that are often perceived as some of the highlights of life: sex, marriage, and parenthood. Malthus equated additional births with misery, particularly for the poor (2018 [1803]).

Malthusian Demography

Malthus, an English clergyman and a professor of history and **political economy**, published "An Essay on the Principle of Population as it affects the future improvement of society" in 1798. His essay influenced many classical sociologists, including Auguste Comte, Herbert Spencer, and Émile Durkheim (Trovato 2015). He also had a crucial impact on demographic policies and the debate about causes of **poverty** and welfare provisions.

Before the **Industrial Revolution**, a time marked by major scientific and technological changes in Europe and North America in the eighteenth and nineteenth centuries, both birth rates and death rates were high globally. As a result, the **population growth rate** – which indicates the rate at which the number of individuals in the population was changing within a specific time period – was low, and the world population grew slowly. While women had many children, most of them died young due to infectious diseases, famines, and wars. Global population growth changed drastically around the time of the Industrial Revolution and thereafter. Food production increased, public health interventions that limited the spread of infectious diseases intensified, and **standards of living** – a measure of economic well-being that indicates the level of wealth, material goods, and services that people have access to – improved. These changes led to a decline in the **mortality rate**, the number of deaths per 1,000 people in a population. Fertility, however, generally remained relatively high for some time. This led to substantial population increases.

Malthus, who lived around the time of the Industrial Revolution, was deeply concerned about population growth. Malthus (2018 [1803]) put forward two propositions. The first is that food is necessary for survival. The second is that humans have a powerful instinct to reproduce. Malthus believed that it is a universal natural law that living organisms (including human beings) would – if unconstrained – multiply indefinitely. However, the need for food puts a limit on such growth, as food production can't keep up with population increase. Malthus believed that population increases geometrically (e.g., 1, 2, 4, 8, 16, 32, 64, 128, etc.), while food production increases arithmetically (e.g., 1, 2, 3, 4, 5, 6, 7, 8, etc.). Malthus argued that unchecked population growth would lead to food shortages. Such shortages in turn would create constant checks on population by leading to misery and deaths due to famine, war, and diseases. It is important to point out that, historically, famines were common (Malthus 2018 [1803]). Famine killed 2.8 million people in France (or 15 per cent of the population) between 1692 and 1694; 20 per cent of the population in Estonia in 1695; and 25 per cent to 33 per cent of the people in Finland in 1696 (Harari 2017, 4).

Malthus advocated for "moral restraint" – abstinence from sex and delayed marriages – to keep population size in balance with food supply (Malthus 2018 [1803]). Consistent with the religious sentiments in England at the time, Malthus was opposed to the use of contraception or abortion as a way for couples to limit their number of children. He regarded abstinence from sex and delayed marriage as morally superior measures to contraception or abortion to control population growth (Caldwell 1998). Malthus also opposed providing relief to poor people or to those suffering from famine or malnutrition. He feared that such assistance would lead to early marriage, high fertility, food shortages, and ultimately more deaths and misery (Caldwell 1998; McNicoll 1998).

Critiques of Malthus

Malthus's essay had a long-lasting impact on discussions of population growth. However, Malthus failed to consider the effects of the Industrial Revolution on the increase in food production. The global population increased more than sevenfold between the time Malthus wrote his essay and 2017. However, at the same time, **infant and child mortality** sharply declined, and standards of living, in general, have dramatically improved. While Malthus disapproved of contraception and abortion, he failed to foresee how the adoption of contraception rather than "moral restraint" would bring fertility levels down. Ironically, despite Malthus's objection to birth control, his writings provided justification for the birth control movement, which led to the creation of family-planning programs designed to reduce fertility rates worldwide.

Among Malthus's fierce critics was nineteenth-century German philosopher and economist Karl Marx, who, along with Friedrich Engels, advanced a critique of **capitalism** and called for its overthrowing. Marx argued that population growth is not inherently negative; rather, the consequences of population growth depend on the way in which a **society** is organized in terms of the production and distribution of food, goods, and services. Marx argued that overpopulation and poverty are features of capitalism. **Capitalists** – those who own the **means of production** such as factories and raw material – are motivated to maintain "an industrial **reserve army**," an oversupply of people who are unable to find work. Such "excess" population allows for capitalists to keep the wages of the workers down and consequently increase their own profits (Trovato 2015). Stated differently, overpopulation and poverty are not due to food shortage; rather, they are symptoms of inequalities inherent in capitalist economies. Capitalism encourages the maintenance of an "excess" number of people who are excluded from participation in the labour force and whose existence facilitates the perpetuation of the meagre wages of workers and, consequently, their poverty.

Neo-Malthusian Demography

Despite the critique of Marx and others, Malthus's theory of population growth remained influential. The fear that population growth was outstripping the food supply and other resources intensified in the 1960s and 1970s as mortality rates in developing countries declined significantly and the global human population reached three billion around 1960 (United Nations 2017a). In 1968, **neo-Malthusian** Paul Ehrlich published the doom-and-gloom bestseller *The Population Bomb*, in which he predicted large-scale famines and a substantial rise in death rates as a result of unchecked population growth. He furthermore called for urgent interventions to reduce birth rates (Ehrlich 1968). Ehrlich's gloomy predictions failed to materialize thanks in part to the **Green Revolution**, which led to a remarkable increase in food production because of the use of high-yield crops, pesticides, fertilizers, and other technological advancements in agriculture (Lam 2011). It is important to point out that the Green Revolution has many critics, who argue that it contributed to loss of biodiversity, ecological degradation, as well as social and economic damage, particularly to small and communal farmers (Becker 2013; Cullather 2010).

The global human population continues to increase, reaching 7.6 billion in 2017. It is projected to reach about 10 billion in 2050 (United Nations 2017b). Recently, Hall and Day (2012) renewed the Malthusian argument that our planet cannot sustain any more population growth because of the depletion of non-renewable energy sources (such as fossil fuels), overpopulation, and the extensive use of fertilizers and pesticides to bolster food production. Boserup (1965, 1981) and Simon (1981, 1996), among others, disagree, arguing that population growth has occurred in tandem with progress in science and technology and that population growth may have, in fact, served as a stimulus for advancements in technology that have led to increases in food production and improved standards of living. **Neo-Marxists** also criticize neo-Malthusians for focusing primarily on population while disregarding the huge disparities between and within countries in the distribution of resources as well as ignoring the legacy of colonization, imperialism, wars, and globalization (Trovato 2015).

The debate about global population growth has important policy implications. If population growth is seen as the cause of poverty and hunger, then governments and international organizations should focus on reducing fertility rates particularly in poor countries. However, if overpopulation and poverty are understood to be the consequences of an unjust economic system and ill distribution of wealth between and within countries, then we need to primarily address the role of the capitalist system, colonization, imperialism, and exploitation. As discussed previously, there are also those who see population growth as beneficial to humanity or what Simon (1981, 1996) calls the "ultimate resource." Regardless of one's position vis-à-vis population growth, the simple fact remains that global population increases are the result of the difference in the number of births and the number of deaths in the world.

Spring Babies: Trends in Fertility

Fertility symbolizes new life and growth; for many other animal species, spring is the season of giving birth and raising young babies, as Susan Machum demonstrated in her discussion of agrarian time in the previous chapter. Fittingly, spring is also the season of peak human births in European countries such as Sweden, where the number of newborns is highest in the spring (March to May) (Lam and Miron 1994). Almost all human populations are characterized by seasonality of births, although the seasonal patterns differ from region to region depending on environmental, cultural, and economic factors (Lam and Miron 1994). The seasonality of births has persisted in contemporary times (Lam and Miron 1996) despite the increased use of modern contraception and the remarkable decline in fertility. Demographers measure fertility by the number of children born per woman. Globally, in 1800, women had, on average, about six children during their lifetime (Lee 2003). In 2017, women, on average, were expected to have about 2.5 children by the end of their reproductive years (i.e., around age 49) although there are significant national variations (Population Reference Bureau 2017). Women are having fewer children in all seasons.

The Demographic Transition Theory

The decline in fertility has occurred gradually, although the timing and the pace of the decline differed between and within countries. One of the dominant theoretical perspectives in demography that sought to explain this demographic change from high fertility and mortality rates to low fertility and mortality rates is the **demographic transition theory**, first introduced by Warren Thompson in 1929 and further developed by Frank Notestein and Kingsley Davis in 1945. According to the demographic transition theory, countries go through four stages. In stage one, both fertility and mortality rates are high and fluctuating, resulting generally in very low population growth. In stage two, mortality starts to decline following **industrialization** and **modernization**, due to improvements in nutrition and public health interventions, while fertility remains high. As a result, there is substantial population growth. In stage three, economic and cultural changes associated with industrialization and modernization lead to fertility decline. However, the number of births is still higher than the number of deaths. The population continues to increase exponentially in size. In stage four, both fertility and mortality are low, and population growth rates are again very low.

All countries in the world have passed at least stage one. One of the main measures of fertility is the **total fertility rate** (TFR), which is the average number of children that a woman is expected to have during her child-bearing years (15–49 years) assuming that the current age-specific fertility rates continue to prevail. Niger exemplifies stage two of the demographic transition in which the **under-five mortality rate** – the probability that a newborn would die before reaching the age of five years – declined. However, the fertility rate remains very high, with a TFR of 7.3 children per woman in 2017 (Population Reference Bureau 2017). Other countries, such as Egypt (TFR of 3.3) and Kenya (TFR of 3.9), represent stage three, in which fertility rates have declined but are still relatively high (Population Reference Bureau 2017). The populations of these countries are expected to continue to grow in the near future. Countries such as France, New Zealand, and Sweden, with a TFR of 1.9 in 2017 (Population Reference Bureau 2017) currently signify stage four: mortality is low and fertility is around or slightly below **replacement-level fertility**, which is the level of fertility at which a population replaces itself from one generation to another (a TFR of 2.1 is considered replacement-level fertility for highly industrialized countries). These wide variations in fertility rates over time and across countries are due to differences in levels of industrialization and **urbanization**, women's educational attainment and career prospects, the monetary and non-monetary costs of having children, access to contraceptives, attitudes and **norms** regarding marriage and child-bearing, and government and workplace policies.

While the demographic transition theory has been extremely influential, it has numerous shortcomings. First, it assumes that countries will follow a linear path from stage one to stage four. It presupposes that the demographic experience of non-European countries (e.g., sub-Saharan African countries) will replicate that of Europe and North America despite vast differences in historical, geopolitical, and cultural contexts. It also presumes that the final stage of the demographic transition is characterized by equilibrium, in which fertility and mortality are low and total fertility rate is around replacement level. However, this is not necessarily the case. Total fertility rates in a number of countries, such as Italy, Singapore, South Korea, and Spain, have been around 1.2

or 1.3 children per woman – well below replacement-level fertility – for many years (Population Reference Bureau 2017).

The Second Demographic Transition Theory

In 1986, Ron Lesthaeghe and Dirk van de Kaa proposed the **second demographic transition theory**, a conceptual framework that describes and explains contemporary demographic changes such as below replacement-level fertility, postponement of marriage and child-bearing, and the increase in divorce, cohabitation, and childlessness in highly industrialized countries (Lesthaeghe 2011). Lesthaeghe attributed these demographic phenomena to the rise of **secularization**, in which religious beliefs are no longer the dominant basis of societal norms, as well as **individualism**, which refers to an increased emphasis on self-fulfilment and pursuit of individual interests. While the demographic transition theory focused primarily on industrialization and modernization as the causes of demographic change, the second demographic transition theory stressed the role of ideational change due to the increase in secularization and the rise of individualism (Zaidi and Morgan 2017).

Summer Weddings: Marriages and Common-law Unions and Demography

Summer, with its nice weather and longer days, is a popular season for love and weddings, as detailed by Ondine Park in chapter sixteen. It is estimated that about 67 per cent of weddings in Canada in 2015 occurred between June and September. August is the most popular month, with around 23 per cent of all weddings (O'Brien 2015). An expensive, luxurious wedding has become the new status **symbol**, signalling the couple's "attainment of a prestigious, comfortable, stable style of life" (Cherlin 2004, 857). Yet despite this prestige, there has been an overall global delay and decline in marriage.

Age at first marriage has been rising worldwide (United Nations 2011), as men and women spend longer periods attaining education and/or pursuing economic opportunities. The increasing expectation that couples, especially men in some countries, should be financially secure before getting married has led to the postponement of marriage. In Canada, the average age at marriage was 31.0 years for men and 29.6 years for women in 2008 (Milan 2015). These trends give credence to the second demographic transition theory.

Although globally it has been increasing over time, age at first marriage is generally much lower in non-highly industrialized countries. The limited industrial and post-industrial development in these countries constrains the education and career opportunities of young men and women, and alternatives to marriages, such as cohabitation, are often uncommon and frowned upon. Based on 2012–16 data, the median age at first marriage for women was less than 18 years in a number of Asian and African countries, including Niger, Bangladesh, Chad, Ethiopia, and Nepal (Demographic and Health Surveys Program 2018).

The rise in age at first marriage is occurring alongside a shift in the meaning of marriage (Cherlin 2004). Traditionally, marriage has served as an economic contractual arrangement based on the interests of the families of the bride and the groom and as an **institution** through which to bear and rear children (Cherlin 2004; Coontz 2004). Beginning in the early twentieth century, there was a shift toward companionate marriages that centre on emotional and sexual satisfaction and commitment between spouses. Since the 1960s, however, companionate marriage has been losing ground to individualized marriage, which is characterized by an emphasis on self-development, personal growth, and individual fulfilment (Cherlin 2004). This shift is occurring particularly in Australia, Europe, North America, and New Zealand. Another significant demographic change is that an increasing number of women in highly industrialized countries are purposefully foregoing having any children. This is unprecedented; childlessness has historically been viewed as a "tragedy and economic hardship" (Comacchio 2014, 24–25). However, childlessness is now increasingly accepted as a viable life choice.

Given the dramatic transformations in the functions of marriage, legal marriages have been declining. **Common-law unions** or **consensual unions**, in which couples live together without being legally married, have been on the rise, particularly in Australia, Europe, North America, and New Zealand. The percentage of couples living common-law has increased in Canada, from 6.3 per cent in 1981 to 21.3 per cent in 2016. The increase has been even more dramatic in Quebec, where the percentage of common-law couples increased from 8.2 per cent in 1981 to 39.9 per cent in 2016 (Statistics Canada 2017a). The percentage of non-marital births, which refers to births in which the mothers are not legally married, has also increased substantially over time. In 2015, non-marital births accounted for over 55 per cent of all births in Bulgaria, France, and Norway (Eurostat 2018).

The historical transformation of the institution of marriage continued with the legalization of same-sex marriage in many countries. The Netherlands was the first country in the world to legalize same-sex marriage in 2000. By 2017, same-sex marriage was legal in Belgium, Spain, Canada, South Africa, Norway, Sweden, Iceland, Portugal, Argentina, Denmark, Uruguay, New Zealand, Brazil, France, England and Wales, Scotland, Luxembourg, Finland, Ireland, Greenland, the United States, Columbia, Germany, Malta, and Australia (Pew Research Center 2017). In 2016, about one per cent of all married or common-law couples in Canada were same-sex couples (Statistics Canada 2017e).

Autumnal Divorce

In the life course, the summer season of love often winds down into the autumnal season of divorce. While all marriages and unions eventually end, either through death, separation, or divorce, the latter is also a demographic phenomenon that is surprisingly seasonal. Family lawyers in Canada report that filing for divorce peaks in September, following the summer holidays, as well as in January, following the Christmas holidays. Individuals who strategically wait until September or January to initiate divorce proceedings are typically those who have been unsatisfied in their marriages and contemplating divorce for a number of years (Bielski 2011). They often wait so that their families could have one last summer vacation or Christmas holidays together before filing for divorce, especially since summer vacation and Christmas holidays are considered inappropriate times to end relationships. Autumn is a more suitable time.

Prior to the 1960s, divorce was generally uncommon. The interdependence between spouses and women's economic dependence on their husbands meant that marriage was women's most viable life strategy; women often could not afford to leave their husbands (Luxton 1980). Until the late nineteenth century, married women in Canada and England did not have the right to manage their own personal property, including their wages, and they were legally incapable of engaging in contractual agreements related to business or commerce in their own names (Backhouse 1988). In Canada, married women were banned from working for the federal government until 1955 (Ursel 1992, as cited in Guppy and Luongo 2015). The barriers to paid employment for women exacerbated women's economic dependence on men, making divorce seem less possible. There were also strong cultural and religious norms discouraging divorce. Couples who got divorced were stigmatized, and obtaining a divorce was very difficult legally in many countries. Restrictions on divorce started to ease in the late 1960s in Australia, Europe, North America, and New Zealand, a period characterized by changes in societal attitudes, increased secularization, a rise in women's participation in the paid labour force, and a surge of **social movements** like second-wave feminism, the civil rights movement, the anti–Vietnam War protests, and the LGBTQ rights movement.

Canada enacted its first federal divorce law, the Divorce Act, in 1968. Under this law, individuals were required to provide proof that one of the spouses committed one of the grounds for divorce, such as adultery, cruelty, rape, or same-sex sexual acts (Douglas 2008; Sev'er 2011). The Divorce Act of 1968 also introduced no-fault divorce, which allowed couples to divorce in cases of permanent breakdown of their marriages based on specific conditions, such as addiction and imprisonment. However, in such cases, spouses were required to have been living separately for at least three years before they could file for divorce (Douglas 2008). The 1986 Divorce Act reduced the required period of separation in the case of no-fault divorce to one year (Douglas 2008). Divorce rates increased tenfold between 1968 and 1987, then decreased slightly in the early 1990s and have been relatively stable since (Milan 2015; Sev'er 2011).

Demographers estimate that about 38 per cent of the marriages entered into in Canada in 2008 will end in divorce within 25 years of marriage (Milan 2015). Statistics on divorce do not fully reflect the extent of the breakdown of intimate relationships, though, as the dissolutions of long-term cohabitating (common-law) relationships, which generally have higher rates of dissolution, are not captured in divorce statistics (Sev'er 2011; Statistics Canada 2018a).

Winter Mortality

The cycle of human life often ends in the winter; deaths in winter exceed that of any other season. The positive association between cold weather and mortality was known at least as early as the fifth century (Keatinge 2002). Excess winter mortality ranges between 5 per cent and 30 per cent in most countries (Curwen 1991, as cited in Healy 2003). In 2013, the number of deaths in Canada during the winter season was 16 per cent higher than in the summer (Statistics Canada 2017b). Cold temperatures trigger biomedical reactions in the body that exacerbate diseases, especially those of the circulatory system and respiratory system, and increase the risk of mortality (Keatinge 2002). The elderly are particularly susceptible to cold weather and the increased risk of death in winter.

Life Expectancy and the Industrial Revolution

While we will all die one day, we now generally live much longer than at any previous time in history. An important demographic measure of mortality is **life expectancy at birth**, a measure that incorporates the risk of death at various ages at a specific year. In 1700, global life expectancy was around 27 years (Lee 2003). In 2017, life expectancy was over 80 years in many highly industrialized countries like Canada, Sweden, and Japan – a remarkable increase of about 53 years (Population Reference Bureau 2017).

Prior to the nineteenth century, infant and child mortality were globally very high. Infant and child mortality were still high at the beginning of the Industrial Revolution in Europe, as urban centres were dirty and crowded, and buildings lacked indoor plumbing and waste management systems. The belief that filth was the cause of diseases led to massive clean-up campaigns and the development of sewage disposal in European cities around the mid-nineteenth century (Kunitz 1987); these efforts reduced mortality rates. Between the mid- and late nineteenth century, the **germ theory**, which identified microorganisms as the cause of infectious diseases rather than filth itself, started to gain traction in Europe and North America. This led to disease-specific interventions such as isolation, vaccination, administrating anti-toxins, and the introduction of water treatment systems (Kunitz 1987). The Industrial Revolution also led to improvements in nutrition and overall standards of living (McKeown and Record 1962). As a result, infant and child mortality sharply declined, and life expectancy increased in Europe and North America. A decline in infant and child mortality did not generally occur in Asia, Africa, and South America until after World War II, when interventions such as immunization and oral rehydration therapy, as well as newly discovered drugs such as penicillin, were introduced.

The Epidemiological Transition Theory

As infectious diseases declined, non-infectious chronic and degenerative diseases became the leading causes of death globally. In Canada, the current leading causes of death are cancer and heart diseases, which accounted for about half of all deaths in 2016 (Statistics Canada 2018b). Omran (2005 [1971]) developed the **epidemiological transition theory** to explain the historic shift from deaths predominantly occurring at infancy and childhood from famine and infectious diseases to deaths at old age due to chronic and degenerative diseases (Trovato 2015). Life expectancy increased from around 20 to 30 years in the period prior to the Industrial Revolution to around 50 years by early 1920, and then to about 70 years by the 1960s in highly industrialized countries (Omran 2005 [1971]; Trovato 2015). Life expectancy continued to increase in the late twentieth century and early twenty-first century due to declines in **age-specific death rates** at old age (i.e., death rates for those aged 65 and over). The onset of chronic and degenerative diseases has shifted to older ages, especially in highly industrialized countries, due to advances in medical technology and public health measures (Olshansky and Ault 1986). In 2017, life expectancy at birth for women reached 89 years in San Marino (the highest in the world), 87 in Japan, and 84 in Canada (Population Reference Bureau 2017). However, there are large national disparities in this measurement. In 2017, life expectancy at birth for men was below 55 years in a number of sub-Saharan African countries, such as Chad, Côte D'Ivoire, Nigeria, and Sierra Leone, while it was over 80 years in Iceland, Italy, Japan, Luxembourg, Norway, Singapore, Sweden, and Switzerland (Population Reference Bureau 2017).

The epidemiological transition theory is a useful model for describing the historic shift in the causes of mortality over time; however, it assumes that there is a linear and irreversible increase in life expectancy. It does not envision a scenario leading to the stagnation or decline in life expectancy, as has happened in sub-Saharan Africa due to HIV/AIDS and in Russia following the collapse of the Soviet Union and the consequent erosion of the social and economic safety net and the increase in alcohol consumption. The epidemiological theory also does not address the wide racial, ethnic. and socio-economic disparities in mortality and life expectancy within nations. In Canada, life expectancy at birth for 2017 was estimated at 64 years for Inuit men and 73 years for Inuit women, while the corresponding numbers for the total Canadian population was 79 years for men and 83 years for women; a staggering difference of 15 years in the case of men and 10 years in the case of women (Statistics Canada 2015).

An important consequence of the increase in life expectancy and especially the decline in fertility is that the percentage of people aged 65 and above has been significantly increasing in highly industrialized countries. In other words, countries like Canada are increasingly populated by people in the winter of their lives. This phenomenon is referred to as **population aging**. The percentage of people aged 65 and over in Canada doubled from 8 per cent in 1971 to 16.9 per cent in 2016 (Statistics Canada 2012, 2017d). This demographic shift requires sociologists and policy makers to ask many questions about how to support an aging population.

A related issue that continues to generate intense debate is whether life expectancy will continue to increase or whether we have reached the limit. Further substantial increases in life expectancy would require medical breakthroughs that would reduce mortality at old age, as infant and child mortality is already very low in highly industrialized countries. Some demographers point out that obesity, unhealthy lifestyles, and, more recently, the opioid epidemic and emerging infectious diseases will dampen future increases in life expectancy or even reverse the trend. For instance, there was a slight decline in life expectancy for men in the United States in 2015 and 2016 (Kochanek et al. 2017; Xu et al. 2016). Others argue that life expectancy will continue to increase at the same pace and that advancement in longevity research will allow for the slowing or even reversing of aging in humans in the near future (Vaupel 2010).

Conclusion

The human life cycle corresponds with the four seasons. In European countries like Sweden, spring is a season for birth; summer is the season for love and weddings, while the beginning of fall is marked by an uptick in divorce. Finally, there is a greater likelihood of death in winter.

While the cyclical nature of the life course presents a calming stability, demographically, the world today is very different from Malthus's time not only in terms of the number of people alive but also in terms of fertility, marriage, and mortality rates. Globally, fertility has declined from about six children per woman in 1800 to about 2.5 children per woman in 2017, and life expectancy increased from about 27 years in 1700 to 70 years for men and 74 years for women in 2017 (Lee 2003; Population Reference Bureau 2017). An increasing number of men and women in highly industrialized countries are postponing or even foregoing marriage in favour of cohabitation or other living arrangements. Marriage has also generally become less stable. Questions about population growth, inequality in the distribution of wealth and resources, and the sustainability of the environment continue to generate passionate year-round debate. And while births, unions, separations, and deaths seem as natural as the changing seasons, demographers demonstrate how these phenomena are deeply impacted by social, economic, technological, and ideational changes.

Questions for Critical Thought

1. Do you think that Malthus's arguments and views are relevant today?
2. How can the data used by demographers, such as censuses, vital statistics, and sample surveys help us to answer questions about seasonal demographic phenomena?
3. Should countries try to reduce high fertility? If so, how? If not, why?

4. Is low fertility in countries such as South Korea, Japan, Italy, and Spain a problem? Should countries with low fertility encourage their citizens to have more children? Why or why not?
5. Should society invest in research and medical technology to increase life expectancy to 100 years or even 150 years? Why or why not?

References

Armstrong, Louis. 1968. "What a Wonderful World." Lyrics. https://www.lyrics.com/lyric/1623275/Louis+Armstrong/What+a+Wonderful+World.

Backhouse, Constance B. 1988. "Married Women's Property Law in Nineteenth-Century Canada." *Law and History Review* 6 (2): 211–57. https://doi.org/10.2307/743684.

Becker, Stan. 2013. "Has the World Really Survived the Population Bomb? (Commentary on 'How the World Survived the Population Bomb: Lessons from 50 Years of Extraordinary Demographic History')." *Demography* 50 (6): 2173–81. https://doi.org/10.1007/s13524-013-0236-y.

Bielski, Zosia. 2011. "Hello September, So Long Spouse." *Globe and Mail*, September 1. https://www.theglobeandmail.com/life/relationships/hello-september-so-long-spouse/article592926/.

Boserup, Esther. 1965. *The Conditions of Agricultural Growth*. Chicago: Aldine.

———. 1981. *Population and Technological Change: A Study of Long-Term Trends*. Chicago: University of Chicago Press.

Caldwell, John C. 1998. "Malthus and the Less Developed World: The Pivotal Role of India." *Population and Development Review* 24 (4): 675–96. https://doi.org/10.2307/2808021.

Cherlin, Andrew J. 2004. "The Deinstitutionalization of American Marriage." *Journal of Marriage and Family* 66 (4): 848–61. https://doi.org/10.1111/j.0022-2445.2004.00058.x.

Comacchio, Cynthia. 2014. "Canada's Families: Historical and Contemporary Variations." In *Canadian Families Today: New Perspectives*, 3rd ed., edited by David Cheal and Patrizia Albanese, 22–42. Don Mills: Oxford University Press.

Coontz, Stephanie. 2004. "The World Historical Transformation of Marriage." *Journal of Marriage and Family* 66 (4): 974–79. https://doi.org/10.1111/j.0022-2445.2004.00067.x.

Cullather, Nick. 2010. *The Hungry World: America's Cold War Battle against Poverty in Asia*. Cambridge: Harvard University Press.

Curwen, Michael. 1991. "Excess Winter Mortality: A British Phenomenon?" *Health Trends* 22: 169–75.

Demographic and Health Surveys Program. 2018. *Median Age at First Marriage [Women]*. 25–49, custom data acquired on June 1, 2018. https://www.statcompiler.com/en/.

Douglas, Kristen. 2008. *Divorce Law in Canada*. Library of Parliament Current Issue Review 96-3E.

Ehrlich, Paul. 1968. *The Population Bomb*. New York: Ballantine Books.

Eurostat. 2018. *Marriage and Divorce Statistics*. http://ec.europa.eu/eurostat/statistics-explained/index.php/Marriage_and_divorce_statistics#A_rise_in_births_outside_marriage.

Guppy, Neil and Nicole Luongo. 2015. "The Rise and Stall of Canada's Gender-Equity Revolution." *Canadian Review of Sociology* 52 (3): 241–65. https://doi.org/10.1111/cars.12076.

Hall, Charles A.S., and John W. Day, Jr. 2009. "Revisiting the Limits to Growth after Peak Oil." *American Scientist* 97 (3): 230–37. https://doi.org/10.1511/2009.78.230.

Harari, Yuval Noah. 2017. *Homo Deus: A Brief History of Tomorrow*. New York: HarperCollins Publishers.

Healy, Jonathan D. 2003. "Excess Winter Mortality in Europe: A Cross Country Analysis Identifying Key Risk Factors." *Journal of Epidemiology and Community Health* 57 (10): 784–89. https://doi.org/10.1136/jech.57.10.784.

Keatinge, W.R. 2002. "Winter Mortality and its Causes." *International Journal of Circumpolar Health* 61 (4): 292–99. https://doi.org/10.3402/ijch.v61i4.17477.

Keats, John. 1819. "The Human Seasons." Representative Poetry Online, University of Toronto Libraries. https://rpo.library.utoronto.ca/poems/human-seasons.

Kochanek, Kenneth D., Sherry L. Murphy, Jiaquan Xu, and Elizabeth Arias. 2017. *Mortality in the United States, 2016*. NCHS Data Brief no 293. Hyattsville, MD: National Center for Health Statistics. https://www.cdc.gov/nchs/products/databriefs/db293.htm.

Kunitz, Stephen J. 1987. "Explanations and Ideologies of Mortality Patterns." *Population and Development Review* 13 (3): 379–408. https://doi.org/10.2307/1973132.

Lam, David. 2011. "How the World Survived the Population Bomb: Lessons from 50 Years of Extraordinary Demographic History." *Demography* 48 (4): 1231–62. https://doi.org/10.1007/s13524-011-0070-z.

Lam, David A., and Jeffrey A. Miron. 1994. "Global Patterns of Seasonal Variation in Human Fertility." *Annals of the New York Academy of Sciences* 709: 9–28. https://doi.org/10.1111/j.1749-6632.1994.tb30385.x.

———. 1996. "The Effects of Temperature on Human Fertility." *Demography* 33 (3): 291–305. https://doi.org/10.2307/2061762.

Lee, Ronald. 2003. "The Demographic Transition: Three Centuries of Fundamental Change." *Journal of Economic Perspectives* 17 (4): 167–90. https://doi.org/10.1257/089533003772034943.

Lesthaeghe, Ron. 2011. "The 'Second Demographic Transition': A Conceptual Map for the Understanding of Late Modern Demographic Developments in Fertility and Family Formation." *Historical Social Research* 36 (2): 179–218.

Luxton, Meg. 1980. *More than a Labour of Love. Three Generations of Women's Work in the Home*. Toronto: Women's Press.

Malthus, Thomas Robert. 2018 [1803]. *An Essay on the Principle of Population: The 1803 Edition*. Edited by Shannon C. Stimson. New York: Yale University Press.

McKeown, Thomas, and R.G. Record. 1962. "Reasons for the Decline of Mortality in England and Wales during the Nineteenth Century." *Population Studies* 16 (2): 94–122. https://doi.org/10.1080/00324728.1962.10414870.

McNicoll, Geoffrey. 1998. "Malthus for the Twenty-First Century." *Population and Development Review* 24 (2): 309–16. https://doi.org/10.2307/2807976.

Milan, Anne. 2015. *Marital Status: Overview, 2011*. Ottawa: Statistics Canada. http://www.statcan.gc.ca/pub/91-209-x/2013001/article/11788-eng.htm.

O'Brien, Jen. 2015. "Wedding Trends in Canada 2015." *WeddingBells*. https://weddingbells.ca/planning/wedding-trends-in-canada-2015/.

Olshansky, S. Jay, and A. Brian Ault 1986. "The Fourth Stage of the Epidemiologic Transition: The Age of Delayed Degenerative Diseases." *Milbank Quarterly* 64 (3): 355–91. https://doi.org/10.2307/3350025.

Omran, Abdel R. 2005 [1971]. "The Epidemiological Transition: A Theory of the Epidemiology of Population Change." *Milbank Quarterly* 83 (4): 731–57. https://doi.org/10.1111/j.1468-0009.2005.00398.x.

Pew Research Center. 2017. "Same-Sex Marriage around the World." http://www.pewforum.org/2017/08/08/gay-marriage-around-the-world-2013/.

Population Reference Bureau. 2017. *World Population Data Sheet.* Washington, DC: Population Reference Bureau. http://www.prb.org/pdf17/2017_World_Population.pdf.

Rault, Wilfried, and Arnaud Régnier-Loilier. 2016. "Seasonality of Marriages, Past and Present." *Population* 71 (4): 675–99. https://doi.org/10.3917/popu.1604.0719.

Sev'er, Aysan. 2011. "Marriage-go-around: Divorce and Remarriage in Canada." In *Canadian Families: Diversity, Conflict, and Change*, 4th ed., edited by Nancy Mandell and Ann Duffy, 243–73. Toronto: Nelson Education.

Simon, Julian L. 1981. *The Ultimate Resource.* Princeton: Princeton University Press.

———. 1996. *The Ultimate Resource 2.* Princeton: Princeton University Press.

Statistics Canada. 2012. *Seniors.* http://www.statcan.gc.ca/pub/11-402-x/2011000/pdf/seniors-aines-eng.pdf.

———. 2015. *Life Expectancy.* https://www.statcan.gc.ca/pub/89-645-x/2010001/life-expectancy-esperance-vie-eng.htm.

———. 2017a. *Families, Household and Marital Status: Key Results from the 2016 Census.* http://www.statcan.gc.ca/daily-quotidien/170802/dq170802a-eng.htm.

———. 2017b. *Mortality: Overview, 2012 and 2013.* http://www.statcan.gc.ca/pub/91-209-x/2017001/article/14793-eng.pdf.

———. 2017c. *Population Size and Growth in Canada: Key Results from the 2016 Census.* https://www.statcan.gc.ca/daily-quotidien/170208/dq170208a-eng.htm.

———. 2017d. *Population Trends by Age and Sex, 2016 Census of Population.* http://www.statcan.gc.ca/pub/11-627-m/11-627-m2017016-eng.htm.

———. 2017e. *Same-sex Couples in Canada in 2016.* http://www12.statcan.gc.ca/census-recensement/2016/as-sa/98-200-x/2016007/98-200-x2016007-eng.cfm.

———. 2018a. *Common-law Couples Are More Likely to Break Up.* https://www.statcan.gc.ca/pub/11-402-x/2011000/chap/fam/fam02-eng.htm.

———. 2018b. *Deaths, Causes of Death and Life Expectancy, 2016.* https://www150.statcan.gc.ca/n1/daily-quotidien/180628/dq180628b-eng.htm.

Trovato, Frank. 2015. *Canada's Population in a Global Context: An Introduction to Social Demography.* Don Mills: Oxford University Press.

Ursel, Jane. 1992. *Private Lives, Public Policy: 100 Years of State Intervention in the Family.* Toronto: Women's Press.

US Census Bureau International Database. 2017. *Population Pyramid Graph – Custom Region – Canada.* https://www.census.gov/data-tools/demo/idb/region.php?N=%20Results%20&T=12&A=separate&RT=0&Y=2016&R=-1&C=CA.

United Nations. 2017a. *World Population Prospects: The 2017 Revision*, custom data acquired on December 18, 2017.

———. 2017b. *World Population Projected to Reach 9.8 Billion in 2050, and 11.2 Billion in 2100.* https://www.un.org/development/desa/en/news/population/world-population-prospects-2017.html.

———. 2011. *World Marriage Patterns.* http://www.un.org/en/development/desa/population/publications/pdf/popfacts/PopFacts_2011-1.pdf.

Vaupel, James W. 2010. "Biodemography of Human Ageing." *Nature* 464 (7288): 536–42. https://doi.org/10.1038/nature08984.

Xu, Jiaquan, Sherry L. Murphy, Kenneth D. Kochanek, and Elizabeth Arias. 2016. *Mortality in the United States, 2015*. NCHS data brief no 267. Hyattsville: National Center for Health Statistics. https://www.cdc.gov/nchs/products/databriefs/db267.htm.

Zaidi, Batool, and S. Philip Morgan. 2017. "The Second Demographic Transition Theory: A Review and Appraisal." *Annual Review of Sociology* 43: 473–92. https://doi.org/10.1146/annurev-soc-060116-053442.

13 Alternative Spring Break: The Politics of Doing Good in a Globalized World

NATHANIEL LAYWINE and ALAN SEARS

LEARNING OUTCOMES

After reading this chapter, you should be able to:

- identify the contradictions of alternative spring break by reflecting on the complex relationship between making a difference for others and for yourself through volunteer activities
- describe how post-secondary education has been reorganized around neoliberal practices
- explain how the unequal power dynamics that exist between the Global North and Global South have emerged due to a history of colonialism
- define hidden curriculum, and explain this concept through a discussion of alternative spring break programs
- critically evaluate the dominant frame of international development work and ask questions about who benefits and who loses through processes of globalization

Introduction

The words "spring break" tend to conjure up escapist images of beaches, bathing suits, and beer for university students who are granted a week's break from classes during their busy winter semester. Spring break follows the rhythm of American universities' semesters and takes place toward the end of March. Here in Canada, we officially dub this break time "reading week" – although students know better and often use more honest terms like "slack week." This break takes place around the last week or two of February, at about the midpoint of the winter semester, when the spring weather is imminent but has not yet appeared. Despite the difference in names, the **rituals** of spring break are still widely known, understood, and practised by Canadian students, many of whom opt to head to the beach in tropical locales such as Florida, Central America, or the Caribbean, participating in the most pervasive image of spring break as hedonistic party time (Josiam et al. 1998; Lee, Maggs, and Rankin 2006; Sönmez et al. 2006).

The Global South in Representations and in Reality

Although the pressure of making money through paid employment means that for many this week is not actually as slack as they might hope, students can still vicariously experience the spring break lifestyle through the annual MTV spring break special programming on television, which, since 1986, has showcased this trend of teenagers drinking, dancing, and otherwise partying in beautiful locales, apparently without a care for their studies or the worlds around them. Even though the American station airs this special during spring break as opposed to reading week, which is technically a different season, it has still contributed significantly to the Canadian reading week experience by setting the standard for perceived fun among university students.

Spring break destinations are located primarily in South and Central America, Africa, and many parts of Asia. These areas of the world are sometimes called developing or underdeveloped nations. This terminology would suggest that these countries are less far along a path of economic and social development based on the model of Europe and North America. Arif Dirlik (2015) is one of many writers who prefers the language of the **Global South** based on hemispheric location, as it does not presume a single path of development or obscure the histories of conquest and violence that have entrenched relations of **poverty** and global inequality.

The imagery of tropical paradises in the Global South is appealing, but this only depicts a very small slice of these places. These images act as **systems of representation**, including language, signs, and **symbols**, that produce or construct meaning about the images that are not necessarily natural or inherently accurate (Hall 1997). Alongside the tropical paradise system of representation is another that casts the Global South as a place of perpetual suffering from problems like violence, disorder, disease, natural disasters, and general instability. We hear about suffering in the Global South in news media, in classrooms teaching international development studies, viral videos, and various ad campaigns for charitable organizations. Celebrities endorse humanitarian campaigns and rock stars play benefit concerts for particular causes and conflicts, or even for general, ongoing problems like hunger or poverty. The benefit of sociological inquiry is that it allows us to look beyond these systems of representation, which seem to be "common sense" or ordinary fact, by using methodical and systematic approaches to test our perception of everyday experiences through observation, theories and social **scientific methods** (Sears and Cairns 2015).

It is true that the tropical locations throughout the world where spring break travel tends to take place face complex, multi-dimensional social, political, and economic challenges that are not immediately apparent while on a beach holiday. Broadly speaking, these challenges are examples of **social inequality** – the disproportionate distribution of wealth, resources, and opportunities to a privileged few, while the vast majority lack the necessities to lead secure, comfortable, and fulfilling lives. Inequality can exist in a number of different ways that are often not readily seen by vacationers on the beach, ranging from sub-poverty pay scales to political violence and international aggression.

Each set of images are only partial truths. While problems of violence, disorder, and poverty do exist within the Global South, these representations do not show the resilience of this region's communities, the vibrant cultures that exist there, or the diversity of daily experiences that make up the realities of billions of people across the world.

In these "common sense" images, locals are positioned as passive victims who are incapable of improving their own circumstances and who require intervention from the outside for salvation from their own lives (Shohat and Stam 1994).

The defining characteristic of the Global South, and the explanation for its various challenges, is its history of **colonialism**: the conquest and direct control of these countries by others. Throughout the fifteenth to twentieth centuries, European colonizers brutally conquered and occupied much of the rest of the world to amass wealth through trade, acquire new resources, and expand their empires by imposing direct rule over the **Indigenous** peoples who originally inhabited this land. It is difficult to address the scale of changes that colonization made to Indigenous peoples' lives and livelihoods, as colonizers often violently took the land and resources through warfare, enslaved the locals, and imposed foreign systems of government and law that outlawed traditional religious and cultural practices. The legacies of colonialism continue, as movements toward nationhood have left the former colonies impoverished and economically reliant upon their former colonizers. Today, much of the world's wealth is concentrated in former colonizer nations (the **Global North**), and among a small elite sector within the Global South (Dirlik 2015). These conditions also created the systems in which workers in the Global South must find work in the Global North under the exploitative conditions of the SAWP, as discussed by Hennebry, Celis Parra, and Daley in chapter four.

Alternative Spring Break

Alternative spring break (ASB) is oriented toward addressing precisely the issues that a hedonistic beach vacation ignores. An increasing number of students are electing to spend their mid-semester breaks volunteering to help others in communities that they perceive as vulnerable. University administrators, **not-for-profit organizations**, and student participants imagine ASB as providing opportunities to spend the break from studies in more seemingly meaningful and worthy activities. Although ASB experiences can take place within the local community of the student, the term is conventionally used within the **volunteer tourism** industry, which caters to students' desire to travel abroad. Volunteer tourists are considered "those tourists who, for various reasons, volunteer in an organized way to undertake holidays that might involve aiding or alleviating the material poverty of some groups in **society**, the restoration of certain environments or research into aspects of society or environment" (Wearing 2001, 1). These experiences are thought to promote **values** of community-driven service, **global citizenship**, and **reflective practice**, among others. As the University of Western Ontario, frames it, "We consider them to be global experiences, due to the intercultural exchange involved within the group and community" (University of Western Ontario 2018). A not-for-profit organization that coordinates volunteer tourism, including ASB programs, frames the experience as a combination "of travel and adventure with multiple opportunities for personal and professional growth... also a great way to give back to the local community" (Projects Abroad 2018).

Common volunteer gigs include working in child care (in orphanages, classrooms, libraries, community centres, or after-school programs) as teachers, nurses, or playmates; working in infrastructure development by either building structures for communities, renovating or upgrading the homes of community members (e.g., by building ecological stoves/fridges), or beautifying neighbourhoods by cleaning up parks or painting local municipal buildings. Some students may work on conservation programs, in close proximity with wild animals or natural parks/reservations, while others might work in health care, social work, or research institutions, if they have the relevant particular skills or are studying in relevant fields. Not only does this activity seem worthwhile to volunteering students, but it also claims to offer the chance to participate in forms of learning that are richer than those normally encountered in the classroom. On the face of it, alternative spring break seems like a significant improvement to beach party culture, offering not only a more worthwhile activity but also a valuable experiential learning opportunity. But this story is not that simple. Despite their intentions, alternative spring break participants might not be doing much good for the communities they visit. Take a minute and consider, for example, what it might mean for you to travel to another country to help a community that struggles with issues related to poverty, lack of resources, and other social issues. How would you know where to begin? And how would you know that your efforts were going to be successful?

I (Nathaniel, one of the authors of this chapter) realized this challenge when I conducted the **fieldwork** for my PhD dissertation in key sites of volunteerism in Peru, a nation in South America that receives over three million tourists annually (World Bank 2018). I conducted **qualitative research** interviews with 32 volunteers from January to March of 2015. A number of the volunteers in this study participated in short-term placements during February and March (summer in Peru). Several volunteers had hoped to teach classes, but nationwide, all of the schools were closed for summer vacation. The inability to make the desired contribution of helping to teach kids was due to prioritizing the volunteer's schedule of spring break over the needs of the Peruvian organizations or communities.

The Hunger for Experiential Learning

By the time most students get to university, they have spent more of their life in a classroom than any other space, except perhaps bed. Students get used to the classroom model of learning, which is based on listening to an expert teach from the front of the room (Sears and Cairns 2015). Certainly, the classroom can be an important part of learning processes, but many of the most important things people know were not learned in the classroom. Children learn their first language by using it. The incentive for learning is not a grade or a gold star, but the ability to meet your wants and needs that comes from being able to name things and express oneself. Similarly, many other key life skills that determine our basic well-being and happiness are not developed in the classroom. Has anyone ever learned sex from sex education?

The classroom developed as the dominant place of learning as compulsory education – education provided by the **state** and required of all of its citizens. Compulsory education was provided not so much because everyone needed certain forms of knowledge like reading, writing, and arithmetic to get through their everyday lives; rather, people needed to be prepared for their place in paid employment, family relations, and the state (Lloyd and Thomas 1998; Sears 2003). It was not necessarily the content of the lessons but the "**hidden curriculum**" that prepared people to accept authority – for example, habituating children to a strict schedule or to raising their hands to speak. The "hidden curriculum" is made up of "those non-academic but educationally significant consequences of schooling that occur systematically but are not made explicit at any level of the public rationales for education" (Vallance 1983, 11).

Classroom instruction, by its very nature, focuses on a very small number of skills, such as the ability to sit still and listen rather than moving and exploring the world physically through the body. Elspeth Stuckey (1991) argues that the disproportionate focus on literacy in classroom settings is "a system of oppression that works against entire societies as well as against certain groups within certain given **populations** and against certain individual people" (64). Specifically, many scholars, including Albanese (chapter twenty, this volume), have identified how the hidden curriculum in many school systems privileges middle- and upper-class values, knowledge, and **traditions**. By contrast, **Indigenous ways of knowing**, the epistemologies discussed by Zoe Todd in chapter one, based on the intimate knowledge of an ecosystem through experience and storytelling, tend to be marginalized. It is not surprising that many students crave other ways of learning when they are in **institutions** of post-secondary education, given that classroom education tends to be freighted with a hidden curriculum that prizes obedience, deference to experts, and the acquisition of second-hand knowledge stored in written form rather than first-hand knowledge through sensory engagement with the world.

Alternative spring break satisfies the cravings many students may feel to learn experientially, through engaging with the world, rather than passively and abstractly through listening and reading. This desire for experiential learning intersects with career anxieties among many liberal arts students, who may be concerned about how university is preparing them for what comes next in their lives. Universities are seeking to prove the relevance of education that may seem rather other-worldly to students by connecting students' hunger for experiential learning to the project of incorporating ideals of **global citizenship education** into post-secondary curricula. If they are willing and able to pay the costs, students can spend entire semesters or school years living and working abroad in any number of different countries while earning credit for their travels.

Theorizing Alternative Spring Break

Our theoretical framework draws on **critical theory**, which aims to identify, critique, and change relationships of power and domination in society, as well as **social movement theory**, which seeks to understand how, why, and in what form groups of individuals or organizations come together to carry out, resist, or undo a social change. Through **radical pedagogy**, or teaching practices that try to help students recognize structures of power and domination, we also address questions pertaining to **experiential education**, the philosophy that students who learn through direct experience in a field and reflect upon their work in the field will increase their skills, abilities, and level of knowledge in ways that classroom-based learning cannot replicate. We also draw on **postcolonial theory** to examine the legacies of colonialism and imperialism throughout the Global South, as well as the consequences of these legacies within the current world order, including **post-development discourse**, which considers structures of international development (e.g., foreign aid, philanthropy-based practices like volunteer tourism) to reflect the ongoing control that the Global North maintains over the South.

Our methodology draws on qualitative interpretive analyses of volunteer experience. This kind of research asks open-ended, exploratory question to try to determine how and why social phenomena occur, and our analyses here are informed in part by Nathaniel's ethnographic fieldwork in Peru. **Ethnography** systematically studies people and cultures through fieldwork-based observation and analysis. In Nathaniel's case study, this involved **participant observation** (watching study participants, who, in this case, were volunteers, as they go about their daily tasks on the job and in the communities where they work) and interviewing (asking participants a series of questions about their lives and experiences, in order to incorporate their own perspectives in the study).

History of International Volunteering

The origins of volunteer tourism may be traced back to the role of missionaries and religious groups in doing service work overseas during the time of direct European colonization throughout the fifteenth to twentieth centuries (Rennick and Desjardins 2014). Since the age of **Enlightenment** in Europe, the goal of promoting human welfare and alleviating peoples' suffering around the world, otherwise known as **humanitarianism**, has been an important goal among a population that was becoming increasingly concerned with human rights and individual freedom. Yet historical humanitarian practices have a dark and violent underside. Colonizers assumed that by imparting their own value systems, beliefs and practices, they were helping to "civilize" Indigenous people, who needed to be saved from themselves. Locals were rarely consulted about the imposition of these new ways of life and were violently coerced into fitting the European model of civilization.

Many nations in the Global South gained their independence over the period of the nineteenth and twentieth centuries, becoming official **nation-states**. Although they won formal independence, the previous centuries of violence, resource exploitation, and a unidirectional flow of wealth from the South to North meant that these new nation-states remained largely dependent upon the more powerful and affluent nations (Prebisch 1950; Singer 1975), relying on assistance in the forms of loans, aid, and relief packages. Postcolonial critics worry that structures of colonialism remain intact even today through these practices of international development (Escobar 1995; Ferguson 1994).

We understand in Canada that we have privileged lives compared to others throughout the world, and it is our duty as Canadians to help others (Hébert 1996; Wagner 2008). The Canadian government has contributed money and resources toward international development initiatives since the 1960s, including programs that send citizens abroad to act as ambassadors of goodwill, or through Canada's Volunteer Cooperation Program (VCP), which, in their words aims to "represent a human face on development initiatives" undertaken by the Canadian government (Canadian International Development Agency 2005, 43).

Although the government of Canada set a precedent for funding young volunteers to travel abroad, it has never funded ASB programs. Rather, universities and the private sector have stepped up their promotion of these experiences for students within the last two decades. For universities, ASB experiences fit with an increasing trend of promoting global citizenship education among students (Cameron 2014; Epprecht 2004). There are many reasons universities seek to include a global citizenship education component to their curricula: Educators and university administrators broadly understand travel opportunities to impart students with the aptitude to understand and address complex issues facing the Global South and the world, while developing their own skills and professional credentials for the international job market (Jorgenson and Schultz 2014; Tiessen and Epprecht 2014).

Does Everybody Win?

Generally, travel-abroad experiences through universities offer some sort of course credit for students. However, there is also an increasing number of private-sector companies that exist to recruit and match prospective travellers with potential host organizations and communities in the Global South. These companies are usually not affiliated with universities, but are hired by non-profit organizations to locate students to volunteer within communities.

Evidence suggests that this type of travel is generally less effective in achieving community goals, as volunteers divide their time between communities and other tourist activities while travelling, and less attention is placed on specific learning outcomes or goals for volunteer participants (McGehee and Andereck 2008; Wearing and Lyons 2008).

Nevertheless, the volunteer tourism industry is growing rapidly, and ASB projects are just one segment. An independent tourism industry consultancy group based in Europe, Tourism Research and Marketing (TRAM) (2008), suggests that 1.6 million tourists participate in volunteer programs each year, collectively spending somewhere between $2.66 billion and $3.25 billion. Included in this expenditure is a vast network of recruitment strategies: travel/study abroad fairs in convention centres, recruiters who come to university campuses, e-mail campaigns, and social media pages. Volunteers can select where they will volunteer, what specific activities they will or will not undertake, and the time frame in which they will travel. Although the flexibility of choice is appealing to volunteers, it means that some projects may receive an abundance of volunteers while others may be left in the lurch. Nathaniel observed in Peru that the proximity to popular tourist sites like national parks, with well-known networks of hiking trails, and Machu Picchu, tended to have much higher concentrations of volunteers. Meanwhile, more rural and isolated communities received volunteer assistance much less frequently.

While the Canadian government broadly defines the primary goal of volunteer-abroad excursions as building the capacities of local organizations and community members (Canadian International Development Agency 2005), some scholars, like geographer David Guttentag, have remarked that interventions in these communities result in impacts that are not immediately apparent but nevertheless harmful. Guttentag (2009) suggests that volunteer interventions neglect locals' needs and Indigenous knowledge. They may impede development projects through the unsatisfactory completion of tasks if volunteers are not properly trained or skilled at their position or if volunteers are not available when they are needed by the project or organization. They risk disrupting local economies, driving up prices of goods and services to profit from wealthy tourists, a process that can even contribute to increasing poverty rather than alleviating it. On top of this, these projects rarely undergo independent or external evaluations. So the actual net benefits for community stakeholders remain somewhat speculative (Benson 2011; Tiessen and Heron 2012).

Although it might be hard for volunteers to realize it, coordinating the logistics for big groups can prove to be quite a burden on the organizations that host them. Since the flow of volunteers can be quite sporadic, volunteer coordinating organizations find themselves stuck between trying to recruit help during low season and dealing with a large of influx of volunteers who need to be housed, fed, scheduled, and otherwise accommodated. One volunteer coordinator at a children's daycare centre explained that she was so understaffed during the low season for tourists that she found herself on some days standing out in the town's central plaza – a main attraction for tourists – handing out fliers for her organization, trying to recruit volunteers off the street to spend a day or two volunteering in the daycare centre. This desperation to fill volunteer positions risks allowing unqualified or unsuitable volunteers to take positions where young people are under their care. The logistics of volunteer management can likewise take up much of these organizations' time and resources, and it may actually impede progress on projects intended to help the communities. As another volunteer coordinator for a community centre that runs programming for youth in a rural Andean community expressed to Nathaniel, "I'm very aware, from a host's perspective, how much energy it takes on my part to work with volunteers.... Volunteers all have needs. And everyone at the community centre all has needs! I can't take care of it all, so it's hard when volunteers lack a certain amount of independence."

When you think about it, it would actually be a very tall order to fill for spring breakers to solve the world's issues during their holidays. Underprivileged communities in the Global South face difficult, ongoing problems like widespread poverty, political instability, or threats to ecological sustainability. These are complex problems deeply woven into the fabric of the dominant economic and social systems. It would require massive resources to address these systemic problems and it is difficult to imagine that a week-long visit by a well-intentioned volunteer is going to do much in the face of deep structural problems. Serious approaches to solving deep-set problems that are in many ways the legacy of colonialism and global inequality require instead a focus on solidarity and partnership that is founded on the **agency** of people in the Global South and the deployment of resources on a scale that exceeds that of individual philanthropy.

What Do Volunteers Take from the Experience?

Given this reality, sometimes the volunteer experience is more about the feeling of being helpful than about actually making a difference in an underprivileged community (Chouliaraki 2012). These feelings of being helpful are the basis of the volunteer tourism industry and the core of marketing tactics that end up defining volunteers' expectations (Vodopivec and Jaffe 2011). Volunteers expect to feel like they have made a difference in the lives of others, even when this may be impossible during a short trip abroad. While ASB projects aim to celebrate justice and international cooperation, they may, in the end, be propagating an industry that is based on satisfying the desire for positive humanitarian feelings among participants. Nathaniel's interviews in Peru revealed that the experience of volunteering was often more about the emotional impact on the volunteer than the help produced for the host community. One volunteer, Jane, age 21,[1] noted, "Before I came here I was a bit of a drunk, just partying all the time. And I was starting to feel kind of guilty about it. Like I was making a fool of myself but I didn't know what to do to change my path. And then I decided to come here!" Another, Miriam, 23, said, "One of the reasons for me to come here and then travel on my own was so that I could feel confident and that I'm independent. So when I do go back, and I'm surrounded

1 All names have been changed to protect the identity of the interviewees.

again by a large network of family and friends, I can be independent and I can do things on my own." Mitchell, 19, commented, "I'm a pre-med student. So volunteerism and community outreach with under-served peoples is kind of an obligation of a physician. Medical schools want you to foster that mentality and engrain the importance of that." These volunteers reveal that the decision to volunteer had as much to do with their own desires to transform and develop as individuals as their desire to assist communities in Peru to transform or develop the communities they found there.

We must ask: what are the actual benefits that volunteers receive beyond the pleasures of a trip to the South during the winter months? And what are these spring breakers actually learning? Some point to these experiences as "journeys of the Self" (Wearing and Lyons 2008), wherein volunteers come to learn as much about their own thoughts, beliefs, and abilities as they learn about other cultures. The experience allows volunteers to develop their own characters – to transform, gain independence and autonomy, heighten confidence, and exercise newfound abilities – through the act of helping others. However, some critics argue that the educational component lacks substance, as a volunteer's encounter with community members doesn't, by itself, lead to a better appreciation of the community's culture or of the historical conditions of its poverty. Instead, volunteers tend to try to cope with the experience of witnessing poverty first-hand by employing various interpretations that don't fully recognize the hardship that impoverished people experience. Kate Simpson has noted the "poor-but-happy" attitude adopted by volunteers, who believe that community members are accustomed to their lives of poverty and therefore are unbothered by their impoverished circumstances (Simpson 2004, 688). Although this exposure to different cultures and lifestyles may provide educational moments, responses such as these indicate that participants do not deeply learn about these different cultures, but instead project their own values and assumptions onto the experiences of others (Sin 2009). E.L. Crossley (2012) has noted in a similar study that volunteers commonly report that they feel lucky or fortunate for their own material wealth or the privilege they enjoy in Canada. But framing the experience in terms of luck reveals how little participants learn about global political or economic structures that allow for this discrepancy in power and privilege to occur in the first place. Global poverty is not a matter of luck, but rather the result of several hundred years of colonization and exploitation, as well as ongoing systems of political and economic domination. Despite these encounters between volunteers and local community members, volunteers are engaging in very little self-reflexivity. These findings call into question the presumed profundity of a volunteer's self-transformation.

Catering to volunteer experiences reflects a turn to **neoliberalism**, "a theory of political economic practices that proposes that human well-being can best be advanced by liberating individual entrepreneurial freedoms and skills within an institutional framework characterized by strong private property rights, free markets and free trade" (Harvey 2005, 2). The role of the state in the neoliberal model is not to remedy inequities – for example, through social programs – but to reinforce market relations in all areas of life, undermining other ways of meeting our wants and needs that are not organized around exchange. The implementation of neoliberal policies around the world have brought funding cuts to public services and international aid programs, the selling off of public spaces, and the use of the market model to reorganize public institutions, including universities.

In the context of international development, neoliberal policy-makers undermine the idea that providing international assistance to help meet human needs is a function of governments and established aid agencies. In the post–World War II order, governments in the Global North, who were able to mobilize massive financial resources far greater than any charity organization, assumed responsibility for providing direct assistance to the decolonizing nations of the Global South, in order to both reduce inequalities and weaken the appeal of the Soviet system in the Cold War context (Williams 2013). In the neoliberal era since the 1980s, the focus has shifted to the expansion of trade combined with private philanthropy, centring on the notion that addressing global inequality is a personal responsibility to be addressed through charity and volunteerism. Volunteer tourists are now attempting to do in one- to two-week time slots, and with minimal resources, what governments and grassroots organizations have been working on for decades: eradicating global poverty and creating sustainable, healthy livelihoods for those in need.

Conclusion

Students often hope that these international volunteer experiences provide genuinely transformative moments in their own learning processes. This rich learning experience, however, does not necessarily guarantee that ASB volunteers are doing good in the world or that they themselves are experiencing deep transformation. Alternative spring break offers a deeply problematic model of experiential learning. Real experiential learning combines some sort of action in the world with deliberate reflection and interchange to make sense of what happened.

If experiential learning is to be part of a genuine transformative process, it cannot simply confirm common sense but should also disrupt and challenge it (Sears and Cairns 2015). ASB draws on the basic scripts of colonialism, casting the volunteers as active agents and the host communities as helpless and needy. This resonates with 500 years of colonialism that cast the invaders from the Global North as makers of history and the peoples of the Global South as unable to act for themselves.

Genuine experiential learning must be a combination of experience with deliberate learning through reflection. Vygotsky and Cole (1978) argued that learning is necessarily social and there is a gap between what individuals can figure out on their own and what they can learn through interchange with others. Experiential learning therefore needs to be processed socially through engagement with others, and participants themselves must actively challenge the assumption that their own presence for a limited period of time will substantially help the community that is hosting them. They can, in that limited time span, open themselves to really learning from their hosts, listening to their own stories and paying attention to their understanding of the world. Deliberate learning from their host communities would provide a foundation for building relations of solidarity and working toward some common vision of justice.

Questions for Critical Thought

1. How was the alternative spring break (ASB) model argued to fail, both in its capacity to provide transformative experiences for student volunteers and in its capacity to be a meaningful source of support for poverty-stricken communities in the Global South?
2. How are the shortcomings of ASB to its volunteers and to communities needing support interrelated (i.e., having to do with the contradiction highlighted by the authors)?
3. Who do you think benefits the most from the existing neoliberal framework for aid provision and the marketing of programs such as "alternative spring break"? Who benefits the least? Consider both short- and long-term benefits and losses.
4. Think of a time when you were either a tourist outside your local community or when you witnessed tourists vacationing in your local community. What are some of the ways in which tourists change or influence the local communities to which they travel? After reading this chapter, do you think of the activities of tourists differently?
5. Do you think the alternative spring break model could be tweaked or redesigned to better respond to the needs of aid recipients and the hopes of volunteers? Could the existing contradictions be resolved?

References

Benson, Angela M. 2011. "Volunteer Tourism: Theory and Practice." In *Volunteer Tourism: Theoretical Frameworks and Practical Applications*, edited by Angela Benson, 1–6. New York: Routledge.

Cameron, John D. 2014. "Grounding Experiential Learning in 'Thick' Conceptions of Global Citizenship." In *Globetrotting or Global Citizenship? Perils and Potential of Experiential Learning*, edited by Rebecca Tiessen and Robert Huish, 21–42. Toronto: University of Toronto Press.

Canadian International Development Agency. 2005. *The Power of Volunteering: A Review of the Canadian Volunteer Cooperation Program Evaluation Report, Final Report.* Gatineau: Canadian International Development Agency.

Chouliaraki, Lilie. 2012. *The Ironic Spectator: Solidarity in the Age of Post-Humanitarianism.* Cambridge: Polity Press.

Crossley, Émilie. 2012. "Poor but Happy: Volunteer Tourists' Encounters with Poverty." *Tourism Geographies: An International Journal of Tourism Space, Place and Environment* 14 (2): 235–53. https://doi.org/10.1080/14616688.2011.611165.

Dirlik, Arif. 2015. "Global South." In *Concepts of the Global South: Voices from Around the World*, edited by Andrea Wolvers, Oliver Tappe, Tijo Salverda, Tobias Schwarz, 13–14. Cologne: Global South Studies Centre.

Epprecht, Marc. 2004. "Work-Study Abroad Courses in International Development Studies: Some Ethical and Pedagogical Issues." *Canadian Journal of Development Studies* 25 (4): 687–706. https://doi.org/10.1080/02255189.2004.9669009.

Escobar, Arturo. 2012. *Encountering Development: The Making and Unmaking of the Third World*. Princeton: Princeton University Press.

Ferguson, James. 1994. *The Anti-politics Machine: "Development," Depoliticization, and Bureaucratic Power in Lesotho*. Minneapolis: University of Minnesota Press.

Guttentag, David. 2009. "The Possible Negative Impacts of Volunteer Tourism." *International Journal of Tourism Research* 11 (6): 537–51. https://doi.org/10.1002/jtr.727.

Hall, Stuart. 1997. "The Work of Representation." *In Representation: Cultural Representations and Signifying Practices*, edited by Stuart Hall, 13–74. London: Sage in association with the Open University.

Harvey, David. 2005. *A Brief History of Neoliberalism*. Oxford: Oxford University Press.

Hébert, Jacques. 1996. *Hello, World!: On Canada, the World and Youth*. Translated by Jean-Paul Murray. Vancouver: Talon Books.

Josiam, Bharath M., Perry J.S. Hobson, Utah C. Dietrich, and George Smeaton. 1998. "An Analysis of the Sexual, Alcohol, and Drug-Related Behavioural Patterns of Students on Spring Break." *Tourism Management* 19 (6): 501–13. https://doi.org/10.1016/S0261-5177(98)00052-1.

Jorgenson, Shelane, and Lynette Schultz. 2012. "Global Citizenship Education (GCE) in Post-Secondary Institutions: What is Protected and What Is Hidden under the Umbrella of GCE?" *Journal of Global Citizenship Education & Equity Education* 2 (1): 1–22. http://journals.sfu.ca/jgcee/index.php/jgcee/article/view/52.

Lee, Christine M., Jennifer L. Maggs, and Lela A. Rankin. 2006. "Spring Break Trips as a Risk Factor for Heavy Alcohol Use among First-Year College Students." *Journal of Studies on Alcohol*. 67 (6): 911–16. https://doi.org/10.15288/jsa.2006.67.911.

Lloyd, David, and Paul Thomas. 1998. *Culture and the State*. London: Routledge.

McGehee, Nancy G., and Kathleen Andereck. 2008. "'Pettin' the Critters': Exploring the Complex Relationship between Volunteers and the Voluntoured in McDowell County, West Virginia, USA, and Tijuana, Mexico." In *Journeys of Discovery in Volunteer Tourism: International Case Study Perspectives*, edited by Steven Wearing and Kevin D. Lyons, 12–24. Cambridge: Elsevier.

Prebisch, Raúl. 1950. *The Economic Development of Latin America and its Principal Problems*. Lake Success: United Nations Department of Economic Affairs.

Projects Abroad. 2018. "Alternative Spring Break Trips – Spring 2018." https://www.projects-abroad.org/volunteer-projects/alternative-spring-break/.

Rennick, Joanne B., and Michel Desjardins. 2014. "Towards a Pedagogy of Good Global Citizenship." In *The World is My Classroom: International Learning and Canadian Higher Education*, edited by Joanne B. Rennick and Michel Desjardins, 3–15. Toronto: University of Toronto Press.

Sears, Alan. 2003. *Retooling the Mind Factor: Education in a Lean State*. Aurora: Garamond Press.

Sears, Alan, and James Cairns. 2015. *A Good Book, in Theory: Making Sense Through Inquiry*. 3rd ed. Toronto: University of Toronto Press.

Shohat, Ella, and Robert Stam. 1994. *Unthinking Eurocentrism: Multiculturalism and the Media.* London: Routledge.

Simpson, Kate. 2004. "'Doing Development': The Gap Year, Volunteer-Tourists and a Popular Practice of Development." *Journal of International Development* 16 (5): 681–92. https://doi.org/10.1002/jid.1120.

Sin, Harng Luh. 2009. "Volunteer Tourism – 'Involve Me and I Will Learn'?" *Annals of Tourism Research* 36 (3): 480–501. https://doi.org/10.1016/j.annals.2009.03.001.

Singer, Hans Wolfgang. 1975. *The Strategy of International Development: Essays in the Economics of Backwardness.* London: Macmillan Press.

Sönmez, Sevil, Yorghos Apostolopoulos, Chong Ho Yu, Shiyi Yang, Anna Mattila, and Lucy C. Yu. 2006. "Binge Drinking and Casual Sex on Spring Break." *Annals of Tourism Research* 33 (4): 895–917. https://doi.org/10.1016/j.annals.2006.06.005.

Stuckey, J. Elspeth. 1991. *The Violence of Literacy.* Portsmouth: Boynton/Cook.

Tiessen, Rebecca, and Mark Epprecht. 2014. "Introduction: Global Citizenship Education for Learning/Volunteering Abroad." *Journal of Global Citizenship & Equity Education* 2 (1): 1–12. http://journals.sfu.ca/jgcee/index.php/jgcee/article/view/54/27.

Tiessen, Rebecca, and Barbara Heron. 2012. *Creating Global Citizens? The Impact of Learning/Volunteer Abroad Programs; Final Report.* Ottawa: International Development Research Council.

Tourism Research and Marketing (TRAM). 2008. *Volunteer Tourism: A Global Analysis.* Arnhem: ATLAS Publications.

University of Western Ontario. 2018. "Alternative Spring Break: Program Overview." http://asb.uwo.ca/about/program_overview.html.

Vallance, Elizabeth. 1983. "Hiding the Hidden Curriculum: An Interpretation of the Language of Justification in Nineteenth Century Education Reform." In *The Hidden Curriculum and Moral Education: Deception or Discovery?*, edited by Henry Giroux and David Purpel, 9–27. Berkeley: McCutchan Publishing.

Vodopivec, Barbara and Rivke Jaffe. 2011. "Save the World in a Week: Volunteer Tourism, Development and Difference." *The European Journal of Development Research* 23 (1): 111–28. https://doi.org/10.1057/ejdr.2010.55.

Vygotsky, L.S., and Michael Cole. 1978. *Mind in Society: The Development of Higher Psychological Processes.* Cambridge: Harvard University Press.

Wagner, Eric. 2008. "The Peaceable Kingdom? The National Myth of Canadian Peacekeeping." *Canadian Military Journal* 7 (4): 45–54. http://www.journal.forces.gc.ca/vo7/no4/wagner-eng.asp.

Wearing, Stephen. 2001. *Volunteer Tourism: Experiences That Make a Difference.* New York: CABI.

Wearing, Stephen, and Kevin Lyons. 2008. *Journeys of Discovery in Volunteer Tourism: International Case Study Perspectives.* Cambridge: CABI.

Williams, David G. 2013. "The History of International Development Aid." In *Handbook of Global Economic Governance*, edited by Manuela Moschella and Catherine Weaver, 233–48. London: Routledge.

World Bank. 2018. *International Tourism, Number of Arrivals.* http://data.worldbank.org/indicator/ST.INT.ARVL.

14 Supermoms and Bumbling Dads: How Mother's Day and Father's Day Cards Perpetuate Traditional Roles in the Home

ALISON THOMAS and ELIZABETH DENNIS

LEARNING OUTCOMES

After reading this chapter, you should be able to:

- understand how adopting a sociological perspective can make it possible to think critically about familiar features of everyday life, such as greeting cards
- explain the value of using both quantitative and qualitative data in research involving content analysis
- describe the part played by the mass media as one of several agents of socialization that communicate cultural norms and values regarding gender roles in society
- explain how the persistence of traditional gender stereotypes in popular culture contributes to sustaining an unequal division of domestic labour
- apply the concept of the "second shift" to an understanding of gendered labour

Introduction

In spring each year, shopping malls throughout North America invite us to purchase cards, flowers, and other gifts as gestures of appreciation for the mothers and fathers in our lives. Mother's Day (the second Sunday in May), established in the United States in 1914, and Father's Day (the third Sunday in June), officially recognized much later, in 1972, have become important commercial events throughout North America. Hallmark, one of the major greeting card manufacturers, reported sales of 113 million cards for Mother's Day and 72 million for Father's Day in 2016, with only Christmas and Valentine's Day card sales exceeding these numbers. The societal expectation that North Americans should all in some way mark Mother's Day and Father's Day each year indicates that this is a cultural

norm – a widespread **social practice** based on shared **values** – which in this case are those of affectionate respect and appreciation for what parents do for their families.

Most people simply take such familiar aspects of our **society** for granted, yet sociology invites us to adopt a different perspective and to *make the familiar strange*, as Peter Berger (1963) suggested in his book *Invitation to Sociology*. This means re-examining all such taken-for-granted features of our everyday lives and asking a variety of questions about them that can lead us to a deeper understanding of how our society works. We might have noticed the growing commercialization of Mother's Day and Father's Day and wonder how this may reflect the importance of consumerism in our society. We might also be curious to know why sales of Mother's Day cards are so much higher than those for Father's Day.

In this chapter, we demonstrate the value of adopting a sociological perspective by exploring how Mother's Day and Father's Day cards portray the roles played by women and men in their families and, based on our analysis of the images and messages the cards contain, we explain how these contribute to the perpetuation of traditional **gender** roles in the home.

The Gender Revolution and the "Second Shift"

The starting point for our study was our interest in how families allocate responsibility for paid and unpaid work, a topic that has been important in sociology for many decades. For much of the twentieth century, people expected that when women married they would leave whatever paid employment they may previously have had to become full-time housewives and – in due course – mothers. While women became responsible for housework and child care, their husbands took on responsibility for supporting them and their children as the sole family breadwinner. Talcott Parsons and Robert Bales (1955) as well as other sociologists regarded this so-called "breadwinner-homemaker" family, with its clearly differentiated roles for each gender, as an efficient arrangement, ideally adapted to the North America of the 1950s. As a **structural functionalist**, Parsons believed that each of society's component parts, including the family unit, performed a necessary function for society as a whole and that within families, each adult had their own distinct part to play. However, by the 1960s, feminists such as Betty Friedan (1963) were giving voice to the growing dissatisfaction that many women experienced with the role of housewife, arguing that women were unable to achieve their full potential while confined to the domestic sphere. While Friedan and many others saw paid employment as a way for women to demonstrate their capabilities and achieve equal recognition with men in the public sphere, some feminist theories also emphasized its importance in freeing women from economic dependence on men within marriage (Lorber 2012).

The cumulative impact of the women's movement on public opinion from the 1960s onward, coupled with changes to the economy that opened up new employment opportunities for women (especially the availability of part-time work), encouraged growing numbers of married women to find paid work outside of the home in the decades that followed. This was hailed as a major revolution in gender roles. However, by the 1980s, it had become apparent that this revolution was incomplete and, in Arlie Hochschild's words, had "stalled." In her influential 1989 book, *The Second Shift,* Hochschild noted that although more and more women were contributing to the household income, most men had not made any corresponding increase in their share of unpaid work in the home (child care, cooking, cleaning, laundry and so on). This, she argued, meant that the majority of women were now effectively working one shift of paid work outside the home followed by a "**second shift**" of unpaid work at home. Meanwhile, most men continued to assume that their working day was over once they arrived home and that "helping out" with domestic chores was optional (Oakley 1981). As Hochschild and others have pointed out, an unfair division of household labour such as this is liable to decrease marital satisfaction, and so this inequality has potentially serious implications for marital stability (Frisco and Williams 2003).

Some 30 years later, although men now do somewhat more household work than they did in the 1980s, Canadian statistics continue to show that women still carry the main responsibility for domestic labour of all kinds (Houle, Turcotte, and Wendt 2017; Marshall 2006, 2011), and a recent reassessment of the status of the **gender revolution** (Guppy and Luongo 2015) concluded that it remains stalled, in part for this very reason. Unsurprisingly, women's double burden (and the resulting struggle to balance both paid work and family obligations) continues to be a major source of dissatisfaction and economic inequality for women (Statistics Canada 2016). This is demonstrated across different contexts, including in farm families (as detailed by Susan Machum in chapter eleven), during the holidays (explained by Heidi Bickis in chapter five), and during summer vacations (explored by Tonya K. Davidson in chapter seventeen).

Mass Media Images of Parental Roles

A variety of factors can be seen to contribute to this unequal **household division of labour**, such as differences in the hours of paid work that women and men do as well as the income that they earn from their employment (Kan, Sullivan, and Gershuny 2011; Latshaw 2011). However, cultural ideologies (sets of shared beliefs) also play a part in shaping people's behaviour. Popular beliefs about what are the "normal" and appropriate roles for mothers and fathers to play in the home underpin cultural **norms** that influence the way people act. Those who deviate from these norms may experience negative consequences or **sanctions**. For example, fathers who request parental leave may experience disapproval from employers (Rudman and Mescher 2013). Beliefs about gender roles are communicated to us throughout our lives via various **agents of socialization**, starting with our family members and going on to include peer-group influence, our educational experiences and, importantly, our exposure to **mass media**. So, growing up, we learn not only from observing how our own parents and other real-life role models divide domestic responsibilities but also, increasingly, from images and ideas about gender roles that we encounter through print media such as newspapers and magazines, through broadcasting (radio, film, and television), and via the internet. Sociologists argue that media images do not merely reflect social reality but, rather, they communicate a selective version of that reality that emphasizes some aspects and ignores others (McQuail 2010). Given the exposure that we nowadays have to mass media of various kinds, this means that the images they provide us with can exercise considerable influence over how we perceive the social world around us. So, what kinds of ideas about parental roles are provided for us in the media?

For most of the twentieth century, the mass media in the **Western** world portrayed women and men as occupying very different roles within the home, consistent with the demographic prevalence of the **breadwinner-homemaker family** (Coontz 2005). For example, in the 1950s and 1960s, married women were invariably depicted as the "happy housewife" in magazines, advertising and in television shows such as *Leave it to Beaver*, while the so-called "working mother" was either invisible or was represented as a bad mother (Ferguson 1983). However, as times changed and sharply differentiated gender roles began to blur, media representations had to adjust accordingly. By the 1970s and 1980s, the mass media, led by women's magazines, were starting to recognize the working mother as a positive role model for the modern woman (Walker 2000) and this more favourable depiction helped encourage the steady increase in the numbers of married women taking up paid work outside the home (Ferguson 1983). By the end of the twentieth century, the mass media had recognized this trend and embraced the image of the multi-tasking "supermom," juggling both paid work and domestic chores (Johnston and Swanson 2003), as the central figure in the contemporary dual-earner family.

Cultural images of fathers have also changed over time, although a consistent feature has been the father's responsibility as family breadwinner. A number of distinct father roles were apparent over the course of the twentieth century, with the idea of the father as stern patriarch and head of the household gradually giving way to that of father as mentor, role model, and playmate (LaRossa 1997; Pleck 1987). However, starting in the 1980s, the mass media began hailing the emergence of a new, more nurturing style of fathering (Coltrane and Allan 1994), with the suggestion that this so-called "**new father**" would be "at least as adept at changing diapers as changing tires" (Furstenberg 1988,193). In spite of encouraging signs that increasing numbers of young fathers are now becoming more engaged in family work of all kinds (Chesley 2011; Marshall 2011; Patnaik 2015), the major cultural shift in father involvement that was predicted back in the 1980s has still not yet occurred (Latshaw 2011). Why, then, did that early wave of mass media enthusiasm for the new father not replicate what had happened with media endorsement of working mothers and translate into widespread acceptance of involved fathering as a new norm?

Theorizing the "Lag" Between the Culture and the Conduct of Parenthood

In 1988, sociologist Ralph LaRossa observed that there is an important difference between what he termed the *conduct* and the *culture* of parenthood. The ***conduct* of parenthood** is quite simply what mothers and fathers actually do (including both paid and unpaid work to support their families), whereas the ***culture* of parenthood** refers to how their roles are represented to us through culture – including through the mass media. LaRossa pointed out that although married women had taken on paid employment well before the media embraced the idea of the "working mother," by the 1980s the *conduct* and the *culture* had converged. By contrast, he argued that the idea of the "new father" was being promoted by the media long before it had become at all common for men to actually seek this level of involvement in parenting – in other words, the *conduct* of fatherhood lagged some way behind the *culture* of the "new father." In essence, his analysis suggested that when media images are too far removed from people's own perceptions of everyday reality, they lack credibility and will be less influential.

Our own interest in examining how well the contemporary *culture* of parenthood matches the *conduct* of parenthood began in 2006 and drew inspiration from a study by LaRossa and his colleagues that looked at the depiction of mothers and fathers in newspaper comic strips published on Mother's Day and Father's Day (LaRossa et al. 2000). This gave us the idea to similarly compare Mother's Day and Father's Day greeting cards in order to see how they portrayed the roles that mothers and fathers play within their families and, for example, whether or not they now included images of both working mothers and "new fathers."

Researching Greeting Cards

A perennial problem with studying mass media content is that it may not be easy to know how the images or ideas they communicate actually influence people's behaviour (LaRossa et al. 2000). For example, though we are all exposed to the influence of advertising in various forms, it would be unwise to assume that images of young fathers baking cookies in the kitchen with their children in IKEA catalogues have any direct influence on men's behaviour, nor could we expect to measure this from sales of their kitchen cabinets. Likewise, finding evidence that contemporary parenting advice books feature more attention to fathers' participation in child care does not guarantee that any couple buying such a book will necessarily follow its advice and involve the father more (Lupton and Barclay 1997). In other words, the prominence of particular images of fathers in the mass media (*culture*) cannot readily be translated into measurable evidence of their popularity or their influence on people's behaviour (*conduct*).

However, studying Mother's Day and Father's Day greeting cards makes it possible to get closer to assessing the relationship between the *culture* and the *conduct* of motherhood and fatherhood. Like both advertising and parenting advice literature, greeting cards provide a barometer of prevailing societal views of parenting roles (Cacioppo and Andersen 1981; Jaffe 1999; West 2007). The range of cards produced each year is based on extensive market research and sales analysis by card manufacturers (Bolton 2004). Noticing which cards sell well in one year will be the basis for the card companies' decisions on what to produce the following year (Cacioppo and Andersen 1981).

FIGURE 14.1 A Father's Day card display (above) and Mother's Day card display (opposite). Photo credit: Alison Thomas

Indeed, unlike sales of IKEA kitchen cabinets, cards provide a fairly direct indication of the degree to which people relate to these images of mothers and fathers, since they are products that customers buy precisely because of the images they offer. People choose cards that they identify as providing a personally meaningful and appropriate message about motherhood or fatherhood, as experienced (or desired) within their own family (Jaffe 1999). However, it is equally important to note that in the process of browsing the racks and selecting a card to buy, individuals will typically be exposed to a number of other cards featuring various different representations of parental roles, all of which in some way may contribute to shaping their general perceptions of motherhood and fatherhood.

Our Study

In the weeks preceding Mother's Day and Father's Day 2006, we[1] catalogued the full range of Mother's Day and Father's Day cards in each of the two major retail card stores (Carlton Cards, a division of American Greetings, and Hallmark Cards) in a major shopping mall in an outer suburb of Vancouver, Canada (Thomas and Dennis 2008).

1 In addition to us, our research team consisted of five undergraduate research assistants recruited from our respective institutions whom we trained to collect and analyze the card data.

This was a **mixed-methods research** study, involving both quantitative and qualitative data collection and subsequent **content analysis**. We recorded detailed information on each card, using pre-printed data sheets with various **coding** options that we had prepared in advance, based on an earlier pilot study. Our coding included noting whom each card was designed to be sent by (e.g., child or partner) and whether it was humorous or serious in tone. We also wrote down the exact wording of the messages and described the images in order to have a detailed descriptive record of each card. In 2016, we carried out a more limited follow-up study in the same stores to assess how much had changed in that 10-year period.

Our analysis of the data started with a simple quantitative classification of the cards, noting the distribution of cards across different categories (for example, cards from different senders, humorous versus serious cards). This enabled us to get an overall sense of how similar or different cards are for Mother's Day and Father's Day. We then proceeded to do a qualitative analysis of the card messages and images to identify distinct themes.

For each occasion, there were over a thousand card designs available, all arranged in easily identifiable sections within a special display area, with labels such as "Mother from Daughter," "Mother-Religious," "Dad from Son," "Husband-Humorous" (see figure 14.1). Since many of these cards were for grandparents, aunts, uncles, and others, we decided to focus only on cards designed to be given to mothers and fathers by their children or partners, which resulted in a focused **sample** of 1,054 Mother's Day cards and 940 Father's Day cards.[2]

Findings

Quantitative Analysis

From our quantitative analysis, we found that just over half of the cards for both mothers and fathers were designed to be sent by their children (53.7 per cent), 15.3 per cent were designed to be given by a spouse or partner, and 27.7 per cent were worded in such a way that they could be given by anyone. We also found that even though the majority of cards for both mothers and fathers could be classified as serious in tone, more than twice as many cards for fathers were humorous (39.6 per cent), compared with cards for mothers (17 per cent). There were also some interesting gender differences in the distribution of cards in each of these categories. Overall, there were considerably more cards designated specifically for daughters to give, compared with sons (184 versus 115), and although there were equal numbers of cards from sons and daughters for their mothers (72 in each case), there were nearly three

2 Our 2016 follow-up study yielded a focused sample of 1,316 Mother's Day and 1,144 Father's Day cards.

Table 14.1 Distribution of Mother's Day and Father's Day cards categorized by sender and tone (numbers and %)

	Cards for Mother's Day (MD)			Cards for Father's Day (FD)			
	Tone of card			Tone of card			
	Serious (%)	Humorous (%)	MD totals	Serious (%)	Humorous (%)	FD totals	Totals
Cards from children	**82.9**	**17.1**	**55.6% (587)**	**65.3**	**34.7**	**51.5% (484)**	**53.7% (1071)**
From daughter	90.3	9.7	6.8% (72)	75.0	25	11.9% (112)	9.2% (184)
From son	66.7	33.3	6.8% (72)	58.1	41.9	4.6% (43)	5.8% (115)
From child/ren (unspecified)	82.7	17.3	32.9% (347)	61.1	38.9	26.3% (247)	29.8% (594)
From both/group	90.6	9.4	9.1% (96)	68.3	31.7	8.7% (82)	8.9% (178)
Cards from spouse/partner	**84.2**	**15.8**	**13.9% (146)**	**71.9**	**28.1**	**17.0% (160)**	**15.3% (306)**
Cards from family pet	**30.0**	**70.0**	**0.9% (10)**	**9.1**	**90.9**	**2.3% (22)**	**1.6% (32)**
Cards from others (e.g., friend, sibling)	**72.4**	**27.6**	**2.8% (29)**	**50.0**	**50.0**	**0.4% (4)**	**1.7% (33)**
Cards from anyone (unspecified)	**85.5**	**14.5**	**26.8% (282)**	**49.3**	**50.7**	**28.7% (270)**	**27.7% (552)**
Totals	83.0	17.0	100.0 (1054)	60.4	39.6	100.0 (940)	100.0 (1994)

times as many cards to be given by daughters to their fathers, compared to cards from sons (112 versus 43).

Qualitative Analysis

In our qualitative analysis, we wanted to look more closely at what these cards revealed about the roles mothers and fathers are assumed to play within the family and so we decided to focus only on those with a message (and/or imagery) that referred to the receiver's characteristics as a mother/father and/or to the quality of the relationship between sender and receiver. This reduced our sample to 415 Mother's Day cards and 537 Father's Day cards. By studying the images and the text in these cards, we were able to identify a number of distinct themes, each corresponding to a different aspect of the roles that mothers and fathers are shown to play in the lives of their children and partners.

Expressing Appreciation in Mother's Day Cards

Since the vast majority of Mother's Day cards (83 per cent) were serious in tone, expressing straightforward appreciation for mothers, it was not surprising to find that the most prominent theme in cards from any sender was that of the mother who is consistently loving and caring. Mothers are praised for their thoughtfulness, for all the caring "little things" that they do for their family, and for always "being there" to support them. The importance of enduring motherly love is further emphasized in cards that identify it as the "glue" holding the family together and that portray the mother herself as the heart of the family. In other words, even in an era in which the majority of mothers spend much of their time engaging in paid work outside of the home, they continue to be identified symbolically as the nucleus of home and family.

In addition to recognizing the importance of mothers' love, many cards included recognition of their other attributes – such as their wisdom, strength, and courage – and thank them for teaching their children these virtues by setting a good example. Another commonly occurring theme in cards designed to be given by older children (both daughters and sons) is the special character of the mother-child bond, with frequent reference to the idea that the mother can also be a friend to her children as they grow older.

In acknowledging all of the things that mothers do for their families, many cards applaud their ability to juggle multiple tasks at once and some even list the various things mothers do for their families (e.g., "give rides, cook and clean, dry tears, pick up laundry, cheer spirits, tend injuries"). In all, over half of all Mother's Day cards we studied made reference, in some form or other, to the work mothers do and how much it is appreciated. These messages reflect an appreciation of what Patrizia Albanese identifies as "**intensive mothering**" in chapter twenty. Yet it was rare to find cards with explicit recognition that this multi-tasking may also include paid work outside the home (an exception to this

Table 14.2 Examples of themes expressing appreciation in Mother's Day and Father's Day cards

Theme and card identification	Visual imagery	Text
Example 1 (MD card) **The working mom** Hallmark MD 206-2 (2006)	Comic strip series of images of a woman busy in various work and home settings.	"A Mother's job is tough and tiring. Watch her go – she's awe-inspiring! After all the hours she works while putting up with total jerks, she comes back home to do some more – like tackling every household chore."
Example 2 (MD card) **Motherhood as the most important job** Carlton CM0010-01P (2006) Carlton CMD02010-02F (2016)	Flowers in a vase.	"The most important job in the world doesn't offer an hourly wage or days off.... But it does offer priceless memories and many wonderful moments of joy.... Always remember there's no more important job than the one you do every day."
Example 3 (MD card) **The imperfect housewife** Hallmark MOA 709-7 (2016)	Floral design framing text: "A hundred years from now, no one will care how clean our kitchens were or if all the laundry got folded."	Inside: "What will matter then is what has always mattered most ... the love that filled our homes and the people who filled our lives."
Example 4 (FD card) **Father as provider** Carlton CCF21215-10F (2016)	Photo of canoe on lake with mountains beyond.	"You have to love a Dad who works hard to make sure his family has everything they need."
Example 5 (FD card) **The protective father** Carlton CCF 21214-11F (2016)	Design framing text: "Part of being a Dad is asking these questions: 'How was school today?' 'What time will you be home?'"	Inside: "It's amazing how many ways there are for a Dad to say 'I love you' through the years.... Thanks Dad – Love you too."
Example 6 (FD card) **The hands-on, nurturant father** Carlton CCF 21656-01K (2016)	A series of whimsical images of a cartoon bear father caring for infant bear.	"Here's to the men who rock the world ... and pace the floors and lose the sleep ... and change the diapers and find the blankies ... and wipe up the spills – and love every minute of it."

is Example 1 in table 14.2). While the invisibility of their paid employment does not correspond to the realities of most Canadian women's lives in the twenty-first century, it is not surprising that for Mother's Day, the emphasis should be on appreciating the work that women still also do in the home in their more traditional (second-shift) role as caring mothers and capable housewives (see Dillaway and Paré 2008). Indeed, some cards explicitly contrasted the paid and unpaid work that mothers do, stressing the idea that being a mother is in itself the most important (and toughest) job a woman can have – one that they do all day and every day, out of love for their family. This theme was represented in a variety of ways, some serious (see Example 2) and others comical – even including images of women tackling household chores in full combat gear!

An interesting variation on the theme of motherly love that we noticed emerging in our 2016 data was that of the mother as an imperfect housewife (see Example 3), whose love for her family is more important than having an immaculately clean home. Given the evidence that women are in fact spending less time on housework than in the past, cards like these offer reassurance that a sticky kitchen floor does not mean that a woman is not a good mother and suggest a possible lessening of the expectation that all mothers should aspire to be supermom.

Expressing Appreciation in Father's Day Cards

Fathers (like mothers) are thanked for being important as teachers and role models, and they are often also portrayed as a "guiding light" in their children's lives – a message sometimes underlined in symbolic images of lighthouses on rocky shores. Traditional ideas about fathers' responsibility for providing for and protecting their families were also prominent in these cards and were frequently depicted as the practical ways in which fathers demonstrate their love (see Examples 4 and 5).

Though cards such as these indicate recognition that fathers care *about* their children, far fewer gave any indication that they actively did the practical work of caring *for* them, and cards portraying men explicitly as nurturing, involved fathers were relatively uncommon in both 2006 and 2016. Cards designed for the first-time father (such as Example 6) are the ones most likely to depict the father's active involvement in child care of any kind, and a number of these even make explicit his participation not just in the more appealing hands-on activities such as tucking in small children at bedtime, but also in diaper changing. (This is noteworthy, as it is seldom referred to in Mother's Day cards – it is simply taken for granted that that is something mothers do!)

While many Father's Day cards are clearly designed to be given by adult children with a mature appreciation of the roles that their father played as they were growing up, a common theme in cards designed to appeal specifically to younger children is the idea of the father as a playmate, a friend with whom they can have fun. This is quite unlike the depiction of friendship found in Mother's Day cards, where it is cards from adult daughters that are most likely to refer to having a close friendship with their mother.

Many of these themes showing appreciation for fathers were combined in cards that identified fathers as heroes or superheroes. In cards from children, the father's heroism was typically identified with his status as a role model, protector and provider to his family, and as somebody to look up to, even in adulthood. However, cards from partners also expressed appreciation for his practical acts of domestic heroism, such as unblocking toilets. In 2016, we also found a new theme emerging, typically in cards from the partner, expressing the idea that most men are trying hard to be good dads, even if they aren't perfect.

Humour in Mother's Day and Father's Day Cards

As we have seen, though there are many similarities between the messages in Mother's Day and Father's Day cards, there are also some striking differences between them. Not only were there pronounced differences in the proportions of cards using humour for Mother's Day and Father's Day, but the kind of humour employed in funny cards reveals further interesting differences.

Humorous Mother's Day cards that poke fun at mothers generally do so with affectionate, light-hearted recognition of the same stereotypical views of motherhood that are celebrated in the serious cards, such as Mom the multi-tasker, the all-knowing wise mother, and "motherly advice"; one even joked about Mom always "being there" when things go wrong, concluding, "Face it, Mom: You're a jinx!" These cards too thus serve to reinforce cultural expectations of the good mother. Cards that make fun of the sender tend to reflect similar ideas about the important role the mother plays in managing their life (see Example 7, table 14.3) and, somewhat surprisingly, many cards from husbands to their wives made jokes about the balance of power and responsibility in the home, typically acknowledging the mother as the responsible parent (see Example 8). In fact, a considerable number of funny Mother's Day cards feature more or less explicit comparisons between the capable mother and incompetent father (see Example 9). Even among humorous cards, there are few that suggest anything negative about the mother or her competence – although in 2016, we did find a few cards referring to how mothers deal with the strain of coping with everything by resorting to self-medication through alcohol or imaginary drugs such as "Screwitol."

In contrast to the use of humour in Mother's Day cards, many Father's Day cards make the father the butt of their jokes, gently mocking his limited fishing skills, golfing talents, or his competence as a "home handyman." As with Mother's Day cards, many cards draw upon the same images of fatherhood as the serious cards, such as the father as role model, but poke fun at them. While the humour in these cards often appears benign and affectionate, in some there is also a hint of disrespect for the more "traditional" role of the father as an authority figure within the family (as in Example 10). Many of the cards we found for the father-to-be or for new fathers were also humorous, mainly featuring jokes about men's reliance on women to manage practical child care of all kinds. Echoing what we found in Mother's Day cards, a number of cards joked about fathers being subordinate to mothers (see Example 11). However, of the many humorous cards that poked fun at father **stereotypes**, the most obviously disrespectful were those portraying the father as an idle couch potato and all-round slob, as in Example 12. Numerous cards also referred to fathers burping, scratching, snoring, and a remarkable number joked about fathers farting!

While the majority of funny Father's Day cards (54 per cent) make fun of fathers themselves, this is not the case with Mother's Day cards, where the joke is either against the sender of the card (35 per cent) or against the father (35 per cent), and only 27 per cent target mothers. This discrepancy should come as no surprise, since a similar pattern is apparent in other forms of popular culture, such as television shows and advertisements. These routinely employ humorous depictions of male domestic incompetence

Table 14.3 Examples of humorous themes in Mother's Day and Father's Day cards

Theme and card identification	Visual imagery	Text
Example 7 (MD card) **Joke against sender (child)** Carlton AM 16459-01P (2006)	Cartoon image of teenage boy standing in untidy bedroom, with the caption: "Mom, where would I be without you?"	Inside: "Probably buried under 500 lbs of junk in my room!"
Example 8 (MD card) **Joke against sender (partner)** Carlton CCM 15036-03K (2016)	Cartoon mother and father bear. "To my wife: since this is Mother's Day, you just relax and I'll take care of everything."	Inside: "By the way, where is everything?"
Example 9 (MD card) **Mothers as more capable than fathers** Hallmark ZMD 607-2 (2006)	Comic-strip style multi-tasking mother with the caption: "Being a mom isn't easy."	Inside: "If it was, dads could do it."
Example 10 (FD card) **Mocking the "traditional" dad figure** Hallmark FD259-3 (2006)	Multi-page folding card with a caption and "stereotypical" father image for every letter of the alphabet.	"Being a Dad is as easy as ABC! Ask your mother; Because I said so; Close that door; Do I look like a bank? Eleven does not mean 11:45," et cetera.
Example 11 (FD card) **Mothers in charge of the family** Carlton CCM 02015-10 (2016)	No images, only text. "Stuff you ask Mom" – followed by various questions, such as: "What's for dinner?" "When is it my turn?" "Do I have to go to bed?"	Inside: "Stuff you ask Dad" – followed by a single question: "Where's Mom?"
Example 12 (FD card) **Couch-potato dad** Carlton GF45042-09L (2006)	Cartoon-style images of multiple possible gifts for dad (e.g., clothing, tools, gadgets) and a child's face with question marks over it.	"For Father's Day I wanted to get you something a guy like you could really use.... But I couldn't find a remote with a 'bring me a beer' button."

to suggest that men should not be trusted in the home, yet they seldom mock women's abilities (Robinson and Hunter 2008; Scharrer et al. 2006).[3] In fact, many social scientists have noted a contemporary culture of "male-bashing," which makes fun of men in a way that would be regarded as sexist if it were directed toward women (Nathanson and Young 2001).

3 For example, in 2008–2009 a CBC reality series entitled *The Week the Women Went* featured the women of a small community being enticed away from their homes for a week by the show's producers, leaving their male partners to take care of the home and family, with TV cameras rolling to document the domestic chaos that was predicted to follow. (Needless to say, the producers ensured that it did – at least in the households that they chose to feature.)

Assessing the Cultural Impact of Greeting Cards

As noted earlier, the most prominent differences that we found between Mother's Day and Father's Day cards are that the majority of cards designed for mothers express straightforward appreciation (83 per cent), whereas nearly 40 per cent of those for fathers are humorous and poke fun at fathers themselves. Does this suggest that our culture is simply less comfortable expressing sentimental feelings toward our fathers than to our mothers, leading us to fall back on jokiness instead as way of connecting? (This pattern seems particularly pronounced when we look at the differences between cards for sons and daughters to give to their fathers. See table 14.1.)

While that is one possible explanation for this difference in tone, the current prevalence of jokes about fathers being secondary to mothers in the home, both here and in various other forms of mass media, may also be an indicator of the transitional era in which we find ourselves, with previously **gendered** roles in the process of dissolving. On the one hand, these jokes may be evidence that as a society we are beginning to agree that some aspects of the more traditional styles of fatherhood are worth laughing at – and rejecting – in favour of contemporary models of more involved fatherhood. However, it is also possible that laughing at "bumbling dads" serves merely to reinforce popular beliefs that we still need to rely on women to run the home; in which case, it is not a very progressive message at all. Both analyses seem plausible in a diverse society in which people may hold quite different opinions about the desirability of change in the household division of labour.

Relating our research findings back to the issue of the *culture* versus the *conduct* of parenthood, we suggest that one reason for the apparent lack of impact of the early wave of mass media attention to the "new father" may be that since the 1980s we have been exposed to rather more mixed messages about male involvement in the home, as seen in the cards discussed here. While some do show fathers providing hands-on care to their young children, the great majority portray men in much more "traditional" father roles, including that of family breadwinner. By contrast, mothers' paid work is almost entirely invisible in these cards, and instead it is their role as primary caregiver and housewife that is highlighted. This emphasis on gender-differentiated roles (which was just as apparent in 2016 as in 2006) is also consistent with what has been found in various studies of contemporary parenting advice in books, newspapers, and magazines, in which mothers are still assumed to take primary responsibility for routine child care while fathers participate in fun activities with their children (e.g., Sunderland 2000, 2006; Schmitz 2016; Wall and Arnold 2007). This distinction is captured very clearly here, in two cards that consist of definitions of what mothers and fathers represent:

> "A Mother: someone who gives and cares and works and worries.... Who keeps going and giving and running around ... and caring and helping and saving the day." (Hallmark MD 524-6)

> "What is a Daddy? A daddy helps fix things, buys ice cream, plays games ... hugs you and finds time – to spend being your daddy and being your friend!" (Carlton AF0527-02P)

In other words, instead of the *conduct* of fatherhood changing to catch up with the *culture*, the *culture* itself appears to have reversed course to some extent, bringing the range of images of fatherhood it presents closer to what most men actually do. Might this lowering of expectations for men to become fully engaged "new fathers" actually make it easier for them to make a more gradual shift toward greater involvement in family work?[4] Though there is evidence that younger men are more likely to get involved in child care and housework than preceding generations (Battams 2016; DeGeer, Carolo, and Minerson 2014), the generally slow pace of change indicates that it is still likely to be a long time before it becomes the norm for men to share any form of family work equally with women (Marshall 2011). With little evidence of change in greeting card representations of parenting roles over a 10-year period, it will be interesting to see what role cards and other media images may play in promoting (or ignoring) a more equal household division of labour in the next decade.

Conclusion: Greeting Cards as an Indicator of the Stalled Gender Revolution

Many sociologists have identified the ongoing inequity in household labour as a major factor in the "stalled" gender revolution (e.g., Hochschild 1989; Latshaw 2011), and researchers continue to investigate why gender roles in the home seem so slow to change. One approach examines the role of mass media in presenting images of parental roles that influence public attitudes and behaviour (distinguishing the *culture* and the *conduct* of parenthood) and focuses on whether these images are supporting or hindering change, particularly in men's involvement in the home (e.g., LaRossa et al. 2000; Robinson and Hunter 2008).

To illustrate this approach, we reported our research examining Mother's Day and Father's Day cards, which found that rather than challenging old gender stereotypes and promoting more equal roles, these (in common with other forms of mass media) are still mainly reinforcing the domestic status quo. If, as Cacioppo and Andersen (1981) argue, greeting cards can be assumed to represent what the public want to buy, the prevalence of jokes about fathers' domestic incompetence (alongside praise for the supermoms who can "do it all") suggests to us that our society is still not yet ready to accept fully interchangeable family roles for women and men. We are still very much stuck in a "stalled" gender revolution.

4 LaRossa and colleagues (2000) drew attention to periodic fluctuations over time in depictions of mothers and fathers and so anticipated this kind of reversal. LaRossa (1988) also argued that the gap between media images of the idealized "new father" and what most fathers were actually contributing to family work was causing marital friction, meaning that presenting more realistic images of father involvement should help lessen this.

Questions for Critical Thought

1. Has this chapter changed the way you look at greeting cards? What other special-occasion cards might you examine if you wanted to further explore gender stereotypes?
2. Looking at the figures in table 14.1, what do you notice about the number and the tone of cards available for daughters and sons to give to their mothers and fathers? How might we explain the differences we see here?
3. As powerful agents of socialization, the various forms of mass media are the subject of extensive sociological investigations. Which forms of mass media do you think are the most powerful?
4. How does the concept of the "second shift" correspond with patterns you observe in your everyday life?
5. If you wanted to use greeting cards to help promote a more equal division of domestic labour, what images and messages would you employ? How do you think the characteristics associated with being a good mother contribute to a "second shift" for women?

Acknowledgements

The study described in this chapter was made possible by research funding from our respective institutions, Douglas College and the University of the Fraser Valley. We very much appreciate their support.

References

Battams, Nathan. 2016. "Modern Fathers Reshaping the Work–Family Relationship." *L'Institut Vanier de la famille/Vanier Institute of the Family*, June 13. http://vanierinstitute.ca/modern-fathers-reshaping-workfamily-relationship/.

Berger, Peter L. 1963. *Invitation to Sociology: A Humanistic Perspective*. Garden City: Anchor Books/Published by Doubleday and Company, Inc.

Bolton, Rachel. 2004. "Dads are Heroes: Important, Influential, Inspiring." *Hallmark Pressroom*.

Cacioppo, John T. and Barbara L. Andersen. 1981. "Greeting Cards as Data on Social Processes." *Basic and Applied Social Psychology* 2 (2): 115–19. https://doi.org/10.1207/s15324834basp0202_3.

Chesley, Noelle. 2011. "Stay-at-Home Fathers and Bread-Winning Mothers: Gender, Couple Dynamics and Social Change." *Gender and Society* 25 (5): 642–64. https://doi.org/10.1177/0891243211417433.

Coltrane, Scott, and Kenneth Allan. 1994. "'New Fathers' and Old Stereotypes: Representations of Masculinity in 1980s Television Advertising." *Masculinities* 2 (4): 43–66.

Coontz, Stephanie. 2005. *Marriage, a History: from Obedience to Intimacy, or How Love Conquered Marriage*. New York: Viking.

DeGeer, Ian, Humberto Carolo, and Todd Minerson. 2014. "Modern Fatherhood: Paternal Involvement and Family Relationships." *The Vanier Institute of the Family: Transition* 44 (2): 9–12.

Dillaway, Heather, and Elizabeth Paré. 2008. "Locating Mothers: How Cultural Debates about Stay-at-Home Versus Working Mothers Define Women and Home." *Journal of Family Issues* 29 (4): 437–64. https://doi.org/10.1177/0192513X07310309.

Ferguson, Marjorie. 1983. *Forever Feminine: Women's Magazines and the Cult of Femininity*. London: Heinemann.

Friedan, Betty. 1963. *The Feminine Mystique*. New York: W.W. Norton.

Frisco, Michelle L., and Kristi Williams. 2003. "Perceived Housework Equity, Marital Happiness, and Divorce in Dual-Earner Households." *Journal of Family Issues* 24 (1): 51–73. https://doi.org/10.1177/0192513X02238520.

Furstenberg, Frank F. 1988. "Good Dads/Bad Dads: The Two Faces of Fatherhood." In *The Changing American Family*, edited by A. Cherlin, 193–218. Washington, DC: Urban Institute Press.

Guppy, Neil, and Nicole Luongo. 2015. "The Rise and Stall of Canada's Gender-Equity Revolution." *Canadian Review of Sociology* 52 (3): 241–65. https://doi.org/10.1111/cars.12076.

Hochschild, Arlie Russell, with Anne Machung. 1989. *The Second Shift: Working Parents and the Revolution at Home*. New York: Viking.

Houle, Patricia, Martin Turcotte, and Michael Wendt. 2017. "Changes in Parents' Participation in Domestic Task and Care for Children from 1986 to 2015." *Spotlight on Canadians: Results from the General Social Survey*, June. Statistics Canada Catalogue no. 89-652-X. http://www.statcan.gc.ca/pub/89-652-x/89-652-x2017001-eng.htm.

Jaffe, Alexandra. 1999. "Packaged Sentiments: The Social Meanings of Greeting Cards." *Journal of Material Culture* 4 (2): 115–41. https://doi.org/10.1177/135918359900400201.

Johnston, Deirdre D., and Debra H. Swanson. 2003. "Invisible Mothers: A Content Analysis of Motherhood Ideologies and Myths in Magazines." *Sex Roles* 49 (1): 21–33. https://doi.org/10.1023/A:1023905518500.

Kan, Man Yee, Oriel Sullivan, and Jonathan Gershuny. 2011. "Gender Convergence in Domestic Work: Discerning the Effects of Interactional and Institutional Barriers from Large-Scale Data." *Sociology* 45 (2): 234–51. https://doi.org/10.1177/0038038510394014.

LaRossa, Ralph. 1988. "Fatherhood and Social Change." *Family Relations* 37 (4): 451–57. https://doi.org/10.2307/584119.

———. 1997. *The Modernization of Fatherhood: A Social and Political History*. Chicago: University of Chicago Press.

LaRossa, Ralph, Charles Jaret, Malati Gadgil, and G. Robert Wynn. 2000. "The Changing Culture of Fatherhood in Comic-Strip Families: A Six-Decade Analysis." *Journal of Marriage and the Family* 62 (2): 375–87. https://doi.org/10.1111/j.1741-3737.2000.00375.x.

Latshaw, Beth A. 2011. "The More Things Change, the More They Remain the Same? Paradoxes of Men's Unpaid Labor since 'The Second Shift.'" *Sociology Compass* 5 (7): 653–65. https://doi.org/10.1111/j.1751-9020.2011.00391.x.

Lorber, Judith. 2012. *Gender Inequality: Feminist Theories and Politics*. 5th ed. New York: Oxford University Press.

Lupton, Debora, and Lesley Barclay. 1997. *Constructing Fatherhood: Discourses and Experiences*. Thousand Oaks: SAGE.

Marshall, Katherine. 2006. "Converging Gender Roles." *Perspectives on Labour and Income* 18 (3): 7–17.

———. 2011. "Generational Change in Paid and Unpaid Work." *Canadian Social Trends* 92: 13–24.

McQuail, Denis. 2010. *McQuail's Mass Communication Theory*. Thousand Oaks: SAGE.

Nathanson, Paul, and Katherine K. Young. 2001. *Spreading Misandry: The Teaching of Contempt for Men in Popular Culture*. Kingston: McGill-Queen's University Press.

Oakley, Ann. 1981. *From Here to Maternity: Becoming a Mother.* Harmondsworth: Penguin.

Parsons, Talcott, and Robert Freed Bales. 1955. *Family, Socialization and Interaction Process.* Glencoe: Free Press.

Patnaik, Ankita. 2015. "'Daddy's Home!' Increasing Men's Use of Paternity Leave." *Council on Contemporary Families*, April 2. https://contemporaryfamilies.org/ccf-briefing-report-daddys-home/.

Pleck, Joseph H. 1987. "American Fathering in Historical Perspective." In *Changing Men: New Directions in Research on Men and Masculinity*, edited by Michael Kimmel, 351–61. Thousand Oaks: SAGE.

Robinson, Bryan K., and Erica Hunter. 2008. "Is Mom Still Doing It All? Reexamining Depictions of Family Work in Popular Advertising." *Journal of Family Issues* 29 (4): 465–86. https://doi.org/10.1177/0192513X07310311.

Rudman, Laurie A., and Kris Mescher. 2013. "Penalizing Men Who Request a Family Leave: Is Flexibility Stigma a Femininity Stigma?" *Journal of Social Issues* 69 (2): 322–40. https://doi.org/10.1111/josi.12017.

Scharrer, Erica, Daniel D. Kim, Ke-Ming Lin, and Zixu Liu. 2006. "Working Hard or Hardly Working? Gender, Humor, and the Performance of Domestic Chores in Television Commercials." *Mass Communication and Society* 9 (2): 215–38. https://doi.org/10.1207/s15327825mcs0902_5.

Schmitz, Rachel M. 2016. "Constructing Men as Fathers: A Content Analysis of Formulations of Fatherhood in Parenting Magazines." *Journal of Men's Studies* 24 (1): 3–23. https://doi.org/10.1177/1060826515624381.

Statistics Canada. 2016. *Spotlight on Canadians: Results from the General Social Survey: Satisfaction with work-life balance: Fact Sheet.* Catalogue no. 89-652-X2016003. Ottawa: Statistics Canada. http://www.statcan.gc.ca/pub/89-652-x/89-652-x2016003-eng.htm.

Sunderland, Jane. 2000. "Baby Entertainer, Bumbling Assistant and Line Manager: Discourses of Fatherhood in Parentcraft Texts." *Discourse and Society* 11 (2): 249–74. https://doi.org/10.1177/0957926500011002006.

———. 2006. "'Parenting' or 'Mothering'?: The Case of Modern Childcare Magazines." *Discourse and Society* 17 (4): 503–27. https://doi.org/10.1177/0957926506063126.

Thomas, Alison, and Elizabeth Dennis. 2008. "Angels, Heroes ... and Slobs: How Do Representations of Gender and Family Work in Mother's Day and Father's Day Cards Help Explain the 'Stalled Revolution'?" Paper presented at the annual conference of the Canadian Sociological Association, Vancouver, BC.

Walker, Nancy A. 2000. *Shaping our Mothers' World: American Women's Magazines.*

Wall, Glenda, and Stephanie Arnold. 2007. "How Involved Is Involved Fathering? An Exploration of the Contemporary Culture of Fatherhood." *Gender and Society* 21 (4): 508–27. https://doi.org/10.1177/0891243207304973.

West, Emily. 2007. "When You Care Enough to Defend the Very Best: How the Greeting Card Industry Manages Cultural Criticism." *Media, Culture and Society* 29 (2): 241–61. https://doi.org/10.1177/0163443707074255.

15 Rites of Spring: Multiculturalism and the Celebration of Vaisakhi in Vancouver

BONAR BUFFAM

LEARNING OUTCOMES

After reading this chapter, you should be able to:

- describe how religions are dynamic social phenomena that have been shaped by the modern structures of empire and the nation-state
- explain how ghettos and ethnic enclaves form in urban spaces through processes of discrimination and spatial segregation
- describe how Vaisakhi celebrations represent the complex local histories of Sikh and South Asian communities in Metro Vancouver
- explain how religious, cultural, and political rituals create different forms of social cohesion and division
- evaluate the different political, social, and cultural meanings of multiculturalism and understand why it is important to recognize these differences

Introduction

I grew up in a sleepy suburb of Victoria, British Columbia, where my favourite local **ritual** was the Oak Bay Tea Party, which was held over the first weekend in June. Its marquee event was the midway carnival, but my most vivid memories surround the parade that kicked off the celebrations. Every year, my family would get to the parade route early to eke out the same stretch of sidewalk to watch the passing cavalcade of cars, floats, and high school marching bands. As a kid, I thought nothing of the ritual and ceremony of the occasion or of the kinds of local **identity** and community solidarity that were displayed through these celebrations, similar to the Santa Claus parades discussed in this book's introduction. Much of the Tea Party's ritualism was steeped in images of genteel British **culture**, including its choice of the Mad Hatter as the event's mascot, which reflects the kinds of identity cultivated in this upper-middle-class municipality that had been formed through the **dispossession** of **Indigenous** land.

Parades often have very complex relationships to the places in which they are staged. Some parades, like the Oak Bay Tea Party, try to assert a common local or **national identity** for that place (Brickell 2000). In these circumstances, the floats, marching bands, and other entries in the parade try to communicate some sense of the collective **norms** and **values** of the people who frequent those neighbourhoods. As a kid, my other points of reference for parades were the Fourth of July parades featured on television sitcoms like *The Wonder Years,* where they appeared as a ritual of national cohesion that brought people together according to their shared sense of American identity. In other contexts, parades are staged by minority groups to express and combat their exclusion from a given place. For instance, St. Patrick's Day parades were first held in the nineteenth century to challenge the **discrimination** faced by Irish immigrants by establishing a more visible and collective presence in their communities. Pride parades have also been a way for **queer** communities to combat **homophobia** by reclaiming public space for sexual minorities (Brickell 2000).

This chapter examines the complex relationships to place that are created through the annual **Vaisakhi** parades in Metro Vancouver, which happen in Surrey and Vancouver over two consecutive Saturdays in April. Vaisakhi parades commemorate the founding of the Sikh Khalsa – the new spiritual order of Sikhs that was established in 1699 (Ballantyne 2006). The parades also mark a Punjabi harvest season, when crops like rabi and barley are gathered in this region of the Indian subcontinent. While it is tempting to think of Vaisakhi as a religious practice, in this chapter I suggest that we should also think of these celebrations as social and political rituals that are deeply connected to **place.** Sociologists use the concept of place to make sense of the complex attachments that people form to particular spaces like neighbourhoods, cities, and **nation-states.** I examine how Vaisakhi is shaped by different practices of **multiculturalism** that reflect connections to Canada as a distinct place that fosters certain kinds of identity. This requires some explanation of how multiculturalism exists as (1) a demographic reality, (2) a pluralist vision of social change, (3) a set of vernacular practices that occur in contexts of plurality, and (4) a set of government policies that sanctioned new patterns of immigration and images of national identity (Keith 2005; Mackey 2002; Thobani 2007). I also examine how Vaisakhi parades are tied to the neighbourhoods in which they are staged, places that have been shaped by processes of social and spatial segregation. Through these processes of segregation, areas of south Vancouver and south Surrey have become **ethnic enclaves,** a term used by sociologists to describe neighbourhoods where certain minority groups are statistically overrepresented relative to the rest of the **city** (Keith 2005; Walks and Bourne 2006).

In this chapter, I draw on my ongoing **qualitative research** on the changing political circumstances of Sikh and South Asian communities in Metro Vancouver. When I use the term "political," I am not only referring to the workings of state institutions but also to the broader struggles over power and inequality that shape the social circumstances of groups like local Sikh communities. For this project, I analyzed various newspapers and magazines to see how these communities are represented in the media, collected historical documents from state archives that show how government institutions treated and interacted with these communities, and undertook observational **fieldwork** at Vaisakhi celebrations in Vancouver and Surrey. By integrating the information from these sources, I am able to explain how these seasonal celebrations reflect broader social and political processes that have shaped Sikh and South Asian communities in Metro Vancouver.

Sikhi and the Complex Category of Religion

In 2011, there were roughly 23 million Sikhs around the world (Mandair 2013). Nearly three-quarters of this **population** live in the Punjab region of the Indian subcontinent, where Sikhi first emerged in the fifteenth century. I use the term "**Sikhi**" rather than the more common word "Sikhism" because its connection to the Punjabi word *sikhna* ("to learn") better reflects the ongoing experience of learning that is prioritized in Sikh scriptures and practices (Mandair 2013). Sikhi is focused on the teachings of 10 successive gurus – a title given to people devoted to the spiritual emancipation of their followers. The last of these gurus, Guru Gobind Singh, founded the Sikh Khalsa by standardizing a series of rites that must be followed to initiate people into the distinct order of Amritdhari Sikhs. Men and women who are Amritdhari Sikhs typically show their identity by wearing five **symbols** of their initiation into the Khalsa: a steel bracelet (*kara*), undergarments (*kachera*), uncut hair (*kesh*), combs (*kangha*), and a ceremonial dagger (*kirpan*) (Ballantyne 2006). Of course, not all people who practise Sikhi are a part of the Khalsa tradition, nor do all Amritdhari Sikhs show their identities in the same way (Nayar 2008).

Various symbols of Sikh identity figure prominently in the Vaisakhi parades, which are organized by the local **gurdwaras**. The Khalsa symbol (*Khanda*), which was formalized in the early twentieth century, appears on flags, signs, and T-shirts throughout the parade route (see figure 15.1). In each parade, the marquee entries are the *nagar kirtans*, processions of people who recite hymns as they walk through the community. At the front of this procession is a truck with musicians playing these hymns, with the principal book of Sikh scripture (*Guru Granth Sahib*) in the compartment above the driver. To understand the social realities of **religion** at events like these, many sociologists have used the ideas of Émile Durkheim.

Émile Durkheim (1857–1917) was a French sociologist credited with formalizing the discipline of sociology through his research on the rise of modern societies (as discussed in chapters seven and eight of this book). Durkheim was writing about a time of great societal change in Western Europe, which also had significant repercussions around the world. As he witnessed people moving en masse into cities, he came to define modern

FIGURE 15.1 Vancouver Vaisakhi Parade, 2015. Photo credit: Bonar Buffam

societies in terms of their heterogeneity (the mingling of social differences in cities), **industrialization** (increased factory production), and secularity (which he associated with the decreased prominence of organized religion). In his book *The Elementary Forms of Religious Life,* Durkheim (2008) draws on anthropological studies of so-called "primitive" societies to identify the rudimentary and universal features of religion as it is practised around the world. Contemporary scholars have critiqued Durkheim for the problems that plague his analysis. We should be cautious about perpetuating racist distinctions between "primitive" and "advanced" religions, which present Indigenous peoples as uncivilized and historically backward. These kinds of representations have been used to deny political autonomy to Indigenous peoples and justify different forms of violence against them (Simpson 2014). Others have questioned whether religion is actually a universal category, raising valid concerns that such a conclusion rests on **Eurocentric** assumptions that make all religions fit certain Judeo-Christian parameters (Masuwaza 2005); this critique is explained in more detail later in the chapter. What Durkheim (2008) offers is some recognition of the social dimensions of religion, as well as the complex dynamics that affect how we categorize social phenomena (Cooper 2017; Smith 2004). Unlike many of his contemporaries, who dismiss religion as a mere lie or illusion, he suggests that religion persists across various places because it serves real, determinate social purposes and reflects and informs specific values, concerns, and interests. For the sake of this chapter, I want to show how Durkheim's definition of religion can help explain the complex ways in which religion, culture, and politics intersect during Vaisakhi celebrations.

Early in his book, Durkheim (2008) defines religion as a "unified system of beliefs and practices relative to sacred things, that is to say things set apart and forbidden – beliefs and practices which unite into one single moral community called a Church, all those who adhere to them" (44). In this passage, Durkheim suggests that the shared realities of religious groups are a function of how they envision and preserve the sacred – those symbols (e.g., the Star of David, the *Khanda*) and objects (e.g., communion wafers and *kirpans*) that have a special significance to the group. The sacred quality of these things is expressed and maintained through ritual practices that ensure they are "set apart" from the rest of reality, which is classified as "profane" or "mundane." Yet Durkheim clarifies that no symbol or object is innately sacred; they acquire this sacred significance through the collective practices of the specific community of believers. For Durkheim, the ritualistic character of these collective practices is critical to the continuation of religion as they renew the group's ties across periodic intervals of time and ensure that people continue to see themselves as a part of this group. Using Durkheim's ideas, we can see how Vaisakhi celebrations do not merely express Sikh values and **traditions**; each year, the rituals that surround Vaisakhi also work to reinforce and redefine the collective ties of Sikh communities in the Lower Mainland.

It would be a mistake to imply that religious communities are the only groups engaged in these kinds of rituals. After all, this book is focused on many of the different seasonal rituals that structure social life in Canada, only some of which are connected to religion. The fans of professional sports teams discussed by Nicole Neverson in chapter ten are bound together by different gameday rituals, many of which centre on team **logos** and colours that take on a sacred significance. The practice of watching hockey games at pubs and sports bars has a ritualistic quality that is similar to the religious rites described by Durkheim. Canadian **nationalism** is also dependent on people's continued "religious" orientation to certain symbols (e.g., the maple leaf) and values (e.g., freedom and diversity), which are reinforced through rituals that are both mundane (e.g., the singing of the national anthem) and spectacular (e.g., Canada Day celebrations). Insofar as Durkheim's ideas illustrate the religious character of modern social life, they work against the secular tendency to treat religion as though it is categorically distinct from politics, culture, and other realms of modern **society** (Asad 2003). In this regard, Durkheim's ideas are helpful for understanding how Sikh practices cannot be analyzed apart from broader cultural and political processes, an idea repeatedly affirmed in Sikh studies scholarship.

Recent research in the field of Sikh studies questions whether the category of religion accurately reflects how Sikhi has been practised apart from the influence of the British Empire and European notions of religion. Such understandings position the traditions of Judaism and Christianity as the models for all religion (Mandair 2009). Until the mid-nineteenth century, Sikhi was not practised outside Punjab, the northwest region of the Indian subcontinent in which it originated. From 1849 to 1947, Punjab was a colony of the East India Company and the British Empire (Ballantyne 2006). These imperial institutions dramatically impacted the way Sikhi was understood and practised.

According to Mandair (2009), Sikhi does not easily fit with standard categories of religion; it only came to be understood as a religion, "Sikhism," because it was made to fit Judeo-Christian notions of religion by European philosophers, anthropologists, and Sikh reformers. This transformation of Sikhi into a religion had multiple consequences. It affected how people classified sacred objects and shaped the practices that were deemed necessary to protect that sacred status. It also changed how people understood and identified themselves as "Sikhs" (Mandair 2009). Under British rule, people's relatively fluid cultural practices were categorized into distinct and rigid religious identities: "Sikh," "Muslim," and "Hindu" (Ballantyne 2006).

It was also during British rule over Punjab that some Sikhs travelled to Canada and other British colonies like Australia and Singapore, sometimes as part of anti-colonial movements that sought to challenge British imperialism and bring about self-rule in India (Mawani 2012; Mongia 2018). In Canada, Sikh institutions like gurdwaras have served multiple political functions that are not reducible to religion. For instance, in the early twentieth century, gurdwara leaders were instrumental in advocating for changes to immigration restrictions faced by Sikh and Indian populations and for demanding the enfranchisement of Indian-Canadians, who were summarily banned from voting in Canadian elections until after World War II (Nayar 2008).

While Durkheim's theory of religion helps illuminate the collective dimensions of social life, it would be a mistake to think of Sikh communities in BC as a single homogenous group. To assume that there is such a unified group of Sikhs is especially problematic given how Sikhi has been politicized in the wake of campaigns to create a separate Sikh nation state known as Khalistan. After India gained national independence from Britain in 1947, some Sikh groups demanded the creation of a sovereign country in Punjab, a region of the Indian subcontinent that spans the border of Pakistan and India (Axel 2001). In 1984, when these separatist movements were acquiring momentum, India's prime minister, Indira Gandhi, ordered a military siege of the Golden Temple in Amritsar, a gurdwara in Punjab that many Sikhs regard as their most important and sacred institution (Ballantyne 2006). This siege instigated a series of violent retaliatory events, including the bombing of two Air India flights allegedly orchestrated by certain Sikh separatist groups operating in BC. Over the last 30 years, divisions have emerged within local Sikh communities over people's different positions on these Khalistani movements. While some Sikh groups have criticized the use of violence to realize an independent nation state, others have questioned whether Sikh communities in Canada should support this cause at all (Nayar 2008). Vaisakhi parades have been a catalyst for these divisions when participants include imagery that praises one of the Air India bombers as a Sikh martyr, imagery that has been denounced by Sikh community leaders and Canadian politicians who have appeared at the parades.

Vaisakhi celebrations have also come to feature other political rituals of protest and public education. In 2015, the week after the Vancouver Vaisakhi parades, Indian prime minister Narenda Modi was scheduled to address people at the Ross Street Temple, prompting an array of local groups to erect a banner on Fraser Avenue that read "No Compromise on Canadian and Human Values. You are not welcome." That same year,

FIGURE 15.2 Vancouver Vaisakhi Parade, 2016. Photo credit: Bonar Buffam

the Mamta Foundation, a local non-profit organization devoted to helping impoverished children, entered a float in the Vancouver parade that politicized **gender** inequalities in Sikh and South Asian communities. Prominent on the float is an image of the tenth Sikh guru along with the words "you are not to associate with those who kill their daughters," a message that presents gendered violence as antithetical to Sikhi (see figure 15.2).

Across all of the political rituals that take place during Vaisakhi parades, Sikhi works in a manner that complicates prevailing European categories of religion, which assume it can be separated from the political (Mandair 2013). Even though "Sikhism" is recognized and understood as a distinct religion, its practise has become inextricably linked to a variety of political projects and practices. In the next section of this chapter, I explain how Vaisakhi has become the venue for political rituals more directly connected to the Canadian nation-state.

Multiculturalism and National Political Rituals

There has been no shortage of politicians at recent Vaisakhi celebrations in Metro Vancouver. Along the parade route on Main Street, political parties from across the spectrum set up tables to hawk their platforms and distribute paraphernalia that is branded according to their party's trademarked colour (see figure 15.3). At the stages

FIGURE 15.3 Political party tables at the Vancouver Vaisakhi Parade, 2015. Photo credit: Bonar Buffam

constructed for dance and musical performances, politicians like BC's former premier, Christy Clark, and then-federal minister of immigration, Jason Kenney, have delivered speeches about Canada's legacies of diversity and multiculturalism. In the following section, I explain how the presence of political figures at these celebrations exemplifies the varied political rituals that characterize Vaisakhi, many of which centre on the different meanings of multiculturalism.

Multiculturalism as Ideology and as Policy

Multiculturalism is broadly understood to be a type of **pluralist ideology** that values and cultivates cultural differences within a given political environment (Mackey 2002). In the decades after World War II, this notion of multiculturalism emerged in countries like Canada and the United Kingdom to counter enduring racial ideologies. Racial ideologies assume that there are innately different groups of people that can be distinguished and classified according to their worth and humanity (Gilroy 2000; Goldberg 2009). Sociologists often contrast the desired outcomes of multiculturalism and **assimilation**, that latter of which expects minority groups to abandon their cultural identities and practices to become more like the majority group (Bloemraad 2006; Mackey 2002). In the face of growing demands for equality and civil rights, multiculturalism promised, at least in principle, a new vision of coexistence premised on the cultivation and celebration of cultural difference (Fleras 2011). Insofar as Vaisakhi celebrations serve as a forum for the public expression of Sikh and Indian cultural practices, their recurrence exemplifies this pluralist ethos of multiculturalism.

Multiculturalism is also used to describe government programs and policies that are guided by this pluralist ideology. In Canada, Prime Minister Pierre Trudeau is credited with formalizing multicultural policies in 1971 by further diversifying immigration sources and establishing programs to encourage minority groups to maintain their cultural practices (Mackey 2002). Prior to this, people from India were subject to various immigration restrictions that denied or restricted their capacity to (a) enter Canada and (b) acquire full rights of citizenship, explicit restrictions that were not removed until after World War II. It was multicultural policies that helped give Indians more opportunities to immigrate to Canada (Nayar 2012). Of course, critics of more recent immigration systems rightly suggest that the ostensibly neutral criteria used to judge who can immigrate to Canada continue to discriminate against people from the **Global South** (Bannerji 2000; Thobani 2007).

Multicultural policies have also tried to cultivate the diverse cultural practices of minority groups in Canada; this objective sets these policies apart from those focused on assimilation, which force minority groups to adopt the cultural norms and practices of the majority group (Bloemraad 2006). During my research at the national archives in Ottawa, I found an array of successful proposals for funding from the federal government's multicultural programs. Dated between the early 1970s and mid-1980s, these proposals were submitted by organizations across Canada looking to promote Sikh, Punjabi, and Indian cultural practices and, in some instances, share them with the broader Canadian public. By looking to disseminate these practices beyond minority communities, these proposals run counter to public perceptions that multicultural programming has only promoted the isolation of cultural minorities.

Insofar as Vaisakhi celebrations serve as a forum for the public expression of Sikh and Indian cultural practices, their recurrence each year exemplifies the pluralist ethos of multiculturalism. While Vaisakhi does not occur under the formal auspices of multicultural policies, the scale of these celebrations requires the co-operation of municipal authorities. In 2013, Vaisakhi was one of four celebrations that was granted civic parade status by the City of Vancouver, which guarantees the organizers a certain level of funding and tactical support from the city. Municipal, federal, and provincial politicians also make a point of demonstrating their commitment to multicultural diversity by taking part in the Vaisakhi celebrations, either by appearing in the parade or speaking to participants at the parade tents. In fact, the ubiquitous presence of politicians at these events has spawned criticisms that politicians are merely pandering for the so-called ethnic vote, leading some to suggest that Vaisakhi is yet another example of multiculturalism run amok. More conservative critiques of multiculturalism suggest that its ethos of diversity has stifled criticism of what they call barbaric cultural practices and practices that dilute Canadian values. Such accusations are contradicted by evidence that suggests minorities continue to face cultural and economic marginalization as well as more intense public scrutiny of cultural differences (Fleras 2011; Jiwani 2006; Thobani 2007).

Vernacular Multiculturalism

Yet it would be a mistake to reduce the multicultural dimensions of Vaisakhi parades to the policies and practices of state actors, given how these celebrations reflect and facilitate certain forms of **vernacular multiculturalism**, a term I use to refer to the unpredictable and informal ways in which cultural practices change as they collide and intersect under conditions of demographic diversity. Ordinarily, the term "vernacular" signifies a kind of dialect or language that is spoken in a particular region but has not necessarily been formalized or received any kind of institutional recognition. Here, the term "vernacular multiculturalism" refers to the overlooked processes of cultural change, improvisation, and intermixture that occur in spaces of ethnic and cultural plurality (Gilroy 2005; Keith 2005). These forms of multiculturalism are often overlooked when there is too much focus on official, state-based understandings of multiculturalism. Sociologists have criticized multicultural state programming for reinforcing notions of culture that are fixed in time and place (Bannerji 2000; Fleras 2011; Thobani 2007). That is, because the programming emphasizes the preservation of cultural traditions, minority groups are often made to feel that their cultural practices are irrelevant or out of place in contemporary social contexts. Conversely, by analyzing more vernacular forms of multiculturalism, we can pay attention to the ways in which cultural practices are fluid, ever-changing, and disputed by various social actors.

The vast number of different cultural practices that take place during Vaisakhi make these celebrations excellent vantage points to examine vernacular forms of multiculturalism. At Vaisakhi celebrations, different cultural practices overlap and intersect in unpredictable ways. *Kirtans*, dance performances, and other cultural practices will resonate differently with the audiences at these events based on the range of perspectives of the people there. It would be a mistake to reduce this plurality of experiences and practices to the abstract and sometimes calcified notions of culture common to state policies of multiculturalism. Vaisakhi celebrations feature an abundance of colours, sounds, smells, and tastes that create the kind of convivial atmosphere that Gilroy (2005) suggests is characteristic of multiculturalism's promise. Gilroy uses the term "conviviality" to capture the lively and exciting ways in which cultural differences can intersect, overlap, and produce new identities and practices in contexts where plurality exists.

This aspect of vernacular multiculturalism is especially evident in how food circulates during Vaisakhi celebrations. Each year, I have seen businesses, families, and community organizations handing out a variety of food and drink to the celebrations' participants: bottles of water, cups of chai, slices of pizza, samosas, plates of rice and curry, as well as samplings of sweets like *gulab jamun*. The practice of sharing food within and outside of gurdwaras has a long history in Sikhi. Yet compared to the more scripted forms of multiculturalism that are featured in news stories about Vaisakhi, the informality and personal care that characterize these practices also exemplify the spirit of vernacular multiculturalism.

Rituals of Place-Making

Metro Vancouver's Vaisakhi celebrations have complex relationships to the neighbourhoods in which they are staged. That these events have assumed such a large scale, attracting nearly 600,000 people in 2017, is a consequence of the historic presence of Sikh and South Asian communities in the Lower Mainland, which were among the first of these communities in North America (Nayar 2008). Vaisakhi parades commemorate and reinforce this historical presence, particularly in neighbourhoods that have been shaped by processes of residential segregation.

Spatial Segregation

Because Vaisakhi parades are organized around local gurdwaras, their specific locations in the region reflect the changing geographies of settlement and segregation experienced by Sikh and South Asian populations. The region's first gurdwara was opened in 1904 by the Burrard Inlet, near where most of the first Sikh migrants lived and worked in the lumber mills. By the 1960s, this pattern of residential concentration had shifted, and most Sikh and South Asian people were living in south Vancouver's Sunset neighbourhood (Nayar 2008). At the time, the area's lower residential density offered less expensive housing to these residents as well as the opportunity to minimize their exposure to the discrimination and exclusion they experienced elsewhere in Vancouver (Indra 1979). Part of the neighbourhood became known as the Punjabi Market because it housed restaurants, grocers, and clothing stores that catered to a predominantly Indian, and especially Sikh, clientele. To reflect this shift in the city's geography, south Vancouver's Ross Street Gurdwara opened in 1970, a change marked by a *nagar kirtan* that travelled between the two gurdwaras.

The formation of the Punjabi Market is an example of spatial segregation. Urban sociologists study patterns of spatial segregation, often to explain the formation of distinct city spaces like central business districts, "skid rows," **ghettos**, and ethnic enclaves (Pattillo 2013; Wacquant 2008). Black ghettos in American cities are the most widely researched instance of segregation and can be traced to the turn of the twentieth century, when African-Americans leaving the American South were subjected to new forms of social and economic discrimination in the industrialized cities of the American Northeast and Midwest. Ghettoized areas formed through the systematic manner in which African-Americans were denied housing in **white** neighbourhoods and subjected to harassment, surveillance, and violence if they crossed the demarcated boundaries of the ghetto (Wacquant 2008). Urban sociologists claim that, because these boundaries have been so heavily protected and policed, many ghettoized areas develop their own infrastructures that duplicate the institutions that exist beyond their borders, a process referred to as **institutional encasement** (Wacquant 2001).

The Punjabi Market neighbourhood more closely resembles the categorical features of an ethnic enclave than a ghetto. Ethnic enclaves are urban spaces where minority groups are disproportionately concentrated, but they are nonetheless characterized by less intense and enduring forms of **stigmatization** and **territorial confinement** than ghettos. In some instances, residence in ethnic enclaves is framed as a voluntary choice, independent of larger structures of **race** and **social class**. In Toronto and Montreal, ethnic enclaves like Little Portugal and Greektown have been more temporary sites of segregation, where immigrants reside before they are incorporated into the city's broader social fabric. While the relative absence of research on the Punjabi Market complicates any definitive categorization, there is no evidence to suggest that its boundaries have been policed with the same intensity as ghettoized areas. The Punjabi Market also lacks the same degree of institutional encasement as most ghettos. Yet the boundaries that have distinguished south Vancouver and Surrey as ethnic enclaves must still be viewed as evidence of the formal and informal practices of discrimination experienced by many South Asian people in the area (Buffam 2013, 2019; Frost 2011; Indra 1979; Johal 2007).

Place-Making and the Punjabi Market

Vaisakhi celebrations are one way in which Sikhs' enduring connections to this neighbourhood are remembered and recreated. With the recent growth of urban tourism, municipal authorities have employed different forms of place-based marketing to draw consumers to ethnic enclaves like Greektown in Toronto and Banglatown in London, United Kingdom. This process transforms histories of exclusion into commodified **narratives** of diversity, promoting the fixed notions of culture associated with state visions of multiculturalism (Keith 2005). Around the nucleus of the Punjabi Market, special street signs have been erected that mark the specific history of the area. In 2008, the provincial government of BC announced plans to create a $3 million India Gate to commemorate this history as well as market the area to tourists, serving a similar function as the gate in the city's Chinatown. Certain aspects of Vaisakhi can be understood in a similar vein; after all, the Punjabi Market Business Association sponsors one of the main tents in which politicians address the crowd of participants on Main Street.

In south Vancouver, Vaisakhi parades have acquired a new significance against growing concerns that community ties to the neighbourhood have been severed by the growth of the nearby City of Surrey as the social and residential hub of Sikh and South Asian communities (Nayar 2012). Beginning in the 1970s, more suburban cities like Delta, Richmond, and Surrey drew increasing numbers of Sikh and South Asian people, despite some early resistance from their predominantly white, working-class residents (Johal 2007). The growing suburbanization of the city's South Asian populations has put a significant strain on the stores and restaurants in the Punjabi Market that had once catered primarily to Sikh and South Asian clientele. In December 2016, the nucleus of the Punjabi Market along Main Street featured empty storefronts peppered with "for lease" signs or applications for rezoning. Against this tide of suburbanization, Vaisakhi parades work to publicly assert an enduring connection between local South Asian communities and the changing place of the Punjabi Market.

Conclusion

In April 2001, the *Vancouver Sun* published an editorial that waxed poetic about the plurality of religious and secular rituals that mark the passage of spring in Vancouver. At one point in the editorial, the reporter asserts that

> [f]or the Christians in our midst, Easter is the most poignant religious milestone of the year. Good Friday marks the day of the crucifixion of Jesus Christ, followed two days later by his joyous resurrection. For Jews, Pesach – or Passover – commemorates the ordeals of the Jews' slavery in Egypt.... For Sikhs, this weekend is the anniversary of the day followers adopted the symbols of their faith and it is celebrated by parades. Even nature worshippers can find reason to commemorate mid-April, as the time the skunk cabbage blooms and the bears begin to emerge from hibernation. (A14)

In this passage, similarities are identified between Vaisakhi and other ostensibly religious holidays on the basis of common symbolic features. Each symbolizes some experience of endurance, whether of religious persecution or of the hazards of winter, which frames these holidays as springtime rituals of rebirth and rejuvenation.

Vaisakhi celebrations cannot be understood as strictly religious celebrations, even if they exemplify the religious dimensions of social life as they were analyzed by Émile Durkheim. The specific manner in which culture, power, and place intersect during Vaisakhi celebrations complicates the categorical distinctions that are typically drawn between religion, society, and politics. These parades have served as a medium to express political dissent about the practice of Sikhi in and beyond the Canadian context, reframing traditions as dynamic and contested elements of everyday life. As staging grounds for different visions and endorsements of plurality, Vaisakhi celebrations are at once a function of state policies of multiculturalism and a vehicle for the emergence of more vernacular forms of multiculturalism that foment new cultural practices and modes of intercultural expression. The ritualized practices that are so central to the parades are also reflective *and* productive of collective attachments to place, which are, in turn, an effect of shifting processes of segregation and suburbanization.

Questions for Critical Thought

1. What are the multiple meanings of the concept of multiculturalism? Explain and provide an example for each of these different meanings.
2. What seasonal rituals in Canada have overt and covert Christian associations? What do these rituals say about how religion is performed in Canada?
3. Explain how Durkheim conceives of the religious character of social life. What other social groups and rituals have this religious quality?

4. How do sociologists define the concept of place? What social practices are used to create a sense of place in the neighbourhoods and cities where you have lived?
5. Considering the concepts of ghettos, ethnic enclaves, and institutional encasement, what kinds of physical and symbolic boundaries distinguish neighbourhoods in the cities where you have lived?

References

Asad, Talal. 2003. *Formations of the Secular: Christianity, Islam, Modernity*. Stanford: Stanford University Press.

Axel, Brian Keith. 2001. *The Nation's Tortured Body: Violence, Representation and the Formation of a Sikh "Diaspora."* Durham: Duke University Press.

Ballantyne, Tony. 2006. *Between Colonialism and Diaspora: Sikh Cultural Formations in an Imperial World*. Durham: Duke University Press.

Bannerji, Himani. 2000. *Dark Side of the Nation: Essays on Multiculturalism, Nationalism and Gender*. Toronto: Canadian Scholars Press Inc.

Bloemraad, Irene. 2006. *Becoming a Citizen: Incorporating Immigrants and Refugees in the United States and Canada*. Berkeley: University of California Press.

Brickell, Chris. 2000. "Heroes and Invaders: Gay and Lesbian Pride Parades and the Public/Private Distinction in New Zealand Media Accounts." *Gender Place & Culture* 7 (2): 163–78. https://doi.org/10.1080/713668868.

Buffam, Bonar. 2013. "Public Demands: Law, Sanctuary, and the Eventual Deportation of Laibar Singh." *Sikh Formations* 9 (1): 29–37. https://doi.org/10.1080/17448727.2013.799728.

———. 2019. "Documentary Practices: Race, Bureaucracy, and the Legal Regulation of Gurdwaras in British Columbia." *Sikh Formations* 15(3–4): 396–410. https://doi.org/10.1177/14624740122228276.

Cooper, Travis. 2017. "Taxonomy Construction and the Normative Turn in Religious Studies." *Religions* 8: 270–95. https://doi.org/10.3390/rel8120270.

Durkheim, Émile. 2008. *The Elementary Forms of Religious Life*. Translated by Karen E. Fields. Oxford: Oxford University Press.

Fleras, Augie. 2011. *Racisms in a Multicultural Canada: Paradoxes, Politics and Resistance*. Kitchener: Wilfred Laurier University Press.

Frost, Heather. 2010. "Being Brown' in a Canadian Suburb." *Journal of Immigrant & Refugee Studies* 8 (2): 212–32. https://doi.org/10.1080/15562948.2010.480880.

Gilroy, Paul. 2005. *Postcolonial Melancholia*. New York: Columbia University Press.

———. 2000. *Against Race: Imagining Political Culture Beyond the Colour Line*. Cambridge: Harvard University Press.

Goldberg, David T. 2009. *The Threat of Race: Reflections on Racial Neoliberalism*. Malden: Wiley-Blackwell Publishing.

Indra, Doreen M. 1979. "South Asian Stereotypes in the Vancouver Press." *Ethnic and Racial Studies* 2 (2): 166–89. https://doi.org/10.1080/01419870.1979.9993261.

Jiwani, Yasmin. 2006. *Discourses of Denial: Mediations of Race, Gender, and Violence*. Vancouver: University of British Columbia Press.

Johal, Gurpreet Singh. 2007. "The Racialization of Space: Producing Surrey." In *Race, Racialization and Anti-racism in Canada and Beyond*, edited by Johnson Genevieve Fuji and Randy Enomoto, 179–205. Toronto: University of Toronto Press.

Keith, Michael. 2005. *After the Cosmopolitan? Multicultural Cities and the Future of Racism*. New York: Routledge Press.

Mackey, Eva. 2002. *The House of Difference: Cultural Politics and National Identity*. Toronto: University of Toronto Press.

Mandair, Arvind-Pal Singh. 2009. *Religion and the Spectre of the West: Sikhism, India, Postcoloniality and the Politics of Translation*. New York: Columbia University Press.

———. 2013. *Sikhism: A Guide for the Perplexed*. London: Bloomsbury Press.

Masuzawa, Tomoko. 2005. *The Invention of World Religions, or, How European Universalism was Preserved in the Language of Pluralism*. Chicago: University of Chicago Press.

Mawani, Renisa. 2012. "Specters of Indigeneity in British-Indian Migration, 1914." *Law and Society Review* 46 (2): 369–403. https://doi.org/10.1111/j.1540-5893.2012.00492.x.

Mongia, Radhika 2018. *Indian Migration and Empire: A Colonial Genealogy of the Modern State*. Durham: Duke University Press.

Nayar, Kamala. 2012. *The Punjabis in British Columbia: Location, Labour, First Nations, and Multiculturalism*. Montreal: McGill-Queen's University.

———. 2008. "Misunderstood in the Diaspora: The Experience of Orthodox Sikhs in Vancouver." *Sikh Formations* 4 (1): 17–32.

Pattillo, Mary. 2013. *Black Picket Fences: Privilege and Peril Among the Black Middle Class*. Chicago: University of Chicago Press.

Simpson, Audra. 2014. *Mohawkus Interruptus: Political Life Across the Borders of Settler States*. Durham: Duke University Press.

Smith, Jonathan Z. 2004. *Relating Religion: Essays in the Study of Religion*. Chicago: University of Chicago Press.

Thobani, Sunera. 2007. *Exalted Subjects: Studies in the Making of Race and Nation in Canada*. Toronto: University of Toronto Press.

Vancouver Sun, 2001. "A Time to Celebrate Our Diversity and Renewal." *Vancouver Sun*, April 13, 2001, A14.

Wacquant, Loïc. 2001. "Deadly symbiosis: When Ghetto and Prison Meet and Mesh." *Punishment & Society* 3 (1): 95–134. https://doi.org/10.1177/14624740122228276.

———. 2008. *Urban Outcasts: A Comparative Sociology of Advanced Urban Marginality*. London: Polity Press.

Walks, R. Alan and Bourne, Larry S. 2006. "Ghettos in Canada's Cities? Racial Segregation, Ethnic Enclaves and Poverty Concentration in Canadian Urban Areas." *Canadian Geographer* 50 (3): 273–97.

Summer

While summer can feel like the shortest season in Canada, it stretches into the rest of the year through memories and longing. Summer is idealized as a long, unbroken stretch of leisure time characterized by easy living, openness, and freedom from both the physical limitations of surviving in a challenging natural environment and the ordinary constraints of daily life in **society**. The summers of childhood, in particular, evoke images as relaxed days of independence and liberty. But this image of carefree summer is constantly confronted by the ongoing reality of social embeddedness, interrelations, and conflict.

One of the ways in which the idea of summer as a time of freedom is contradicted is in the common obligation experienced especially by young adults to spend every weekend of summer attending weddings. In chapter sixteen, Ondine Park considers the **ritual** of the white wedding – the culturally dominant form of the marriage ceremony. As Park discusses, while such weddings are imagined as celebrating the unique love of distinctive individuals, the ways in which this ritual is marked are far from expressions of uniqueness, being instead highly influenced by cultural and consumer images and expectations; moreover, the kind of love that is celebrated is far from universal but rather **heteronormative**, the reiteration of dominant **norms** of gender and sexuality that celebrate and **normalize** heterosexuality. These norms are learned through processes of **socialization** into **culture**.

In chapter seventeen, Tonya K. Davidson explores how expectations and experiences of summer cottages in Canada are often premised on the idea that people have access to extended, unstructured summer breaks from school to spend on a lake in a private second home. But as Davidson discusses, these images present middle- and upper-class leisure activities as a cultural norm to which all should aspire. Moreover, "cottage country" in Canada constitutes places imagined to be appropriately used as a landscape of enjoyment for **white** settlers within the context of a **settler-colonial** state, at the expense of local **Indigenous** uses of this land. In reality, Indigenous people, other local folk, and seasonal cottagers often have different expectations and experiences of the same landscape.

In chapter eighteen, Paul Joosse also discusses tension between local residents – and their desires for a safe, livable community – and the interests of oil companies that seek to use the land in ways that bring them into conflict with the residents and creates animosity between residents. While protests and **social movement** activities may happen at any time of year, the case Joosse highlights in this chapter ominously invokes summer. In the summer of 2010, anonymous letters protesting the **fracking** done by the natural gas company EnCana in Tomslake, British Columbia, were delivered to the media threatening of a coming "hot" summer. This was after a series of unsolved bombings had occurred the previous year. Joosse analyzes the ways in which the anti-fracking movement, which is oriented toward challenging the use of environmental resources, as well as our relationships to both the economy and the state have been understood or **framed**.

In contrast to the heated terrain of political contest and conflict, for many, summer is marked by a cooler (i.e., more air-conditioned and frivolous) seasonal **tradition**: anticipating, lining up for, and enjoying a summer blockbuster movie. In chapter nineteen, Benjamin Woo uses the blockbuster to illustrate how society and media mutually influence each other in a process called "**mediatization**." As Woo explains, media are not separate from our real lives, encountered discretely from time to time. Rather, our entire world is mediated: We exist within media. Summer, as all seasons, is likewise experienced within mediated social worlds. As many chapters in this section (and throughout the book) explore, our understandings of socially appropriate seasonal rituals, and our expectations of what joys and difficulties a season will bring, are shaped by our engagements with and messages from various media.

Finally, in chapter twenty, Patrizia Albanese considers the ways in which **social class** informs how children experience summer in her analysis of the **summer setback**. The summer setback describes the loss, during the summer break, of learning that children gain during the school year. Albanese explores how the ways in which parents structure their children's summers are largely based on economic and **cultural capital**, so that some children thrive and are enriched while others are set back.

Like all seasons, summer is experienced in very intimate biographical and biological ways, yet it simultaneously shapes and is shaped by broader **social structures** and meanings. Our feelings about summer shape ideas about who we are and what we value as individuals and collectively. Despite an image of freedom and self-indulgence in which one may shed layers of clothes and social constraints, such summer freedoms are not experienced equally in Canada. As the chapters in this section show, access to land, justice and protection, childhood leisure and growth, love, and inclusion in dominant norms, **values**, and meanings are all contested in the long, hot days of summer.

16 Wedding Season: The White Wedding as a Cultural Ritual of Heteronormativity

ONDINE PARK

LEARNING OUTCOMES

After reading this chapter, you should be able to:

- describe Peter Berger's understanding of sociological thinking
- explain how the white wedding is a key ritual of contemporary social life that expresses dominant norms, values, and culture while also helping to define and justify the same norms, values, and culture
- identify the key characteristics of culture, including that it is socially produced, shared and learned (through socialization and the influence of agents of socialization), and cumulative and ever-changing
- use the concepts of hegemony, dominant ideology, gender, and hetero-normativity to interpret other rituals or significant social interactions, or representations of these
- analyze the ways in which culture and traditions, like weddings, can reinforce and justify inequality and stratification

Defamiliarizing the White Wedding through Satire and Sociology

> Summer is well underway which means you've probably heard wedding bells ring ... a few times. Yes, its [sic] wedding season folks.
>
> – Mehta 2014

The wedding is a highly important **ritual** in contemporary **Western** societies. It is "the most conspicuous of the few remaining rituals" and has only become more popular and prominent over the course of the twentieth and twenty-first centuries (Carter and

Duncan 2016, 1; Engstrom 2012, 1). The dominant form of this key ritual is the **white wedding**. If you imagine a "typical" wedding, perhaps one you have been to or seen in North American, British, or Australian TV shows or movies, you're probably picturing a white wedding. This is the kind of lavish marriage ceremony that is associated with romantic love, an elaborate white bridal gown, a structured ceremony involving a procession of the bride and the exchange of vows, gold rings, and a ceremonial kiss, and an extravagant, tiered wedding cake. Typically, it begins with a ritualized engagement proposal featuring a diamond ring and often ends with a luxurious honeymoon involving travel. This is the most celebrated, desired, and **normative** version of this important cultural event. To say this is normative is to say that this is the version of the wedding that is taken to be the model or standard by which other weddings are judged: "The white wedding has become the standard for the ritual of marriage" (Engstrom 2012, 1). The wedding is so significant as a ritual in North America that an entire season of the year, summer, is often understood as "wedding season" even though there is no coordination among individuals or by official **structures** (such as a recognized religious or statutory holiday during the summer) to organize this "season." Rather, what makes summer the season of weddings is a combination of the sheer number of weddings that occur during those months – 65 per cent of weddings in Canada occur in the four months of summer from June to September (Patel 2014) – and the general cultural expectation that weddings occur in summer.

Playing off these factors, the news and entertainment website *BuzzFeed* released a spoof video in the style of a horror movie trailer entitled "Wedding Season is Coming" (Ward et al. 2015). The video depicts a group of young adult friends coming to the frightening realization that wedding season is upon them and, one by one, everyone around them is getting married. Their panic mounts as this unrelenting "epidemic" begins to overtake them, and they are inundated with wedding invitations and expectations. One friend even finds himself seemingly at the whim of an irrepressible force that conspires to get him down on bended knee before his girlfriend, presenting her with a diamond ring that has mysteriously found its way into his hand. Faced with the possibility of a wedding proposal, she runs away, screaming in terror. As he writhes on the grass while screaming "no, no, no, this isn't mine," he experiences excruciating flashes of a vision of a wedding cake being cut. While most people are unlikely to experience wedding season with quite such an intense sense of impending doom, the video is effective at satirizing familiar experiences around weddings.

A Sociological Approach toward the White Wedding

Satire and sociology share a similar orientation to looking at ordinary aspects of social life that we might take for granted and paying unusual attention to them to consider them anew. As American sociologist Peter Berger (1963) describes, "the excitement of sociology" comes from taking a familiar situation or scene and being "brought up against an insight that radically questions everything one had previously assumed about this familiar scene" (22). As a result, the "familiar now seems not quite so familiar any more" (Berger 1963, 22). In a comparable way, the satirical video presents common experiences of wedding season and makes them unfamiliar, even frightening. In the video, the many scenes of warm, sunny weather strongly suggest that the oncoming wedding season corresponds to summer – a season of the year that, because of its association with weddings, becomes replete with formal obligations and social expectations. This is the sense of wedding season that we see in etiquette and advice guides that provide tips on how to "survive" months of attending other people's weddings (e.g., ACCC 2019; Singh 2013). "Wedding Season is Coming" also implicitly casts wedding season as a season of one's life (as discussed by Rania Tfaily in chapter twelve): It depicts one's own wedding as an irresistible (perhaps even unstoppable) life event, as if to suggest that, like seasons, having a wedding is an unavoidable, inevitable period through which everyone must eventually pass. In this way, the video can be interpreted to mean that wedding season is both the summer season and a season of life – both being inescapable periods of time. In addition to these two takes on what "wedding season" might mean, a third aspect of the wedding to which the video draws attention is the familiarity of its key elements. We see just the most minimal of features of a formal proposal, bridal outfit, and wedding cake, and yet we can easily recognize each of these and understand that they represent vital aspects of the wedding despite their caricature as unwelcome, sinister intrusions.

"Wedding Season is Coming" leaves us with the sociological excitement (or terror) of defamiliarizing conventions, which we often think of as normal, proper, natural, or inevitable for weddings. And this is as far as the satirical video goes. But for Berger, thinking sociologically cannot stop there. The sociologist must recognize and interpret particular, individual circumstances or events in relation to larger social, cultural, and historical conditions in which that particular situation is located. The sociologist needs, further, to engage in a process of "seeing through" the official, ordinary, conventional ways of making sense of the world to recognize that what we might think of as social reality has many layers of meaning, wherein the "discovery of each new layer changes the perception of the whole" (Berger 1963, 23). Thus, for Berger, there is a "debunking tendency" in sociology (38) – an approach that holds open the possibility that there are other ways to understand social life or social situations that might potentially be uncomfortable or troublesome, especially for the official ways of accounting for social life. This process of seeing through can be used along with the **sociological imagination** proposed by American sociologist C. Wright Mills (1959) to gain a fuller sociological perspective. (See also the introduction for discussions of Berger and Mills.) The sociological imagination involves the ability to recognize that individual experiences and larger social processes and historical forces mutually inform and mutually constitute each other. Thus, some problems an individual might experience – those that we can understand as **social issues** – though they may be extremely intimate and internal, may have their origins not in the personal flaws, actions, or ideas of the individual but rather in the specific conditions of that person's larger social, cultural, and historical context.

At the same time, the social world and historical circumstances can be better understood by recognizing the individuals and the experiences within **society** of the individuals who comprise a particular social world at a particular moment in time.

In this chapter, I apply such a sociological orientation to look at some of the characteristics of the normative white wedding and discuss the larger conditions that help us to make sense of it. In considering the white wedding in this chapter, I pull together and draw upon academic wedding literature and theoretically analyze a variety of popular cultural sources in order to explore and understand the white **wedding-industrial complex** (a concept I will explain shortly). In addition to "Wedding Season is Coming," popular sources include newspapers, magazines, and websites as well as movies and TV shows. My site of inquiry is primarily limited to the cultural mainstream of Canada, the United States, and, to a lesser extent, Britain: These are Anglo-American societies that generally share histories of and engagements with the white wedding ritual, and they are the nations primarily covered in the wedding literature I have used.

Culture and Socialization; Or, How General Ideas Become a Specific Event

Learning from Culture

How does any marrying couple come to know of, and be able to work through, all of the expectations and decisions required to design and execute such an important and elaborate ritual as the white wedding? While it is largely up to each individual couple (and especially the bride) to create their ritual almost as if from scratch, they are able and encouraged, even compelled, to draw from their culture to help guide this process.

The couple learns from their culture. **Culture**, as British **cultural studies** scholar Raymond Williams (1989) described, is "a whole way of life" of a people (4). It includes the beliefs, ideas, images, behaviours, practices, **symbols**, language, and material things and places shared by a group and that help to define the group. Importantly, culture also includes **norms** and **values**. Norms are rules within society that guide how we are expected to be and act. A culture's norms are based on its values, which are the collective standards that the culture uses to make judgments on morality (goodness), aesthetics (beauty), usefulness, desirability, and worthiness. With white weddings, although the couple ostensibly makes each of the multitude of decisions on their own (for example, which cutlery, songs, vows, napkins, venue, meals, and guests to select?), they draw on their culture in doing so. Culture is socially produced and socially shared: People participate in culture together. Each generation passes down culture to the next and is obliged to do so. A crucial way in which this cultural transmission occurs is through **socialization**. As discussed in this book's introduction and in chapters three, ten, and twenty, socialization is the lifelong, active process of learning one's culture and developing the skills and habits necessary for participating in that culture.

Aiding in the process of socialization are **agents of socialization**: the people and **institutions** that influence individuals as they learn how to fit into their culture. Family and peers – those individuals who are immediately in the couple's lives – have both direct and indirect influence on the couple. Direct influences might include explicitly saying and showing what the couple should do, think, and feel ("you must invite your cousins"; "this is the happiest day of your life"). Indirect influences can include encouraging (or demanding) individuals, since childhood, to adopt the values of the culture as their own, such as developing a sense (or not) that marriage is a natural, desirable, and inevitable path in one's **life course**. In addition to family and peers, education is also a key socializing agent. In the case of socialization into the role of white wedding bride and groom, expert sources act in this educational role. Individuals such as bridal gown salesclerks (Corrado 2002) or jewellers, photographers (Lewis 1998), religious leaders or other officiants, or wedding-oriented media, such as guidebooks, magazines, and websites, help to educate the couple in the various intricacies of the wedding structure and details. Media, and culture in general, are also agents of socialization. These contribute to the socialization of individuals into norms and expectations surrounding weddings by providing the ideas, images, and scripts, of what romance, proposals, weddings, and social roles (such as the groom role or the bride role) could and should look like and how they ought to be enacted. Individuals also socialize themselves. The couple draws on their own thoughts and experiences of having attended weddings and interacted with generalized social expectations about weddings.

The Wedding-Industrial Complex

In the contemporary Anglo-American world, many of these cultural elements have been mobilized into the wedding-industrial complex (a concept derived from the more common idea of the military-industrial complex; see also **prison-industrial complex** in chapter two) to produce a sense that the white wedding is just what normal people do and naturally want in order to get married and to be proper adults. The concept of the wedding-industrial complex refers to the deep entanglement of the wedding ritual and **capitalist** interests. This concept highlights the mobilization and deployment of an immense array of commercial interests and capitalist industries (Ingraham 1999; see also Boden 2003; Engstrom 2012; Freeman 2002; Howard 2006; Kingston 2004; and Wallace 2004). This relationship could be seen as mutually beneficial, in that industry supplies the needed provisions (goods, services, spaces) for the ritual and, in turn, profits from the ritual. However, it is problematic in that the relationship produces an increased reliance on the industry for cultural expertise and to define norms around weddings; moreover, motivated by profit seeking, the industry is driven to influence individuals' and general cultural expectations toward ever-costlier weddings. For many cultural observers, the wedding has itself become an industry (Boden 2001, 1.2), "a machine fueled by the profit motive and lubricated by myth" (Kingston 2004, 33).

The wedding-industrial complex includes the wedding industry – businesses that offer the goods, services, and people who are directly related to the wedding (and thus directly profiting from the wedding), such as wedding trade shows, bridal gown and formal wear shops, wedding planners, reception and ceremony venues, jewellers, stationers, bakeries, florists, liquor stores, and honeymoon destinations. This industry is worth $300 billion globally – including $55 billion in the United States (Bourque 2017) and $5 billion in Canada (Patel 2014). It reinforces its own importance through things like wedding-planning checklists or schedules, which provide a normative timeline of proper consumption. For example, according to a *Brides* wedding-planning checklist, in an "ideal" 12-month engagement, the bride should determine the wedding budget and select venues 12 months prior to the wedding, hire vendors 11 months prior, buy her wedding dress nine months prior, book the honeymoon five months prior, choose a cake four months prior, and so on (Kellogg, Price Olson, and Mooney DiGiovanna 2020). Nearly every major point on the timeline involves a major purchase. In other words, wedding planning is presented as a carefully orchestrated and properly timed series of consumption decisions.

In addition to the wedding industry, the wedding-industrial complex also includes **mass media** and culture in general, which are mobilized to reflect the value, desirability, and appropriateness of the white wedding, to **normalize** the white wedding, and to support the wedding-industrial complex. These cultural elements help to forward and naturalize certain ideas, such as the notion that getting married is the normal, right, and only way to legitimate a romantic or sexual relationship; that the way to confirm true love is by having what is imagined to be a proper wedding; that getting married is the clearest demonstration of having achieved full and meaningful adulthood; and that the correct and desirable way to do all of this is through the particularly elaborate and costly white wedding. In Canada, the average cost of a wedding is between $30,000 (Patel 2014) and $50,000 (Wilford 2018). Media that does this work of reflecting, promoting, and normalizing values around weddings can include wedding industry media such as magazines, movies, books, websites, television shows about brides or weddings; however, even media that are not specifically geared toward weddings and culture generally also does this work. The wedding of British Prince Harry and Meghan Markle in 2018 and Prince William and Catherine Middleton in 2011 are prime examples of this phenomenon, as these weddings became protracted media spectacles with widespread coverage in not only wedding-related media but also TV, internet, and print news, lifestyle reporting, and celebrity news, fashion magazines, gossip magazines, and more. The wedding-industrial complex is able to realize greater profit and power not only through increasing the elaborateness and complexity of this particular celebration, but also through normalizing the white wedding in culture in general.

Adding to and Changing Culture, and the Limits Due to Hegemony

The marrying couple learns from culture – but culture is also cumulative, and in producing and performing the ritual of the white wedding, the couple adds to it. This also means that culture is ever-changing. People, individually and collectively, may strengthen, change, or discard the meaning, value, or purpose of any element of culture to suit new uses, interpretations, and social, cultural, and situational conditions. The couple contributes to culture by affirming, contesting, or rejecting what a wedding must look like, how a groom is required to act, what a bride's responsibilities ought to be, what parents should do, and so forth. If they successfully pull together a wedding that is recognizable as a white wedding, then the couple helps to reproduce and strengthen the idea of the white wedding as a norm and adds to the collective image of what a wedding could and should be. If they successfully contest or reject conventions of a white wedding, then they help to challenge and possibly change the white wedding or even offer innovative ideas about the wedding ritual.

However, even though culture is subject to change and transformation, there are still dominant norms, values, and structures in operation. Thus, for example, although cultural conventions and **traditions** around weddings might transform (and have indeed changed) over time, and individual weddings can be highly personalized, this ritual must still be understood in relation to the particular cultural and social context in which it is located and which gives meaning and significance to the event and to the couple's relationship. As Emily Fairchild (2014, 364) notes, "a couple cannot simply make sense of the ceremony for themselves, but they are held accountable to the expectations of family and friends regarding what a wedding is, appropriate roles for men and women, and what the ritual elements mean." Most importantly, the white wedding produces and reproduces some key dominant ideologies – that is, the norms, values, and ideas that form the status quo. These dominant ways of interpreting, interacting within, and organizing society are hegemonic. **Hegemony** is a concept that Marxist philosopher Antonio Gramsci (1971) developed to describe the way that the dominant (or ruling) class of people that holds power within society uses ideas and culture to try to maintain control of society and its people. Marxist scholars help us to recognize that society is structured to be unequal; that is, society is stratified. **Stratification** describes the organization of society according to a hierarchy of classes of people, which embeds inequality into the very structure and operation of society. For Marxists, it is clear that this inequality serves the interests of the ruling class, which benefits from having greater access to and control over resources, including material resources, power, prestige, and the advantages of living in society. This inequality oppresses what Gramsci (1971) called "the great masses of the population" (12). This subordinated class has inconsistent, less, or no access to these social goods. How does the ruling class maintain this inequality and hold on to its authority? For one thing, it is able to mobilize the coercive arms of the **state,** such as the police, prisons, and the military to force people to submit to its rule. However, Gramsci (1971) argued that, rather than relying on violence, the dominant group is able to maintain its ongoing rule by manipulating the rest of the **population** into consenting on an ongoing basis to their own subordination. The ruling class is able to make their ideas, values, and worldview into the **dominant ideology** – a system of beliefs that supports the dominant class in its rule and that justifies the inequality that maintains its domination. The exercise or threat of violence and the show of force is not as necessary when people willingly agree and even feel committed to the dominant ideology.

This might seem a far-fetched idea to apply to weddings, which, even if you don't really like them, probably generally seem like nice occasions. After all, weddings and the resulting marriages don't appear to be a way in which inequality is maintained as an alternative to the explicit use of violence, right? And anyway, don't most people like weddings (even if they don't admit it)? Don't people freely and eagerly choose to express their love through weddings? And, for the most part, aren't people generally pretty happy and honoured to be able to celebrate their friends' and family members' achievement? These questions reveal the subtle way hegemony works. Dominant ideology can be said to be hegemonic when it is seen as the only normal, proper, and moral way to make sense of or organize the social world: Behaviours, attitudes, or values that serve the interest of the dominant class are seen to be simply natural or inevitable.

"Seeing Through" Wedding Season

> Sociology involves a process of "seeing through" the facades of social structures.
>
> – Berger 1963, 31

Can we take up Berger's challenge to discover other layers of social life, in order to "see through" the official hegemonic version of the white wedding and perceive it differently? How can we apply our sociological imagination to understand the relation between individual experiences and larger social forces? One question we might ask to start this work is: what – if any – dominant ("official") ideologies are upheld in the white wedding? Does this ritual hide or produce inequalities? In the remainder of this chapter, I will discuss two ideological structures that produce and maintain inequality: **gender** and **heteronormativity**.

The Proposal Ritual

The beginning of the white wedding ritual is the proposal. Although it is not part of the wedding-day ceremony, it is nevertheless an integral moment in the white wedding ritual – and one of the most crucial, setting everything else in motion. The official proposal is most recognizable when the man suddenly gets down on one knee, presents the woman with a velvet box in which a diamond ring is nestled and, naming the woman by her full legal name, utters in strangely clear, formal, and contractual language, "will you marry me?" The socially expected reaction to this bejewelled proposal is for the woman – who, despite her surprise, is otherwise quiet and motionless – to become overwhelmed by emotions of happiness and love, and, with tears in her eyes, to state unconditionally "yes," holding out her finger so that he may place the ring on it. Any other response or reaction by the woman (such as a deferral, a negotiation, or a refusal) is considered awkward, humiliating, or heartbreaking for the man, particularly if he made the proposal a public spectacle. As neuroscientist Dean Burnett (2016) mused in an article for the *Guardian*, "The question at the end of this [public proposal] is not just 'Will you marry me?'; it could be seen as 'Will you refuse to marry me and risk harsh judgement from all these strangers, who know nothing about you apart from the fact that you have a partner who just went to extreme efforts to impress you so obviously cares about you greatly, and will likely be utterly heartbroken and humiliated if you refuse?'" (n.p.). We see a bleak example of this in a story that made the rounds on social media in 2018: A man convinced the video-game company Insomniac Games to include his marriage proposal to his girlfriend in their new *Spiderman* video game. Before the game was released in September 2018, the woman had broken up with the man as, from her perspective, the relationship had been deteriorating over the course of months and years (Rouner 2018); but the proposal remained embedded in the game. The man's one-sided version of the experience, embellished with damaging fabricated details and framed as a "heart-breaking" jilted-lover story (Rouner 2018), was circulated around social media. In reaction, the woman was "swamped" with so much harassment that "all of her social media accounts have been deleted" (Manavis 2018). The abuse over social media this woman received illustrates that cultural rituals are expected to follow particular patterns and coercive force can be unleashed when dominant expectations and norms are not upheld. One of these expectations is around gender.

Hegemonic Gender Norms

The engagement ritual exemplifies gender norms. *Gender* describes the expectations about masculinity and femininity that each of us regularly encounters and to which we are all expected to conform in our everyday ways of being, feeling, and doing. Dominant understandings of gender are based on a belief in a **gender binary** – the social belief and expectation that there are two, and only two, genders (men/boys and women/girls). These two genders are believed to be unambiguously distinct from and even opposed to each other. Each gender is believed to have characteristics (masculinity or femininity) and socially approved (some might say socially mandated) norms that are specific to that gender and that properly belong only to one or the other gender but not both. According to these dominant gender norms, there is very little consideration for other genders or even the possibility that other genders might exist, or that gender might not be a useful category at all. (For example, as Nicole Neverson points out in chapter ten, in sports, athletes and teams are divided most basically by gender – men's *or* women's sports – and then, after that, by skill level, age, or weight.) In the binary way of thinking about gender, men are expected to be masculine and women are expected to be feminine. So, if you are a man, you must embody masculinity, behave in masculine ways, and do and want masculine things. You must not be feminine or act, think, or desire in ways that are feminine. Although norms around gender appear as if they are natural and obvious, these expectations about how each gender should act and what each should value, emulate, or even think, feel, or desire are actually historically, culturally, group-, and situationally specific. Across history, across cultures, and across groups, there have been and are many ways of being **gendered**. Moreover, gender is something that individuals accomplish on a continual basis in specific situations, not something inherent to our bodies. Through **interactions** with each other and with social institutions and expectations, we learn about gender from our culture and what it means to be "properly" gendered. As individuals, we both intentionally and unintentionally uphold and conform to gender, or we don't. Thus, there are many variations on gender, and a person's way of being gendered may change from moment to moment or context to context. However, while there are many forms of masculinity and femininity and many ways of being masculine or feminine, as with other elements of culture, there are also normative forms, which are both dominant and most highly valued on a hierarchy of gender.

Hegemonic masculinity is a concept developed by gender theorist R.W. Connell to describe the currently most culturally dominant ideal way of being a man (Connell 1987, 2005; Connell and Messerschmidt 2005). Hegemonic masculinity is at the pinnacle of the gender hierarchy and confers both material and immaterial privileges to those who are perceived as fulfilling this ideal. As an expression of dominant ideology, all men must strive to be hegemonically masculine even though most, by definition, cannot realize this ideal. The qualities of hegemonic masculinity shift according to prevailing cultural norms and values (Connell and Messerschmidt 2005), but characteristics typically attributed to it in its current configuration include expectations that men should always be independent, aggressive, physically and emotionally strong and in control, meaningfully employed, and sexually dominant (Connell 1987; Kivel 2003). Within the current mainstream Canadian context, a hegemonically masculine man must be able-bodied, white, employed, and an adult, and not gay, a woman, or feminine. In contrast, the normative form of femininity, **emphasized femininity**, does not confer additional power to women who successfully embody this ideal. It is, instead, an accentuated form of femininity that women may adopt (intentionally or unintentionally) in order to try to navigate the structural and experiential disadvantages conferred upon women in general within a system of **patriarchy**. Expectations of this dominant form of femininity dictate that women should appear to be (or actually be) frail, nurturing, emotionally and socially supportive, agreeable, and available, enthusiastic, and accommodating to men's desire.

Negotiating Gender Norms and Individual Agency

Let's return to our imagined romantic couple – our man on bended knee and our woman happily weeping. How is the proposal scenario illustrative of norms around gender? It mobilizes dominant and heightened social expectations about masculinity and femininity. According to the gender binary, and hegemonic masculinity in particular, men are supposed to be in control, be self-directed, and to act with agency. **Agency** refers to the ability to act according to one's thoughts and will – rather than according to inevitability or constraint – in order to produce a result in the world. In the proposal, we see it is the man who acts and is in control throughout. He plans the proposal, decides that it is going to happen (including when, how, and where), gets down on his knee, and speaks the proposal. Illogically, this act of agency is based on doing what a man is *expected* to do, not necessarily what he might want to do. Some men may relish planning and performing the proposal. However, others may prefer to have a rational conversation with their partner about marriage or may be too shy or anxious to want to engage in such a stressful performance. Some men may be physically or cognitively unable to enact the "official" version of the proposal or to endure the lengthy and draining ordeal of the planning and execution of the wedding; others may be financially unable to fulfill expectations of the diamond ring and an elaborate ceremony. In line with impositions of emphasized femininity, the woman, in contrast, accommodates the proposal by being present but is not enabled, for the most part, to decide whether or how the proposal will happen. She can only react; that is, she is not able (or supposed) to be agentic. Yet even if she is genuinely overwrought with emotions (as she is supposed to be), she is nevertheless expected to facilitate, passively but enthusiastically, a successful proposal with grace and kindness. If a woman does not fulfill or challenges these norms, she can face negative social consequences, as, for example, we saw with the woman who did not accept the proposal embedded in the Spiderman videogame.

The proposal reproduces cultural norms of gender by enacting and celebrating these expectations and thereby legitimating, strengthening, and reaffirming these norms as proper, worthy, and good. The enactment of the "official" proposal is informed by previous knowledge about cultural and social norms and values, but it also transmits and adds to these. We see similar enactments of gendered expectations throughout the white wedding; for example, in the "giving away" of the bride by her father or parents, or in the officiant giving permission to the groom that he "may kiss the bride," or in the groom covering and "guiding" the bride's hand as they cut the wedding cake together. In each instance, women are expected to passively comply and be physically and culturally done to, while men are expected to initiate, lead, and act.

Heteronormativity

One thing I hope you have been wondering (possibly even been getting annoyed about) in reading this is why I've described this all in terms of a relationship between a man and a woman. In Canada, same-sex couples have legally been able to get married since 2005 and we have seen increased and more positive portrayals of same-sex relationships, marriages, and even white weddings in popular culture (e.g., Cam and Mitch in *Modern Family*, 2014; Callie and Arizona in *Grey's Anatomy*, 2011). Nevertheless, there continues to be a general cultural assumption and expectations that the white wedding ritual occurs as a marriage between a woman and a man, a bride and a groom, a white dress and a black tuxedo.

As feminist theorist Judith Butler (1990) has influentially argued, our widely held social norms about gender and sexuality are assumed to be directly connected, along with sex, in what she calls the heterosexual matrix. This matrix is a set of interrelated assumptions and expectations that we use to make sense of "genders, bodies, and desires" (Butler 1990, 151). This model describes the common set of assumptions that is applied in social life to "make sense" of bodies. Specifically, there is a general expectation that all people are gendered; not only are they gendered, but their gender is directly linked to and evidence of their sex, which is understood as a binary biological category – either male or female. This gender binary is organized on a hierarchy where masculinity is not only understood as being opposed to, but also more valued than, femininity. This opposition and valuation is based on compulsory heterosexuality (Butler 1990). **Compulsory heterosexuality** is a concept originally developed by feminist author Adrienne Rich (1980) to describe the primary social expectation that everyone is (or should be) heterosexual and that society should operate with heterosexuality as the only normal and morally acceptable sexuality. As Butler argues, gender only makes sense when you already assume that, and act as if, everyone is naturally heterosexual because the idea of heterosexuality is understood as the sexual attraction to and coming together of *opposite* sexes. Compulsory heterosexuality also describes the way that such normative expectations become institutionalized – that is, embedded within the very operation of society – regulating "those kept within its boundaries as well as marginalizing and sanctioning those outside them" (Jackson 2006, 105).

main argument

The white wedding is ultimately a ritual of heteronormativity: it privileges the dominance of heterosexuality and affirms its coherence, as well as the gender binary that heterosexuality constructs (Bartholomay 2018; Berlant and Warner 1998), and, in doing so, it reinforces compulsory heterosexuality as a norm and heteronormativity as a value. Thus, whereas heterosexual white weddings might be thought of derisively as "cookie cutter" – that is, tediously conventional and conforming strictly to norms – gay and lesbian weddings always require at least a minimal degree of diverging from dominant cultural expectations. (For example, who proposes? Who wears what? Which partner gets "given away" or walked down the aisle – or do both? Who kisses whom?) Heterosexual couples may question these conventions and personalize the details but gay and lesbian couples must decide how they will fit themselves into a ritual that is fundamentally premised on excluding them. As wedding scholar Ewa Glapka (2014) summarizes, "wedding conventions erase homosexuality from the culture and reproduce entrenched gender binaries" (55). The white wedding not only takes heterosexuality and gender binaries for granted, thus participating in heteronormativity, but it likewise helps to make these seem both normal and worthy of celebration.

Conclusion

The white wedding is arguably our single most important social ritual in contemporary North American society. It is one of the few rituals that is broadly recognizable, widely celebrated within mass media and culture generally, and, with its simple basic structure, promises to be available to be taken up by anyone regardless of specific **identity** or affiliation. This version of the wedding is often seen as the ideal, most complete, most correct, and most traditional expression of the wedding ritual. In other words, it is the dominant, normative form. As a social ritual, the white wedding is also an event that expresses cultural ideals and helps define a particular set of values, aesthetics, norms, and ideas as important, desirable, right, and good. More than this, it not only reflects society's dominant ideals, but it helps to define and even justify them; for example, the white wedding also expresses and reproduces heteronormativity and problematic, constraining gender norms.

The video "Wedding Season is Coming," with which I began this chapter, ends with one of the friends standing in a darkened room looking at herself in a mirror. Bedecked with a white veil and a small bouquet of flowers, she eerily sings "Here Comes the Bride," turns to look directly in the camera and asks, "Will you marry me? Will you?" The suggestion is that none of us can escape wedding season – either spending the entire summer season at weddings or, at some point, finding ourselves passing through the wedding season of life. The inevitability with which this is presented effectively illustrates the compelling but not always recognized workings of socialization.

If we consider wedding season with our sociological imagination and try to see through the familiar story, we can ask some strange questions. For example, if summer is wedding season, and weddings largely work to reproduce the hegemonic cultural expectations into which we are socialized, then is summer, by virtue of the ubiquity and normativity of weddings, a season given over to preserving, championing, and reproducing hegemonic cultural ideals? If we remember that weddings are culturally interpreted to demonstrate true love, commitment, and adulthood, the significance of the wedding's hegemonic status becomes even clearer in its exclusion and harmful judgment: If you must wed to be an adult, then how are those who cannot wed or will not wed positioned within the social world we collectively and actively produce and reproduce?

Questions for Critical Thinking

1. What is the white wedding and what is sociologically significant about it? What is the wedding-industrial complex? What is its relationship to hegemonic orientations toward weddings?
2. What are agents of socialization? Identify four of the key socializing agents. What role do they play in the white wedding?
3. Can you apply the concepts of hegemonic masculinity and emphasized femininity to understand other parts of the white wedding ritual beyond the proposal?
4. How would you explain the heterosexual matrix? How is this related to the white wedding?
5. How might white weddings help to reinforce social inequality and stratification? For example, take a look through a popular bridal magazine or website: Do you see racialized or Indigenous brides featured on the cover or in ads as "normal" brides, or are they shown only as exceptions? Do you see any representation or discussion of brides, grooms, or guests who have any kind of disability or illness? If you do come across non-dominant group representations, what is the context of their representation?

References

American Consumer Credit Counseling (ACCC). 2019. "ACCC on How to Survive Wedding Season." *ConsumerCredit.com*, May 3. https://www.consumercredit.com/about-us/press-releases/2019-press-releases/accc-on-how-to-survive-wedding-season.

Bartholomay, Daniel J. 2018. "What, Exactly, Are We Measuring? Examining Heteronormativity in Relation to Same-Gender Marriage." *Sociology Compass* 12 (3): e12563. https://doi.org/10.1111/soc4.12563.

Berger, Peter. 1963. *Invitation to Sociology: A Humanitistic Perspective*. New York: Anchor Books.

Berlant, Lauren, and Michael Warner. 1998. "Sex in Public." *Critical Inquiry* 24 (2): 547–66. https://doi.org/10.1086/448884.

Boden, Sharon. 2001. "'Superbrides': Wedding Consumer Culture and the Construction of Bridal Identity." *Sociological Research Online* 6 (1): 1–14. https://doi.org/10.5153/sro.570.

———. 2003. *Consumerism, Romance and the Wedding Experience*. New York: Palgrave MacMillan.

Bourque, Andre. 2017. "Technology Profit and Pivots in the $300 Billion Wedding Space." *Huffington Post: The Blog*, December 6. https://www.huffingtonpost.com/andre-bourque/technology-profit-and-piv_b_7193112.html.

Burnett, Dean. 2016. "Public Proposals: True Romance or Unwarranted Coercion?" *Guardian* online, August 16. https://www.theguardian.com/science/brain-flapping/2016/aug/16/public-proposals-true-romance-or-unwarranted-coercion-olympic-podium-proposal.

Butler, Judith. 1990. *Gender Trouble: Feminism and the Subversion of Identity*. New York: Routledge.

Carter, Julia, and Simon Duncan. 2016. "Wedding Paradoxes: Individualized Conformity and the 'Perfect Day.'" *The Sociological Review* 65 (1): 1–19. https://doi.org/10.1111/1467-954X.12366.

Connell, Raewyn W. 1987. *Gender and Power*. Sydney, Australia: Allen and Unwin.

———. 2005. *Masculinities*. 2nd ed. Berkeley: University of California.

Connell, Raewyn W., and James W. Messerschmidt. 2005. "Hegemonic Masculinity: Rethinking the Concept." *Gender & Society* 19 (6): 829–59. https://doi.org/10.1177/0891243205278639.

Corrado, Marisa. 2002. "Teaching Wedding Rules: How Bridal Workers Negotiate Control over Their Customers." *Journal of Contemporary Ethnography* 31 (1): 33–67. https://doi.org/10.1177/0891241602031001002.

Engstrom, Erika. 2012. *The Bride Factory: Mass Media Portrayals of Women and Weddings*. New York: Peter Lang.

Fairchild, Emily. 2014. "Examining Wedding Rituals through a Multidimensional Gender Lens: The Analytic Importance of Attending to (In)consistency." *Journal of Contemporary Ethnography* 43 (3): 361–89.

Freeman, Elizabeth. 2002. *The Wedding Complex: Forms of Belonging in Modern American Culture*. Durham: Duke University Press.

Glapka, Ewa. 2014. *Reading Bridal Magazines from a Critical Discursive Perspective*. London: Palgrave MacMillan.

Gramsci, Antonio. 1971. *Selections from the Prison Notebooks of Antonio Gramsci*. Edited and translated by Quintin Hoare and Geoffrey Nowell Smith. New York: International Publishers.

Howard, Vicki. 2006. *Brides, Inc.: American Weddings and the Business of Tradition*. Philadelphia: University of Pennsylvania Press.

Ingraham, Chrys. 1999. *White Weddings: Romancing Heterosexuality in Popular Culture*. New York and London: Routledge.

Jackson, Stevi. 2006. "Gender, Sexuality and Heterosexuality. The Complexity (and Limits) of Heteronormativity." *Feminist Theory* 7 (1): 105–21. https://doi.org/10.1177/1464700106061462.

Kellogg, Kristi, Anna Price Olson, and Jessie Mooney DiGiovanna. 2020. "The Ultimate Wedding-Planning Checklist and Timeline." *Brides*, January 16. https://www.brides.com/story/brides-wedding-checklist-custom-wedding-to-do-list.

Kingston, Anne. 2004. *The Meaning of Wife*. Toronto: HarperCollins Publishers Ltd.

Kivel, Paul. 2003. "The 'Act-Like-A-Man' Box." In *Masculinities: Interdisciplinary Readings*, edited by Mark Hussey, 69–72. Upper Saddle River: Prentice Hall.

Lewis, Charles. 1998. "Working the Ritual: Professional Wedding Photography and the American Middle Class." *Journal of Communication Inquiry* 22 (1): 72–92. https://doi.org/10.1177/0196859998022001006.

Manavis, Sarah. 2018. "The Depressingly Familiar Viral Story of the 'Heartbroken Nerd' and a Spider-Man Video Game." *New Statesman*, September 13. https://www.newstatesman.com/science-tech/internet/2018/09/depressingly-familiar-viral-story-heartbroken-nerd-and-spider-man.

Mehta, Rupa. 2014. "Wedding Season: Tying Your Own Emotional Knots." *Huffington Post: The Blog*, July 22. https://m.huffpost.com/us/entry/5608961.

Mills, C. Wright. 1959. *The Sociological Imagination*. New York: Oxford University Press.

Patel, Nisha. 2014. "Wedding Costs Can Be Trimmed with a Few Simple Tricks." *CBC News*, July 26. https://www.cbc.ca/news/business/wedding-costs-can-be-trimmed-with-a-few-simple-tricks-1.2718135.

Rich, Adrienne. 1980. "Compulsory Heterosexuality and Lesbian Existence." *Signs* 5 (4): 631–60. https://doi.org/10.1086/493756.

Rouner, Jef. 2018. "The Other Side of the Spider-Man Proposal Story," *Houston Press*, September 10. https://www.houstonpress.com/news/the-spider-man-proposal-easter-egg-has-a-darker-side-10842784.

Singh, Natasha. 2013. "Advice for Guests: How to Survive Wedding Season on a Budget." *Canadian Living*, July 10. https://www.canadianliving.com/life-and-relationships/weddings/article/advice-for-guests-how-to-survive-wedding-season-on-a-budget.

Wallace, Carol McD. 2004. *All Dressed in White: The Irresistible Rise of the American Wedding*. New York: Penguin Books.

Ward, Patrick, Quinta Brunson, Zach Evans, and Justin Tan. 2015. "Wedding Season is Coming." *BuzzFeed*, March 27. https://www.buzzfeed.com/patchesrward/wedding-season-is-coming.

Wilford, Denette. 2018. "What is the Average Cost of a Wedding in Canada?" *Slice*, April 23. https://www.slice.ca/love/photos/average-cost-wedding-canada/#!canadian-wedding-cost-honeymoon

Williams, Raymond. 1989. "Culture is Ordinary." In *Resources of Hope: Culture, Democracy, Socialism*, 3–14. New York: Verso.

17 Summer in Cottage Country: Expectations and Experiences of Canadian Nature

TONYA K. DAVIDSON

LEARNING OUTCOMES

After reading this chapter, you should be able to:

- describe how Ontario's cottage country is a result of the dispossession of land from Indigenous peoples
- define classism, conspicuous consumption, and conspicuous leisure
- define and be able to identify the characteristics of gentrification
- analyze how experiences of visiting summer cottages are gendered
- analyze cottage inheritance and intergenerational social mobility with a sociological imagination

Introduction

"When the day arrives a little earlier, and lingers a little later, you can be sure it's summer" begins the narration of a 2015 Walmart commercial. A fully packed SUV with a canoe on the roof arrives at a lakeside house; scenes show young children and adults fishing, swinging on ropes and jumping into the lake, canoeing, and making s'mores. The narration continues, "And for this bounty, so little is expected in return, only that we find ways big and small to milk every last second of it, to use a little imagination, and make a whole lot of memories. Low prices, every day on everything you need to get away from it all. Walmart." The commercial ends with the crowd of summer revellers lighting sparklers, the magic of summer at the cottage confirmed. Every long weekend in the summer in my home province of Ontario – the reference point for this chapter – radio and television traffic reports and weather forecasters suggest that many, seemingly most, of my neighbours are packing their hatchbacks full of Frisbees and potato salad to head off to "the cottage." In just one week last spring I noticed a "cottage reading" display at my local bookstore, listened to a segment on the CBC Radio show *Day 6* dedicated to books to read at the cottage, and, at popular chain restaurant Jack Astor's, I was given the "cottage" summer menu.

These invocations of "the cottage" seem to rely on an assumption that everyone has access to a cottage that they enjoy in the summer. Despite **consumer culture** and popular culture's assumptions of a universal Canadian (or at least Ontario) summer cottage experience, according to Statistics Canada data, only 8.2 per cent of Ontarians owned a cottage in 2003 (Harrison 2013, 247). Of course, many more Ontarians and Canadians enjoy cottages as friends of cottage owners or as renters. The summer cottage celebrated in the Walmart commercial has a particularly Ontario aesthetic. Because of a long tradition of Ontario-centrism in the Canadian imaginary (demonstrated most clearly in the use of the iconic Ontario-Quebec maple leaf in nationalist symbolism), the Ontario summer often problematically stands in for the Canadian summer. In Ontario there are multiple "cottage countries," including the Muskokas, which are on the shores of Georgian Bay and adjacent to Algonquin Park, and the Kawartha Lakes region, which is bordered by the granite Canadian Shield. In other provinces like Saskatchewan, British Columbia, and Newfoundland, the cottage equivalent is known as the "cabin." Cabin-going may share characteristics with "going to the cottage" in Ontario; however, this chapter focuses on the Ontario cottage as it is produced in the Canadian imagination.

In what follows, I detail how cottage ownership and enjoyment in Ontario is the result of histories of **dispossession** of land from **Indigenous** peoples as a form of **settler colonialism**. I then explore how assumptions about cottage ownership can be read as expressions of **classism** and **conspicuous consumption**, and I follow this by explaining how the quintessential Ontario summer cottage experience has also historically been gendered, experienced differently for men and women. Finally, the frequently fraught expectations of cottage inheritance can be best understood by employing a **sociological imagination** that allows us to see how generational differences and **intergenerational social mobility** shape attitudes about family cottages. The arguments in this chapter are based on a reading of other sociologists' ethnographic research (Harrison 2013), **content analysis** and a critical reading of travel memoirs (Thorpe 2011), and **quantitative research** on second-home ownership (Jansson and Muller 2004; Marsh and Griffiths 2006). All of this analysis will demonstrate how spending time at the cottage during the summer should not be understood as a taken-for-granted or universally enjoyable experience in Ontario or, more broadly, Canada.

The Ontario Cottage and Settler Colonialism

Going to the cottage joins other idealized Canadian summer pastimes, like camping and canoeing, that promote Canada as a land of wilderness and Canadians as attuned to and reverent of their natural environment. Jocelyn Thorpe (2011) describes the concept of

social nature as: "the mechanisms through which nature appears separate from culture in order to make it clear that the nature-culture binary is a cultural product that has benefited some groups at the expense of others" (194). In other words, our understanding of nature is anything but natural; nature is constructed and imagined for us through particular sets of social ideas. The social nature of Ontario cottage country was and is only possible through the dispossession of the land from Indigenous people. Cottage country in Ontario is often on unceded Indigenous land, meaning it is on land that European settlers inhabited without ever signing treaties with the original Indigenous inhabitants. In some cases, cottages are on land that Indigenous communities have leased long-term. Dispossession of land from Indigenous peoples was and continues to be the basis of settler colonialism in Canada. Thus, the centrality of owning cottages to the Ontario summer imagery supports the logic of settler colonialism and a specifically **white** English-Canadian orientation toward nature.

In cottage country, settler colonialism takes two forms: going to the cottage is a practice where Indigenous people and Indigenous land rights are actively forgotten, simultaneously **Indigeneity** is often imagined in these spaces in ways that serves the interests of settler colonialism. Specifically, in cottage country, the minimal representations of Indigenous people that exist are often anachronistic, and caricatured like the racist "cigar store Indian" figures of the past.

Representing Cottage County as Terra Nullius

In the 1920s, the Group of Seven, a group of landscape artists based in Ontario, was instrumental in shaping how Canadians imagined the Canadian wilderness. Their paintings were characterized by wild, unpeopled landscapes, the Canadian Shield, and northern woods, and they were clear depictions of ***terra nullius***: an empty land ripe for white settlement (see Unger, chapter nine; Blomley 2004; Razack 2002). Nicholas Blomley (2004) suggests that maintaining the logic of *terra nullius* requires constant vigilance and spatial practices such as planning, naming, and mapping. In early settler writing on cottage country, Indigenous people were either imagined as absent – one travel writer wrote of Temagami that it was "untrammeled by the foot of man, unsullied by his hand" (in Thorpe 2011, 204) – or as primitive and stuck in the past. The celebration of the Ontario cottage lines up with the logic celebrated in the Group of Seven's paintings; it glorifies the landscape as if it was vacant and available for settler colonial use and enjoyment. The ideas surrounding the moral, aesthetic, and socializing value of an Ontario cottage allow for the ongoing dispossession of land from Indigenous people in a way that is presented as **naturalized**, peaceful, and as a site for **primary socialization** – good for children.

Today, going to the cottage continues to be a summer experience predominantly enjoyed by white people. From her ethnographic research in the Haliburton region of Ontario, Julia Harrison (2013) explains that the whiteness of the Haliburton cottagers influenced their understandings of and attachments to their cottage. Haliburton cottagers exhibited a certain slippage into the presumption of their right to own – and retain – a cottage for future generations of their Canadian family. In Harrison's study, Haliburton cottagers expressed both presumptions that they had the right to own the cottage properties in the present and would continue to access the resources needed to own the properties for future generations (159).

Over time, owning family, for many, cottages became imagined as a birthright, as white settlers came to view their cottage properties as a "spiritual homeland" (Grant 2008, M.1). The whiteness of cottage country is maintained when Indigeneity is invoked only to bolster the natural background but expelled and understood as an encroachment on proper land usage when Indigenous people work toward **sovereignty**.

Daniel Francis (1992) defines the "imaginary Indian" as an anachronistic Indigenous figure created through a European imagination and circulated through stories, summer camps, books for children, product branding, and sports **logos**. This figure has dominated how mainstream white **society** views Indigenous people. Philip Deloria (1998) has written about how there is a long history of white people "playing Indian" in the United States. Since the American Revolution, through the 1950s and the countercultural 1960s and 1970s, white Americans have fetishized Indigenous difference as a way to define their own cultural and individual identities. He write that "[a]lthough these performances have changed over time, the practice of playing Indian has clustered around two paradigmatic moments – the Revolution, which rested on the creation of a national identity, and modernity, which has used Indian play to encounter the authentic amidst the anxiety of urban industrial and postindustrial life" (7). While discussing a different national context, "playing Indian" has taken on a similar resonance in Canada and in cottage country. In cottage country, Indigeneity is welcomed at the level of the imaginary. For example, the word "Kawartha," a Mississauga word for "bright waters and happy lands" was "first coined in 1885 in response to a request by tourism promoters to the Mississauga people of Curve Lake for a name to describe the region.... It is not clear whether the native people already used this word to identify this area, or whether it simply originated in response to the request" (Marsh and Griffiths 2006, 220).

"Wild Rice is Anishinaabe Law"

While cottage country welcomes Indigenous names and some material culture, Indigenous peoples and land claims are often met with hostility. In the summer of 2016, people driving up to Ontario's Pigeon Lake, northeast of Toronto, in the Kawarthas, would have passed a billboard that read: "*Anishinaabe manoomin inaakonigewin gosha*" meaning, "wild rice is Anishinaabe law," illustrated with stalks of the *manomin* plant. The billboard was part of the larger Ogimaa Mikana (Reclaiming/Renaming) Project curated by Susan Blight and Hayden King. *Manomin* (the Ojibwa word for a grain commonly known as wild rice) has been a staple of the local Ojibwa diet since time immemorial. In the Kawarthas, this billboard deliberately spoke to what was being called the "rice wars," which had been ongoing since 2007 (Jackson 2016). For the past decade, some cottage owners had become upset that their cottage landscapes were being altered by

FIGURE 17.1 *"Anishinaabe manoomin inaakonigewin gosha,"* from the Ogimaa Mikana (Reclaiming/Renaming) Project by Susan Blight and Hayden King. Photo credit: The Ogimaa Mikana Project (https://ogimaamikana.tumblr.com/)

the ongoing and expanding cultivation of *manomin*. The upset cottagers started a group called "Save Pigeon Lake" and in 2015, cottagers complained because one *manomin* harvester, James Whetung, was seeding the lake with a motor boat instead of a traditional canoe. Whetung had a licence and treaty rights that gave him access to the lake. As a response to the cottagers' concerns, in a Parks Canada settlement, cottagers were allowed to clear a 100-by-100-square-foot area free of rice by their shores (Sachgau 2015).

Like in other cottage countries, Indigeneity is permissible (and even exploited) at the level of imagery, in the form of tourism marketing and vague notions of the region's past. However, in the face of present Indigenous claims, many respond with a strong sense of entitlement to beaches for their own leisure. When harvesting, Whetung describes that "[t]hey just come down to yell racial slurs and threaten us ... [saying that] if we don't get out of there, they're going to call the cops every five minutes until [they] drag us out of there" (quoted in Jackson 2016, n.p.). The *manomin* harvest represents Indigenous sovereignty, food sovereignty, and community building. However, in the historic production of this region's social nature as cottage country for white settlers, the wild rice stocks that the Anishinaabeg relied on became increasingly threatened, first through the building of the settler-colonial infrastructure for the Trent-Severn Waterway in 1837, 1856, and 1880, and then by the release of carp into the lakes in the 1870s (Jackson 2016).

For Whetung, Blight, and King, *manomin* harvesting is central to local Indigenous culture and food security, both in the past and in the present. For some of the present cottagers, however, the social nature of cottage country should be one managed for the leisure practices of the white settler cottagers: a space where both Indigenous peoples and their present engagements with the land are expelled. This story demonstrates how the social nature of cottage country has been created and maintained to affirm the dominance of white cottagers.

The Classism of Cottages

Cottage ownership and enjoyment is also clearly stratified within non-Indigenous society along the lines of **social class** and **gender**. Not in cottage country but in the heart of downtown Toronto, I visit condominiums for sale. One tiny condo that boasts a Juliette balcony and a barebones rooftop terrace is staged, awaiting my visit. The staging includes copies of *Cottage Life* magazine fanned out on the living room coffee table. The so-called cottage life is incongruent with the tenor of the apartment building, suggesting to me that cottages are clearly aspirational objects. In other words, the real estate customers interested in purchasing this tiny condominium likely could not afford an expensive second home; however, the cottage life is presented to complement a dreamy lifestyle imagined to be bought alongside this condo. Bruce Ravelli and Michelle Webber (2010) define classism as "an ideology that suggests that people's relative worth is at least partly determined by their social and economic status" (165). Privileging summer cottage-going over other more accessible forms of summer leisure can be understood as a reflection of classism, whereby the expensive cottage life is seen as the ideal form of leisure and those who can afford it are seen to be enjoying Ontario summers properly. In this staged condo, the imagined cottage life is clearly celebrated as an idealized form of leisure.

Conspicuous Cottages

In many parts of Canada, cottage ownership is an exemplary form of conspicuous consumption. Living and writing at the turn of the twentieth century in the United States, Thorstein Veblen (2007) noticed a radical shift in consumption practices. While for many decades Americans had been strongly influenced by a Calvinist asceticism that included not splurging on material goods, by the late nineteenth century, Americans were beginning to purchase luxury goods for the sake of owning luxury goods, a practice Veblen referred to as conspicuous consumption. Flaunting newly purchased consumer products was a way for individuals to demonstrate that they had excess wealth and, in fact, their wealth was so secured (it was such old money) that they did not need to work or appear to be working. Family cottages are frequently passed down through generations; owning a cottage thus clearly signals that cottagers have some access to what is commonly understood as old money. Of course, not all cottages, especially cottages not in the greater Toronto area, fit the following analysis. Many enjoy inexpensive, modest cottages as cabins or hunting or fishing camps. However, the cottages sold in *Cottage Life*, invoked in Walmart commercials, imagined when weather reporters report the weekend forecast as good or bad for "the weekend at the cottage," and pictured on Jack Astor's menus take on the aesthetic of these more luxurious, conspicuously enjoyed second homes.

For Veblen, conspicuously consumed items were also less functionally useful than their cheaper versions. Unnecessarily high heels and excessively fast cars are two contemporary examples of conspicuous consumption. Cottages, while varying in level of comfort, are also prized for being remote and offering opportunities for some sort of restorative manual labour. Cottages are not functionally convenient leisure destinations; they are prized in part for their symbolic value. And presented alongside other commodities – books, vacations, cocktail mixes, clothes – the summer cottage is another **commodity** bought, sold, and fetishized within contemporary consumer culture.

Veblen also coined the term **conspicuous leisure** to refer to demonstrating one's ability to not work through the flashy use of leisure time. While owning and going to a cottage is cost prohibitive to many, it is also time prohibitive to even more Canadians. Owning, maintaining, and enjoying a second home, especially a second home that is remote and not winterized, demands both material and time resources. In Canada today, leisure time is a luxury – in fact, in a recent study, Ontarians take on average 13 vacation days, despite having access to (on average) 17 paid vacation days (Byers 2016). Most Ontarians, even when they are owed vacation time, feel financial or other pressure to keep working. In light of this, months spent at an expensive second summer home are indeed conspicuous.

Over 100 years ago, Veblen noticed that one of the downsides of this type of **consumption** was that people without great economic means would emulate the wealthy in their consumption practices, creating a type of trickle-down consumption practice. In her contemporary reading of Veblen, Juliet Schor (2015) argues that conspicuous consumption is more present and more dangerous in the twenty-first century, and she names the practice of consuming as if you have access to old money "**upscale emulation**" (253). Upscale emulation in the twenty-first century is much more economically devastating than it was in the 1900s for two reasons. First, the gap between the rich and the poor has expanded exponentially. In the 1920s – the heyday of robber barons, glitz, and the Great Gatsby – the richest man imaginable, John D. Rockefeller, made 7,000 times the income of the average worker. In 2008, the top twenty-five hedge fund managers – people in charge of an economic system that collapsed, devastating millions of Americans – made on average a little over $1 billion each, 24,000 times the average American (McQuaig and Brooks 2010, 7). Second, Schor explains that we are no longer just comparing ourselves to the richest family in town, but to celebrities, who are even further removed from our everyday lives. Our sense of what good leisure is and what we are entitled to, or should aspire for, is entirely out of whack with our economic realities.

In the most popular cottage regions in Canada, cottages (including many of the cottages touted in *Cottage Life* magazine) are prohibitively expensive. In 2015, a report by Royal LePage demonstrated that while there is a range of cottages in Canada, in some places like the Muskoka region of Ontario, Mont-Tremblant in Quebec, and the Gulf Islands in British Columbia, the average cottage costs half a million dollars. Meanwhile, a Statistics Canada report in March 2015 showed that the debt load for Canadian families was at an all-time high, at 163 per cent of disposable income (debt-to-income ratio) (Parkinson 2016). With these financial realities, owning a home *and* a million-dollar second home is not a reasonable goal for middle- and even upper-middle-class Canadian families. Assuming cottage ownership is a cultural norm (as everyday talk often does) encourages a type of upscale emulation.

Celebrity Cottages

Like other practices of conspicuous leisure, spending summers at the cottage is a practice endorsed by celebrities. Celebrities including Goldie Hawn and Kurt Russel, Tom Hanks, and Steven Spielberg all have cottages in Ontario's Muskoka region. The August 2015 issue of *Vogue* magazine featured an invitation to Cindy Crawford's "private island retreat," a deluxe cottage in Muskoka to which Crawford's family arrives by sea plane. Crawford herself describes the area: "Every house here is a Ralph Lauren ad already" (Haskell 2015, n.p.). The décor of her retreat is described as

> a warmly appointed chalet with brass lanterns, miniature canoes, and dream catchers made by the local Ojibwa tribe. The seat of an old leather club chair is upholstered in a Pendleton blanket, and a credenza from a bar Rande once owned in Aspen stands beside a lounger from a former house of Cindy's in DeKalb, Illinois, the town where she grew up. (Haskell 2015, n.p.)

Not just an emblem of conspicuous consumption, Crawford's cottage also problematically reduces Indigeneity to ambiance. The dream catchers, within the context of this celebrity cottage, reinforce the "imaginary Indian" trope described by Daniel Francis (1992) and could be read to be operating in the tradition of what Deloria (1998) identifies as "object hobbyists" – people who, emerging in the mid-twentieth century, enjoyed collecting Indigenous artifacts and saw Indigenous people as "objects of desire, but only as they existed outside of American society and modernity itself" (135). When understood sociologically, Crawford's private island retreat, presented as aspirational, reinforces dominant classed and racialized values.

Private Lakes versus Public Pools

Aspirational summer leisure like Ralph Lauren–styled cottage retreats are celebrated culturally and invoked in all of the expressions of cottage-focused assumptions that began this chapter. However, these cottage-going assumptions mean that the summer leisure activities of the un-cottaged masses, people coming from all social classes, in hot cities and suburbs often go ignored and underfunded. While cottages are private property and enjoyed with chosen company, public pools are both deeply intimate and public. Suzie O'Brien and Imre Szeman (2014) suggest that "[t]he state of public swimming pools has historically been, and continues to be, a microcosm of the wider North American society" (278). In 2008, the Toronto District School Board announced that they would be closing a number of their pools. Reflecting on her childhood summers learning to swim in Lake Superior and speaking to the recent cuts to public swimming pools, author Margaret Atwood (2008) responded to the pool closures in a newspaper article:

> But why can't they learn in a lake, as I did? Many people used to swim in Lake Ontario, before it got so polluted that if you went in with two eyes you'd come out with three. We're told that water quality's improving, but there's a way to go yet; and even if the lake were totally purified, it's too cold for swimming in all but three months of the year. But isn't that enough time to learn? Kids do it at summer camp. Yes, those whose parents can afford it – who are a small fraction of the Toronto total. Which leaves us with: Rich kids swim, poor kids sink. (n.p.)

Atwood here highlights the classism in assuming that all Canadian children have ready access to lakes to learn to swim. In many cases, spending time at a lake is a luxury, while public pools are designed for and used by broader society. Collectively presuming everyone is at a cottage enables disinvestment in summer leisure activities in the places where most Canadians live – hot, sticky cities. Underfunding public summer leisure activities exacerbates the classed ways in which children's summers are actually, as Patrizia Albanese explains in chapter twenty, "often experienced as a financial and logistical strain on parents, and a source of great stress" (this volume, p. 346).

The Townies versus the Citidiots

The classism imbedded in cottage love can also be understood as an expression of an urban and rural or small-town divide. **City** dwellers crave experiences in and with nature in ways that people living in the country and in small towns (people who wake up to the sounds of tree toads every morning) might. While there is a significant rural middle class who do own or have access to cottages, it is also largely people from cities who have the disposable income to spend on a second home (Halseth and Rosenberg 1995).

A friend of mine, a third-generation Muskoka local, describes tensions in Bracebridge, Ontario, between "townies" and what the locals call "citidiots." Townies drive trucks, mid-priced cars, wear plaid and jeans. Citidiots drive Audis, or pull speedboats behind their utility vehicles, wear deck shoes with khakis, Lululemon yoga pants, brand-name sunglasses. According to my friend, tensions become most visible in the grocery store parking lot, a shared space where cottagers tend to block parking spots with their speedboats.

Bracebridge is located in the middle of Ontario's Muskoka district. In the context of **deindustrialization** marked by a decline in manufacturing jobs in the region, cottagers provide a lot of employment for the locals between May and September. Many other locals are employed in the tourist service industry. However, tourism and the cottage construction businesses are seasonal and precarious. In fact, for many years the tourism industry has relied on workers from the temporary foreign worker program to fulfill many of the seasonal, precarious jobs in the region (Brownlee, 2018).

Cottagers bring with them a seasonal form of **gentrification**. Neil Smith (2000) defines gentrification as the "reinvestment of CAPITAL at the urban centre, which is designed to produce space for a more affluent class of people than currently occupies that space" (294). In Bracebridge, locals face seasonal cottager-led gentrification. Every spring new businesses pop up on the city's main street – pet accessory stores, bakeries selling $7 butter tarts – and locals take bets on which business will make it through the slower fall and winter seasons. Meanwhile, local staples like the hardware store have been pushed out. This type of gentrification demonstrates another aspect of classism – how the interests of the wealthier seasonal visitors are privileged over the needs of locals.

Cottage-led gentrification is even the bane of more established cottagers. In a recent letter to the editor of Toronto's *NOW* magazine, one cottager from the eastern Ontario region of Prince Edward County laments:

> There's been a lot of press about the exodus of Torontonians to "the county," as in Prince Edward County. I'm happy that people enjoy it. My husband grew up there and I've been visiting the family cottage there since 1974. After a couple of inroads by McDonald's and Tim's, I'm concerned that hipsters and wannabe winemakers will finally put an end to the peaceful, rural place it's always been. I'm sure the Drake in Wellington, the new owners of the Hayloft and many restauranteurs think they're fitting in, but do they get that it's not just Queen

> Street very far east? Once they've weathered the isolation and lack of visitors during the long, cold winter, I suspect many will give up and go home, where they can grab a cab to the next new hot restaurant. I hope so. (L. Cummins, Toronto, *NOW*, September 3, 2015)

In this letter, the tension we see isn't between local full-time inhabitants and summer cottagers or between **settler** and Indigenous populations, but, rather, between long-term cottagers and more recent cottagers.

While cottagers bring cash for fancy cupcakes, they are less likely to contribute to the maintenance of local infrastructure. Throughout the 1980s, the only public transit in Bracebridge was the kitschy, tourist-oriented trolley that brought passengers to the "Santa's Village" amusement park. One dilemma for cottage regions is that

> since cottage area services are based on seasonal occupancy, conversion to year-round housing puts tremendous pressure on the local environment and infrastructure. Too often the costs of cottage conversion, including pollution control, road access, winter snow removal, water supply, and garbage collection, are not anticipated in cottage area planning. The costs of these services can be substantial, and may easily exceed property tax revenues. (Halseth 2004, 38)

In June 2015, the city of Timmons, Ontario, was grappling with the growing demand to service rural roads that have historically served secondary homes. City counsellor Pat Bamford reportedly said, "So, I have a problem just holus bolus saying we are going to increase our taxes to pay for somebody who has a summer home. Because that is, in a way, a luxury" (in Gillis 2015, n.p.).

Cottagers and locals conflict not just over tax hikes, but over land stewardship, the construction of wind turbines (a cottager's eyesore is a local's revenue source), rice farming, and, in Muskoka, some cottagers disregard the speed limits at the mouth of the river, creating waves that gradually erode the shoreline. In these examples, we can see that the social nature of cottage country has been produced as a space for the affluent and, in some cases, the desires of those with second homes outstrip the needs of the locals living in the cottage country proper. Conspicuous consumption, leisure, and classism shape summer aspirations, labour practices, and peoples' understandings of ownership to these landscapes.

A Cottage of One's Own: Gendered Cottage Experiences

Race and class are not the only ways in which the enjoyment of cottages is structured. Cottage leisure is often also premised on dominant gender **norms**, **heteronormativity**, and family structures. When doing a little real estate sleuthing in the cottage country of Evangola State Park near her home in Buffalo, New York, my sister Stephanie found a cottage that intrigued her; it was much smaller than the others (624 square feet), clearly built before rules were established in the 1990s that dictated a 1,200 square-foot minimum. She looked up the ownership details on the tax website and found a woman listed as the sole owner of the cottage from its building in 1961. She found that interesting, telling me that

> Normally whoever records this data either throws the woman off the deed or lists them as secondary, as "spouse." I looked further and noticed that a couple of decades later another woman was added to the deed, along with the original owner ... I looked the women up and found their obituaries. They were listed as each other's "lifelong friends".... The one was the first foreman at the electrical plant; the other was a national park worker. They died within two years of each other. (Personal communication, June 25, 2016)

Understanding "lifelong friends" as a mid-twentieth century euphemism for **queer**, we can read this story of queer female cottage ownership as unusual because, as many ethnographers have detailed, cottages are often imagined as spaces for heterosexual men and children (Harrison 2013; Thorpe 2011). In her study of travel writing in the nineteenth century that focused on Temagami, Ontario, Jocelyn Thorpe (2011) details how travel writing constructed the Ontario wilderness as a necessary reprieve for white men, a place for them to become "physically and mentally fit like their forefathers, who had been 'hewers of wood and drawers of water'" (205). Journeys into the wilderness of Temagami allowed for men "to take regular breaks from civilization in order to recuperate from the pressures of modern life" (205). Thorpe (2011) cites a 1909 piece of travel writing by a woman who, recalling a hunting trip, wrote, "I went out to call my husband to breakfast, when one of them [a party of hunters from Toronto] exclaimed, 'Is that a woman's voice? Why, we're not out of civilization yet!" (200).

While imagined as spaces of leisure, both men and women work at the cottage. However, their work takes different forms. For men, seemingly emasculated by urban living, the cottage becomes a place where they can pick up saws and axes and dig into manual projects (see Harrison 2013; Jansson and Muller 2003). Cottage country paradoxically both relies on women's work and is a space in which women themselves are imagined as incompatible. Cottage leisure demands a lot of the "**holiday body work**" discussed by Heidi Bickis in chapter five. In other words, women are necessary to make the cottage experience possible, but as the female travel writer highlighted, their very presence threatens the ability to understand cottage country as a place in which to perform rugged masculinity.

An irony of the gendering of the cottage is that, while imagined as a hyper-masculine space, Harrison (2013) explains that in the postwar era in the Haliburton cottage region, women spent more time at their cottages than men did, often arriving right after the end of the school year and not returning until Labour Day weekend; men often came up only for weekends. And unlike the male cottage labour that was understood as a form of therapeutic reclamation, women's work at the cottage was more of the same undervalued domestic toil of their everyday lives, albeit without helpful technological aids (washing machines, dishwashers). As Harrison (2013) notes, the norm of women and children spending the entire summer at the cottage shifted when women became more involved in the paid work sphere (221). Today, despite full-time work, women continue to do a disproportionate amount of social reproduction-based labour: meal preparation, child care, and cleaning. Sociologist Arlie Hochschild (1989) has called this phenomenon the "**second shift**" for women (see chapters five and fourteen). In a 2010 Canadian study, men spent on average 8.3 hours a week doing housework, while women spent an average 13.8 hours a week on these tasks (Statistics Canada in Little et al. 2014, 378). When it comes to the summer cottage experience, we can assume that those sparklers and hot dogs being enjoyed in the Walmart cottage commercial were probably thought of, bought, packed, unpacked, and cleaned up by women; in this way, these **gendered** cottage practices also presume and rely on heteronormative understandings of nuclear families. The queer women's cottage at Evangola State Park suggests a subtle subversion of the gendered logic of how summer cottages are enjoyed.

Cottages for Millennials?

While summers in Canada are short, in nostalgic reminiscences, summer months magically seem to stretch. For many, summer cottages are emotionally saturated landscapes. They are sites of childhood **socialization** and emblems of family lineages both symbolically and economically. While some cottages are lavish and conspicuous second homes, for many, cottages are rustic, modest, and perhaps hard-to-retain family inheritances. Cottage inheritance and cottage loss are both phenomena that can be understood sociologically. While researching cottages, I have been told many emotional stories of cottage loss. After the family cottage near Algonquin Park was sold when she was a child, my friend Heather remembers her childhood full of stories and memories of the lost family cottage. At one point, the family rented a cottage across the lake from the lost cottage and her mom and aunt swam across the lake and sat on the beach of their former cottage, in longing.

Cottages are imagined, experienced, and projected into the future as architectural embodiments of family lineage – in fact, David Gage (2013) suggests that "family cottages are often more stable properties than family homes" (89). In a **survey**-based study of second home owners in the area known as Kvarken in northern Finland and Sweden, Jansson and Muller (1998) found that 10 per cent of second-homeowners gave maintaining links with the "landscape of childhood" as their main reason for having a second home (265). Furthermore, when asked about their future plans for their homes, 66.7 per cent of respondents planned for their second homes to be inherited by their children or grandchildren (Jansson and Muller 1998, 268). The summer cottage, therefore, is imagined in alignment with assumptions about present and future nuclear, heteronormative family relations.

Inheritance is not just a reflection of family relationships, though – it is also a socially structured means of maintaining status-quo class and race relations. Thomas Shapiro's research on baby boomer inheritance in the United States found that

> white inheritance is seven times larger than black inheritance. One third of baby boomer whites in 1989 could count on bequests, compared to only five percent of blacks. White families are four times as likely as blacks to receive a significant inheritance, and of those who do receive inheritances, on average whites inherit $102,167 more than blacks. (Lipsitz 2007, 19)

Inheritance is a common way in which people find themselves cottage owners. Understanding this can help us to comprehend the **racialization** and social classedness of cottage country.

Saturated with family lore and memories generated from family cottages, cottage inheritance can also produce a specific burden on adult children who are living in different economic circumstances, with different access to leisure time, and perhaps different leisure interests than their ancestors. One of the elements of C. Wright Mills's sociological imagination is the ability to contextualize one's life and experiences. Many millennial potential inheritors could likely not imagine inheriting and upkeeping a second home when first homes have become increasingly out of reach. The tensions around cottage inheritance highlight what sociologists call intergenerational social mobility: the differences in social class between different generations of a family (Little et al. 2014, 291).

However, in some urban housing markets (notably Toronto), young millennials are foregoing buying primary residences and instead are pooling funds with siblings, or finding ways to invest instead in cottage properties. A young married couple featured in *Toronto Life*'s "Cost of Living" series are quoted as saying, "We're happy renting for now. We want to buy a cottage before we buy a house, just because we don't think buying a house in Toronto is possible. We don't want to invest our money in a shoebox" (Kupferman 2016, n.p.). In this surprising flip, cottages have become a new possibility for property ownership in the context of inflated housing markets.

Conclusion

In this chapter, I've explored how the suggestion that going to the cottage is the idealized way of spending a Canadian summer continues the imperialist project of dispossessing Indigenous peoples of their land, a process that is often twinned with employing colonial visions of Indigeneity as a marketing scheme. As I've demonstrated here, imagining or proposing that all or most Ontarians spend their summers at the cottage is also a classist presumption. Buying cottages can likewise be a form of conspicuous consumption that leads to unsustainable forms of seasonal gentrification in the local communities.

Celebrating summer at the cottage does not just involve leisure, but also labour, which continues to be gendered when cottage labour is imagined as restorative for men but ongoing invisible domestic work for women. For millennials and subsequent generations, cottage owning cannot be understood as a taken-for-granted inheritance. At the same time, the practice of inheriting cottages underscores how class structures people's access to cottage country.

Every summer I try to get myself invited to my friend's cottage in Quebec. I stock up on corn on the cob, nachos, and coolers at the shop in the nearest town and prepare for a weekend of Settlers of Catan, reading bad magazines, and swimming in the lake. It's always relaxing and fun and I always enjoy the stop for soft-serve ice cream on the drive home. While this chapter has been highly critical of the logic of cottage ownership, cottages can be really great. There can be something rejuvenating about spending time disconnected from the intensities of urban modern life. However, cottages should not be taken for granted as the ideal way to spend an Ontarian or Canadian summer. Instead of being read as "returning to nature," cottage country should be understood sociologically as produced and maintained through a series of social ideas and practices. It epitomizes Thorpe's understanding of "social nature." Settler colonialism, class, and **normative** structures of gender and heteronormativity impact who has access to cottages and how they are experienced. The next time the weather announcer or traffic reporter discusses the weekend forecast in relation to weekends at "the cottage," understand that the ability to enjoy or imagine a summer at the cottage is not distributed equally across our hot, sticky, summer society.

Questions for Critical Thought

1. What are the expectations for summer leisure that you encounter? Can you read these expectations through a sociological lens?
2. Should providing access to summer leisure opportunities (swimming pools, lakes, playgrounds) be understood as a public or private responsibility?
3. In this chapter, cottages are discussed as an exemplary form of conspicuous consumption. What are some other examples of conspicuous consumption and conspicuous leisure that are celebrated in the media, your family, and among your peers?
4. In this chapter, the author cites the paintings of the Group of Seven and the ideas surrounding cottage ownership as contributing to "social nature." In what other ways are our conceptions of nature mediated by social ideas?
5. Did you go to summer camp as a child? Did any summer camp traditions reinforce or challenge the ideas of Indigeneity that are produced in cottage country, as discussed in this chapter?

References

Atwood, Margaret. 2008. "Rich Kids Swim, Poor Kids Sink." *Globe and Mail,* April 19, M1.

Blomley, Nicholas. 2004. *Unsettling the City: Urban Land and the Politics of Property.* New York: Routledge.

Brownlee, Alison. 2018. "'We Still Can't Find People': Labour Shortage Rips across Muskoka." *Hunstville Forester.* July 16.

Byers, Jim. 2016. "Canadians Leave 31 Million Vacation Days Unused Each Year: Study" *Toronto Sun,* October 19. https://torontosun.com/2016/10/19/canadians-leave-31-million-vacation-days-unused-each-year-study/wcm/67eb87e2-3916-4e63-bdd4-cf4d033cd481.

Cummins, L. 2015. "Hands Off 'the County,' Hipsters." *NOW Magazine.* September 5. https://nowtoronto.com/news/letters-to-the-editor/letters-to-the-editor-tory-has-left-station-on-scarborough-s/.

Deloria, Philip. 1998. *Playing Indian.* New Haven: Yale University Press.

Francis, Daniel. 1992. *The Imaginary Indian: The Image of the Indian in Canadian Culture.* Vancouver: Arsenal Pulp Press.

Gage, David. 2013. "Holding on to 'Family Cottages'" *American Journal of Family Law* 27 (2): 89–96.

Gillis, Len. 2015. "Growing Calls to Extend Services to Rural Areas." *Timmins Press,* June 4.

Grant, Kelly. 2008. "Let Us Back into Our Cottages." *Globe and Mail,* August 16, M1.

Halseth, Greg. 2004. "The 'Cottage' Privilege: Increasingly Elite Landscapes of Second Homes in Canada." In *Tourism, Mobility, and Second Homes: Between Elite Landscape and Common Ground,* edited by Colin Michael Hall and Dieter K. Muller, 35–54. Toronto: Channel View Publications.

Halseth, Greg, and Mark Rosenberg. 1995. "Cottagers in an Urban Field." *Professional Geographer* 47(2): 148–59. https://doi.org/10.1111/j.0033-0124.1995.00148.x.

Harrison, Julia. 2013. *A Timeless Place: The Ontario Cottage.* Vancouver: University of British Columbia Press.

Haskell, Rob. 2015. "An Exclusive Look at Cindy Crawford's Private Island Retreat." *Vogue,* August 25. http://www.vogue.com/13290253/cindy-crawford-island-house-canada/.

Hochschild, Arlie. 1989. *The Second Shift: Working Parents and the Revolution at Home.* New York: Viking/Penguin.

Jackson, Lisa. 2016. "Canada's Wild Rice Wars: How a Conflict Over Wild Ricing on Pigeon Lake Is Drawing Attention to Indigenous Rights and Traditional Foods." *Al Jazeera,* February 20. https://www.aljazeera.com/indepth/features/2016/02/canada-wild-rice-wars-160217083126970.html.

Jansson, Bruno, and Dieter K. Muller. 2004. "Second Home Plans among Second Home Owners in Northern Europe's Periphery." In *Tourism, Mobility, and Second Homes: Between Elite Landscape and Common Ground,* edited by Colin Michael Hall and Dieter K. Muller, 261–72. Toronto: Channel View Publications.

Kupferman, Steve. 2016. "We Don't Want to Invest Our Money in a Shoebox: A Young Couple Saves Up for a Cottage." *Toronto Life,* June 30. http://torontolife.com/city/life/cost-of-living-alison-and-zach/.

Lipsitz, George. 2007. "The Racialization of Space and the Spatialization of Race: Theorizing the Hidden Architecture of Landscape." *Landscape Journal* 26 (1): 10–23. https://doi.org/10.3368/lj.26.1.10.

Little, William, Sally Vyain, Gail Scaramuzzo, Susan Cody-Rydzewki, Heather Griffiths, Eric Strayer, Nathan Keirns, and Ron McGivern. 2014. *Introduction to Sociology*. 1st Canadian ed. BC: Open Textbook Project.

Marsh, John, and Katie Griffiths. 2006. "Cottage Country Landscapes: The Case of the Kawartha Lakes Region, Ontario." In *Multiple Dwelling and Tourism: Negotiating Place, Home and Identity*, edited by Norman McIntyre, Daniel Williams, and Kevin McHugh, 219–33. Wallingford: CABI Publishing.

McQuaig, Linda, and Neil Brooks. 2010. *The Trouble with Billionaires: Why Too Much Money at the Top is Bad for Everyone*. Toronto: Penguin Canada.

O'Brien, Suzie, and Imre Szeman. 2014. *Popular Culture: A User's Guide*. Toronto: Nelson.

Parkinson, David. 2016. "Canadian Household Debt Soars to Yet Another Record." *Globe and Mail*, March 11. https://www.theglobeandmail.com/report-on-business/economy/canadians-debt-burden-still-growing-hits-record-in-fourth-quarter/article29172712/.

Ravelli, Bruce, and Michelle Webber. 2010. *Exploring Sociology: A Canadian Perspective*. Toronto: Pearson.

Razack, Sherene. 2002. "When Place Becomes Race." In *Race, Space, and Law: Unmapping a White-Settler Society*, edited by Sherene Razack, 1–20. Toronto: Between the Lines Press.

Sachgau, Oliver. 2015. "Rice Farming in Ontario Lake Sparks Fight over Treaty and Property Rights." *Globe and Mail*, August 28. https://www.theglobeandmail.com/news/national/rice-farming-in-ontario-lake-sparks-fight-over-treaty-and-property-rights/article26155200/.

Schor, Juliet. 2015. "The New Politics of Consumption: Why Americans Want So Much More Than They Need." In *Gender, Race, and Class in Media: A Critical Reader*, edited by Gail Dines and Jean Humez, 251–57. London: Sage.

Smith, Neil. 2000. "Gentrification." In *The Dictionary of Human Geography*, 4th ed., edited by R.J. Johnston, Derek Gregory, Geraldine Pratt and Michael Watts, 294–96. Malden: Blackwell Publishers.

Thorpe, Jocelyn. 2011. "Temagami's Tangled Wild: The Making of Race, Nature, and Nation in Early-Twentieth-Century Ontario." In *Rethinking the Great White North: Race, Nature, and the Historical Geographies of Whiteness in Canada*, edited by Andrew Baldwin, Laura Cameron and Audrey Kobayashi, 193–210. Vancouver: University of British Columbia Press.

Veblen, Thorstein. 2007. *The Theory of the Leisure Class*. New York: Oxford University Press.

18 "The Long and 'Hot' Summer is Coming": Environmental Activism, Violence, and the State

PAUL JOOSSE

LEARNING OUTCOMES

After reading this chapter, you should be able to:

- describe how the state's legitimacy is achieved and potentially lost
- reflect on issues of social inequalities as they pertain to class, the rural/urban divide, environmental justice, and the role of the citizen amid the corporate-state alliance
- understand social movement mobilization from the framing perspective
- describe how natural gas extraction (including fracking) and its attendant dangers are organized and managed in Canada
- apply Max Weber's definition of the "state" to the Canadian state's involvement with the natural gas industry in British Columbia

Introduction

"Time out is over!! The long and 'hot' summer is coming," warned the threatening letter in April 2010 (EnCana Bomber 2010). Addressed to Canadian natural gas giant EnCana Corporation and to several media outlets, everybody knew what the promised "hot summer" implied. Between October 2008 and July 2009, six bombs had gone off – all targeting EnCana's infrastructure in the area surrounding Tomslake, British Columbia. The bombings highlighted a growing friction between a variety of companies that operated in the area and community members – community members who were becoming increasingly worried about the environmental, economic, and social consequences of the rapid expansion of extraction operations in and around the places where they lived and worked.

At the time, I was in the middle of writing my doctoral dissertation about environmentally motivated sabotage and I decided to build this case into my research, trying to understand what had led to this tension, and to understand more generally why protests – and even spates of sabotage – seemed to have a seasonal quality. Why did this "heat" of which the bomber spoke come and pass and then come again periodically, much like the summer months? Although as **crimes** the bombings are officially unsolved, sociological concepts can help us to understand this process of "heating up." The first concept comes from Max Weber, a sociologist who, in the early twentieth century, produced tremendously important sociological work that included, among other things, his influential definition of the **state**.

Defining the "State"

At first glance, the question *what is a state?* may seem so elementary that it doesn't deserve consideration. After all, we already know what a state is, don't we? Canada is a state. The Canadian state is what is responsible for ushering in official **multiculturalism** (as detailed by Buffam in chapter fifteen) and for organizing the migration of seasonal migrant workers (as explained by Hennebry, Celis Parra, and Daley in chapter four). The United States and Mexico are also states. But while we can recognize these as examples, just being able to identify them doesn't give us insight into the defining element of what, exactly, makes a state a state. The interesting thing is that the defining element, for Weber, is not something that would spring to most people's minds when they think, for example, about Canada. For Weber (1958), this defining factor of what constitutes a state is violence. More specifically, he defined a state as "a human community that (successfully) claims the monopoly of the legitimate use of physical force within a given **territory**" (28). Key in this definition are three elements: (a) monopoly over violence, (b) **legitimacy**, and (c) territory. **Monopoly over violence** means that the use of violence is the exclusive privilege of a state actor. Legitimacy means that there are general agreed-upon ideas among the **population** about the "properness" of this use of violence by the state. That is, there is general consensus that it is proper for the state to have a monopoly over violence. Territory refers to the notion that this "legitimate monopoly" over violence is exercised within a particular geographical space.

Why doesn't this idea immediately spring to mind when we think of what makes Canada? Partly, of course, this is because such a notion seems crude or reductive. You might object, for example, and argue that there is *much more* to "Canada" than the threat of violence. Weber would answer that, yes, of course Canada is a robust and complicated place, but he would also maintain that the entire power structure of Canada – what makes Canada a state – does in fact derive, ultimately, from this claim over the power of violence. Even the most minor rules within Canada, Weber would argue, derive from this power. Sure, you could ignore that jaywalking ticket. You could throw out those notices of non-payment that come in the mail about the ticket. Next, you could skip your assigned court date. At some point, however, we all know what will happen. Ultimately, a police officer – someone that the state endows with the legitimate use of physical force – will be knocking at the door.

Defining Social Movements

A second concept to think about in relation to the case study of the EnCana bombings comes from the sociological literature on **social movements**. Social movements are sustained collective actions that seek to make some lasting change within **society**. Social movement literature tries to understand *why* social movements form, why they form *when* they do, *what* makes them successful, and *how* social movements interact with other elements of society, such as the political system, the legal system, the media, and so on. While there are different approaches within **social movement theory**, one influential set of literature pertains to how social issues are **framed** – that is, how our ideas about social issues are shaped in ways that lead people to join together with others to try to effect change within a society. The key writers who pioneered this framing perspective are Robert Benford and David Snow. In an influential article published in 2000, they described three **core framing tasks** with which every social movement will need to engage if they are to be successful as movements. These core framing tasks establish a perspective on the world that is likely to result in **mobilization** – the word that social movement theorists use to describe the transition that people make from being non-active to active participants in social movements. According to Benford and Snow (2000), these core framing tasks include producing three frames. To be successful, a social movement must produce diagnostic frames – frames that, as the name suggests, diagnose what the main problem is, either in society as a whole or in some smaller social community. Having established what the problem is, a movement must develop prognostic frames – frames that tell us what should and can be done with respect to this problem. And finally, the movement must provide motivational frames. These tell us why we should care about the problem, and particularly, why it is important that *you* become involved. These framing tasks operate by trying to change the *way people think* about issues. One interesting feature of this perspective is that different groups of people can operate with entirely different sets of diagnostic, prognostic, and motivational frames. This helps to explain, in part, why different politically motivated groups can align into fundamentally opposed camps, and how the "legitimacy" that we usually give to state violence can be challenged by people who engage in social movements.

Social Movements and the State

These two sets of concepts, from Weber and from Benford and Snow, relate to one another in ways that can help us to understand how challenges to state power become possible. Specifically, if the state's power is framed as legitimate, then those who challenge state power will invariably be diagnosed as the problem. Conversely, if state power is framed as illegitimate, then the state, its actions, and the actions of its partners may be diagnosed as the central problem. Similarly, divergent conclusions will result in terms of the prognoses for action that we may make, and in terms of the motivations we may have for caring about the issue. In our everyday lives, most of us likely don't think about the possibility of challenging state power; the state seems to have a natural, taken-for-granted quality, and the power structure seems frozen in place. For those who harbour hopeful visions for a different society, situations where state power is accepted unquestioningly must seem like a dark winter in which little movement is possible. Periodically, however, the world seems to tilt in such a way that this winter will come to an end. Events and actions coincide in ways that work to thaw power relations, creating a palpable sense of fluidity. It is in these moments that the "hot summer" can begin.

Tomslake and the EnCana Bombings

Backdrop: A Community Divided

Tomslake, a tiny hamlet in northeastern British Columbia, is like many small Canadian towns that have been beset by dwindling economic opportunities. According to residents in the area, the past 40 years have seen a steady decrease in the viability of farming, and since the 1990s an infestation of pine beetles in the forests has severely hurt the logging industry. Where this hamlet's fortunes differ from many other towns (for good or ill, as we will see) is that it sits on the Montney Play – a deposit of 449 trillion cubic feet of natural gas, which is mostly trapped in shale rock. In the past 20 years, this untapped natural resource has become available for extraction, largely a result of new technological developments in drilling and **fracking**. Fracking is a process that involves injecting high-pressure water and chemicals into the ground in ways that crack shale formations, releasing the trapped gas. EnCana Corporation, the largest natural gas extraction company in North America, has over 200 wells in the area around Tomslake. There is fierce competition among several companies who operate in the area, however, and companies can even purchase mineral rights at different geological strata so that, when driving around the area, one can often see multiple companies maintaining surface structures on the same plot of land.

Many people in the community welcome these developments, since natural gas extraction has provided them with an economic lifeline. It is no longer necessary for nearly all young people to move away for jobs, as often was the case prior to the expansion of natural gas extraction at the turn of the century. Now, companies like Talisman, Fortis, Murphy Oil, and EnCana offer well-paying industry jobs locally. Furthermore, although the companies purchase the mineral rights to the natural gas, they still need to negotiate with landowners for surface rights (the rights to put extraction structures on their land). This means that many landowners receive regular payments from companies for allowing access. On top of this, the companies regularly ingratiate themselves to the wider community by making large donations for public facilities. For example, Mike

Bernier, mayor of Dawson Creek, British Columbia (a community 30 kilometres northwest of Tomslake) commented to the *Globe and Mail's Report on Business:*

> Any time you have economic development, you have hassles, but EnCana has bent over backward to support the community. They gave us $500,000 for the naming rights on an entertainment multiplex, and another $250,000 to launch a new arts centre. They've been a really good corporate citizen. (Quoted in McDonald 2009, 47)

It is clear that many community members see the value of having companies operating (often literally) in their backyard.

Some, however, hold a much different view about this industrial development. Rather than a sustainable, long-term economic strategy, this rapid industrial development can be understood as an **economic boom**. An economic boom is a period of rapid growth and profitability across an economy, but one that, by definition, ends, often suddenly. Economic booms tend to have the effect of creating, deepening, and revealing existing disparities between those who benefit from the new economic activity and those who are left out in the cold. I wanted to understand the differences in opinion surrounding the oil and gas activity in the area, and so I paid several visits to Tomslake, attended community meetings, in some cases stayed in community members' homes for a short period of time, and conducted 17 **interviews** with residents in the area. These issues were sensitive in nature, and as a result of the sabotage campaign that was occurring at the time (which will be discussed below), the issue of people's opinions about oil and gas development was all the more sensitive. For this reason, I have removed all potentially identifying information from the quotes that appear below.

Some residents I spoke with were put off by the sheer pace of the development, such as one who remarked that "they're going after this stuff like it's going to rot in the ground." Another mentioned, "I look out over my community at night and it's lit up like a birthday cake" (a reference to the number of gas flares that the person could see spread across the land; see figure 18.1 for an example of a flare stack). Others noted that the increased activity was disruptive to their previously quiet and peaceful existence. In a comment post-scripting a CBC news story in 2008, one Tomslake resident wrote: "How would you like it if every day for the last 10 years Oil Truck[s] ... are passing through your streets that [are] barely big enough to get 2 normal size trucks safely through ... how would you like it if you look outside and see oil rigs all over in and around your community?" (quoted in Joosse 2008a, A7). Other community members noted that the new wealth seemed to spur new social problems within the community itself. I spoke to one local resident who invoked classic images of gold-rush decadence, lamenting: "It all goes up someone's nose, in someone's arm, or in some lady's purse." These were oblique references, she clarified, to "drugs and prostitution."

Chief among their concerns, however, was an environmental hazard. The natural gas in the Montney Play is what people refer to as sour, meaning that it contains hydrogen

FIGURE 18.1 A flare from a gas well, Tomslake, British Columbia. Photo credit: Paul Joosse

sulphide (H_2S). This is a neurotoxin lethal enough to cause death with one breath at a concentrated level (Agency for Toxic Substances and Disease Registry 2006). What makes it even more worrisome to residents are its physical attributes. For one thing, the gas is clear and heavier than air, meaning that it can form pools in low places on a still day. Secondly, although at low concentrations it smells like rotten eggs, at higher concentrations it can burn out the olfactory senses, making it difficult to detect even by smell. This means that, if it escapes from damaged or worn-down gas-line infrastructure – or if it escapes as a result of fracking itself – these concentrated pools would be undetectable. It is common for front-line workers in the natural gas industry to be "knocked down," which is industry parlance for being rendered unconscious from exposure to H2S (Nikiforuk 2001, 21). There have been several leaks in the past, and on November 22, 2010, a well blowout (a failure of the company's well that releases natural gas) at an EnCana site near Tomslake required the evacuation of several residences. The leak killed farm animals and revealed serious inadequacies with EnCana's air detection systems and evacuation procedures (Citizens' Meeting Minutes 2010; see also BC Oil and Gas Commission 2010). Prior to the leak, one resident of Tomslake, in a moment of prescience, confronted a representative from Murphy Oil at a Peace River Regional Hospital District meeting, voicing the complaint that "we don't like knowing we are going to wake up to [a] whistle, have to go outside, figure out where the wind is blowing and run" (quoted in Joosse 2017, 55).

Increased traffic, unease with the influx of a young and male working population, resentment at the encroachment of business interests from neighbouring Alberta, and concerns about the long-term health effects associated with extraction all arose commonly as grievances for residents of the Tomslake area whom I interviewed. EnCana has responded with a publicity campaign called "Courtesy Matters," which aims to improve relations between EnCana's staff and operations and local residents. This campaign is primarily aimed at ensuring that EnCana workers treat locals with courtesy. This means driving more slowly (so as not to kick up dust), not passing dangerously, dealing with roadkill, and counselling their "land men" about how to interact with residents when negotiating with them. When I mentioned the campaign to residents, many of them cynically scoffed, one responding with a play on words: "more like *currency* matters."

Before the bombings, which brought wider attention (my own included) to these issues, residents had tried a number of strategies that played to more traditional channels of political influence to resist the negative activities of these companies. These strategies included letter-writing campaigns, staging town hall meetings with police and industry, and even setting up road blocks that would target industry vehicles, forcing them to reroute (Joosse 2008a). When I interviewed residents, however, many expressed frustrations with their lack of success with these tactics. Aside from the fact that the community itself was divided about the issue, with some of members gauging that the benefits outweighed the aforementioned risks, there was also a common feeling that, given the larger political and economic realities, there was no realistic prospect of improving their situation. In the 2008–9 fiscal year, the BC provincial government collected a record $2.4 billion from the sale of oil and gas land rights (CBC News 2009; see also Simpson 2009). Rural jurisdictions like Tomslake, because of their low populations and low population densities, are unlikely to weigh heavily in politicians' calculations about extraction policies, and local residents are aware of this. One landowner erected a sign on his property that expressed his frustration with this sense that politicians seemed not to care about his interests: "Needed: MLA [Member of the Legislative Assembly] that represents landowners, not energy companies." Another resident responded that "we're the expendable ones," when I asked her to compare the situation of Tomslakers with those who live in urban centres like Dawson Creek. She explained to me that she felt that the safety of her and her family were taking a back seat to the interests of those who lived in the larger **city**.

"Legitimate Authority" and Historical Mistrust

All of this activity seems to have exacerbated what was a pre-existing antagonism between local authorities and the community. Indeed, the difficulties in the **interactions** between police and the people of Tomslake have a long history. The settlement of Tomslake was founded in 1939 by ethnic Germans from the Sudetenland of Czechoslovakia who were mostly members of the Social Democratic Party (SDP) there. Vehemently opposed to the ascendance of Hitler in Germany and of the growing Nazi influence in the region, they felt extremely betrayed – and they were ultimately imperilled – by the Munich Agreement of 1938. This agreement between Great Britain, Germany, France, and Italy handed their lands in Czechoslovakia over to Germany, putting them in Nazi control. As reparation for these actions,[1] members of the SDP who fled were granted permission by Canada to set up two communities in western Canada, one of them being Tomslake. However, the Sudeten **settlers** were met with suspicion and fear by the local community and especially by the local authorities. This was a time of paranoia surrounding political and ethnic sympathies. During this period, Japanese-Canadians were viewed with such suspicion by the state, for fear that they would side with Japan against Canada in the war, that the state subjected them to the confiscation and auctioning off of their assets as well as **internment**. To **intern** someone is to confine them or imprison them, usually for political or military purposes. Historian Mary Drysdale has done some excellent work on the reception that the Sudeten settlers received upon arrival in Canada:

> When war broke out in September 1939, the RCMP arrived in Tomslake to inform the disbelieving immigrants that they were now "enemy aliens." The refugees were fingerprinted, told to carry a white "alien" card and their landed

1 Because Great Britain bore responsibility for this policy of appeasement toward Hitler, Canada, as a commonwealth member state, agreed to grant them land as a reparation for the Munich Agreement.

> immigrants' card with them at all times and to report to the authorities once a week. (2002, 96)

An RCMP document from 1940 expressed concern that they were flying red flags, which were feared to indicate communist sympathies. Ironically, locals were also suspicious of the new residents because of their ethnic-German status, something that raised fears that they may have ties to Nazism (Amstatter 1978; Drysdale 2002) – even if it was clear from their history that they came from an anti-Nazi political party. Writing a report at the time, RCMP intelligence officer E.W. Bavin, who was stationed in the Tomslake area, expressed mistrust about the newly settled immigrants: "While they have not actually engaged in anti-British activities, their attitude is not altogether satisfactory and, on occasion, would almost verge on the point of defiance with respect to their 'rights'" (RCMP 1940, 1). The officer contemplated the feasibility of interning the settlers, but instead, ultimately advocated

> that a responsible official who understands the problem [should] talk to them, pointing out that they are living in a democratic country and it is expected of them not to only respect and obey the laws of our country, but also try to live up to the democratic traditions inherent in our system. (1)

Thus, although subject to suspicion, the Sudeten settlers' situation was not comparable to the treatment of Japanese-Canadians; nevertheless, from historical documents and from my interview with two of the last remaining first-generation Tomslakers, it is clear that, while they were grateful to Canada for their opportunity to come here, they also were at times bitterly aware of the irony of the suspicions they faced. This historical distrust in authorities was clearly something that shaped the present mistrust of police, as agents of the state – something that we will explore in the next section.

The Investigation and the Resistance

On October 7, 2008, someone sent three threat letters from a Canada Post outlet in Dawson Creek to *Coffee Talk Express*, a newsletter that circulates in the area, to the *Dawson Creek Daily News*, the region's newspaper, and to EnCana Corporation. The identical anonymous letters claimed to be advocating on behalf of the people of Tomslake and demanded that "EnCana close down [its] operations ... and leave the area" (EnCana Bomber 2008). This letter was followed by six bombing attacks against EnCana sites between October 12, 2008, and July 4, 2009, and two more sets of letters from the bomber, one of which warned EnCana that things may "get worse for you and your terrorist pals in the oil and gas business" if they refused to make plans to pull out of the area (EnCana Bomber 2009). All the attacks were fairly minor in terms of the actual damage caused to gas-line infrastructure, and the bomber claims to have been taking steps to minimize the threat to people, assuring the public that the bombings

FIGURE 18.2 A blast site with visible EnCana signage warning about poisonous gas, Tomslake, British Columbia. Photo credit: John Lehmann/Globe and Mail via The Canadian Press.

were "minor" and "controlled" (EnCana Bomber 2009). EnCana, claiming millions of dollars in losses due to interruptions in its production, hired extra security and offered rewards – first \$500,000, then \$1 million dollars – in an effort to apprehend the bomber. These were the largest monetary rewards in Canadian history (see figure 18.2).

The RCMP also took the matter very seriously. During the investigation and in their public statements, they described the bombings as "**domestic terrorism**." They also devoted considerable resources to the investigation and deploying their Integrated National Security Enforcement Team to the area (Joosse 2009). This team is a special counterterrorism task force that includes staff from the RCMP, Canadian Border Services Agency (CBSA), the Canadian Security Intelligence Service (CSIS), and representatives from municipal police services. At one point, 250 investigators were working on the case. By calling it terrorism and investigating it as such, the police were conveying that it is a matter of extreme concern. It should be noted, though, that there is a lack of consensus in the academic literature about what constitutes "terrorism" (Schmid and Jongman 1988). Despite this, most academic definitions view terrorism as something that is conducted by non-state actors (see, for example, Giddens 2004, 6). Such definitions accord with Max Weber's thinking about the state that monopolized the legitimate use of violence: violence conducted by the state, even if it "terrorizes" citizens, is not considered by most analysts to constitute terrorism. One common notion expressed about the concept of terrorism is that one person's "terrorist" is another person's "freedom fighter." Anti-Apartheid revolutionary Nelson Mandela, for example, was once regarded by US President Ronald Reagan and UK Prime Minister Margaret Thatcher as a terrorist, before he became president of South Africa and was awarded the Nobel Peace Prize. In legal terms, the Criminal Code of Canada, section 83.01 defines terrorism as an act that "in whole or in part for a political, religious, or ideological purpose, objective, or cause" is done with the intention of intimidating the public "with regard to its security, including its economic security, or compelling a person, a government or a domestic or an international organization to do or to refrain from doing any act."

Despite the resources that were deployed by the RCMP, the covert nature of the attacks – and the fact that they seemed to be carried out by a small group of individuals who were difficult to detect (Joosse 2007, 2012, 2020) – seriously impeded the investigation.

During the investigation, the RCMP has consistently maintained in public the theory that those responsible for the bombings were local residents, and they expressed frustration that the local community seemed to be uncooperative with their investigation, even in the face of ongoing bombing attacks. RCMP spokesperson Tim Shields publicly entertained the possibility that the bomber was of Sudeten heritage, pointing to the use of the word "territory" and "home lands" by the bomber in the first threat letter, saying: "we know that the Tomslake area was once referred to, especially after the Second World War, as the Sudeten homeland, and the word 'territory' was also included in that description of Tomslake at that time" (quoted in Vanderklippe and Stueck 2009; also see Joosse 2009).

Over the course of the investigations, the authorities interviewed nearly every community member, sometimes upwards of eight or nine times. They asked for DNA **samples**, handwriting samples, and for people to take polygraph tests (Arsenault 2011; Crawford 2009; Hainsworth 2010; Joosse 2009; Thompson 2009). Writers such as Brian Hutchinson (2009) of the *National Post* wrote that these investigative strategies created a "land of suspicion" that bred distrust among community members and exacerbated the existing misgivings of police. Adding to this distrust were some of the deceitful and heavy-handed tactics that police used in their investigation. Tamara Cunningham, a local journalist, wrote a story for the *Dawson Creek Daily News* recounting how one RCMP officer impersonated a reporter during the investigation (Cunningham 2008). Another practice that was much discussed within the community was when officers reputedly would "'accost people at their places of work and yell at them, denouncing them loudly in public places as the bomber'" (Gratl, quoted in Crawford 2009, 4). In December 2008, the police held a press conference to publicize a specially created tip line and webpage (dawsoncreekbombings.com), encouraging the public to visit and offer information (Joosse 2008b). It was later revealed that the RCMP had been collecting personal information from the local internet provider, whom they contracted to host the site, extracting names and addresses of people who had simply looked at the site (as the RCMP had directed the public to do), and they then used this information to guide them to residents for questioning (Joosse 2009).

In the absence of progress in their efforts, it appears that investigators were also looking for leads in the local and national newspapers. A common experience among residents was that if a resident gave a press interview in which they expressed dissatisfaction with the gas operations in the area, they would find themselves being interviewed by police shortly thereafter (Brooymans 2009; Hainsworth 2010; Trumpener 2012). This led to a further shut-down of public discussion. Reporter Hanneke Brooymans wrote that "[m]any people approached by *The [Edmonton] Journal* declined to say anything at all about development in the area and about the bomber," and one man with whom she spoke would not comment "for fear of becoming a target of RCMP interrogations, harassment and phone tapping" (Brooymans 2009, A1, A3). During the investigations themselves, RCMP spokesperson Tim Shields lamented that residents were "literally running away from the investigators whenever they see them" (quoted in Bergland 2009, A1). To many residents, it seemed unjust that they would come under criminal suspicion simply because they were expressing what they felt to be legitimate political and safety concerns about the activities of natural gas companies.

On the political front, the sum total of all of this activity has been a chilling effect on people publicly expressing opposition to industry. Tim Ewert, a local organic farmer, said in a press interview that police tactics had "virtually silenced" the local movement that had been resisting the operations of the gas companies. In an interview a year and a half after the bombings stopped, Ewert noted that:

> People were having a lot of unwelcome visits by the police, being hauled off to the police station for many hours of interrogation, totally upsetting their lives.... There was a lot of unhappiness about what was going on with the oil and gas industry–the intrusion, the risk ... I know people who were very active in their concerns about the oil and gas industry who have not said a peep for several years. (CBC News 2011, n.p.)

One of the research participants maintained that this suspicion resulted from close teamwork between EnCana and the police, who would often appear in press conferences together. Feeling unduly targeted, this resident maintained:

> The people being targeted in the investigation are those who have had the guts to ask for some answers from EnCana about safety issues. No one else has even been questioned. No one from EnCana or any of their prior employees. Only those on a list given to the RCMP from EnCana that were a visible presence both in Kelly Lake and Tomslake. People who tried to exercise their freedom of speech. People who had educated themselves to the industry and had concerns about what was happening.

The public communicative strategies of the police and EnCana, which most often involved joint press conferences, did little to disabuse residents of the notion that there was an intertwining of state and corporate interests in the investigative thrust pursued by the RCMP. Social theorist Jurgen Habermas (1976) described such intertwining between the state and corporate interests as "**state capitalism**," which "recoupl[es] the economic system to the political" (36). In Habermas's view, "[t]he State apparatus no longer, as in liberal capitalism, merely secures the general conditions of production ... but is now actively engaged in it" (36). While not expressing their perceptions in those terms, it is clear that many residents felt that the political and corporate interests had merged to the extent that they felt their government no longer spoke for them.

Conclusion

As of this writing, the police have yet to charge anyone in connection with the EnCana bombings. This of course results in what is in some sense an unsatisfactory plot line, leaving the "whodunit" mystery unsolved. Nevertheless, there may be ways to "solve" the case in sociological terms – or at least to use sociological concepts to gain some insight into why things unfolded the way they did.

At the beginning of the chapter, I asked you to think about the case through two specific concepts. The first was framing theory from Benford and Snow (2000), with their diagnostic, prognostic, and motivational framing tasks. In light of the above case, we can see that there were fundamentally different diagnoses about what the central problem was. Some residents viewed industry and its activities as the problem, and they faulted the close relationship between the state and industry as the reason that the problem could persist. As a result, they had very different prognoses about what needed to be done. For them, the issue was to decouple the state-corporate power alliance described by Habermas in his concept of state capitalism. Moreover, they had a set of motivational frames that drew on their prior mistrust of state power (from their historical experiences of betrayal by the state as Sudeten refugees), their sense of environmental spoilage and worries about safety, and feelings of injustice about how economic benefits were flowing disproportionately toward urban populations and not toward those who actually had to accommodate surface structures on their land. By contrast, others diagnosed the main problem as being the bombing campaign itself – and the residents who seemed unwilling to aid police in their investigation of the bombings. Along with this separate diagnostic frame came a different prognosis: it was important, they felt, for the police to use ever-more intensive investigative strategies to solve the crimes of the bombings. One can see how these different sets of frames correspond to one more basic distinction relating to one's position about the legitimacy of the state itself.

Here, there is a connection with Weber who, as we read previously, defined the state as the group that can successfully monopolize the legitimate use of violence in a given territory. The deployment of the RCMP and the Integrated National Security Enforcement Team clearly indicates that the bombings were being understood as a challenge to the monopoly of the use of violence and, therewith, to the **sovereignty** of Canada itself.

Legitimacy also seems to have been relevant here. In liberal democracies such as Canada, the legitimacy of state power derives from a social contract between citizens and those who hold authority over them. This is the idea that citizens give over certain authority to agents of the state because those agents of the state promise to defend certain public goods.

In this chapter, I hope you've been able to see that states, rather than being natural, unchanging entities, are actually contested formations of power. Their continued existence is very much dependant on the legitimacy that they manage to acquire from citizens, and, like the seasons, this legitimacy is something that can come and go. The "long and hot summer" that the EnCana bomber referenced therefore does not just refer to friction within a community, or to the explosive power of bombs; it was a reference to a sustained challenge being made to state power itself.

Questions for Critical Thought

1. How did the elements of Weber's definition of the state give shape to the interactions that are evident between EnCana, the police, and community members?
2. Imagine that you are a police officer in charge of investigating the EnCana bombings. Given Weber's notion that legitimacy can be won or lost, how would you approach the task of cultivating or maintaining such legitimacy?
3. What are examples from the case study – either explicit ones that you can directly see, or implicit ones that you sense are in operation – about how a variety of important social issues are being "framed"?
4. Territory is an important element of Weber's definition of the state. How did the concept of territory play out in this case? How is rural territory different from urban territory here? How have historical notions of territory become meaningful in the way that the EnCana bombings have played out?
5. Finally, while the bomber threatened a "long and hot summer," no new bombings have taken place since that last threat letter. It seems, therefore, that rather than a sustained challenge to the state's monopoly on violence, there has been a "return to normal" – a normalcy that involves residents continuing with their ambivalence toward the activities of natural gas extraction companies. Under what conditions do you think that this "long and hot summer" could become a reality?

References

Agency for Toxic Substances and Disease Registry. 2006. *ToxFAQ™ for Hydrogen Sulfide*. CAS no. 7783-06-4. Atlanta: Agency for Toxic Substances and Disease Registry, Division of Toxicology and Human Health Sciences. https://www.atsdr.cdc.gov/toxfaqs/tfacts114.pdf.

Amstatter, Andrew. 1978. *Tomslake: History of the Sudeten Germans in Canada*. Saanichton, BC: Hancock House.

Arsenault, Chris. 2011. *Loud Bangs and Quiet Canadians: Power, Property Relations and Anti-EnCana Sabotage in Northeastern British Columbia, October 2008 – August 2009*. Master's thesis, University of British Columbia.

Benford, Robert D., and David A. Snow. 2000. "Framing Processes and Social Movements: An Overview and Assessment." *Annual Review of Sociology* 26 (1): 611–39. https://doi.org/10.1146/annurev.soc.26.1.611.

Bergland, Andrew. 2009. "RCMP Alienate Allies in Bombing Case." *Dawson Creek Daily News*, July 17, A1.

BC Oil and Gas Commission. 2010. *Failure Investigation Report: Final report on the Nov. 22, 2009 Failure of Piping at Encana Swan Wellsite A5-7-77-14 L W6M*. November. http://www.bcogc.ca/document.aspx?documentID=1026&type=.pdf.

Brooymans, Hanneke. 2009. "Climate of Fear Grips Gas Country." *Edmonton Journal*, September 7, A1, A3.

CBC News. 2009. "BC Oil and Gas Rights Sales Net Record 2.4B." *CBC News*, March 26. https://www.cbc.ca/news/canada/british-columbia/b-c-oil-and-gas-rights-sales-net-record-2-4b-1.776419.

———. 2011. "BC Pipeline Bombings 3 Years Old with No Charges Laid: One Alberta Man Arrested and Released during the Investigation." *CBC News*, October 12. http://www.cbc.ca/news/canada/british-columbia/b-c-pipeline-bombings-3-years-old-with-no-charges-laid-1.985126.

"Citizens' Meeting Minutes." 2010. Public meeting held at Pouce Coupe Senior's Hall, January 14. Pouce Coupe, BC.

Crawford, Tiffany. 2009. "RCMP Accused of Harassment in Bombing Probe." *Chetwynd Echo*, July 17, 4.

Hainsworth, Anne. 2010. "CTV W-Five: The Suspects." CTV W-Five, produced by Anne Hainsworth, aired January 25.

Cunningham, Tamara. 2008. "Police Officer Impersonates Journalist at Latest Pipeline Bomb Site." *Dawson Creek Daily News*, November 5, A1.

Drysdale, Margaret. 2002. *Three times betrayed: The Sudeten Germans of Tomslake, BC*. Master's thesis, University of Victoria.

EnCana Bomber. 2008. "To EnCana and all other oil and gas interests…" Letter to *Dawson Creek Daily News*, October 7.

———. 2009. "EnCana, You Simply Can't Win This Fight because You Are on the Wrong Side of the Argument…" Letter to *Dawson Creek Daily News*, July 15.

———. 2010. "EnCana, Time-Out is Over!!" Letter to *Dawson Creek Daily News*, April 15.

Giddens, Anthony. 2004. "The Future of World Society: The New Terrorism." Lecture at the London School of Economics, November 10. https://digital.library.lse.ac.uk/objects/lse:boh708tuk.

Habermas, Jürgen. 1976. *Legitimation Crisis*. Boston: Beacon Press.

Joosse, Paul. 2007. "Leaderless Resistance and Ideological Inclusion: The Case of the Earth Liberation Front." *Terrorism and Political Violence* 19 (3): 351–68. https://doi.org/10.1080/09546550701424042.

———. 2008a. "Is It Only a 'Crazed' Individual Behind Pipeline Bombings?" *Vancouver Sun*, November 24, A7.

———. 2008b. "RCMP Blows Pipeline Bomb Investigation." *Calgary Herald*, December 15, A9.

———. 2009. "Investigation Eroding Confidence." *Saskatoon Star Phoenix*, August 12, section A6.

———. 2010. "Ludwig's Arrest May Have Had More to Do with Olympics than Evidence." *Edmonton Journal*, January 12, A12.

———. 2012. "Elves, Environmentalism, and 'Eco-Terror': Leaderless Resistance and Media Coverage of the Earth Liberation Front." *Crime, Media, Culture* 8 (1): 75–93. http://dx.doi.org/10.1177/1741659011433366.

———. 2017. "Leaderless Resistance and the Loneliness of Lone Wolves." *Terrorism and Political Violence* 29 (1): 52–78.

———. 2019. "Narratives of Rebellion." *European Journal of Criminology*. https://doi.org.10.1177/1477370819874426.

McDonald, Jake. 2009. "The First Letter Arrived on Oct. 10. The Explosion Went Off TWO Days Later." *Globe and Mail*, September 25. https://www.theglobeandmail.com/news/national/the-first-letter-arrived-on-oct-10-the-explosion-went-off-two-days-later/article4214905/.

Nikiforuk, Andrew. 2001. *Saboteurs: Wiebo Ludwig's War Against Big Oil*. Toronto: Mcfarlane, Walter and Ross.

RCMP. 1940. Memo from E.W. Bavin, Superintendent, Intelligence Officer to the Commissioner of the Immigration Department (ref. no. D 945-1-Q-113).

RCMP. 2009. "Dawson Creek – Recent Blast Not Likely Related to Gas Infrastructure Explosions." Press release, June 22, 2009.

Schmid, Alex, and Albert Jongman. 1988. *Political Terrorism: A New Guide to Actors, Authors, Concepts, Data Bases, Theories and Literature*. Oxford: North Holland.

Simpson, Scott. 2009. "BC Records Massive $370M in Gas Auction Results." *Vancouver Sun*, October 22.

Thompson, Michelle. 2009. "Grandma a Likely Bomber?" *Edmonton Sun*. July 26.

Trumpener, Betsy. 2012. "Pipeline Police Alberta." CBC radio segment for *Daybreak North*. June 13.

Vanderkilppe, Nathan, and Wendy Stueck. 2009. "Bomber's Second Letter Taunts EnCana, RCMP." *Globe and Mail*, July 17. https://www.theglobeandmail.com/news/national/bombers-second-letter-taunts-encana-rcmp/article1200265/.

Weber, Max. 1958. "Politics as a Vocation." In *Max Weber: Essays in Sociology*, edited and translated by H.H. Gerth and C. Wright Mills, 77–128. New York: Oxford University Press.

19 The Summer Blockbuster: Sociology of Media and Media Sociology

BENJAMIN WOO

LEARNING OUTCOMES

After reading this chapter, you should be able to:

- define and identify examples of media
- describe some common approaches to researching media and communication
- define blockbusterization; understand the seasonality of this phenomenon
- evaluate the usefulness of the four different components of the media theory pyramid
- apply the concept of mediatization to various forms of media engagement

Introduction

You've been waiting for this for months – ever since they first announced the remake, reboot, or sequel to that thing you love. You followed along with the casting news and images from the set, culminating in a series of special covers of *Entertainment Weekly* or *Vanity Fair*. The first trailer blew you away, and you've had high expectations ever since the teaser for the trailer was leaked from the Comic-Con panel last July. For the last couple weeks, as the tie-in merchandise has started rolling out, the cast has also been making the rounds on late-night talk shows, sharing funny stories and new, exclusive clips. You saw photos from the red-carpet premiere in London or Shanghai or Sydney, but then you shut down your social media to avoid spoiling the big reveal. Some will wait to see it on Netflix, but you *need* to see it on the big screen with popcorn in hand and a room full of strangers who will laugh and gasp and cheer along with you. So, here you are, waiting in line on opening night to see the summer's biggest blockbuster with a hundred of your newest friends – some of them even came in costume. You hope there's a post-credits scene or two to set up the next one!

Does this experience of going to the movies sound at all familiar to you? It's certainly how many people in Hollywood would like you to interact with their products. It might, equally, be a strange or off-putting account – that's an important difference to which we'll return later – but a great deal of time, talent, and money is spent to convince us that we should care about these cinematic spectacles.

As media scholar Mark Deuze (2011) puts it, we no longer live *with* media but *in* media, and this presents two challenges for social scientists. The first is to analyze media sociologically, and the second is to account for media's presence in the rest of sociology. In this chapter, I look at the summer blockbuster movie as a media object and use it to explore the **sociology of media** and communications. After introducing some concepts from media studies, I review the history, economics, and aesthetics of the blockbuster movie. Why are certain kinds of films treated in this peculiar way, and why are they so closely associated with the summertime? Following some recent research on the reception of Peter Jackson's Hobbit trilogy (Davis et al. 2016; Michelle et al. 2017), I then consider "**blockbusterization**" as the outcome of several media-oriented **social practices** undertaken by media companies and audiences alike.

Media and Mediatization

Defining Media

In everyday speech, we often reduce media to "the media," treating a range of major mass-media companies in different industries as if they were a single, more or less homogenous **institution**. But take a moment to notice all the media present in your immediate environment or spend a day tracking all the different ways you use media, and you will soon find that "the media" contains multitudes.

The word "medium" comes from the Latin for "the middle" or "in between," just as medium is the size in between small and large or a mediator tries to get two parties to a conflict to "meet in the middle." Media are things that stand in between. Some – what we might call media of perception – stand in between us and the world, enabling us to collect sense data about our environment. They include telescopes, microphones, and remote sensors. Others – media of communication – stand in between us and other people. They include words, images, and music, and all the means recording, transmitting, and retrieving them. Every medium of communication is a "recipe," with specific technologies, institutions, and cultural forms as its ingredients (Grossberg et al. 2006, 13). For example, sending a letter to a friend requires language and writing, one or more postal services to deliver it, and the conventions that influence how you compose it; alternately, making a call on your cell phone requires mobile telephony, wireless service providers and the government agencies that regulate them, and an understanding that phones are for interpersonal communication rather than broadcasting concerts and that we answer by saying "hello" rather than "ahoy." Pioneering Canadian media theorist Marshall McLuhan (1964), who coined slogans like "the medium is the message" and "the global village," argued that media extend innate human capabilities. Media of perception extend our senses, while media of communication extend our voices, allowing us to share our thoughts and feelings with people who are distant from us in either space or time – McLuhan even suggested that the wheel is a medium because it extends the human foot. As new media enter **society**, these tools change us: McLuhan argued that their capabilities disrupt taken-for-granted modes of perceiving and processing information and introduce new ones, fundamentally altering our experience of the world.

Defining Mediatization

It is perhaps no surprise, then, that new media – beginning with faster printing presses for newspapers and magazines in the nineteenth century and continuing through the twentieth century with the development of radio, cinema, television, and so on – were seen by social scientists as urgent phenomena to be studied. Distinct from media that enable two-way communication between a small number of people, **mass media** are designed for mass communication, enabling a single sender to reach very large audiences. Mass media tend to be expensive to produce and they incorporate few, if any, mechanisms for feedback or dialogue. These features raised fears that governments and corporations might use them to manipulate the masses of ordinary people, subverting democracy and promoting dangerous behaviours or **values**. The sociologists, psychologists, critics, and philosophers who tried to understand these transformations laid the foundations of communication and media studies as an academic field. Scholars today use the term **mediatization** to describe the processes through which media and society influence one another. A domain of social life like politics, work, or the family becomes mediatized when media and their needs become taken-for-granted parts of ordinary social life (Couldry and Hepp 2017). Civil society groups using glossy advertising campaigns to promote their causes, a teenager carefully composing an Instagram-worthy photo, and political parties selecting leaders based on who comes across best on TV rather than who has the best ideas are all examples of mediatization in action. Like other social institutions, media tend to get reified over time. Reification means that something that is socially constructed has been misrecognized as natural and unchanging. Something that has been reified fades into the background of everyday life. It is media research's job to make us aware of media again so we can understand and, if necessary, change how they work in our society.

The Media Theory Pyramid

Different traditions of media research seek to do this by focusing on different aspects of the media. Media sociologist Nick Couldry (2012) defines four broad approaches that make up what he calls the "**media theory pyramid.**" The four vertices of the pyramid are medium theory, the political economy of communication, textual analysis, and socially oriented media theory. **Medium theory** conceptualizes media as technologies with objective physical qualities: They are heavy or light, durable or fragile, cheap or expensive, simple or complicated, and so on. These qualities can be expressed as a set of affordances (things they make relatively easy or intuitive to do) and constraints (things they make relatively difficult or even impossible to do). The key question for medium theorists like McLuhan is, what difference does the medium make? That is, how does that fact that we are using one medium rather than another alter our experiences and expectations about the world?

The **political economy of communication** tradition emphasizes the economic and political institutions that govern media systems. In line with Marxian analyses of **capitalism**, political economists are typically concerned by the concentration of power in a small number of media companies. They ask who has control over the media and how their interests diverge from the public's. If someone wanted to understand why their cellphone rates are so expensive, why certain political perspectives dominate the news, or why certain sports dominate the sports broadcasts (as discussed by Nicole Neverson on chapter ten), they could examine the **political economy** of those industries.

Textual analysis views media as cultural forms that carry meaning and shape people's beliefs and ideologies. Using textual analysis, we can analyze the form and aesthetics of films, magazine ads and video games, just as literary scholars analyze poems and novels. This approach helps us understand how the media messages we are exposed to are put together so we can be more critical of them. Alison Thomas and Elizabeth Dennis' analysis of Mother's Day and Father's Day cards in chapter fourteen demonstrates this form of analysis.

Finally, **socially oriented media theory** draws attention to how media interact with everyday social life. Here, the key research question is: what people are doing with media? Someone might draw on socially oriented media theory to understand the role media play in other social processes and domains. Sonia Bookman uses a version of this approach in her discussion of how people use Instagram and Twitter to express their affection for the pumpkin spice latte in chapter three.

Crucially, these four approaches suggest *complementary* ways to study media, not competing schools of thought. They are stronger together; whenever we turn one point of the media theory pyramid upwards, bringing one set of ideas, concerns and questions into focus, it necessarily rests on a foundation of the other three (Couldry 2012). Consequently, you may notice that I employ arguments grounded in all four perspectives in the rest of this chapter to analyze the summer blockbuster as a medium.

Blockbusters

When it was released in 1975, Stephen Spielberg's *Jaws* became the first film to make more than $100 million. It is typically credited as the first summer blockbuster

(Buckland 2006). We routinely use this category to describe some of Hollywood's productions, but what does it actually mean? Like all Hollywood movies, blockbusters rely on technologies for recording and playing back images and sound to create a life-like impression of movement; they are made by a system of production companies and studios, using mostly unionized labour in highly structured roles, and distributed to theatre chains, television channels, and streaming services; and they are produced with an understanding that certain kinds of audiences want and expect certain kinds of things from the movies they see. But blockbuster movies add some extra ingredients to the mix: they make heavy use of digital visual effects; they are tied into merchandising and cross-promotion deals with toy manufacturers, fast-food restaurants, and other companies; and there are specific genres that are more likely to be treated as blockbusters than others. The summer blockbuster is a specific kind of media phenomenon we can explore using the conceptual tools of media research.

Blockbusters: The Look, the Hook, and the Book

Most media markets are winner-take-all economies, where a small number of individuals reap most of the benefits. In the publishing, record, and television industries, for instance, the handful of highly visible, bestselling books, hit records, or top-rated TV shows – the so-called "short head" – are vastly outnumbered by their less-successful competitors, who make up the "long tail" of the distribution (Anderson 2004). Media companies have to make enough profit on a few hits to make up for their many losses. But not just any hit is a blockbuster. For example, a film like *Justice League* (Zack Snyder 2017), which was widely considered a flop due to underperforming expectations and weak reviews despite turning a modest profit, can still be recognized as a blockbuster. The blockbuster operates as a quasi-genre and, like other film genres (e.g., comedies, Westerns, thrillers), signals to viewers what kind of moviegoing experience they can expect (Neale 1990). Blockbusters are *movies that are designed to be hits*. But, whereas blockbusters were once exceptional products in larger, more diverse slates of film releases, after *Jaws*, they "increasingly became Hollywood's standard or *dominant* practice of filmmaking" (Buckland 2006, 11). According to Warren Buckland (2006), blockbusters are defined by high production and marketing costs, on the one hand, and high revenues, on the other hand (17). This creates a vicious circle: Big budgets necessitate big returns, but the strategies employed to make and market blockbusters are themselves very costly. Bigger and bigger hits – with more famous stars, more dazzling special effects, and more intense advertising campaigns – are needed to make up the costs of all the misses in the studio's slate. In order to attract the large audiences and cross-promotional partners that they need to recover their costs, film studios typically design would-be blockbusters around a single, easily encapsulated and appealing premise, or what is known as a "high concept":

> The high concept film is designed to maximize marketability and, consequently, the economic potential at the box office. This marketability is based upon such factors as stars, the match between a star and a project, a pre-sold premise (such as a remake or adaptation of a best-selling novel), and a concept which taps into a national trend or sentiment. (Wyatt 1994, 15)

Basically, filmmakers and studio executives build movies around high concepts in an attempt to create reliable products that can be easily promoted in posters, trailers, and short TV commercials. Blending a textual analysis of blockbuster aesthetics with a political economist's understanding of how these films respond to studios' economic needs, film and media scholar Justin Wyatt (1994) argues that high concepts, comprising what he calls "the look," "the hook," and "the book," are a tool for product differentiation in the entertainment **marketplace**. By the look, Wyatt means an aesthetic influenced by advertising and music videos. The hook is a memorable marketing message that appeals to multiple audience segments. Here, "high concept" echoes the related idea of the "four-quadrant" movie that has something to interest men and women under the age of 25 and above it. Finally, the book represents a reduced or simplified **narrative** that is supported by conventional plots and characters or pre-existing, familiar intellectual property and sustained through spinoffs and tie-ins. By emphasizing a cool aesthetic style, easily communicated marketing messages that interest multiple demographic groups, and a narrative that is made easily digestible through some combination of genre conventions and familiar characters and premises, studios try to give consumers reasons to choose their film over their competitors' offerings. However, Wyatt's definition of high-concept filmmaking also includes films like *Grease* (Randal Kleiser 1978) and *The Rookie* (Clint Eastwood 1990), which most people probably wouldn't describe as blockbusters no matter how successful they were.

Fantastic Action

Other film scholars and critics have pointed to several characteristics that typify blockbuster movies as a distinct media object. In order to see if their arguments can be supported, I undertook a **secondary data analysis** of available industry figures. That means I am taking publicly available information produced by (in this case) the film industry and analyzing it for my own purposes. While industry statistics and indicators can sometimes be difficult to locate, incomplete or vague in their definitions of what exactly they measure, they are often our only record of how media are made and who they reach. I took a list of the top-grossing films of each decade from Tim Dirks's *filmsite.org* as of December 2017 (Dirks n.d.). This website has been relied upon as a reference by film critics and cinephiles for over 20 years. Since 2008, it has been owned by the same parent company as the cable channel AMC ("American Movie Classics"). Dirks compiled a list of "all-time box office hits" by decade; for our purposes, collecting the top movies *by decade* is preferable to looking at the top movie of each year because some years have multiple high-performing blockbusters. Starting my analysis with the June 1975 release of *Jaws* gives us a total of 105 films, with the most recent being 2017's *Wonder Woman*. I then looked up release dates and domestic box office revenues from the website *Box Office Mojo*, a widely used source for box office data. Canada and the United States constitute a single market for film distribution, so all figures are given in US dollars. Since the value of money changes over time due to inflation (e.g., one dollar would buy a lot more bread in 1970 than it does today), I adjusted the box office revenues for inflation using the US Bureau of Labor Statistics Consumer Price Index inflation calculator. This gives us a better basis for comparing the films' commercial success across decades. For example, adjusting for inflation moves the original *Star Wars* from forty-sixth place in the rankings with domestic box office revenues of just over 300 million 1977 dollars to first place with slightly more than 1.2 billion 2017 dollars; however, it doesn't account for changes that are specific to the film market, such as 3D, IMAX, and other premium-priced formats – imagine how much more *Star Wars* might have made if people could have paid extra to see it in UltraAVX. Finally, in order to look for patterns in film performance, I also coded the films based on their genre and whether they were remakes, sequels, or spinoffs (see table 19.1). My analysis of these data will help us understand what kind of films end up as blockbusters.

Perhaps most importantly, blockbusters favour action and visual spectacle over character development and dialogue. First, by fully exploiting the scale of a theatre's projection technologies, they give viewers a motivation to go see the film in cinemas rather than waiting for it to be released on home video, streaming services, or on broadcast television. Second, they circulate more easily in the increasingly important global film marketplace. Today's big-budget productions need moviegoers all around the world in order to turn a profit, and films heavy in explosions and battle scenes are less reliant on cultural context to understand and require less work from translators than comedies or tense interpersonal dramas. Genres featuring what we might call "fantastic action" – that is, a mix of spectacular action sequences with science-fiction, fantasy, or other supernatural tropes – generally meet both requirements. In figure 19-1a, we can see that the proportion of the top-grossing films based in fantastic action genres increases sharply after 2000. Moreover, the 47 fantastic-action films make an average of $499 million in domestic box office revenues, adjusted for inflation, versus $427 million for the other 58 films in our list.

Sci-fi, fantasy, and comic-book superhero movies not only occasion stunning visuals that take full advantage of advances in digital special effects and 3D projection but also bring familiar (or "pre-sold") characters and settings to the table. Indeed, of the top-grossing movies of each decade since *Jaws*, 74 were adaptations, remakes, reboots, sequels, prequels, or spinoffs of some existing source material. What's more, there has been a steady increase in the number of adaptations and sequels over time, as can be seen in figure 19-1b. While they only made up half the top-grossing films of the 1980s, virtually all of the most successful movies of the 2000s and 2010s are based on a pre-existing franchise or intellectual property. Looking at the 100 highest-grossing

Table 19.1 Example of secondary data analysis: Release date, box office, and author's coding for first 20 films in dataset

Title	Year	Release date	Unadjusted box office	Adjusted box office	Genre	Adaptation/ Sequel	Both genre and adaptation/sequel
Star Wars: Episode IV	1977	May 25	$307,263,857.00	$1,222,910,150.86	1	0	0
Jaws	1975	June 20	$260,000,000.00	$1,159,600,000.00	0	1	0
Star Wars: Episode VI	2015	Dec. 18	$936,662,225.00	$974,128,714.00	1	1	1
Titanic	1997	Dec. 19	$600,788,188.00	$919,205,927.64	0	0	0
E.T.	1982	June 11	$359,197,037.00	$905,176,533.24	0	0	0
Avatar	2009	Dec. 18	$749,766,139.00	$854,733,398.46	1	0	0
Jurassic World	2015	June 12	$652,270,625.00	$678,361,450.00	1	1	1
Marvel's The Avengers	2012	May 4	$623,357,910.00	$666,992,963.70	1	1	1
Star Wars: Episode I	1999	May 19	$431,088,295.00	$633,699,793.65	1	1	1
The Dark Knight	2008	July 18	$533,345,358.00	$618,680,615.28	1	1	1
Star Wars: Episode VI	1983	May 25	$252,583,617.00	$616,304,025.48	1	1	1
Star Wars: Episode V	1980	May 21	$209,398,025.00	$605,160,292.25	1	1	1
Jurassic Park	1993	June 11	$357,067,947.00	$603,444,830.43	1	1	1
Grease	1978	June 16	$159,978,870.00	$585,522,664.20	0	1	0
Shrek 2	2004	May 19	$441,226,247.00	$569,181,858.63	0	1	0
Raiders of the Lost Ark	1981	June 12	$212,222,025.00	$558,143,925.75	1	0	0
Beverly Hills Cop	1984	Dec. 5	$234,760,478.00	$549,339,518.52	0	0	0
Spider-Man	2002	May 3	$403,706,375.00	$549,040,670.00	1	1	1
Forrest Gump	1994	July 6	$329,694,499.00	$543,995,923.35	0	1	0
Rogue One	2016	Dec. 10	$532,177,324.00	$542,820,870.48	1	1	1

Data courtesy of filmsite.org and BoxOfficeMojo.com

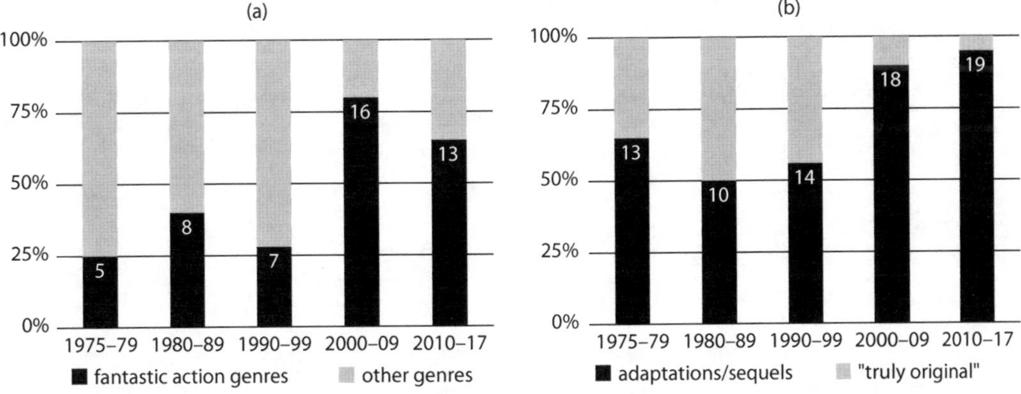

FIGURE 19.1 Proportion of top-grossing films by decade since June 1975 that (a) feature "fantastic action" and (b) are adaptations, prequels, sequels, reboots, or remakes, versus "truly original." Data courtesy of filmsite.org and BoxOfficeMojo.com.

films released each year between 2005 and 2014, Stephen Follows (2015) found that the 39 "truly original" films (i.e., *neither* an adaptation of some specific source material *nor* related to pre-existing intellectual property) tended to have lower budgets and to make less money than ones derived from existing properties. While there have always been successful films based on other media – think of *Gone with the Wind* (Victor Fleming 1939), *The Ten Commandments* (Cecil B. DeMille 1956), and most of Alfred Hitchcock's filmography – Follows's analysis confirms that Hollywood has become more reliant on pre-existing intellectual property over time. Literature (20 per cent), other films and television series (18 per cent), and comic books (6 per cent) are the raw material of today's entertainment economy, grist for the blockbuster mill (Follows 2015). Adaptations and reboots benefit from consumers' existing **brand** awareness; marketers don't have to explain what a James Bond or Star Trek movie is all about. Many of them also already have dedicated and organized fan bases that can be counted upon to build up anticipation and "buzz" on behalf of the production. (Although managing the expectations of disappointed or disgruntled fans can also present problems.) Finally, sci-fi and fantasy novels, superhero comic books, and TV series all involve (to greater or lesser degrees) expectations that stories will continue over a number of episodes. Each successful film in a blockbuster franchise or mega-franchise feeds into and drives audiences to the others. For example, the Marvel Cinematic Universe (MCU) capitalized on the success of *Iron Man* (Jon Favreau 2008) to launch a sequence of films building toward *The Avengers* (Joss Whedon 2012), which both sustained existing mini-franchises and later launched less-known characters like Doctor Strange and Black Panther into films of their own. As of January 2018, the 17 films in the MCU had made an average of $310 million each, and the franchise as a whole has earned over $5 billion in box office revenues alone. Similarly, the rights to adapt the Hunger Games or Harry Potter novels were valuable not only for their name recognition and enthusiastic fans but also for the

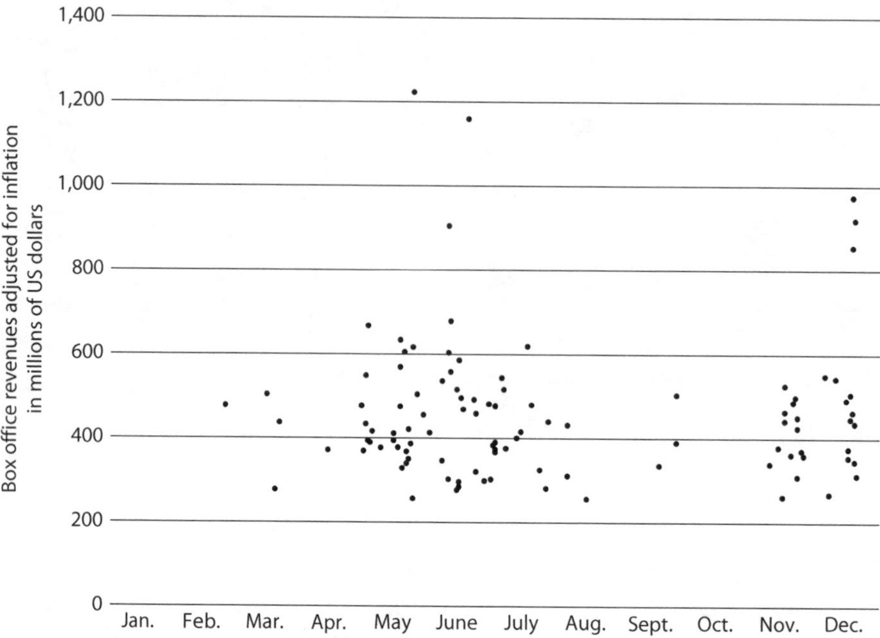

FIGURE 19.2 Top-grossing films by decade since June 1975, by day and month of release and adjusted box office revenue (in millions of US dollars). Data courtesy of filmsite.org and BoxOfficeMojo.com.

promise of four or eight hit movies, respectively. Together, these formal and aesthetic features of the blockbuster film represent an attempt to manage uncertainty and risk in the entertainment marketplace.

The Summer Blockbuster

Beyond tending to have certain features in common, blockbusters also tend to be released at specific times of the year. As discussed earlier by Heidi Bickis in chapter five, historian E.P. Thompson (1967) famously argued that the mechanical clock – a medium of perception – introduced an entirely different conception of time, replacing the cyclical rhythms of agrarian life with an unending, linear succession of identical, abstract units of time. Media similarly introduce distinct temporalities into our lives. For example, the broadcast schedule that placed television shows in specific time slots once defined many people's weeks, whereas subscription streaming services like Netflix now release entire seasons of a show at one time, not only enabling us to watch at our own leisure but also enabling the timeless time of binge-watching. As another example of media's role in anchoring distinctive temporal rhythms, the summer was not always a time for moviegoing: "While people usually spent their summer breaks at the beach or the pool, *Jaws* changed all of that by inviting people out of the hot sun and into the cool movie theaters" (Mokry 2017). There are several good, practical reasons why more movies make more money during the summer: warm weather makes air-conditioned theatres appealing and waiting outdoors in long lines possible; there are multiple holiday weekends; and young people, who typically have more discretionary spending power and are the largest consumers of film tickets (MPAA 2017, 14, 16), are out of school. But the prevalence of blockbusters in the summer is also to some extent a self-fulfilling prophecy on the part of studio executives, distributors, and theatres, who decide when movies will be released. Only five films in our list were released before May, with none coming out in January, and 15 were released in December for the Christmas holidays, but nearly two-thirds of the list – by far the largest cluster of films – came out between May and August. Indeed, seven of the top-ten films, including the two highest-grossing films on the list, were released during this season. (See figure 19.2.) Looking at weekly box-office revenues across all films between 2000 and 2010, Edmund Helmer (2011) also found a spike in the winter months, during which dramas, comedies, and adventure films do best, and a broader peak during the summer months that favours action, comedy, and adventure films. Thus, we can see that summertime has become synonymous not only with moviegoing in general but also with seeing particular kinds of movies. Serious award contenders are often released in the fall and family fare thrives in the winter, but, as industry analyst Paul Dergarabedian says, "Summer is the season of cinematic fast food" (Lemire 2015, para 8).

Blockbusterization as Ritual and Practice

Dergarabedian's fast food metaphor is perhaps the key to the popular conception of the blockbuster, and not just because of the frequent cross-promotions between these two industries. Like fast-food meals, summer blockbusters are highly refined, mass-produced, and mass-marketed commodities. They are highly pleasing – and, thus, very popular – because they focus on a relatively restrained palette of simple but strong sensations (flavours of sweetness and saltiness for the fast-food meals; visual spectacle and feelings of excitement for the films) but are not seen as particularly nourishing or challenging. We may find them enjoyable but deep down we know they're not good for us. This is obviously not a very flattering picture of blockbusters or their audiences, but there is a long history of critics discussing pop culture in these terms. For example, social philosophers Max Horkheimer and Theodor W. Adorno (2002 [1947]) coined the term **culture industry** in the 1940s to critique the production of culture within the mass media of capitalist societies. For Horkheimer and Adorno, **culture** was supposed to elevate us as individuals and collectively, providing experiences that would enable us to be critical of society. The image of a factory that churns out cultural products like General Motors churns out cars and McDonald's churns out chicken nuggets was intended as a shocking contradiction in terms. They wanted to draw attention to what they saw as the pernicious effects of the commercial mass media system in the United States. But, much as people have pointed out that relatively unhealthy food can be an expression of care (Fielding-Singh 2018) or a rational choice (Drewnowski and Specter 2004; Kirkup et al. 2004) for people living in areas where fresh food is limited and expensive, other scholars have tried to balance Horkheimer and Adorno's cynicism about the production of culture. As the **cultural studies** scholar Stuart Hall (1981) famously put it, "That judgement may make us feel right, decent and self-satisfied about our denunciations of the agents of mass manipulation and deception ... but I don't know that it is a view which can survive for long as an adequate account of cultural relationships.... Ordinary people are not cultural dopes" (232). Echoing the socially oriented approach to media research, Hall is saying that while it is easy to dismiss other people's actions as irrational or ill-informed from the outside, we nonetheless need to understand the *reasons* they eat at McDonald's and go to Michael Bay movies.

The Moviegoing Ritual

In order to see what blockbusters mean for the people who engage with them, we need to take up what James Carey (2009 [1989]) called the **ritual view of communication.** When we talk about communication, we typically rely on metaphors that represent meaning or information as a substance that needs to be moved from one place to another, like water moves through the pipes in a building. But although conveying information is indeed an important feature of human communication, it is hardly the only thing we do when we communicate. In everyday life, for example, asking your significant other about their day is not only a request for information but also a way of expressing care for them and maintaining your shared relationship. Similarly, you might go to the movies to spend time with friends, on a date, to pass the time, or simply to escape the summer heat for a few hours, regardless of what's playing. According to Carey (2009 [1989]), communication is not only a carrier of information but is also, and more importantly, a "symbolic process whereby reality is produced, maintained, repaired, and transformed" (19). For instance, when we read the news, we do not simply receive a summary of all the events of the previous 24 hours. Rather, journalists have to prioritize and filter what events they cover, and they necessarily make choices about how to represent them. "News reading, and writing," Carey (2009 [1989]) argues, "is a ritual act, and moreover a dramatic one. What is arrayed before the reader is not pure information but a portrayal of the contending forces in the world" (17). Even the organization of a newspaper (or its website) gives a picture of the world: More of us have jobs than own businesses, so why is there a business section and not a labour one? Why are there sections for style or travel but not the environment? From Carey's ritual view, the news communicates what journalists, editors, and the companies that employ them think is important, and they make those values appear to be natural by representing them day in and day out. The blockbuster can also be analyzed as a communication ritual. In addition to *what* a blockbuster is, we ought to ask *why* a blockbuster is – how, that is to say, do these films enter into people's lives? What values do they dramatize? What effects do they have in terms of how and with whom we spend our time?

The Blockbuster Spectacle

Because of their (literally) larger-than-life status, it might be useful to begin by thinking of blockbusters as what Daniel Dayan and Elihu Katz (1992) call **media events**. These "high holidays of mass communication" (1) are preplanned ceremonies or spectacles that are broadcast live, interrupting the normal flow of television programming and garnering large audiences. Echoing Carey's ritual view, Dayan and Katz (1992) argue that media events like royal weddings, state funerals, trials and hearings, and major sporting events are "symbolic acts that have relevance for one or more of the core values of society," such as patriotism or fairness (12). Depending on their genre, plot, and themes, various movies have different things to say about various social values, but the promotional spectacles leading up to their release, their red-carpet premieres, and the awards shows that celebrate them have a common denominator. As Couldry (2005) suggests, these ritualized events always have relevance for the entertainment industry itself, constructing, formalizing, and marking its meaning in relation to cultural categories like celebrity, glamour, excitement, and **nostalgia**. From this perspective, the media event is the message: the *idea* of the media's importance is ultimately more significant than the content of any individual film we might see.

Blockbusterization in Everyday Life

In their book on audience attitudes towards Peter Jackson's Hobbit film franchise, Carolyn Michelle and her colleagues (2017) develop the concept of blockbusterization to suggest that making a blockbuster is an ongoing process; it doesn't stop when the director says "that's a wrap" but continues through post-production and marketing and involves journalists, critics, and ordinary audience members who all work together to "blockbusterize" the film. Much of the marketing of Hollywood blockbusters is designed to appeal to and mobilize fan communities before they even get to buy a ticket through activities like reading about production news and rumours, watching trailers and other public relations materials, and talking about the films with friends and family (Michelle et al. 2017). For dedicated fans, casting announcements, speculations about the plot, and the release of exclusive preview clips and teasers are occasions to build anticipation for the movie. Fans not only provide studios with a reliable base that can be counted on to show up and buy tickets but also generate positive word-of-mouth that may translate into higher box-office revenues (Meehan 2000). After release, fans continue to produce value by telling friends, purchasing licensed merchandise, attending conventions, and following the stars to future projects. In contemporary mega-franchise filmmaking, studios can draw this process out in cycles that repeat over several years. Recent marketing campaigns for Lucasfilm's retail partners, for instance, have heavily emphasized the Star Wars saga's cross-generational appeal (Meslow 2015).

Digital and social media have given studios and audiences new tools for constructing blockbusters. For example, Twitter recently announced that *Black Panther* (Ryan Coogler 2018) was the most-tweeted-about film of all time (Chuba 2018). In part, this merely acknowledges the role that active social media users played in laying the groundwork for the film's financial success and cultural impact, but the announcement also attempted to construct Twitter as a natural site for accessing what's going on "out there" in society. In doing so, Twitter the company – and the entertainment reporters regurgitating its press release as news – positioned users exclusively as audiences/consumers – neglecting their creativity as authors of tweets and memes and, moreover, flattening out the range of critical conversations the film occasioned about (among other matters) **race**, **identity**, and anti-oppression tactics into a single metric that redirects all that energy into reaffirming the importance of this brand in particular and of corporate entertainment media in general. All of these strategies encourage consumers to adopt habits and social practices that, at the level of everyday life, continually reproduce the social value of media.

Conclusion

This chapter has introduced media as a sociological object, as well as a set of approaches to media drawn from the interdisciplinary fields of media, communication, and cultural studies. If, as Deuze (2011) asserts, we now live *in* media, then we not only need a "sociology of media" that analyzes the media with existing sociological theories and methods but also a "media sociology" that grapples with the mediatization of virtually every facet of social life. In my discussion of blockbusters and blockbusterization, I have tried to show how these two projects overlap and connect. As a media object, the blockbuster film is certainly susceptible to sociological analysis: using medium theory, we could analyze the cinematic apparatus (Baudry 1974); we could examine the political economy of the film industry and trace the imperatives that guide its production and marketing (Wasko 2005); or we could decode films' cultural forms to examine how style and genre are used to signal expectations to the audience (Neale 1990). Together, these perspectives take us some distance in understanding why producers and audiences like blockbuster movies – and why they seem to like them in the summertime.

But blockbuster movies also make up part of the "second nature" of social reality (Lukács 1971), insisting on their own importance and relevance to our lives. I recently bought a bunch of bananas at my local grocery store and was surprised to find when I got them home that one bore a sticker with a picture of an AT-AT, a combat vehicle deployed by the evil First Order in *Star Wars: Episode VIII – The Last Jedi*, and the slogan "STAR WARS: FAITES ÉQUIPE AVEC DOLE" ("Star Wars: Team up with Dole"). The sticker turned that humble banana into a medium carrying an explicit marketing message on behalf of Disney and Dole. By using something as ordinary as my breakfast to generate brand value, it also relayed an implicit message about the importance, ubiquity, and power of media. An example of mediatization and blockbusterization, it showed how Star Wars – a media franchise that comprises television series, video games, comic books, and literal tonnes of licensed merchandise, but which is anchored by some of the most successful movies of all time – works its way into everyday life.

Questions for Critical Thought

1. Individual media are defined by a distinctive recipe of technologies, institutions, and cultural forms. Begin by looking again at the examples discussed in this chapter, then think about some of the media you use or encounter in an average day and list their ingredients in a table like the one below.

Medium	Technologies	Institutions	Cultural forms
Letters (p. 328)	Language, writing system	Postal service	Etiquette
Telephone (p. 328–29)	Transmitters, exchanges, receivers	Telephone companies, telecommunications regulators	Interpersonal uses, etiquette
Movies (p. 331)	Motion picture recording and projection	Film studios, theatre chains, entertainment magazines	Film genres

2. To which of the four approaches to media research discussed in this chapter do you feel most drawn? What are its strengths and weaknesses in comparison to the other approaches making up the "media theory pyramid"?
3. Think about a film you saw recently. What marketing messages or other factors influenced your decision to see that film?
4. Look up the trailer for a recently released blockbuster. How does it signal to prospective audiences what they can expect through the information it presents or through its aesthetics (e.g., narration, music, pace of editing, logo design)? Do you associate any of these signals with specific audience demographics?
5. Reflect on some times when you have been an audience or consumer of media and some when you were an author or creator. For each example, think about who derives benefits from and who pays costs for your engagement with media of communication. On balance, are these exchanges fair?

References

Anderson, Chris. 2004. "The Long Tail." *Wired*, October 1. https://www.wired.com/2004/10/tail/.

Baudry, Jean-Louis. 1974. "Ideological Effects of the Basic Cinematographic Apparatus." *Film Quarterly* 28 (2): 39–47. https://iedimagen.files.wordpress.com/2011/11/baudry-jean-louis_ideological-effects-of-the-basic-cinematographic-apparatus.pdf.

Box Office Mojo (website). Accessed January 25, 2018. https://boxofficemojo.com.

Buckland, Warren. 2006. *Directed by Steven Spielberg: Poetics of the Contemporary Hollywood Blockbuster*. New York: Continuum.

Carey, James W. 2009 [1989]. *Communication as Culture: Essays on Media and Society*. Rev. ed. New York: Routledge.

Chuba, Kirsten. 2018. "'Black Panther' Becomes Most Tweeted-About Movie Ever." *Variety*, March 20. http://variety.com/2018/film/news/black-panther-most-tweeted-movie-ever-1202731499/.

Couldry, Nick. 2005. "Media Rituals: Beyond Functionalism." In *Media Anthropology*, edited by Eric W. Rothenbuhler and Mihai Coman, 59–69. Thousand Oaks: SAGE.

———. 2012. *Media, Society, World: Social Theory and Digital Media Practice*. Cambridge: Polity.

Couldry, Nick, and Andreas Hepp. 2017. *The Mediated Construction of Reality*. Cambridge: Polity.

Davis, Charles H., Carolyn Michelle, Ann Hardy, and Craig Hight. 2016. "Making Global Audiences for a Hollywood 'Blockbuster' Feature Film: Marketability, Playability and *The Hobbit: An Unexpected Journey* (2012)." *Journal of Fandom Studies* 4 (1): 105–25. https://doi.org/10.1386/jfs.4.1.105_1.

Dayan, Daniel, and Elihu Katz. 1992. *Media Events: The Live Broadcasting of History*. Cambridge: Harvard University Press.

Deuze, Mark. 2011. "Media Life." *Media, Culture & Society* 33 (1): 137–48. https://doi.org/10.1177/0163443710386518.

Dirks, Tim. n.d. "All-time Box Office Hits (Domestic Gross) by Decade and Year." *Filmsite*. Accessed January 25, 2018. https://www.filmsite.org/boxoffice2.html.

Drewnowski, Adam, and S.E. Specter. 2004. "Poverty and Obesity: The Role of Energy Density and Energy Costs." *American Journal of Clinical Nutrition* 79 (1): 6–16. https://doi.org/10.1093/ajcn/79.1.6.

Fielding-Singh, Priya. 2018. "Why Do Poor Americans Eat So Unhealthfully? Because Junk Food Is the Only Indulgence They Can Afford." *Los Angeles Times*, February 7. http://www.latimes.com/opinion/op-ed/la-oe-singh-food-deserts-nutritional-disparities-20180207-story.html.

Follows, Stephen. 2015. "How Original are Hollywood Movies?" *Stephen Follows: Film Data and Education*, June 8. https://stephenfollows.com/how-original-are-hollywood-movies/.

Grossberg, Lawrence, Ellen Wartella, D. Charles Whitney, and J. Macgregor Wise. 2006. *Mediamaking: Mass Media in a Popular Culture*. 2nd ed. Thousand Oaks: SAGE.

Hall, Stuart. 1981. "Notes on Deconstructing the Popular." In *People's History and Socialist Theory*, edited by Raphael Samuel, 227–40. London: Routledge & Kegan Paul.

Helmer, Edmund. 2011. "Films for all seasons." *BoxOfficeQuant: Statistics and Film*, April 3. http://boxofficequant.com/films-for-all-seasons/.

Horkheimer, Max, and Theodor W. Adorno. 2002 [1947]. *Dialectic of Enlightenment: Philosophical Fragments*, edited by Gunzelin Schmid Noerr. Stanford: Stanford University Press.

Kirkup, Malcolm, Ronan De Kervenoael, Alan Hallsworth, Ian Clarke, Peter Jackson, and Rosana Perez del Aguila. 2004. "Inequalities in Retail Choice: Exploring Consumer Experiences in Suburban Neighbourhoods." *International Journal of Retail & Distribution Management* 32 (11): 511–22. https://doi.org/10.1108/09590550410564746.

Lemire, Christy. 2015. "40 Years of Summer Blockbusters." *Parade*, May 22. https://parade.com/398498/christylemire/40-years-of-summer-blockbusters/.

Lukács, Georg. 1971. *History and Class Consciousness: Studies in Marxist Dialectics*. Cambridge: MIT Press.

McLuhan, Marshall. 1964. *Understanding Media: The Extensions of Man*. New York: McGraw-Hill.

Meehan, Eileen R. 2000. "Leisure or Labor? Fan Ethnography and Political Economy." In *Consuming Audiences? Production and Reception in Media Research*, edited by I. Hagen and J. Wasko, 71–92. Cresskill: Hampton Press.

Meslow, Scott. 2015. "The Brilliance of *Star Wars*' Marketing Campaign: It's All About You." *The Week*, December 8. https://theweek.com/articles/592226/brilliance-star-wars-marketing-campaign-all-about.

Michelle, Carolyn, Charles H. Davis, Ann L. Hardy, and Craig Hight. 2017. *Fans, Blockbusterisation, and the Transformation of Cinematic Desire: Global Receptions of The Hobbit Film Trilogy*. London: Palgrave Macmillan.

Mokry, Natalie. 2017. "How the Summer Blockbuster Was Born." *Film School Rejects*, June 20. https://filmschoolrejects.com/summer-blockbuster-origins/.

Motion Picture Association of America (MPAA). 2017. *2016 Theatrical Market Statistics Report*. https://www.mpaa.org/wp-content/uploads/2017/03/MPAA-Theatrical-Market-Statistics-2016_Final-1.pdf.

Neale, Steve. 1990. "Question of Genre." *Screen* 31 (1): 45–66. https://doi.org/10.1093/screen/31.1.45.

Thompson, E.P. 1967. "Time, Work-Discipline, and Industrial Capitalism." *Past and Present* 38 (1): 56–97. https://doi.org/10.1093/past/38.1.56.

Wasko, Janet. 2005. "Critiquing Hollywood: The Political Economy of Motion Pictures." In *A Concise Handbook of Movie Industry Economics*, edited by Charles C. Moul, 5–31. New York: Cambridge University Press.

Wyatt, Justin. 1994. *High Concept: Movies and Marketing in Hollywood.* 1st ed. Austin: University of Texas Press.

20 Summer's Gains and Losses: Children, Social Class, and Learning

PATRIZIA ALBANESE

LEARNING OUTCOMES

After reading this chapter, you should be able to:

- define and describe primary and secondary socialization, and agents of socialization
- understand the anxieties surrounding children's summers from a parent's perspective
- explain how the summer break from school impacts working-class and middle-class children differently
- evaluate the merits of adopting a "new sociology of childhood" approach toward understanding children's summers
- evaluate the differences between the concerted cultivation model and natural growth models of parenting

Introduction

I fondly remember being a child on the last day of school before the start of summer holidays. It was a rush – everything was abuzz; we were filled with joy and a sense of looming freedom. Those last-day-of-school feelings were not far off from the reality to come; at least for me, a working-class, immigrant kid. I vividly recall the hot summer days spent riding my bike with my brothers and neighbourhood children through the working-class streets of the old borough of York, in Toronto. We often landed, towels in hand, at the public swimming pool near the local municipal buildings. Or we raced, frantic, through busy streets to what felt like the huge and wildly overgrown urban jungle – Keelesdale

Park – that existed before they built Black Creek Drive through it. We walked for what seemed ages, through back alleys, to reach the local library. And then there was the street-wide hide-and-seek game after dinner. It was summer, and these mundane things seemed like great adventures for us far-from-affluent kids of midtown Toronto.

Summer meant that my working-class immigrant parents worked. Dad laboured in construction some years or at a local factory, and mom sewed – piece-work – for a high-end Yorkville boutique whose "Made in Italy" labels actually meant "Made by an Italian in a Toronto basement." Having mom working at home meant that summer days were our own, and we could do what we pleased until meal time, or until my mom reminded us that we should do a bit of school work, so we don't forget what we learned during the school year. But after a tiny bit of school work, it was back to our adventures on the busy streets of Toronto.

Summer's joy – there are few feelings comparable to it, even into adulthood. But not all summer holidays are alike. Children of diverse backgrounds experience summer and summer holidays differently. In fact, a *New York Times* article noted that "we can indulge our annual illusion of children filling joyous hours with sprinkler romps and robotics camp or we can admit the reality: Summer's supposed freedom is expensive" (Dell'Antonia 2016). Summer holidays are often experienced by parents as a financial and logistical strain and a source of great stress; they are likewise a cause of disorientation, displacement, and disappointment for some children today.

Alas, things seem to have changed compared to when I was a child – at least as I remember it. The logistical strain pointed out in Dell'Antonia's (2016) article reminds us that not all families have a parent who works from home through the summer. On top of this, the streets are believed to be unsafe, and there is growing pressure on parents to ensure that their children are busy and scheduled most days of most weeks. Attending summer camp – day camps or sleepover camps – is incredibly common for most urban middle-class children today. While this is a seemingly convenient form of child care over parts of the summer months, it is not without its stresses for parents.

This chapter will outline some of the challenges that arise from the "freedom" of summer in the **city**. It provides an overview of academic and non-academic literature (the latter being **grey literature**) on parental stressors, childhood obesity, and **summer learning loss**, especially among working-class children. It ends with a challenge to readers to consider alternative approaches and children's views on the matter. It also challenges us to consider what the woes of summer holidays might look like if we built **social structures**, policies, and communities that were more child-friendly.

Today's Summer in the City

For most parents (read: mothers, in many cases), and especially for those living in large urban centres like Toronto, the planning for summer holidays and summer camps typically starts before children begin daydreaming about March Break. In the first week of March, in the city of Toronto, thousands of parents scramble to sign up their children for city-run summer programs – camps, swimming, soccer, and so on. Local newspapers document the annual event like it is a high-stakes lottery, while the media circulate stories of parental woes and sneaky strategies aimed at getting the upper hand and beating the odds. Parents wake up before the crack of dawn. Some dial multiple phones; some sit patiently at their computers – trigger fingers at the ready; others watch the sun rise on a blustery March morning as they stand in line waiting for the local community centre to open so they can begin the registration **ritual**. One of the many recent news accounts reported one mother's approach as follows:

> As soon as it hits 7 a.m., I hit dial, dial, redial, and refresh the browser to get in the website ... I've been pretty successful, but probably at least one out of every two years there's a problem, and that's with all these things going at the same time. (Nursall 2014, n.p.)

Some might label this **intensive mothering**, which includes the idea that mothering should unequivocally centre around the child's needs, or **helicopter parenting** – the hovering and over-focusing on children's needs. The reality is that for many mothers/parents, this is a necessary part of stitching together summer child care for school-aged children who seemingly have nowhere else to go. Child care costs across the country are typically as high as university tuition; safe, high-quality, and reliable care options are not abundant, especially for school-age children, and national and provincial child care policies, with the exception of Quebec, remain unresponsive to the needs of working parents (Langford, Prentice, and Albanese 2017). It is no wonder, then, that parental stress levels are high, national fertility rates are low, maternal employment opportunities are limited, the wage gap persists, and not all children start school on an equal footing.

Today, most mothers are in the paid labour force – most want to be employed, and most also need paid work to make ends meet. In fact, the increase in the labour-force participation rate of women in Canada over the last two decades has surpassed that of women in the United States. A recent Statistics Canada study revealed that in 1997, women's labour-force participation rates in Canada and the United States were almost identical, at about 76 per cent for women ages 25 to 54 (Drolet, Larochelle-Côté, and Uppal 2016). By 2015, that rate had increased to 81 per cent in Canada, while declining to 74 per cent in the United States. The same study found that while Canadian women with lower levels of education recorded significant gains in their labour-force participation rate (Drolet, Larochelle-Côté, and Uppal 2016), many of these women are employed in lower-paid, precarious and part-time service-sector jobs (Cranford, Vosko, and Zukewich 2003). Caring for children stands out as one of the main reasons that women, at times unwillingly, take on part-time employment (Statistics Canada 2016). This, among other factors, contributes to the persistence of the wage gap, why women's pensions are often lower than men's, and why divorce and single parenthood are often more economically devastating for women with children, compared to their ex-partners.

During the school year, most children are safe and attended to most days of the work week. On the other hand, summers prove to be particularly challenging when it comes

Table 20.1 Biggest challenges for Greater Toronto Area (GTA) parents when making summer camp arrangements for their children

Biggest challenges for GTA parents	Percentage of parents
Affordability	49
Fits into parents'/families' schedule	26
Knowing what programs are available	26
Safety	24
Easy to get to/accessible	23
Spaces still available	22
Beneficial for the child	21
Child will be active	17

Source: Survey of 500 GTA parents of 562 children ages 6 to 12, conducted for the Heart and Stroke Foundation of Ontario in May 2010 by Ipsos-Reid Group; Heart and Stroke Foundation, 2010, http://www.newswire.ca/news-releases/schools-outand-so-is-physical-activity-warns-the-heart-and-strokefoundation-544228122.html

to balancing paid work, providing care, and making ends meet for many Canadian families with children. Not surprising, the promise of low-fee or no-fee city-run programs results in high demand for them. The high demand, in turn, puts many of the programs out of reach for a large number of parents. As noted previously, the annual ritual for registering for Toronto's city-run summer programming involves a mad rush for limited spaces, and once those become unavailable, parents' other options typically involve exorbitantly high costs.

A popular website, ourkids.net, reports that the cost of an overnight camp starts at $300 a week and usually runs as high as $1,000 a week; day camps, the cheaper alternative, cost between $35 and $500 per week (Our Kids Media 2016). Clearly, money matters, and it is a source of parental stress. A **survey** by the Heart and Stroke Foundation reported affordability to be the biggest challenge identified by parents in the Greater Toronto Area (GTA) when it came to making summer camp arrangements, and next on the list were challenges around scheduling (see table 20.1). Also on the list were parents' concerns about whether their child would be active (enough). While the survey is silent about other cities in Canada, one can assume that parents living in other large, expensive cities are struggling with the same challenges, while those living in smaller communities likely lament the limited number of options available to them.

Summer's Gains and Losses

Parents' concerns about their children's inactivity over the summer are not unfounded. In fact, Zinkel and colleagues (2013) found that the most common seasonal pattern in six longitudinal studies was that overweight children experienced accelerated weight gain during the summer, which may lead to the development of poor healthy habits and lifestyles as well as longer-term health problems down the road. Baranowski et al. (2014) noted that contrary to popular belief, four physical activity intervention studies demonstrated that school-year fitness improvements were lost during the summer months, with one of these studies showing that physical activity levels actually declined throughout the summer. Wang et al.'s (2015) research results were consistent with prior findings that children gain more weight during the summer, and that healthy habits formed during the school year appear to be "undone" once school ends for the year – and this is especially true for less affluent children, who have limited options when it comes to summer recreational opportunities.

While research reveals that students at all grade and income levels do not meet the recommended amount for exercise or vegetable intake, and they exceeded the recommended amount for screen time and sugar consumption, there were variations in the results pertaining to **social class** (Wang et al. 2015). Research shows that obesity-related risk factors seemed more prevalent among lower-income youth (Wang et al. 2015).

Social class proved to be an important variable when it came to another school-year gain that becomes undone over the summer. Reading has been identified as one skill, in particular, that is vulnerable to **summer setback** or summer learning loss. Research shows that children of more affluent parents, who typically have higher levels of education, build skills over the summer months, while children of less affluent parents lose skills (or "unlearn") when it comes to literacy (Davies and Aurini 2013; Dexter and Stacks 2014; Downey, von Hippel, and Broh 2004; Jalongo 2005; National Summer Learning Association 2016; Pagan and Sénéchal 2014). Jalongo (2005) notes that in the reading research, this is also known as the "summer slump," "summer slide," or the "summer reading gap" – the tendency for children's reading skills to decline during their summer vacation, away from school.

American research has shown that summer learning loss is one of the most significant causes of the achievement gap between lower- and higher-income youth and a strong contributor to high school dropout rates (National Summer Learning Association 2016). The National Summer Learning Association (2016) reports that this summer loss contributes to gaps in public school achievement, but it also affects future college and career success. While gaps in student achievement remain relatively constant during the school year, the gap widens over the course of the summer, such that even by Grade 5, children of lower-income families can find themselves significantly behind children from families with higher **socio-economic status** (SES) (National Summer Learning Association 2016). Socio-economic status (SES) is a measure of a person's social standing, often measured by one's, and/or one's family's income, occupational prestige, educational attainment, and wealth. In other words, it measures the combination of people's access to money, education, occupational prestige, which often reflects variations in wealth, power, authority, and prestige. SES is closely related to the concept of social class, mentioned previously – a common and important concept in sociology that is often linked to social theorists like Karl Marx and Max Weber.

Davies and Aurini (2013) studied literacy growth using a **non-random sample** of 1,376 Ontario children in Grades 1 to 3 during the summers of 2010 and 2011, and they confirmed American findings that there are strong disparities by family socio-economic status. Like others, Davies and Aurini (2013) found that affluent children gained literacy while children from poorer families lost literacy. Jalongo (2005) noted that, as a result, teachers frequently find themselves reviewing or even reteaching reading skills for the first month or two after school recommences in the fall. It is no wonder then that Pagan and Sénéchal's (2014) correlational research shows that the number of books a child reads over the summer months is positively related to the child's achievement in the fall.

Social Class, Socialization, and Cultural Capital

As discussed in this book's introduction and by Ondine Park in chapter sixteen, **socialization** is the lifelong process of inheriting and disseminating **norms,** customs, **values** and ideologies from one generation to the next. Past scholarly work in this area has divided the process into **primary socialization**, which takes place in childhood, and **secondary socialization**, which takes place later in life; however, where one part of the process starts or ends in relation to the other is not always clear. This traditional division also assumes a linearity and homogeneity that rarely reflects the complexities and differences (including those of social class) that so often characterize social life. Scholarship on socialization has typically focused on the role of key **agents of socialization** – families, peers, schools, and the media – some of which we discuss in various parts of this chapter. Each of these are also differently affected by social class.

Lareau (2011) for example, has argued that parenting styles vary by social class. Her work builds on the work of others, like Melvin Kohn (1977), who found that working-class parents (parents who worked in factories, for example), due to the nature of their repetitive and highly regulated work experiences, tended to stress conformity, neatness, obedience, and orderliness in their children. In contrast, middle-class parents, who seemingly had more control and decision-making power over their work, placed more emphasis on their children's independence, self-reliance, and autonomy. Middle-class parents were also seen as more permissive in almost all matters related to their parenting, while working-class parents were more likely to stress stricter discipline. More recent research has found similar differences across social classes (Holloway and Pimlott-Wilson 2014; Lareau 2011), including the **cultural capital** or symbolic capital – the social know-how of generally approved or valued practices, **social status**, and prestige – with which parents equip their children (Bourdieu and Passeron 1977; see also Neverson, chapter ten). In other words, middle-class parents are not only bestowing economic capital and resources upon their children (through their ability to pay for summer camps, tutors, school trips, and other extracurricular activities), but cultural capital as well. This cultural capital or middle-class know-how allows their children to successfully navigate modern, **Western** capitalist economies and our social **institutions** (Bourdieu and Passeron 1977; Gillies 2005; Holloway and Pimlott-Wilson 2014; Lareau 2011).

Middle-class parents possess, wield, and then transmit to their children the cultural know-how to get ahead in modern societies. If in doubt, consider for a moment middle-class parents' dealings with the school system. Weininger and Lareau (2003), for example, found that while not all middle-class parents are equally assertive, they tend to wield educational authority **discourse** (for example, speaking down to teachers from a/n (self) elevated professional position) more effectively, and more overtly challenge the authority of teachers than do working-class parents. Middle-class parents are able to manipulate the educational system to a greater extent, and they are thus able to better advocate on behalf of their children to gain more individualized attention for them (Albanese 2016). In the end, middle-class parents not only possess the economic resources (for tutors, technology, summer camps, special programs, recreation, etc.) to gain advantages for their children, but have the social status, authority, and knowledge of the dominant discourse (an accepted way of looking at/speaking about a subject that is created by people in power) or cultural capital, as well (Albanese 2016).

Annette Lareau (2011) found that middle-class children spent more time engaging in activities organized by adults that stressed public performance and skills development. She argues that middle-class parents use a **concerted cultivation model** of parenting, where they deliberately develop (cultivate) children's talents in order to optimize their position in school, sports, relationships, and, ultimately, their careers. Lareau (2011) found that family life was organized around each child's school and extracurricular activities, and that many extracurricular activities were chosen for their educational value. Parents also encouraged their child's verbal fluency via conversation with adults (also see Albanese 2016).

In contrast, working-class children spent more time on informal play, visiting kin, and "hanging out" as their parents adopted what Lareau (2011) called a **natural growth model**. This natural growth model is less focused on identifying activities aimed at optimizing children's talents. Instead, it means that while parents provide care and safeguards for their children, they place less emphasis on identifying and making available external organized activities to their children (Lareau 2011). Lareau found the working-class model was characterized by a greater separation of children's and adults' spheres, and there was more free-flowing time for kids to create their own activities at their own pace (in contrast to the concerted efforts of middle-class parents to deliberately organize their children's time and activities to maximize skill development). Working-class parents stressed stricter discipline, more physical punishment, and expected more obedience and respect. Children developed verbal fluency from their peers and had closer contact with kin of all generations (Lareau 2011).

Gillies (2005), however, warns us not to assume the **universality** of the imagined success of middle-class parenting and the perceived inadequacies of working-class parents. Along the same lines, Holloway and Pimlott-Wilson (2014) analyzed parenting classes and suggest that these classes are part of a "professionalization" of parenting, which assumes that there is a proper way to parent that can be taught in accredited/accreditable ways, similar to the social process by which trades or occupations transform themselves into professions of high integrity and competence. They also argued that parenting classes tended to promote neoliberal parenting, which has sought to impose modern, capitalist, middle-class values on working-class parents.

In identifying some of the variations in the experiences of parents and children from different social class backgrounds, it becomes obvious that there is no simple, uniform, or linear way to think about children, childhood, child development, or socialization. If social experiences vary along class lines, consider the complexity and variability when we add **gender**, sexuality, **race**, **Indigeneity**, immigration status, ability, and age to the mix. Beyond this, consider how the views of children on such matters and sets of experiences might vary compared to the views of adults. A body of scholars has challenged traditional approaches to the study of children and childhood (see Chen, Raby, and Albanese 2017; Corsaro 2015; James, Jenks, and Prout 1998), and they have come to embody or champion a theoretical and methodological approach that has come to be known as the **new sociology of childhood**.

The New Sociology of Childhood—Considering Children's Views

If we return to the opening of this chapter, we can easily see the natural growth model of parenting exemplified in the brief accounts of some of my summer days, but you may also have noticed the pangs of **nostalgia** and possibly hints of idealized and glorified memories of my childhood. I included what I remember now and what I opted to share with you, many decades later. The reality is that I was a chubby and insecure child, and my parents worked incredibly hard and sacrificed a great deal to make ends meet. Some of the more difficult memories of childhood, most of us choose not to share and often seek to forget.

Much of what we know about the lives of children and childhood reflects adult views and selective adult memories about their childhood. Most research on children and childhood, until relatively recently, has asked adults to reflect back on their childhood or has asked *persons most knowledgeable* (PMKs), typically parents and teachers, to speak on behalf of children (Albanese 2016). Given some of the limitations of these approaches, as exemplified in my aforementioned nostalgic and somewhat distorted memories, this is changing.

The "new sociology of childhood" has emerged to challenge the traditional ways in which we have studied, treated, and often overlooked children as social agents (Albanese 2016; Chen, Raby, and Albanese 2017). As noted, this approach challenges the traditional, homogenous, linear, and at times biological models that assume that things are "done to" rather than "with" children. Much like feminist sociology before it, which advanced in tandem with the women's rights movement, this "new" theoretical understanding of children was created simultaneously with the growth and expansion of the discourse of children's rights. Proponents of global children's rights movements that have spread simultaneously with and in conjunction to the introduction and mass ratification of the United Nations Convention on the Rights of the Child (1989) and of the new sociology of childhood support the view that children are more competent and autonomous than they appear or are given permission or room to be. The new sociology of childhood seeks to overturn adult paternalism that refuses to recognize children's capabilities and rights, not unlike feminist sociologies did for women some decades before (Albanese 2016; Chen, Raby, and Albanese 2017; Corsaro 2015; James et al. 1998). As noted previously, this approach recognizes children as social agents or social actors in their own worlds.

Recognizing children as social actor means recognizing that children do not simply passively adapt to and learn from the **culture** surrounding them, as assumed in traditional developmental and socialization theories, but they actively participate in the cultural routines offered to them in and by their social environments (Albanese 2016; Bühler-Niederberger 2010a, 2010b; Corsaro 2015). Children's own accounts show us that they are active social agents who carry out important social activities that make and remake their relationships and daily lives. As such, children are seen and treated as active reproducers of meaning (they are recognized as reflexive and thoughtful) (King 2007; Mayall 2000, 2002, 2013) and are understood to be able to appropriate, take up, question, challenge, and reinterpret their situations and environments, and so themselves contribute to cultural reproduction and change (Corsaro 2015). Let us consider an example of how this plays out in our discussion of summer and summer learning loss.

Hillier and Aurini (2018) conducted research on summer learning loss through children's own accounts of their summer reading practices. Through **interviews** with elementary-school-aged children, the authors show that children use their own **child capital** – children's own social and cultural capital – to promote reading initiatives and motivate others to help them with their literacy. Hillier and Aurini (2018) document that while parents and siblings play a supportive role, the children in their study were active participants in their literacy learning. They found that children can and do play a large role in supporting literacy learning during summer vacation in ways that compensate for other kinds of disparities at home. That said, Hillier and Aurini (2018) note that while the potential for child capital to shore up some forms of educational disparities is promising, it is not a remedy for summer learning loss. They call for policy and program shifts and interventions, particularly for children from lower-SES backgrounds.

Dare to Dream: Child-Friendly Policies, Programs, and Communities

What might good policies and programs look like for children over the summer? What types of interventions might we consider implementing? At the moment there are numerous summer reading programs run through local and national organizations, schools, community centres, and local libraries. Some have also argued for the end of summer holidays as we know them, opting instead for 12 months of schooling. While some of these programs and options have their merits, it can easily be argued that children do not have to sit in a classroom all year-round, nor do they have to have their faces in books all summer to prevent summer learning loss.

To start, we must recognize that most forms of play involve learning, and not all learning happens in classrooms. Kate MacDonald's (2017) ethnographic work with young children's experiences in an outdoor classroom is an example of the importance of doing research with children for the purpose of social change and of the value of enhancing children's capacity through inquiry-based learning and play, outside of traditional classrooms settings. Free to explore in a safe outdoor environment, children are treated as experts on their own lives and as capable social agents (MacDonald 2017). Might we, as a **society**, be able to replicate such models and approaches on a larger scale, using safe public spaces and funds? Can we build literacy and numeracy into everyday activities and play? Surely it would not take much to reimagine programs and spaces with children in mind. We may even do well to ask children themselves what those might look like.

Ideas like this are not new. UNICEF – the United Nations Children's Fund that works in more than 190 countries and territories to help support children's well-being – for example, for years has maintained a website (http://childfriendlycities.org/) to promote its initiative for the creation of child-friendly cities and communities (CFC; see UNICEF 2014). The CFC website provides information on how to actually build a child-friendly community and includes data on good practices and interventions, relevant publications, and updates on current research and initiatives around the world. Considering such ideas seems a small effort and price to pay for building a more just and equitable society for children from all walks of life.

Conclusion

This chapter opened with a brief nostalgic recollection of my summers in the city as a working-class, immigrant child. While seemingly idyllic, my almost-40-year-old memories likely did not capture the complex reality of what I or my working-class parents were actually feeling and experiencing. The reality for many parents is that summers are a time of great stress and financial strain. Many working-class children eat more, do less, and lose reading skills over the course of the summer compared to during the school year.

The bulk of the chapter provided a discussion of the impact of family income and social class on the experiences of children over the widely anticipated (by children) and often dreaded (by parents) summer holidays. The chapter reviewed Bourdieu's notion of cultural capital, as well as the work of Annette Lareau, who compared parenting among middle- and working-class parents.

We focused particular attention on re-evaluating the research we do with and for children. Following a brief overview of the "new sociology of childhood," you were challenged to begin to rethink Canadian policies and communities from a child's perspective. Since I began on an idyllic note, allow me to end on one as well: I have no doubt that if we begin to envision and implement policies that move us toward a more child-focused and child-friendly society, we may find ourselves living in a society that is a little more just and fulfilling for all.

Questions for Critical Thought

1. To consider how the taken-for-granted aspects of social life are connected to sociological thinking and research, consider how your autobiography might have read if you began writing it when you were 10 years old. What aspects of your childhood might be included that you would not remember or include if you wrote about your childhood when you are 60 years old? Is capturing the views of children important? Why? What is missed if we don't include their voices and views? How does including the voices of children help us rethink our understanding of the world and our sociological theorizing about it?
2. In rethinking what the "freedom" of summer means for some children, should primary and secondary schools operate all year-round, over the full 12 months of the year, eliminating summer holidays? Why? Why not?
3. Reflecting back on your childhood and the childhood of others you know, do you see traces of social class differences in parenting as reflected in the work of Lareau?
4. Apply what you just learned about the new sociology of childhood: You have been hired to build literacy and numeracy skills into everyday activities and play. What kinds of activities might you develop? Who would you engage or consult to help you to develop those activities and skills?
5. You have been appointed the child and youth advocate for your province. What would you do to ensure that spaces, programs, policies, and practices are more child-focused and child-friendly?

References

Albanese, Patrizia. 2016. *Children in Canada Today.* 2nd ed. Don Mills, ON: Oxford University Press.

Baranowski, Tom, Teresia O'Connor, Craig Johnston, Sheryl Hughes, Jennette Moreno, Tzu-An Chen, Lisa Meltzer, and Janice Baranowski. 2014. "School Year versus Summer Differences in Child Weight Gain: A Narrative Review." *Childhood Obesity* 10 (1): 18–24. https://doi.org/10.1089/chi.2013.0116.

Bourdieu, Pierre, and Jean Claude Passeron. 1977. *Reproduction in Education, Culture and Society.* Beverly Hills: Sage.

Bühler-Niederberger, Doris. 2010a. “Introduction: Childhood Sociology – Defining the State of the Art and Ensuring Reflection.” *Current Sociology* 58 (2): 155–64. https://doi.org/10.1177/0011392109354239.

———. 2010b. “Childhood Sociology in Ten Countries: Current Outcomes and Future Directions.” *Current Sociology* 58 (2): 369–84. https://doi.org/10.1177/0011392109354250.

Chen, Xiaobei, Rebecca Raby, and Patrizia Albanese, 70–88, eds. 2017. *Sociology of Childhood and Youth in Canada.* Toronto: Canadian Scholars/Women's Press.

Corsaro, William. 2015. *The Sociology of Childhood.* 4th ed. Los Angeles: Sage.

Cranford, Cynthia, Leah F. Vosko, and Nancy Zukewich. 2003. “Precarious Jobs: A New Typology of Employment.” *Perspectives on Labour and Income* 15 (4).

Davies, Scott, and Janice Aurini. 2013. “Summer Learning Inequality in Ontario.” *Canadian Public Policy* 39 (2): 287–307. https://doi.org/10.3138/CPP.39.2.287.

Dell'Antonia, K.J. 2016. “The Families That Can't Afford Summer.” *New York Times*, June 4. https://www.nytimes.com/2016/06/05/sunday-review/the-families-that-cant-afford-summer.html.

Dexter, Casey A., and Ann M. Stacks. 2014. “A Preliminary Investigation of the Relationship between Parenting, Parent-Child Shared Reading Practices, and Child Development in Low-Income Families.” *Journal of Research in Childhood Education* 28 (3): 394–410. https://doi.org/10.1080/02568543.2014.913278.

Downey, Douglas B., Paul T. von Hippel, and Beckett A. Broh. 2004. “Are Schools the Great Equalizer? Cognitive Inequality during the Summer Months and the School Year.” *American Sociological Review* 69 (5): 613–35. https://doi.org/10.1177/000312240406900501.

Drolet, Marie, Sébastien Larochelle-Côté, Sharanjit Uppal, Canadian Electronic Library (Firm), and Statistics Canada. 2016. “The Canada – US Gap in Women's Labour Market Participation.” *Insights on Canadian Society.* Catalogue no. 75-006-X. Ottawa: Statistics Canada. http://www.statcan.gc.ca/pub/75-006-x/2016001/article/14651-eng.pdf.

Gillies, Val. 2005. “‘Raising the ‘Meritocracy’: Parenting and the Individualization of Social Class.” *Sociology* 39 (5): 835–53. https://doi.org/10.1177/0038038505058368.

Hillier, Cathlene, and Janice Aurini. 2018. “The Summer Reading Blues: Children's Accounts of Summer Literacy Practices.” In *Reading Sociology*. 3rd ed., edited by Patrizia Albanese, Lorne Tepperman, and Emily Alexander. Toronto: Oxford University Press.

Holloway, Sarah, and Helena Pimlott-Wilson. 2014. “‘Any Advice Is Welcome Isn't It?’: Neoliberal Parenting Education, Local Mothering Cultures, and Social Class.” *Environment and Planning* 46 (1): 94–111. https://doi.org/10.1068/a45457.

Jalongo, Mary Renck. 2005. “Editorial: On Behalf of Children: Tutoring Young Children's Reading or, How I Spent My Summer Vacation.” *Early Childhood Education Journal* 33 (3): 121–23. https://doi.org/10.1007/s10643-005-0036-0.

James, Allison, Chris Jenks, and Alan Prout. 1998. *Theorizing Childhood.* Oxford: Polity Press.

King, Michael. 2007. “The Sociology of Childhood as Scientific Communication: Observations from a Social Systems Perspective.” *Childhood* 14 (2): 193–213. https://doi.org/10.1177/0907568207078327.

Kohn, Melvin. 1977. *Class and Conformity: A Study of Values.* Chicago: University of Chicago Press.

Langford, Rachel, Susan Prentice, and Patrizia Albanese, eds. 2017. *Caring for Children: Social Movements and Public Policy in Canada.* Vancouver: UBC Press.

Lareau, Anette. 2011. *Unequal Childhoods: Class, Race, and Family Life*. Berkeley: University of California Press.

MacDonald, Kate. 2017. "'We Can Play Whatever We Want': Exploring Children's Voices in Education and in Research." In *Sociology of Childhood and Youth in Canada*, edited by Xiaobei Chen, Rebecca Raby, and Patrizia Albanese, 70–88. Toronto: Canadian Scholars Press.

Mayall, Berry. 2000. "The Sociology of Childhood in Relation to Children's Rights." *The International Journal of Children's Rights* 8 (3): 243–59. https://doi.org/10.1163/15718180020494640.

———. 2002. *Towards a Sociology for Children: Thinking from Children's Lives*. Buckingham, UK: Open University Press.

———. 2013. *A History of the Sociology of Childhood*. London: Institute of Education Press.

National Summer Learning Association. 2016. "The Need: Why Summers Matter." Baltimore: NSLA.

Nursall, Kim. 2014. "Overwhelming Demand for City Rec Programs Challenge Parents." *Toronto Star*, March 5. https://www.thestar.com/news/gta/2014/03/05/overwhelming_demand_for_city_rec_programs_challenge_parents.html.

Our Kids Media. 2016. "The Cost of Summer Camp: A Look at Camp Costs, Financial Aid, Tax Breaks, and Camp Scholarships." *Our Kids Media*. http://www.ourkids.net/tips-paying-for-summer-camp.php.

Pagan, Stephanie, and Monique Sénéchal. 2014. "Involving Parents in a Summer Book Reading Program to Promote Reading Comprehension, Fluency, and Vocabulary in Grade 3 and Grade 5 Children." *Canadian Journal of Education* 37 (2): 1–31.

Statistics Canada. 2016. *CANSIM Table 282-0013-Labour force survey estimates (LFS), part-time employment by reason, monthly, unadjusted for seasonality (x 1,000)*. Ottawa: Statistics Canada.

UNICEF. 2014. *Child-Friendly Cities*. New York: United Nations. http://childfriendlycities.org/.

Wang, Y. Claire, Seanna Vine, Amber Hsiao, Andrew Rundle, and Jeff Goldsmith. 2015. "Weight-Related Behaviors When Children Are in School versus on Summer Breaks: Does Income Matter?" *Journal of School Health* 85 (7): 458–66. https://doi.org/10.1111/josh.12274.

Weininger, Elliot, and Annette Lareau. 2003. "Translating Bourdieu into the American Context: The Question of Social Class and Family-School Relations." *Poetics* 31 (5–6): 375–402. https://doi.org/10.1016/S0304-422X(03)00034-2.

Zinkel, S.R.J., M. Moe, III, E.A. Stern, V.S. Hubbard, S.Z. Yanovski, J.A. Yanovski, and D.A. Schoeller. 2013. "Comparison of Total Energy Expenditure between School and Summer Months." *Pediatric Obesity* 8 (5): 404–10. https://doi.org/10.1111/j.2047-6310.2012.00120.x.

Glossary

administrative data: data collected for administrative purposes (e.g., education records, medical files, tax records) that can be used in conducting research.

advanced capitalism: a form of capitalism that many identify as beginning in the 1970s and characterizing most industrial nations in the contemporary global economy. It is marked by a shift from manufacturing as the dominant component of the economy to an emphasis on services, **consumption**, and the symbolic (informational, cultural, knowledge) economy.

aesthetic values: how something's appearance, beauty, or ugliness affects one's emotions.

agency: the capacity to act in a given context or to shape aspects of one's world (while inevitably constrained by **social structures**); one's awareness or perception of, and ability to control, one's own actions.

agents of socialization: those people and **institutions** that teach individuals how to fit into their culture. In contemporary Canadian society, these include, most importantly, the family, especially parents (or parent-like figures), peers, education, and media.

age-specific death rates: death rates that are calculated for each age group (rather than for the total **population**, as is the case in the death rate) in a given geographic area and year; the number of deaths in a specific age group (e.g., 65–69 years) per 1,000 people of the same age group.

agrarian time: an understanding of time that corresponds with the physical and environmental needs of agricultural production.

alternative spring break (ASB): a term used within the **volunteer tourism** industry to refer to student volunteer experiences that take place during students' spring break in communities they perceive as vulnerable; it is premised on **values** of community-driven service, **global citizenship**, and **reflective practice**.

anthropomorphize: to attribute human qualities or characteristics to a non-human entity.

anti-positivist: a theoretical perspective that is critical of using **scientific methods** to understand human action and **society**.

appearance work: a type of **body work** that involves the maintenance of bodily appearance to particular cultural standards (e.g., showering, putting on makeup, shaving, cutting nails, wearing certain types of clothes).

archival analysis/archival research: a research method used in history, sociology, and other disciplines that involves accessing and extracting text and other materials from official (e.g., national, provincial, municipal) and unofficial (e.g., family collection) archives.

arts of noticing: a concept advanced by Anna Tsing that refers to the political act of tuning into the world with the explicit goal of making visible the unseen onto-epistemological forces that shape it – including **white supremacy**, **heteropatriarchy**, and **capitalism.**

assimilation: a process through which minority groups adapt to new social contexts by adopting the **values** and practices of the majority group. Assimilation is often juxtaposed with **multiculturalism**, which stresses the value of cultivating plurality.

biological determinism: also called biologism or essentialism, it is the idea that human behaviour, relationships, thoughts, and so on are solely determined by an individual's or group's biological makeup. This contrasts with **social determinism.**

biomedical gaze: mechanisms of surveillance and control over individuals' bodies used by medical experts, generally perceived to be objective and scientific.

blockbusterization: the process by which a film is produced, marketed, and received as a blockbuster. Blockbusters are characterized by high production and marketing costs, with the aim of garnering high revenues.

body-making through work: a type of **body work** that describes how bodies are altered physically and physiologically by the work they do.

body work: a term that encompasses the various ways work is **embodied.** Typically used in the context of paid work, it includes **appearance work, inter-corporeal body work, emotional labour**, and **body-making through work.**

brands: complex market cultural forms used by companies within the context of advanced capitalism. These forms may include images, feeling, and slogans. Brands contribute to the contexts of consumption, company's identities, and consumers' identities.

brand communities: a term developed by Albert Muñiz Jr. and Thomas O'Guinn to describe the specialized community that forms around a brand, involving a particular set of social relations characteristic of a community, yet centred on shared **consumption** experiences, interests, and practices related to a brand.

brand extension: extending a product range or developing a new line of goods and services under a brand.

brand management: the coordination of all branding activity, with the express aim of cultivating brand identity, image and value.

breadwinner-homemaker family: a model of family structure that developed following the **Industrial Revolution** and was dominant throughout the first half of the twentieth century, in which men work outside of the home for pay and women work unpaid within the home.

bullying: refers to behaviours such as harassment, assault, or exclusion that are perpetrated for the purposes of degrading or humiliating an individual.

capitalism: an economic system that involves the production, buying, and selling of goods and services for profit by private companies.

capitalist: as described in Marxist theory, one who owns the **means of production**, such as factories and the raw materials used to manufacture goods.

census: an official count, generally undertaken every five or ten years, of all the people in a **population** used by modern governments to (a) collect information about the populations they govern and (b) shape decisions about **state** policies.

child capital: coined by Cathlene Hillier and Janice Aurini, refers to children's own way of giving value and meaning to their actions. See **cultural capital**.

child mortality rate: the number of deaths of children under five years of age per 1,000 live births in a population.

cisgender: when one's gender identity corresponds with their sex identified at birth, aligning with dominant **gender binaries**.

city: defined by urban sociologist Louis Wirth as a human settlement marked by relatively large geographical area, dense, and heterogenous population. This offers an alternative to a **census** definition of a city that is based primarily on inhabitant numbers and **population** density.

class: see **social class.**

class distinction: a process by which members of a particular **social class** differentiate themselves from members of other social classes to reinforce their own class position.

classical theory: refers to the body of writing that was produced in the late nineteenth and early twentieth century, and which became recognized as influential in establishing and advancing formal sociology. Thinkers associated with this tradition include Émile Durkheim, Karl Marx, and Max Weber, as well as Georg Simmel, W.E.B. Du Bois, Charlotte Perkins Gilman, Harriet Martineau, and G.H. Mead.

classism: class-based **social stratification**; making and acting on assumptions and judgments about people based on a reading of their **social class** position.

climate change: noticeable changes in climate patterns at regional or global levels. These changes are driven by human action, including the use of fossil fuels and the industrial exploitation of natural resources.

clock time: a form of socio-temporal organization based on the strict measurement of discrete units of time (minutes, hours) as represented in various means of measuring time geometrically (e.g., clocks and timetables).

codes of conduct: official guidelines to govern the behaviour, appearance, and **interactions** of individuals (e.g., used by school administrators to regulate student behaviour).

coding: a method used in analyzing data that involves assigning codes to text or other data in a systematic way.

collective bargaining: a process through which workers, organized collectively, discuss and negotiate their relations, particularly terms and conditions of work, with the employer.

collective effervescence: a term coined by Émile Durkheim that describes an energy that emerges when a group of people simultaneously participate in or witness an event. This energy can stabilize a group's identity and confirm individuals' belonging within that group.

colonialism: the policy or practice of conquest and direct control of a **territory** or nation, its peoples, and/or resources by a foreign entity.

commercial appropriation: the borrowing or taking of a cultural image, idea, or practice by a company, as well as the subsequent reworking of that image into something that can be sold or that can support the sale of goods in the **marketplace.**

commodity: any item bought and sold in the **marketplace.**

common-law union/consensual union: a conjugal union involving two persons who have been living together for a period of time without being legally married to each other.

compulsory heterosexuality: the expectation that everyone is (or should be) heterosexual and that **society** should operate with heterosexuality as the only normal and morally acceptable sexuality.

concerted cultivation model: used by Annette Lareau to refer to parenting in which middle-class parents deliberately develop their children's talents in order to enhance their chances of excelling in school, sports, relationships, and, ultimately, their careers. Compare with **natural growth model**.

conspicuous consumption: a concept developed by Thorstein Veblen to describe buying expensive commodities for their value as status symbols rather than their function.

conspicuous leisure: a concept developed by Thorstein Veblen that refers to the practice of demonstrating one's **social class** through flaunting extravagant leisure activities.

consumer culture: a culture oriented toward enjoying, and focusing money and attention on, the purchasing of goods and services. Consumer culture is a particular kind of material culture that has expanded since the latter half of the twentieth century.

consumption: the purchasing and/or use of goods and services.

contemporary theory: generally refers to works from the early to mid-twentieth century to today. It is characterized by a vast and ever-expanding number of theorists and works, none of which is widely agreed upon as canonical or fundamental to the discipline. See also **theory** and compare to **classical theory**.

content analysis: a quantitative and/or qualitative research method that involves analyzing the content of written documents, images (still or moving), or other texts in order to interpret their meaning.

core framing tasks: according to Robert Benford and David Snow, there are three tasks that are used by participants in social movements to frame issues: diagnostic frames, which define a problem that needs to be solved; prognostic frames, which define what should be done about the problem; and motivational frames, which define why we should care about the problem to the point of becoming involved personally. See also **frame**.

craft consumption: a term coined by Colin Campbell to describe a creative form of **consumption** in which the craft consumer uses mass-produced goods as raw materials to create a unique new product for personal consumption.

crime: any behaviour, action, practice, or omission that violates a society's standard as formally defined in its criminal law.

crime scripts: culturally specific ideas about what constitutes a normal **crime**.

criminal entryways: procedures and mechanisms that introduce people to the criminal justice system. This can include how criminal justice systems accuse people of crimes and wrongdoing.

criminalization: the process of constructing particular behaviours, actions, conditions, individuals, or groups of people as problematic and as requiring a response from the criminal justice system.

criminology: the academic discipline dedicated to studying **crime**, criminality, and punishment.

critical approach/critical theory: a mode of interpretation that regards what appears natural and inevitable to be the result of history and various social forces. Using a critical approach to analyse the social world also means trying to understand the world from viewpoints that are marginal or marginalized instead of from those that are common or dominant. See the **Frankfurt School**.

critical weight studies: see **fat studies.**

cultural capital: a concept advanced by Pierre Bourdieu that refers to non-economic assets that enable **social mobility**. Examples can include education, style of speech, dress, or physical appearance.

cultural consumption: the consumption of goods for their expressive qualities in addition to, or instead of, their utility.

cultural studies: an interdisciplinary field of study (drawing from sociology, philosophy, linguistics, media studies, and history) that examines communication and culture. Cultural studies acknowledges that culture is a site and **institution** involving struggles over the meaning of reality.

culture: a whole way of life of a people that includes the **norms**, **values**, beliefs, ideas, images, behaviours, practices, **symbols,** language, and material things and places shared by a group and that help to define the group.

culture and conduct of parenthood: concepts developed by Ralph LaRossa to describe the distinction between how parenthood is represented through culture (e.g., as portrayed through television, parenting advice magazines and advertising) and how it is actually practised (conducted) by ordinary people.

culture industry, the: Max Horkheimer and Theodor Adorno's term for the production of culture, particularly **mass media**, under conditions of **capitalism**. The reference to a single industry demonstrates the significance of corporate media ownership for the production of culture. See also the **Frankfurt School**.

cyberbullying: bullying behaviour perpetrated through online means, such as social media platforms or private messaging.

cyclic time: a term coined by David Lewis and Andrew Weigert to refer to the cultural time structures that repeat in endless cycles, including the day, week, and seasons, and that are used to organize social life. This is distinct from **linear time**.

dark figure of crime: unreported **crime** that is not captured in **official crime statistics**.

deindustrialization: the process in which a society's economy moves away from industrial manufacturing and toward service and knowledge-based industries. The process of deindustrialization began in North America in the 1960s.

demedicalization: the resistance to and movement away from the dominance of medical authority in everyday life.

demographic transition theory: a theory of how **populations** change from a demographic regime with high rates of **fertility** and **mortality** to one with low rates of fertility and mortality following **industrialization** and **modernization**. During this transition, populations grow exponentially as mortality declines while fertility remains initially high, and they then stabilize when fertility rates decline.

demography: the study of human populations, including the study of population size, growth rate, causes, and consequences of population change. The three main demographic processes are fertility, mortality, and migration.

de-stigmatize: see **stigma**.

deviance/deviant: a term used to describe an attitude, behaviour, practice, condition, individual, or group of people that violates the social **norms** of the society in which the violation occurs.

discourse: as used by **poststructural theory**, the term refers to the predominant yet often implicit way of expressing and organizing knowledge, including thoughts, beliefs, ideologies, and understandings. Discourse is produced and maintained within given historic and social conditions through relations of power.

discrimination: actions that either directly or indirectly deny rewards or resources to individuals or groups. These actions are often motivated, either intentionally or unintentionally, by stereotypes or other prejudices. Compare with **prejudice**.

disenchantment: a concept developed by Max Weber to describe the waning of a sense of mystery, meaning, and magic from everyday life; it is associated with modern **rationalization**, wherein the world is regarded as increasingly knowable, predictable, and controllable.

disenfranchisement: the removal of rights from citizens, such as the ability to vote.

dispossession: the act of taking away someone's land, one of the key mechanisms of **colonialism**.

division of labour: division of work into distinct spheres of activity, distributed to different workers, family members, or group members.

doctrine of discovery: a principle of international law that stipulated that political entities can lay claim to lands that are uninhabited by Christian peoples or by the subjects of a European Christian monarch.

domestic terrorism: terrorism that arises from within a **nation-state**, in contrast to foreign terrorism, which originates from outside state borders.

dominant ideology: a system of beliefs and values that supports the dominant class in their rule and justifies inequality that maintains their domination. See also **ideology**.

dual burden: the workload of people, usually women, who are engaged in both paid labour and significant amounts of unpaid domestic labour.

economic boom: a period of rapid growth and profitability across an economy.

embodied: describes how people live in and through their bodies; thoughts, feelings, and actions cannot be separated from the bodies in which they take place.

embodiment paradigm: a theoretical perspective that refuses the distinction between the social and the biological and sees bodies as both social and biological without reducing this to **biological determinism**.

emotional labour: a concept forwarded by Arlie Hochschild that refers to the management of feelings by suppressing or changing how one actually feels. It is often used to explain how managing and producing emotion is an additional requirement of many paid jobs.

emphasized femininity: a concept developed by gender theorist R.W. Connell to describe an accentuated form of femininity that some women adopt in order to adapt to the structural and experiential disadvantages conferred upon women within the system of patriarchy.

empiricism: the perspective that knowledge about the world is derived from experiencing the world through the senses, scientific observation, and study.

Enlightenment, the: intellectual movement between the sixteenth and eighteenth centuries that was marked by intense philosophical, scientific, technological, social, and historical change. This intellectual movement emphasized the individual as a political and social agent, as well as the use of reason rather than deferring to tradition or authority for the development of knowledge.

epidemiological transition theory: a theory that explains the shift following **industrialization** and **modernization** in the causes and patterns of diseases and deaths – the theory posits that in pre-industrial societies infectious diseases are a dominant cause of death, while in industrialized societies, degenerative and chronic diseases are a dominant cause of death.

episteme: Michel Foucault's term for a set of ideas that shape how knowledge is understood in a particular period.

epistemic diversity: a concept advanced by Achille Mbembe that positions myriad

epistemes as equally important in decolonial knowledge creation endeavours (disrupting the **universality** of Western European philosophical approaches).

epistemology: the field of study that asks: What is knowledge? What is knowable?

ethnic enclaves: urban areas with disproportionate concentrations of ethnic or **racialized** minorities. The term is typically used to designate neighbourhoods that have endured less intense **stigmatization** and **territorial confinement** than **ghettos**.

ethnography: the study of culture by methods that usually include extensive **fieldwork**, **participant observation**, and **interviews**. Etymologically, ethnography derives from Greek, meaning writing about (*graph*) the folk or the people (*ethnos*).

eugenics: a set of beliefs in the racial and genetic superiority of certain races, and a set of practices that attempt to "improve" the genetic stock of a people through reproductive policies and interventions.

Eurocentric: judging other cultures, societies, beliefs and **social practices** from the perspective of **Western** and European superiority.

experiential education: educational practices premised on the value of first-hand knowledge attained through sensory engagement and direct experience with the world; this is contrasted with educational models whereby students learn in a classroom from an expert.

fat shaming: attitudes and actions that are based on and reproduce the idea that fat is inherently bad and shameful. For example, even the suggestion that "fat" is always an insult and should be euphemized using terms like "curvy" is a form of fat shaming.

fat studies: a field of study that focuses on the cultural and social meanings associated with fatness and with different body types.

feminist theories: theories that explain social phenomena in terms of the gendered organization of **society** and corresponding unequal relations of power. See also **patriarchy**.

feminization: when an aspect of social life becomes seen as strictly the domain of women or the realm of the feminine and, as a result, in the context of patriarchal societies, is devalued.

fertility: in the field of demography, the number of children per woman.

field: a sociological term coined by Pierre Bourdieu that refers to a space or place that is organized around relationships of power. A field is governed by distinct sets of rules and understandings that those who engage in the field accept or resist.

fieldwork: a **qualitative research** method in which researchers seek to understand a community, cultural location, or practice through **participant observation,** conducting in-depth **interviews**, and taking detailed notes to document their observations and experiences.

food miles: the physical distance that any particular food travels from where it is produced to where it is consumed.

food supply chain: the **commodity** path that food takes from the point of production through distribution to consumption.

fracking: a process of extracting natural gas that involves the injection of water or other liquids under high pressure to crack the shale rock in which gas is trapped.

frame: an interpretive schema that organizes the way that we view the world.

Frankfurt School: an interdisciplinary group of Western Marxist scholars who developed philosophical critiques of capitalist **society** and modernity, originally at the Institute for Social Research in Frankfurt, Germany, and later fleeing to the United States in the early 1930s to escape the Nazis. See **critical approach/theory**.

frontier law: informal legal relations that, until the 1800s, were shaped spontaneously through

interactions between colonial powers (English and French), corporations (Hudson's Bay Company and the North-West Company), and the various **Indigenous** nations throughout the land known as Canada.

functionalism: a theoretical approach by which social processes and **institutions** are considered necessary to maintain a social system. See **structural functionalism.**

gender: a culturally specific hierarchical categorization of people into gender categories based on presumed social differences (usually understood to be derived from essential biological differences). See **gender binary**.

gender binary: the social belief and expectation that there are two, and only two, genders (men/boys and women/girls), which correspond with a belief that there are only two biological sexes (male and female) that are unambiguously distinct from and even oppositional to each other; accordingly, these each have characteristics (masculinity or femininity) and socially approved (some might say socially mandated) **norms** that are specific for each gender and that properly belong only to one or the other gender but not both.

gender revolution: the transformation of women's status in **society**, as their presence in the workplace increased dramatically from the 1960s onward and they obtained legal equality with men.

gendered: a term used to describe how behaviours, feelings, jobs, dress, roles, and so on are defined as either feminine or masculine and seen as appropriate for either men or for women.

genealogy: a form of critical theorizing that traces the history of and context for the emergence of specific forms of knowledge (perceptions, stereotypes, predominant social discourses) and examines the social, historical, and political relationships between knowledge, people, and social institutions (legal, political, economic).

genetically modified organisms (GMO): organisms, particularly food, that have been altered at the molecular level by adding genes from one species into another in a manner that does not occur in nature.

gentrification: a process where middle- and upper-middle class people move into a neighbourhood that has historically been inhabited by working-class people and transform the area to reflect middle-class **tastes** and economic realities.

germ theory: a theory of the origin of infectious diseases that emerged in the late nineteenth century; it maintains that infectious diseases are caused by microorganisms such as bacteria and viruses.

ghettos: urban areas where ethnic and racialized minorities have been confined within territorial boundaries, often subject to negative **stereotypes** that stress the violence and criminality that may occur there.

global citizenship: a policy or ideal whereby all people would be granted civic rights and human rights more generally, as members of a global **society** (as opposed to any single **nation-state**). This would guarantee the right of marginalized groups to human rights and full citizenship; it universalizes the struggle for citizenship.

global citizenship education: educational practices that recognize the struggle for citizenship among oppressed and vulnerable **populations** and that universalize the struggle for citizenship and human rights more generally. Incorporated into curricula, students may earn credits for travelling abroad to promote ideals of **global citizenship**.

global food system: a complex system that includes the production, distribution, and consumption of food around the world.

globalization: the process of integrating more regions of the world economically, politically, and culturally. This process was accelerated by the histories of the trans-Atlantic slave trade and colonization and gave rise to a system of global inequality. See also **Global North** and **Global South**.

Global North: refers to nations predominantly located in the northern hemisphere; previously referred to as "developed" or "First World." These countries include Canada, the United States, and European nations, but also Australia and New Zealand.

Global South: refers to nations located mainly in the southern hemisphere; previously referred to as "developing," "underdeveloped," or "Third World." These include nations in Latin America, Africa, and most of Asia. The Global South does not include Australia or New Zealand.

Green Revolution: The remarkable increase in food production due to the use of high-yield crops, pesticides, fertilizers and other technological advancements in agriculture that impacted the **global food system** beginning in the 1960s.

grey literature: written materials, including reports, research, and other technical writing, produced by organizations outside of traditional academic publishing. The quality of grey literature tends to vary considerably, so it should be evaluated with care and used with caution when doing sociological research.

gurdwaras: Sikh temples. In British Columbia, gurdwaras also serve a variety of civic, political, and social roles that are not strictly reducible to **religion**.

hegemonic brandscape: a term coined by Craig Thompson and Zynep Arsel to describe the significant influence of a dominant, global brand (such as Starbucks) on local competitors (in terms of the way they configure their branded environments, for example) and the meanings consumers make of their experience with these brands and their branded spaces.

hegemonic masculinity: a concept developed by **gender** theorist R.W. Connell that describes the most culturally dominant form of masculinity at the top of a gender hierarchy, and which confers individual and group privileges, including being seen as "properly" masculine.

hegemony: a concept developed by Marxist philosopher Antonio Gramsci to describe the way in which the dominant (or ruling) class of people who hold power within **society** maintains control of society by using ideas and culture to manipulate the subordinate class to comply and consent to their rule. This contrasts with domination, which uses coercive and violent force in order to secure compliance.

helicopter parenting: a contemporary style of parenting that over-focuses on a child's real or perceived needs.

heteronormativity: the set of ideas and practices that affirm the dominance of and **normalize** heterosexuality as well as the **gender binary** that heterosexuality constructs.

heteropatriarchy: a form of social organization in which cisgendered heterosexual men have social, financial, and political control.

hidden curriculum: **norms**, values, attitudes, principles, and ways of understanding taught to students throughout their educational experiences that are not formally part of an academic program and are often unacknowledged and conveyed implicitly. The hidden curriculum helps to reproduce dominant cultural **values** and structures.

historical sociology: a field of sociology that focuses on past societies, the history of our current social conditions, and social change over time. This field often relies on **archival research** as well as **interviewing** methods.

holiday body: a term used to describe how holidays are **embodied** in paradoxical ways. For example, bodies are organized and imagined during holidays as both resting and working simultaneously.

holiday body work: the **body work** required during holidays – that is, body work activated during a particular time (e.g., a long weekend) and in relation to a particular **ritual** (e.g., Thanksgiving).

homophobia: irrational aversion, fear, or hatred of homosexuality or of gay men or lesbians. See also **compulsory heterosexuality** and **heteronormativity**.

household division of labour: the way in which unpaid work within the home (including housework and child care) is allocated; in heterosexual couples, this is often based on gendered **norms** around work.

humanitarianism: promotion of human rights and welfare, individual freedoms, and the alleviation of suffering around the world.

iconic brands: a term coined by Douglas Holt to refer to cultural brands that offer identity **myths** that have significant value in a **society**; as such, they become widely shared, prominent cultural **symbols.**

identity: refers to how individuals understand themselves and how others interpret them, in relation to the social world. One's identity includes understandings of, and relations to, social **norms**, practices, and structures such as **gender**, **race**, class, and nation. See also **self-identity** and social identity.

ideological parasite: the way cultural brands draw on existing cultural ideas to establish brand symbolism and meaning.

ideology: a system of belief (not always accurate) that people use to make sense of the social world and their experiences in it. An ideology creates taken-for-granted or "common-sense" notions about how the world is organized and how it works. See also **dominant ideology**.

Indigenous/Indigeneity: refers to the original peoples of a **territory**; people who have had relationships with the land since time immemorial.

Indigenous Place-Thought: a concept advanced by Vanessa Watts that understands humans, non-humans, land, and place as thinking, interrelated and co-constituted.

Indigenous ways of knowing: vast array of traditional knowledge systems held among Indigenous people, typically characterized by intimate knowledge of an ecosystem gained through direct experience, storytelling, and oral history.

individualism: an ideology that individuals are in charge of their own destinies, self-sufficient, and fully responsible for themselves.

industrial capitalism: refers to a system of economic production and consumption that emerged with the **Industrial Revolution.** Preceded **advanced capitalism**.

industrialization: a process that is marked by a shift to industrial (factory manufacturing-based) ways of production, often accompanied by increased **urbanization.**

industrial Revolution: the period of time in the late eighteenth to mid-nineteenth century characterized by major technological, social, and economic changes, including the development of new energy resources that revolutionized work and production; this led to the development of factories and massive migration from rural areas to cities.

infant mortality rate: the number of deaths of infants under one year of age per 1,000 live births in a **population**; child mortality rate refers to the number of deaths of children under five years of age per 1,000 live births in a population.

institutional encasement: the process through which ghettoized areas develop a duplicate set of services (e.g., medical, commercial, legal) that mirror those existing in the broader city.

institutions: groups of people that have organized toward a common purpose. Large, powerful, and highly organized social institutions include: **religion**, education, and the **state**.

intensive parenting (mothering): a contemporary style of parenting that includes at least three central philosophies: that mothers are the best people to care for their children, that mothering should centre around the child's needs, and that raising children should be considered wholly fulfilling for parents.

interaction rituals: as defined by Erving Goffman, conventional exchanges that take place between people in face-to-face situations, whereby each honours and affirms the social existence of the other.

interactions: exchanges between two or more individuals that collectively form the foundation of **society**.

inter-corporeal body work: a form of **body work** that involves working on or for other human bodies through direct contact (e.g., doctors) or indirectly (e.g., working with bodily waste).

intergenerational social mobility: changes in **social class** between generations. See **social mobility**.

intern/internment: to intern is to confine a specific population for political reasons.

intersectionality/intersections (of social categories): a critical approach developed by Kimberlé Crenshaw that analyzes the multiple aspects of social location as intertwined, producing differential experiences of privilege and marginality and different life chances. These aspects of social location include **social identity** (such as **gender**, **racialization**, **social class**, ability, sexuality), as well as institutions and structures.

interview: method whereby a participant is asked questions by a researcher. Researchers analyze the participants' answers as data. Interviews can be structured (a **quantitative** method) or semi-structured or unstructured (**qualitative** methods).

kin: a term, most frequently used in anthropology, referring to one's relatives.

law: a codified and enforceable set of regulations that govern individual conduct in a **society**.

law and order perspective: a set of beliefs and policies that advocate for strong sentences for people who commit **crimes**, including increasing incarceration, **zero-tolerance** policies, and minimum sentencing rules.

legitimacy: refers to the perceived rightness or properness of authority.

life chances: a concept developed by Max Weber to describe people's unequal access to resources like food, education, work, and leisure opportunities as determined by social class position and status group.

life course: the process of change and socialization an individual experiences over the course of their life that reflects the interaction between the individual's development and their social, cultural, and historical context.

life expectancy at birth: the average number of years that a person is expected to live from birth to death based on the prevailing age-specific death rates in a **population** at a given time.

logo: a **symbol** designed to be a stand-in for a business or organization.

marketplace: the place (virtual or physical) where goods and services are exchanged – bought, traded, and sold. The marketplace is an important element of the broader economy in **society**.

mass media: technologies of reproduction and transmission that enable a single sender to simultaneously reach large or "mass" audiences, or the institutional press that uses these technologies to disseminate information and entertainment. The flow of information typically runs from sender to receiver with little to no opportunity for feedback.

master status: a term coined by Everett Hughes that refers to the single defining label or demographic category that is perceived as or assumed to be most significant over all others, typically applied to a **population** or person.

material culture: physical objects created and/or used within a culture – for example, tools, toys, flags, or buildings.

means of production: the things needed to produce goods. This includes machines, buildings, raw materials, and other resources.

mechanical solidarity: a type of social cohesion, theorized by Émile Durkheim, that is based on likeness; this solidarity exists in societies that are marked by a low division of labour, social homogeneity, and shared worldviews. Durkheim classifies traditional (or non-modern) societies as exhibiting this type of solidarity. Compare with **organic solidarity**.

media events: preplanned ceremonies or spectacles that are broadcast live, interrupting the normal flow of television programming and garnering large audiences. Daniel Dayan and Elihu Katz argue that these events use the media to dramatize and confirm core social **values**.

media theory pyramid: an understanding of media developed by Nick Couldry that includes **medium theory**, the **political economy of communication, textual analysis,** and **socially oriented media theory**.

mediatization: the mutual shaping of media and **society**, mediatization is the process by which domains of social life (such as work, the family, or politics) come to be dominated by the logic of media.

medicalization: the process by which non-medical conditions come to be treated as medical phenomena requiring intervention by medical experts.

medium theory: a theory that identifies connections among a medium's technical qualities, its use, and how it affects people's relation to the world. Medium theory sees any vision of reality and our ability to interact with it as contingent on technologies and their usable qualities.

methods: the specific techniques and processes researchers use to collect, generate, or analyze data about their subject matter. See also **archival analysis/research, coding, content analysis, ethnography, fieldwork, interview, mixed-methods research, participant observation, qualitative research, quantitative research, scientific method**, and **textual analysis**.

methodology: a plan to use specific methods to be able to discover or produce certain kinds of knowledge about a particular facet of social life. The methodology of a study is based on answering larger, more abstract questions pertaining to how one understands the nature of their object of inquiry. See also **methodology**.

migrant farm worker: a person who travels to work seasonally in paid agricultural activities.

mixed-methods research: research that involves collecting and/or analyzing both **qualitative** and **quantitative** data.

mobile sociology: a type of sociology, forwarded by John Urry, incorporating methodological approaches and definitions of society that recognize globalization and transnational networks as the context in which we live and do research.

mobilization: the ability of a **social movement** to "activate" people; gaining their ideological support and recruiting them for participation.

modernization: the process in which a **society** is transformed by processes of capitalist **industrialization, secularization**, and **urbanization.**

monopoly over violence: from political philosophy; describes the ability of one group to obtain exclusive use of physical force. According to Max Weber, statehood is achieved when a group is able to claim such exclusive use of force within a given physical territory.

mortality rate: the rate at which people in a **population** are dying. It is generally expressed as the number of deaths per 1,000 people.

multiculturalism: in Canada, it refers to official **state** policy adopted in 1971 that endorses Canada as a nation with a plurality of cultural traditions; it also refers to everyday celebrations of multiple cultures and the reality that a **society** contains a multitude of cultural traditions.

myth: according to Roland Barthes, a myth is a cultural story that works to **naturalize dominant ideologies**.

narrative: storytelling device that leads toward certain interpretations.

national identity: a nation's sense of itself as a distinct and singular entity, expressed through both non-material culture (myths, anthems, language) and **material culture** (flags, food, dress).

nationalism: identification with, and devoting time and energy in, the interest of the nation.

nation-state: a bounded geographic region governed by a sovereign political power.

natural growth model: used by Annette Lareau to refer to parenting in which working-class parents take a less "hands-on" or focused approach, compared to middle-class parents, on optimizing children's talents. Lareau argues that in this approach, parents provide care and safeguards for their children with less emphasis on external organized activities. Compare with **concerted cultivation model**.

naturalized: in sociology, the process by which social or ideological ideas become presented and accepted as if they are unarguable truths.

neoliberalism: political and economic ideology that privileges the creation of new markets and market relations over state interventions in social welfare. This ideology values private entrepreneurship, private ownership, and individual property rights. In this model, the role of the state is to maximize efficiency, accountability, and market growth, "governing at a distance" rather than directly intervening in matters of social well-being. Neoliberal policies are characterized by the privatization of public goods, the implementation of austerity measures, and the liberalization of trade relations between countries.

neo-Malthusian: adoption of the ideas of Thomas Malthus (eighteenth-century thinker) in the twentieth and twenty-first centuries, with a focus on advocating for human **population** controls.

neo-Marxism: adoption of the ideas of nineteenth-century thinker Karl Marx in the twentieth and twenty-first centuries.

neurodiversity: differences in behavioural and cognitive functioning; those who embrace neurodiversity understand variations among humans to be natural, commonly occurring phenomena, not things to be cured or fixed.

new father: the model of fatherhood popularized by the **mass media** from the 1980s onwards, which suggests that men should become more actively involved in providing care to their children.

new sociology of childhood: a school of thought that began in the 1980s to pay attention to the changing dimensions of childhood in the late twentieth and early twenty-first centuries; it put greater focus on children's voices and attempted to disrupt the logic of adult expertise.

non-random sampling: method used in both **quantitative** and **qualitative research** to choose participants for a study that does not allow an equal probability of being selected. Snowball sampling is a non-random sampling method that relies on key participants to recommend and direct the researcher to potentially relevant participants. This method contrasts with **random sampling**.

normalize: a concept developed by French philosopher Michel Foucault that refers to the process by which a particular identity, behaviour, or idea comes to be regarded within a particular social and historical context as normal and right while other identities, behaviours, or ideas are seen as abnormal, **queer**, wrong, and problematic.

normative: refers to ways of being, acting, and thinking that are generally assumed to be the standard or normal way one ought to be, act, or think and therefore establishes the basis by which other ways of being, acting, or thinking are judged.

norms: rules within **society** that guide how people are expected to behave, feel, dress, interact, and so on. Individuals learn these rules from various agents of socialization. Some norms are formally inscribed into law or other formal regulatory guidelines, such as school dress codes or the Criminal Code of Canada. Norms are subject to contestation and change.

nostalgia: a wistful longing for a particular past.

not-for-profit organizations: organizations that do not pay income tax on money they receive for their organization based on an understanding that any income will be reinvested in the organization to allow it to subsist, as well as that the organization's existence will benefit the larger public instead of being driven by turning a profit for its owners.

official crime statistics: reflect the number of crimes that have been recorded by police departments.

ontology: philosophy that is concerned with the nature of being, asking questions like "what is reality?" and "what exists?"

organic solidarity: a type of social cohesion, theorized by Émile Durkheim, that is based on difference. This solidarity exists in societies that are marked by a high division of labour, social heterogeneity, and interdependence. Durkheim classifies modern, urban, industrial societies as exhibiting this type of solidarity. Compare with **mechanical solidarity**.

panopticism: the process, theorized by Michel Foucault, by which individuals are led to presume they are subjected to constant levels of surveillance by authorities. This assumption makes individuals conform to particular standards of conduct.

paradox of holidays: the idea that holidays are simultaneously a time of rest and a time of labour.

participant observation: a **qualitative research** method in which a researcher partakes in the activities of the group being studied as both a participant and an observer, to understand the internal workings of its culture.

patriarchy: a form of social organization where men, as a group, have greater control over resources in cultural, economic, social, and political realms. This system disadvantages women, **transgender** people, most men (working-class men, racialized men, gay men), and other marginalized groups.

perpetual harvest: year-round availability of foods regardless of their seasonality.

personal crime: any **crime** perpetrated against an individual, such as assault, kidnapping, or murder.

place: the socially determined connections to and associations with space that are created through habitation of that space as well as mediated representations of it.

place branding: marketing practices that celebrate a particular **place**; these practices could be used to brand neighbourhoods, cities, or nations.

pluralist ideology: a political ideology that stresses the virtues and **values** of difference(s).

pluritemporalism: a term coined by Helga Notwotny to acknowledge that many different conceptions of time exist side by side and must be navigated simultaneously.

political economy: an interdisciplinary field of study focusing on the relationship between economic production and consumption, the law, governments, politics, and the media.

political economy of communication: an approach to media studies focusing on the institutions that regulate media. Political economists are typically concerned with the power held by large, for-profit media companies.

politics of recognition: the way in which political and legal institutions and government view different segments of the population and recognize their respective rights.

population: in demography, a group of people who inhabit a specific geographical area at a particular time period. Population can also be defined in terms of specific characteristics, such as age and sex.

population aging: the increase in the percentage of people aged 65 years and over in a population.

population growth rate: the rate at which a population is increasing or decreasing in size. If the number of people entering the population (births and immigrants) is greater than the number of people exiting it (deaths and emigrants), the population growth rate is positive. If the reverse, the rate is negative.

population pyramid: a graphical representation of the population. It shows t he relative numbers of men and women by age group. This representation takes on a pyramid shape when fertility is high.

positivism: a theoretical perspective based on **scientific methods**; it assumes the existence of a singular, fixed reality that can be positively known or definitively discovered pending application of the proper method; the philosophical belief that any rational assertion can be proven through scientific methods.

postcolonial theory: analyzes the legacies and the ongoing conditions of **colonialism** and imperialism, critically examines the political, economic, and cultural conditions they have created.

post-development discourse: analyzes structures of international development (e.g., foreign aid, philanthropy, practices like volunteer tourism) that reflect the ongoing control that the Global North maintains over the Global South.

poststructural theory: largely drawing on the thinking of Michel Foucault, it challenges assumptions about the **universality** of knowledge and taken-for-granted aspects of everyday life; it demonstrates how ways of interpreting the world are historically and culturally specific and how "truth" and ideas about **social identity** are socially produced rather than naturally inherent.

poverty: inadequate access (either relative to others or absolutely) to the material resources (money, food, shelter) necessary for life as well as the social and cultural resources (time, access to leisure opportunities) necessary for well-being.

precarious employment: paid work characterized by conditions of limited or no job security, few or limited workplace benefits, few or no labour protections, and lower wages. See **structural precarity.**

prejudice: attitudes that individuals hold about groups of people, or individuals of those groups, that are motivated by **stereotypes** or other assumptions.

primary data: original data collected by the researcher. See also **secondary data analysis.**

primary sector: the economic sector that encompasses jobs involved in the extraction of raw, natural resources from the environment. It includes farming, fishing, forestry, and mining.

primary socialization: the process of socialization that happens during childhood and socializes children into basic skills (walking, talking, eating), **norms,** and **values.**

prison-industrial complex: infrastructure through which for-profit corporations are increasingly involved in the administration of criminal justice. It also involves the growing use of criminal justice institutions to respond to social problems such as poverty and addiction. However, this infrastructure of policing and incarceration, which values market growth and profit, is seen to create and sustain a demand for more prisoners rather than respond to social problems or address concerns about public safety.

privatized spaces: spaces that are controlled and occupied based on private ownership, from individual homes to commercial businesses, in contrast to collective spaces such as public parks and streets, where all citizens, in theory, have equal access.

property crime: any **crime** that is perpetrated against property, such as theft, arson, or forgery.

pseudofoods: substances that are eaten by people in our **society**, but which some food activists believe to be so devoid of nutritional character that they are only passing as foods. They may also be called "food-like substances."

qualitative research: a form of inquiry in which the researcher asks open-ended research questions, studies small groups of people or bounded phenomena, and seeks to offer rich, idiographic (in-depth) explanations of the social world.

quantitative research: a form of inquiry in which the researcher poses hypotheses about the relationship between variables. This form of research can be used to study large **populations.** The data is collected as or reduced to numerical form and analyzed using statistical methods.

queer: while historically used as a pejorative term, queer has been reappropriated to be used as an umbrella term to refer to all sexual identities and practices that challenge **norms** of **compulsory heterosexuality** and **cisgender** normativity.

race: a hierarchical categorization of humans into groups based on presumed innate biological differences. While the belief in race is not supported by contemporary genetic research (that is, race is not a scientific fact), it does act as a meaningful social category that has consequences of structural and experiential inequality in the social world.

racialization: the process of ascribing ethnic or racial characteristics or identities to individuals, groups, or **social practices.**

radical pedagogy: teaching practices that try to help students recognize structures of power and domination.

random sample: a method used in both **quantitative** and **qualitative research** to choose participants for a study. The selection of a sample from a **population** in such a way that every element, person, or case, as appropriate, has a probability of being selected.

rationalization: the process by which all aspects of social life have become increasingly organized around means-end calculation and technical procedures to maximize efficiency. This is associated with the rise of Western science and bureaucratic methods and forms of social organization, as described by Max Weber.

recidivism: repetition of an activity or behaviour – for example, reoffence when describing **crime.**

reflective practice: the incorporation of methods of self-reflection or self-study into routine activities or work to appreciate how a person's own experiences or social position affects their conduct; especially applied to understanding how one's actions impact others.

religion: social **institutions**, practices, **rituals**, and beliefs that are organized and oriented toward collective understandings of the spiritual, supernatural, or sacred. These practices create communities of believers who share a worldview.

replacement-level fertility: the level of fertility at which a **population** replaces itself from one generation to another. In countries with very low infant and child mortality (such as Canada), replacement fertility is estimated at 2.1 children per woman.

reserve army: also known as reserve army of labour or industrial reserve army; an over-supply of people who are unable to find work. The presence of such a **population** exerts pressure to push the wages of the workers down and consequently increases capitalist profits.

ritual: a deliberate set of actions, such as making a gesture, a statement, or engaging with an object. These actions tend to have a defined order to them and often take place in a specific location.

ritual view of communication: a perspective on human communication introduced by James Carey that emphasizes the cultural **values** that are constructed, negotiated, or confirmed through acts of communication, as compared to the informational content of messages exchanged.

sample: a group of people, texts, or data, that are used to stand in for a larger **population** or data set in a research project.

sample surveys: questionnaires used to obtain data and information from a subset of the **population**. Sample surveys generally aim to have a representative subset (or **sample**) so that the results are generalizable to the whole population.

sanctions: attempts to regulate people's behaviour. Positive sanctions are incentives to follow certain social **norms** and demonstrate social approval. Negative sanctions regulate behaviour, punishing actions or people who do not follow cultural **norms**.

scapegoating: blaming a person or group for a particular misfortune, typically in ways that simplify a more complex problem.

school-to-prison pipeline: refers to a pattern in which students are directly or indirectly funnelled from educational **institutions** into the criminal justice system as a result of policies and practices that merge educational and criminal justice institutions.

scientific method: research that begins with a hypothesis, relies on systematically collecting and analyzing observable data, and aims to arrive at definitive conclusions.

seasonal branding: a subset of branding activity by which corporations establish and maintain their brand's relevance by offering frameworks for seasonal celebration.

seasonal consumption: consumption activity that is directly related to the seasons, including seasonal transitions, holidays, or festivals.

seasonal migrant workers: migrant workers whose work (and migration for work) is dependent on seasonal conditions and is performed during only part of the year.

secondary data analysis: systematic review of existing research on a subject to identify and evaluate common themes and trends; data is not collected first-hand by the researcher (e.g., no contact with participants from whom the data was collected) or gathered through first-hand experience.

secondary sector: the economic sector that encompasses jobs involved in transforming raw, natural resources into products. This includes all jobs in manufacturing.

secondary socialization: the process of socializing people into new roles (student, parent, employee) that is accomplished by various social **institutions** (education, media, **religion**), and peer groups.

second demographic transition theory: a theoretical perspective that describes and explains demographic changes since the late twentieth century, such as delayed marriage, the increasing prevalence of cohabitation, declining marriage rates, the increase in births by unmarried women, and lower than **replacement-level fertility**.

second shift: a phenomenon, first named by Arlie Hochschild, where women who work in the paid workforce, come home and do another "shift" of work by doing a disproportionate amount of the labour of social reproduction (cooking, cleaning, child care). See also **triple shift**.

secularization: understood as the waning practice of **religion** and/or its effect on social and political life; the restriction of religion to the private practices; or the process by which religion becomes isolated as a distinct realm of social life.

self-identity: how individuals think about themselves personally. See also **identity**.

sequential time: understanding of time in which time unfolds in a linear and progressive fashion and structures activities in a particular, necessary order.

settler: see **white settler society.**

settler colonialism: the practices of land **dispossession** and genocide of **Indigenous** peoples that were and continue to be central to the processes of creating a **white settler society**. Settler colonialism also refers to a set of ideas, logic, or ideologies that have shaped and continue to impact how knowledge is created, understood, and disseminated in white settler societies.

sexism: refers to **discrimination**, **prejudice**, or oppression based on categories of sex and **gender**.

Sikhi: a religious, cultural, and political practice that began in the Punjab region in the late fifteenth century. The term is thought to better reflect the practice than the more widely used term "Sikhism."

social bonds: refers to relationships between individuals as well as between individuals and the **society** in which they live.

social class: an aspect of individual and group identity that derives from an individual or a group's access to material resources and social capital as a group.

social constructionism: a theoretical perspective that emphasizes the role of **society** or social relations in the construction of various aspects of social life.

social and cultural identity: an individual's or group's identity, developed through their position within social categories (e.g., class, **gender**, or **race**) and through their cultural connections with others (e.g., interests, neighbourhoods, and experiences). See also **identity**.

social Darwinism: a discredited school of thought suggesting that natural selection occurs not just in nature but also in human societies.

social determinism: the idea that humans are solely determined by **society** and social conditions. Compare with **biological determinism**.

social fact: a concept introduced by Émile Durkheim. It refers to any socially established and instituted way of thinking, acting, or feeling, formal or informal, that originates and exists outside of any individual but has an impact on individuals' lives. Examples include **religion**, suicide, **law**, and fashion.

social inequality: the patterned and ongoing disproportionate distribution of wealth, resources, and opportunities within a **society**.

social issues: according to C. Wright Mills, types of problem for which the causes, consequences, and solutions are social and structural or collective in nature and beyond the control or influence of individuals or their local circumstances. They are, therefore, a matter of public concern.

socialization: the lifelong process of inheriting and disseminating **norms**, customs, language, **values**, and ideologies, providing an individual with the skills and habits necessary for participating in a given culture, **subculture**, and broader **society**.

socially oriented media theory: an approach to media studies that examines how media are used in social processes.

social mobility: movement of individuals, families, or groups in a system of social hierarchy or **stratification**. See also **intergenerational mobility**.

social model of disability: an approach developed by critical disability scholars and disability activists to challenge the dominant medical model, which locates disability within the body of an individual; the social model focuses instead on the potentially disabling effects of the social environment – for example, stairways without ramps that create exclusions for some people.

social movement: a collective of people mobilized to organize and engage in a sustained series of activities, motivated by ideological concerns and/or the pursuit of political, religious, or social justice, in order to challenge the status quo.

social movement theory: seeks to understand how, why, and in what form groups of individuals or organizations come together to carry out, resist, or reverse a social change.

social nature: the idea, forwarded by Jocelyn Thorpe, that what we understand as nature is socially constructed in ways that benefit some at the expense of others.

social practices: a way of characterizing what people do in **society** as meaningful categories of social analysis and explanation. Practices may vary in complexity, but they are always perceived as a meaningful and structured form of social action, as distinct from mere activity.

social solidarity: that which holds or ties a group or **society** together. It is an expression of the group's shared beliefs, common interests, or mutual support necessary for the cohesion of the society. See **mechanical solidarity** and **organic solidarity**.

social status: the relative standing of a person or group, compared with others, in the context of a hierarchical social ordering. According to Max Weber, status refers to someone's access to social prestige. Compare with **social class**.

social structures: patterned social arrangements that may or may not be organized through social **institutions** and that influence, constrain, or enable peoples' behaviours (e.g., gender, class, race).

social time: a concept developed by researchers to recognize and study how people have constructed, measured, used, and valued time in different historical and cultural contexts.

society: the ongoing collective project that human communities produce through patterned interactions. The outcomes of society include language, culture, solidarity, as well as systems of oppression, war, and violence. Societies can refer to groups that range in size from quite small (a small organization, a school club) up to the global society of humanity.

socio-economic status (SES): a measure that combines analysis of education, work experience, and income to rank individuals and groups within a hierarchical structure.

sociology: the systematic study of society and social life. See also **society**.

sociological imagination: a term coined by C. Wright Mills that stresses the importance of considering how any individual life is both embedded in and helps to constitute larger historical processes, and it both takes place within and helps to shape larger social contexts.

sociological theories of crime: explanations of criminal behaviour that locate the cause of **crime** in the dynamics of broader social structures rather than in individuals' idiosyncratic acts of deviance.

sociology of the body: a subdiscipline of sociology that examines the **embodied** nature of social life, including how, as social beings, humans live in and through bodies, and how the body is social.

sociology of food: a subdiscipline of sociology that examines the social conditions of the production and distribution of food in local and **global food systems**.

sociology of health: a subdiscipline of sociology that examines the interaction between health, illness, and **society**, including analyzing how health and illness are defined within specific cultural and historical contexts.

sociology of media: a subdiscipline of sociology that applies sociological theories to analyze media.

sovereignty: complete legal rule over a geographical and political region.

standards of living: a measure of economic well-being that indicates the level of wealth, material goods, and services (including food, nutrition, housing, and health care) to which people in a particular population have access.

state, the: as defined by Max Weber, the state is that group of people who successfully claim an exclusive right (a monopoly) to the use of physical force within a given **territory**.

state capitalism: as defined by Jurgen Habermas, this refers to a type of capitalism where the state actively works to promote and secure the conditions of capitalist production through forming a solid partnership with corporate actors. State capitalism can be distinguished from more "laissez-faire" forms of **capitalism**, in which the state takes a "hands-off" approach to the economy.

statistical analysis: refers to the processes by which **quantitative** data are analyzed to describe patterns, establish associations between different variables, and test theoretical ideas.

stereotypes: broad, persistent generalizations about a group of people, that may form the basis of various forms of prejudice and **discrimination**.

stigma: a characteristic of an individual that is socially regarded in a negative light, such as a physical characteristic; see **stigmatization**.

stigmatization: the process through which people and places are evaluated according to a perceived negative attribute that defines their social value and identity in **society**. An individual or group is stigmatized when this stigma becomes the basis for being treated differently, harassed, devalued or blamed, isolating the individual or group from the larger social group.

stratification: the organization of **society** according to a hierarchy of classes of people; it embeds inequality into the very structure and operation of society. Stratification includes hierarchies based on class, gender, race, sexuality, and ability.

structural functionalism: a theoretical perspective in sociology, associated particularly with Talcott Parsons and Robert Bales, that was most influential in the mid-twentieth century; it proposes that **society** can best be understood as a system of interrelated parts, each of which performs a necessary function to ensure the smooth operation and continuity of society as a whole; see also **functionalism**.

structural precarity: the manner in which job insecurity becomes institutionalized within employment structures (e.g., work conditions created by the state, like employment immigration programs, wage laws). This job insecurity creates differential exposure to workplace injury, violence, and death.

structures: see **social structures.**

subcultures: a smaller cultural group that shares particular interests, **values**, or beliefs that differ from those of the larger cultural group.

summer learning loss/summer setback: the phenomenon where young people lose academic skills over the summer, potentially resulting in an achievement gap; it is largely associated with lower parental income levels and **social class**, and it is believed to be a strong contributor to high school dropout rates because it leads to frustration related to an inability to keep up.

survey: a form of data collection for research purposes whereby a series of standardized questions is asked to individuals through a paper or online format.

symbol: something that stands in for, or represents, something else.

symbolic economy: an economy based on the production, circulation, and **consumption** of cultural images, information, and experiences, as well as the spaces in which these are configured and consumed.

systems of representation: an idea developed by Stuart Hall that describes how cultural meaning is not fixed or inherent; rather, language, signs, and **symbols** produce meaning that is fixed by the users through this system of representation.

taste: as described by Pierre Bourdieu, **consumption** preferences, which usually reflect and express social and cultural identities – for example, as members of a particular **social class** or subcultural group.

***terra nullius*:** a legal principle that defines land as unoccupied if the territory has not previously been claimed by a state, and therefore it can be claimed by another state.

territorial confinement: restricting an individual's or group's movement to a specific space.

territory: in the context of Weber's definition of the **state**, territory is the geographical area within which the state exercises its monopoly over violence. In most cases, territory is coterminous with national borders.

tertiary sector: the economic sector that encompasses jobs involved in providing services. Service sector, civil service, and knowledge-economy jobs are in this sector.

textual analysis: a research method that involves the collection and analysis of textual data. This analysis usually involves **coding** and can include either **quantitative** or **qualitative** methods of analysis.

theory: a system of concepts, ideas, principles, and propositions that is used to make sense of and explain patterns, regularities, and relationships observed in the social world.

theory of practice: a mode of interpreting and describing people's behaviours, the unwritten rules people follow in doing those things, and how these behaviours are both coordinated and the means for performing certain identities. These theories draw on Pierre Bourdieu and Michel Foucault, among others..

third place: used by Ray Oldenburg to refer to a place that is neither work nor home – such as a café, diner, pub, or salon – in which there is social interaction (an exchange of words, ideas, glances, etc.) and a sense of community.

total fertility rate (TFR): the average number of children that a woman is expected to have during her child-bearing years (15–49 years of age), assuming that prevailing age-specific fertility rates remain unchanged.

traditions: those elements of culture that people individually and collectively decide are important enough to keep and pass down to next generations.

transgender: describes a person whose gender identity does not line up with **normative** assumptions of **gender binaries.**

transnationalism: the sustained movement of people, ideas, goods, and capital between nations.

triple shift: a term proposed by Jean Duncombe and Dennis Marsden to describe the added burden of work expected of women; this includes not only paid employment and domestic labour, but the third additional task of engaging in emotional support work. See also **second shift**.

under-five mortality rate: the probability that an infant born in a specific geographic area and year would die before reaching the age of five. See **child mortality rate**.

unions: organized associations of workers formed to protect and further their rights and interests as workers, including things like wages, benefits, and workplace safety regulations.

universality: the idea that people around the world, and throughout different historic eras, have had similar lived experiences; that there is one way to be human; and, moreover, that human experience can be understood using a universal social science.

upscale emulation: a type of **consumption** practice discussed by Juliet Schor in which people with less money imitate the shopping patterns of people who have more money.

urbanization: a process where an increasing proportion of a population is concentrated in cities; also refers to the increased prominence and power of cities in a society's cultural, political, and economic life.

Vaisakhi: a holiday held in April that marks the beginning of the spring Punjabi harvest season as well as the founding of the Sikh Khalsa in 1699.

values: collective standards that a culture uses to judge whether something is good, beautiful, useful, worthwhile, or desirable. A group's values are the basis of their **norms**. Values are subject to contestation and change.

vernacular multiculturalism: refers to the unpredictable everyday practices of cultural transmission and intermixture that occur in contexts of demographic plurality.

vital registration: the system by which governments collect and process information on key demographic events (such as births, adoptions, marriages, divorces, and deaths) in a **population** on a continuous basis.

volunteer tourism: practices whereby tourists volunteer while on vacation, usually for philanthropic reasons.

wedding-industrial complex: the mobilization and deployment of an immense web of commercial and capitalist industries as well as **mass media** and culture in general, all of which service and promote weddings and by which the wedding itself becomes both an industry (primarily organized around profit motives) and a cultural norm.

West/Western: generally refers to regions of the world that include Europe, the United States, Canada, Australia, and New Zealand. Western refers to the **norms, values, traditions**, and **culture** associated with the societies in the West.

white: a socially constructed racial category, established during European **colonialism** and American slavery, that broadly describes the individuals and groups of people of European descent. The definition of white depends on the cultural, political, and social circumstances of a given historic time.

white settler society: societies with white populations that have settled on lands that were violently dispossessed from Indigenous peoples, beginning from the fifthteenth century. Canada, the United States, Australia, and New Zealand are white settler societies.

white supremacy: a system of racial stratification where people who are defined as **white** have dominant institutional power and control over resources. In this system, whiteness is socially constructed as the norm, and the practices, bodies, and cultures of non-white people are either marginalized, ignored, or understood as deviant.

white wedding: a specific type of wedding **ritual** that typically includes a ritualized engagement proposal featuring a diamond ring, an elaborate white gown for the bride, and a luxurious wedding cake. Roughly synonymous with fairy tale or storybook weddings, or the typical American or **Western** wedding.

world systems theory: a theory developed by Immanuel Wallerstein that details how different parts of the world perform different functions within the global economy and have differential opportunities for economic development.

zero-tolerance: an approach whereby punitive action is taken against an individual for any infraction of a law or code of conduct, regardless of any factors that might mitigate the culpability of the individual.

Contributors

Patrizia Albanese is Associate Dean of Research and Graduate Studies in the Faculty of Arts at Ryerson University, Chair of the Board of Directors of the Federation for the Humanities and Social Sciences, and a past president of the Canadian Sociology Association. She is co-author of *Growing up in Armyville* (2016), *Youth & Society* (2011), and *More Than It Seems* (2010); she has authored *Children in Canada Today* (2016) and *Child Poverty in Canada* (2010). She is co-editor of *Sociology: A Canadian Perspective* (2016), *Principles of Sociology* (2014) and *Canadian Families Today* (2018). She has done research on Canada's child care policies and on the well-being of youth in Canadian Armed Forces families.

Heidi Bickis is a sociologist and lecturer living in the United Kingdom. Her research interests include social theory, contemporary art and aesthetics, and body studies. She is currently researching and writing about the social aspects of tiredness and energy.

Sonia Bookman completed her doctoral degree in sociology at the University of Manchester and is currently an associate professor at the University of Manitoba. Her research focuses on issues of branding, urban culture, cosmopolitanism, and consumption, and she has published in journals such as *Space and Culture*, *Journal of Consumer Culture*, and *Cultural Sociology*.

Bonar Buffam is an assistant professor of sociology in the Department of History and Sociology at the University of British Columbia, Okanagan campus. He is currently writing a book, funded by an Insight Grant from SSHRC, that examines the political histories of religious and racialized minorities in Western Canada. His research has been published in journals such as *Theoretical Criminology*, *Social Identities*, *Cultural Studies*, *Sikh Formations*, and the *International Journal of Sociology and Social Policy*.

David Celis Parra (BA, MIPP) is a social analyst and independent consultant focused on transnational and local issues relating to migration and food security risks. With a growing portfolio on these topics, he is currently involved in advancing work on personal finances and long-term financial wellness for local and international groups.

Rachelle Daley is the member engagement officer with the Canadian Council for International Co-operation (CCIC), a coalition of Canadian voluntary sector organizations working globally to achieve sustainable human development, end global poverty, and promote social justice and human dignity for all. Rachelle has numerous years of work experience related to immigration, as a former certified immigration consultant who practised in Canada and Mexico, and as a former staff member of the Canadian Embassy in Mexico.

Tonya K. Davidson works as a sociologist at Carleton University in Ottawa. Her main research interests are Canadian popular culture, material culture, nostalgia, public memory, and monuments. She has published in the *Journal of Canadian Studies*, *Space and Culture*, *The Public Historian*, and *Topia* and co-edited *Ecologies of Affect: Placing Nostalgia, Desire, and Hope* (2011) with Ondine Park and Rob Shields.

Elizabeth Dennis is professor emeritus at University of the Fraser Valley in British Columbia. Beginning with her doctoral research at the University of Toronto, she has focused on the division of household labour throughout her academic career. Professor Dennis specializes in online teaching and learning, and she continues to teach online courses on a part-time basis.

Michael Graydon is an assistant professor of sociology at Algoma University. His research interests include sleep technologies, gay male sexual cultures, lesbian and gay social history, and social movements.

Jenna Hennebry is an associate professor in the Balsillie School of International Affairs and co-founder of the International Migration Research Centre at Wilfrid Laurier University. She has carried out globally comparative research on labour migration governance, migrant worker rights and health, and gender and migration for over 15 years. She has consulted for UN Women, the International Organization for Migration (IOM), and multiple government agencies. Hennebry was recently named to the IOM's Migration Research Experts Syndicate, she is a member of the Canadian Council for Refugees Subcommittee on Migrant Workers, and she is a member of the UN Expert Working Group on Women's Human Rights in the Global Compact for Migration. Her work has informed policy recommendations and rights-based approaches to governance of labour migration at local, provincial, national, regional, and international levels.

Paul Joosse is an assistant professor in the Department of Sociology at the University of Hong Kong. His past work has explored "eco-terrorism," new religious movements, and radicalization in the Somali diaspora in Canada. He also does theoretical work on Max Weber's concept of charisma. Paul's work has been published in *Social Forces*, *Sociological*

Theory, the *British Journal of Criminology*, *European Journal of Criminology*, and the *Journal of Classical Sociology*, among others. He is currently researching the democracy movement in Hong Kong.

Nathaniel Laywine holds his PhD in Communication Studies from McGill University. His research interests include global citizenship education, humanitarian/human rights communications, and critical media studies. He has previously taught courses on international development, cultural studies, and film and worked with such organizations as the National Film Board, Canadian Museum for Human Rights, Experimental Feminist Ethical Collaborative Tools (EFECT), and the Universalia Management Group.

Susan Machum is the dean of social sciences at St. Thomas University in Fredericton, New Brunswick. From 2006 to 2016 she held a Canada Research Chair in Rural Social Justice. Her PhD is in rural sociology from the University of Edinburgh, and throughout her academic career she has researched agriculture, farm women's work, food security issues, the rural-urban interface, and changing rural communities.

Tara Milbrandt is an associate professor of sociology at the University of Alberta's Augustana campus. She teaches courses in social theory, community, media, and visual sociology. Her research interests include social theory, visual culture, and the public sphere. She is currently researching and writing about the relationship between ubiquitous digital photography and the contemporary public sphere.

Nicole Neverson is an associate professor in sociology at Ryerson University. She teaches courses on the sociology of sport, media research methods, and critical media analysis of sports culture. Her current research interests are grounded in the areas of mass media analysis, the mediated representation of marginalized groups, and the sociological aspects of sports. Recently, she collaborated on a project exploring the integration of critical pedagogy in teaching and learning at Ryerson entitled *Inhabiting Critical Spaces: Teaching and Learning from the Margins at Ryerson University.* This project explored how critical knowledge is experienced by students and professors in the classroom.

Alissa Overend is an associate professor in the Department of Sociology at MacEwan University, where she teaches and researches in the areas of health, food, and social equity. Alissa's work has appeared in *Food, Culture, and Society*, *Social Theory and Health*, *Women's Health and Urban Life*, and *Nursing Inquiry.* Her forthcoming book (2021) is entitled *Shifting Food Facts: Dietary Discourse in a Post-Truth Culture.*

Ondine Park is a critical cultural sociologist and social theorist whose research explores the ways in which space, time, and human ways of being are imagined, produced, and challenged. Ondine works as a sessional instructor at MacEwan University.

Heather Rollwagen is an associate professor in the Sociology Department at Ryerson University. Her research explores the intersections of housing studies and criminology; she is currently investigating how ideologies of housing tenure and built form relate to perceptions of neighbourhood safety and crime. Heather teaches courses in the areas of statistics, urban sociology, and introductory sociology, and she has a particular interest in both blended learning and community-engaged learning models of education.

Alan Sears is a professor in the Department of Sociology at Ryerson University. His research is in the areas of sexuality, social movements, and education. His books include *The Next New Left: A History of the Future* and (co-authored with James Cairns) *The Democratic Imagination: Envisioning Popular Power in the Twenty-First Century*.

Rania Tfaily is an associate professor of sociology at Carleton University. She holds a PhD in demography from the University of Pennsylvania. Her research focuses on marriage and fertility, health and aging, and educational inequalities. She has looked at religious differentials in fertility and the relationship between polygyny and HIV. She has also examined racial/ethnic disparities in health in Canada and the United States. Her work on education focuses on the impact of family background on educational inequality and the interrelations between educational inequality and conflicts.

Patricia Thille (PhD in sociology) is an assistant professor in physical therapy at the University of Manitoba. Her research interests include critical weight studies, inequality and inequity in health care, stigma, and pedagogy.

Alison Thomas began her teaching career in the UK, before immigrating to Canada in 1996. She spent eight years teaching in the Department of Sociology at the University of Victoria before joining Douglas College in Vancouver, where she currently teaches courses in introductory sociology, gender, family, and research methods. After many years conducting research on gender and family, she is currently engaged in research on student learning, focusing on how students' exposure to the sociological imagination (a "threshold concept" in introductory sociology) can transform their worldview.

Zoe Todd (Métis) is an associate professor at Carleton University. She is from Amiskwaciwâskahikan (Edmonton), Canada. She writes about fish, art, Métis legal traditions, the Anthropocene, extinction, and decolonization in urban and prairie contexts. In the past, she has researched human-fish relations and arctic food security in the Inuvialuit Settlement Region in the Northwest Territories, Canada. Her current work focuses on the relationships between people and fish in the context of colonialism, environmental change, and resource extraction in Treaty Six Territory (Edmonton, Amiskwaciwâskahikan), Alberta, and the Lake Winnipeg watershed more broadly. In 2018–19 she was a presidential visiting fellow at Yale University.

Matthew P. Unger is an assistant professor of sociology at Concordia University in Montreal. His work encompasses the hermeneutics of criminal accusation, colonial legal imaginaries, sound studies, and ethnography/participant observation within the extreme metal community. He examines how predominant metaphors and symbols structure aesthetic, sonic, and legal imaginaries. His continuing projects focus on accusation and governance, nature and law, and Paul Ricoeur's thoughts on symbols of fault. He is the author of *Sound, Symbol, Sociality: The Aesthetics of Extreme Metal Music* (2016), and he is co-editor of *Accusation: Creating Criminals* (2016) and *Entryways to Criminal Justice: Accusation and Criminalization in Canada* (2019).

Benjamin Woo is an associate professor of communication and media studies at Carleton University. He is the director of the Comic Cons Research Project and the author of *Getting a Life: The Social Worlds of Geek Culture.*

Jen Wrye is a sociology instructor and educational developer at North Island College. Her research interests include food studies, teaching and pedagogy, animal-human relations and social justice studies.

Index

Italic page numbers represent photos/graphs/illustrations.